BIRDS AT MY FEEDER

created by

BOBBIE KALMAN

art by

GLEN LOATES

BOBBIE KALMAN / GLEN LOATES

BIRDS AT MY FEEDER

The North American Wildlife Series

Toronto
New York

CRABTREE PUBLISHING COMPANY

The Glen Loates North American Wildlife Series:
Created by Bobbie Kalman
Art by Glen Loates

Editor-in-Chief:
Bobbie Kalman

Researchers:
Anne Champagne
Christine Arthurs

Writing team:
Bobbie Kalman
Anne Champagne
Christine Arthurs
Janine Schaub
Louise Petrinec
Moira Daly

Editors:

Janine Schaub	Moira Daly
Christine Arthurs	Louise Petrinec
Anne Champagne	Judith Ellis

Illustrations:
Copyright © 1987 MGL Fine Art Limited.
Page 24, 26-27, 53: Elaine Macpherson

Cover design:
Leslie Smart & Associates Limited

Page design:
Stephen Latimer

Computer layout:
Christine Arthurs

Mechanicals:

Halina Below-Spada	Gerry Lagendyk

Printer:
Bryant Press, with special thanks to Arnie Krause

For Erika and Jacques,
my dear friends in Paris

Cataloguing in Publication Data

Kalman, Bobbie, 1947-
    Birds at My Feeder

(The Glen Loates North American wildlife series)
Includes index.
ISBN 0-86505-167-4 (bound) ISBN 0-86505-187-9
(pbk.)

1. Birds - North America - Juvenile literature.
2. Birdfeeders - Juvenile literature. I. Loates, Glen.
II. Title. III. Series: Kalman, Bobbie, 1947-
The Glen Loates North American wildlife series.

QL681.K34 1987 j598.29'22'097

350 Fifth Avenue
Suite 3308
New York
N.Y. 10118

120 Carlton Street
Suite 309
Toronto, Ontario
Canada M5A 4K2

Contents

Birds at your feeder

One of the happiest sounds in the world is a bird's song. Imagine waking up to your very own concert of whistles, chirps, and tweets. If you had a bird feeder in your yard or on your balcony, you would not only hear cheerful singing, you would also learn to recognize many kinds of birds. You might even give them names! The best part of having a feeder, though, is knowing that you are helping birds survive the fall and winter. Putting out seeds, bread, suet, nuts, and other treats might even encourage some birds to nest near your home in the spring.

When do birds feed?

The fall and winter are the most important times of the year to stock your feeder. Although many birds migrate south to find new feeding sites, some will stay if they can find enough food. If you decide to make or buy a feeder, remember that the birds that you feed will come to depend on the food you leave—so it is important to keep your feeder well supplied!

Become a bird watcher

No one becomes an expert bird watcher by reading a book. A bird watcher's knowledge comes from observing birds. This book will, however, help you in a number of ways. You will learn how to make several kinds of feeders so that you can attract the birds in your neighborhood to your home. You will get to know the names and features of the birds that are likely to visit your feeder and learn what they prefer to eat. After you start recognizing these birds, you will find it easier to tell them apart from the more unusual ones that pay you a visit. *Birds at My Feeder* will also tell you about some of the characteristics that all birds share. So, get busy making a feeder and become a bird watcher and a bird buddy.

You could help these chickadees find food during the winter by keeping your feeder well stocked with bird seed.

A bit about birds

a cardinal

Birds have one feature that makes them different from all other creatures—feathers. The ability to fly or lay eggs is not unique to birds. Some mammals can fly, and most reptiles lay eggs. Because birds originated from reptiles, they still resemble their ancient relatives in many ways. They have scales, or **scutes**, covering their legs and beaks just as reptiles do. They are well adapted to living on land just as reptiles are. Birds are similar to mammals, too. They are warm-blooded, which means that their body temperature stays the same despite the weather.

Why do some birds sing?

When people want to know one another, they usually talk. When birds want to communicate, they call or sing to one another. A bird call is made up of many notes in special repeating patterns. In many species only the male sings. His song attracts a mate and also tells other males to stay out of his territory. The best time to hear birds sing is from early spring to midsummer during the mating and breeding seasons. Don't be surprised if you are awakened early in the morning by a symphony of bird songs. Birds like to sing their loudest just as the sun is coming up!

a blue jay

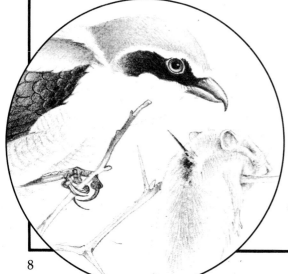

a northern shrike

an oriole

a gray jay landing

How do birds fly?

Everyone has looked up in the sky and wondered what it would be like to fly. How do birds soar so easily through the air? Birds have special features that enable them to fly. Birds do not weigh very much because they do not have teeth, nor a heavy jaw, and their bones are hollow. Therefore they are light enough to glide through the air.

Birds have especially strong hearts and lungs which provide their flying muscles with lots of oxygen. When muscles are fed a rich supply of oxygen, they can work for long periods of time. Of course, feathers also help birds fly. They are light, strong, and smooth. The smoothness of the feathers helps birds fly more quickly and easily.

a red-breasted nuthatch

Learning about bird beaks

Birds' beaks are specially suited to the types of food they eat. Some birds have short, heavy beaks for cracking seeds. The blue jay has an all-purpose beak because its diet is so varied. Some birds have hawk-like beaks for ripping meat, while others have crossbills for removing seeds from cones. Look at each of the bird beaks on this page. Can you guess what each bird might eat? (See page 56 for answers.)

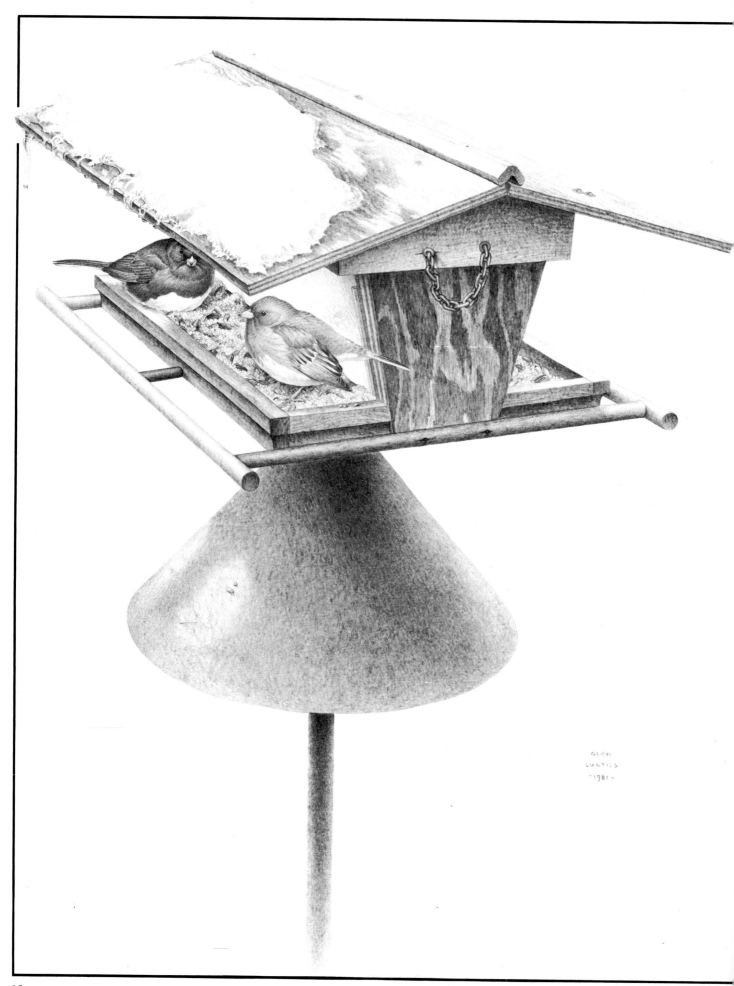

Dark-eyed junco

On those snowy or rainy days when you don't dare poke your nose outdoors, look outside at your bird feeder. You just might see a bunch of dark-eyed juncos braving the bad weather! People sometimes call juncos "snowbirds" because they are often seen scratching at the snow to find seeds. Juncos even take baths in the snow! Sometimes the weather is too rough, though, even for the hardy junco. On stormy summer days this dark-eyed bird often takes cover beneath a flower. It chooses this spot so it can eat the flower's seeds while it is waiting for the storm to clear.

Which junco is which?

At times there may be more than one flock of juncos at your feeder. When it comes time to fly away, the junco has no trouble picking out the members of its own group. Each bird remembers its flock and stays with it.

Ground birds

A junco's gray coat blends in well with the earth and is good protection for a bird that spends a lot of time on the ground. The junco hops around the forest floor looking for seeds and insects. When it is at your feeder, it will often pick up seeds that have fallen to the ground. Even a junco's nest is made in a small hollow in the earth. It is either hidden under tree roots or among tall grass, bushes, or rocks. Long ferns and flowers are pulled over the nest to make a roof.

Ruby-throated hummingbird

Hummingbirds are the world's tiniest birds. Ruby-throated hummingbirds are so small that their nests are the size of walnut shells. These birds hardly weigh more than a small coin, so it is easy for them to stay in the air. Ruby-throats spend most of their time flying from flower to flower collecting sweet nectar. They look for most of their food in flower gardens but tend to make their nests in forest trees. They feed on both tree sap and flower nectar.

Ruby-throats are the only hummingbirds that live in almost all parts of eastern North America. They migrate long distances every year. In the spring as they travel north, hummingbirds visit gardens along the way, just as the new blossoms are opening up.

Helicopter flying

If you have ever watched a hummingbird in flight, you would not be able to see its wings. All you would see is a blur because this tiny bird moves its wings thousands of times a minute. It not only flies forward, backward, up, down, and sideways, it can also hover in one spot like a helicopter. This ability allows the hummingbird to eat while it is flying. As it hovers, it pokes its thin beak into a flower and scoops up nectar with its long, sticky tongue. It can also snatch insects from spiders' webs in the same way.

Magic colors

Although this bird is called the ruby-throated hummingbird, only the male has a red throat. The backs of both the male and female are bright green. Yet the coloring of the hummingbird doesn't always look the same. Sometimes its throat may look black or orange, depending on where you are standing when you are looking at it. Hummingbirds and some other birds have special feathers that seem to change colors right before your eyes. Have you ever seen a piece of crystal? It is made up of many different surfaces, just as the hummingbird's feathers are. All of these surfaces reflect light in different ways, causing us to see different colors.

Feeders for ruby-throats

Because of the ruby-throat's unique diet and feeding habits, this bird requires a special feeder. The best kind of hummingbird feeder is made with a water bottle such as the type you would use to feed a gerbil. Fill it with a solution of one part sugar and three parts water. (It is best to use bottled water rather than tap water.) Remember to change the water every few days! In summer hang the bottle in a shady spot and, if possible, place a sprinkler nearby. Rather than take a bath, hummingbirds like to cool off in a sprinkler's mist.

Red means food!

To attract hummingbirds to the feeder, cut out a flower shape and place it around the neck of the bottle. You may want to color the petals and the bottle's spout with red paint or nail polish because hummingbirds love red. Perhaps they know that red flowers are especially sweet, so "red" means "food" to the ruby-throat.

© GLEN
LOATES
-1985-

Mourning dove

Ooahoo, oo, oo, oo," is the lonely call of the mourning dove. It is named after its sad and mournful song. From the early spring to the end of the summer, the male dove makes this melancholy sound. He sometimes sings a shorter song that sounds like "ooahoo," when he finds a perfect spot for a nest. He may be calling out to a female to take a look at the spot, or he may simply be singing to himself.

Pigeon or mourning dove?

Mourning doves can be found in towns, farms, roadsides, grasslands, and open woodlands. They are particularly fond of pine trees. Even if you startle these birds, they will likely stay where they are, so you may get quite a good look at them. Mourning doves and pigeons are close cousins. You can tell a mourning dove by the white "V" that edges its pointed tail and by its smaller head.

Eating dirt?

In winter most mourning doves feed and roost in flocks of twenty to fifty birds. You can easily attract them to your feeder with cracked corn scattered on open ground. By keeping a close eye on your feeder, you may observe the interesting eating habits of these birds. You will probably see a mourning dove eat a beakful of gravel while munching on the corn. Don't be alarmed! The food and pebbles travel to the mourning dove's **gizzard**, which is its muscular stomach. Because birds do not have any teeth, they need the sand and gravel in their gizzards to help grind the bigger chunks of food into smaller bits.

Mourning doves and many other birds also have **crops** in which they can store food. A crop is a pouch located in the bird's neck. It expands to hold four or five times as much food as the bird's stomach can. Mourning doves don't have to feed often because they can carry a store of food with them.

The frozen apples these grosbeaks are eating are good winter food. Old apples and other fruit are not wasted but are eaten by birds and other animals. Grosbeaks also eat berries and buds in the spring and summer.

Evening grosbeak

Whoever gave the evening grosbeak its name only got it half right! "Gros" means "big" in French. This bird is called "grosbeak" because of its large, strong beak, but the grosbeak is not an evening bird at all! Long ago people thought that it sang in the evening, but we now know that it does its best singing in the morning.

Big appetites

Not only does the grosbeak have a big beak, it also has a big appetite. No wonder so many grosbeaks have fat bodies as well! Maple seeds are their favorite meal, but they also eat many other foods. Sunflower seeds will attract a flock of grosbeaks to your feeder, especially in winter.

The grosbeak's bill is well designed for cracking seeds. The upper part of the bill overlaps and clamps down on the lower part. This slight overlap makes it easier to snap off the shells around seeds. Once the shells are cracked, the seeds just pop right out! Grosbeaks are often seen picking at stones at the sides of roads. Like mourning doves, grosbeaks use these stones to help them grind up the seeds in their gizzards.

Rowdy crowds

Flocks of grosbeaks announce their arrival with loud, ringing "p-teer, p-teer" flight calls. They often come to the feeder in crowds and don't have much patience for other kinds of birds that are already there. Although they allow chickadees, nuthatches, and juncos to stay, they bump other birds off the feeding trough. When most birds see grosbeaks approaching the feeder, they quickly fly away.

Winter outfits

If you ever saw the bottom of an evening grosbeak's foot, you would see that it is covered in ridged cushions that look like the corns people get on their feet. These cushions help the grosbeak grip slippery, ice-covered branches in the winter. Grosbeaks also have a covering of soft, gray down under their brightly colored feathers. This winter underwear shields them from the cold. Grosbeaks need to keep warm because they hardly ever migrate south when the temperature drops. Most prefer to remain in the northern evergreen forests all year long.

Goldfinch

If you were to watch a goldfinch fly away, its flight path might remind you of a rollercoaster ride. This bright yellow bird bobs up and down as it flies through the air, calling out a happy, twittering song.

In July goldfinches sing, "Per-chik-o-ree!" When mating season begins, however, a male's call becomes short and warbling. At nesting time he sings and circles the nest. His job is to protect the eggs and feed his mate whenever she is hungry.

Summer nesters

People don't like prickly thistle patches, but goldfinches love them! Goldfinches eat the tiny, black thistle seeds. They also use the thistle fluff to line their nests. For this reason goldfinches nest in the late summer when there are many thistles around. They also weave their nests with the soft down from poplar and willow trees. Sometimes they even use bark, wool, spiders' webs, and cocoons as nest-building materials. If you follow a female goldfinch carrying any of these things, you may be lucky enough to see a nest being built.

Their favorite seeds

To attract finches to your home, you can buy or build a special finch feeder. A finch feeder is usually a long tube pierced with a few tiny holes and fitted with several perches. It is filled with thistle, or **niger** seed, as it is sometimes called. If you do use these seeds, be sure that they have been oven toasted and cooled. Fresh seeds dropped on the ground under a feeder will grow into a patch of prickly thistles!

Little thieves

If you happen to have sunflower seeds in your regular feeder, you might see goldfinches steal them from other birds. Goldfinches do not like eating sunflower seeds in the shell, so they wait until an expert seed cracker, such as a grosbeak or a purple finch, comes along. When the bird breaks the shell, the goldfinch swoops in and steals the freshly hulled seed before the other bird has a chance to eat it.

Common redpoll

Redpolls spend their summers in the Arctic where there are no trees. In the winter huge flocks move throughout Canada and the United States. They rest on weeds and bushes in winter fields. Of all the songbirds, the hardy redpoll can survive the coldest temperatures. Some people have seen redpolls taking dips in icy streams and burrowing into wet snow.

A feathery mittful

If you want to attract the redpoll to your feeder, you should fill your feeder with millet, hemp, and sunflower seeds. Watch for a tiny bird with a hazy-pink breast and a flashing red patch on its head. This bird is so small it could fit inside your mitten!

Moving north

By mid-March flocks of redpolls leave for the Arctic. They usually build their nests about a meter off the ground in small shrubs. Redpolls construct a loose platform of twigs in the crook of an alder or willow and then make a cup-like nest lined with a cozy layer of ptarmigan feathers.

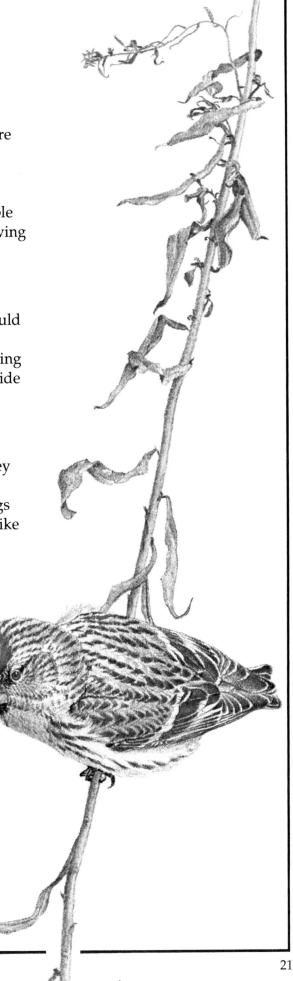

In the winter the redpoll eats the seeds of many kinds of weeds, grasses, and trees. In the summer it catches insects to feed to its young.

Red-breasted nuthatch

Some people think that the white strip above the eye of the red-breasted nuthatch looks like an eyebrow. This marking makes the nuthatch look as if it is wearing a serious frown.

Head-over-heels about food

This lively bird lives mostly in northern pine forests. In the wild the red-breasted nuthatch and its nuthatch relatives have unusual feeding habits. Like many other birds, they eat the creatures that live in the nooks and crannies of trees, such as insects and insect eggs. What makes these birds so unusual is the way they go about finding food. Starting at the top and moving down to the base of the tree, they wind around the trunk and branches with their heads facing toward the ground.

Nuthatches are especially suited to upside-down digging. Other birds scrounge for food in an upright position, using their front claws and stiff tail feathers to hold them in place. Nuthatches don't have these stiff feathers, but they do have three strong claws that extend to the backs of their feet. These claws enable them to cling onto the bark as they make their way down and around a tree.

Tricky nutcrackers

As well as insects, nuthatches eat all kinds of seeds and nuts. You might think that these tiny birds have a difficult time with hard cones and nutshells, but they have developed a trick for opening them up and getting at the soft seeds or nuts inside. A nuthatch often wedges a nut into a small space in the tree bark and pecks at it with its beak until the nut cracks open. You can easily see how the nuthatch got its name!

Year-round feeders

Red-breasted nuthatches are often seen at feeders. In fact, though most of them migrate in the winter, some hardy nuthatches stay behind and rely almost totally on feeder food. They are especially attracted by chopped walnuts and pecans, sunflower seeds, wild birdseed mixtures, and suet.

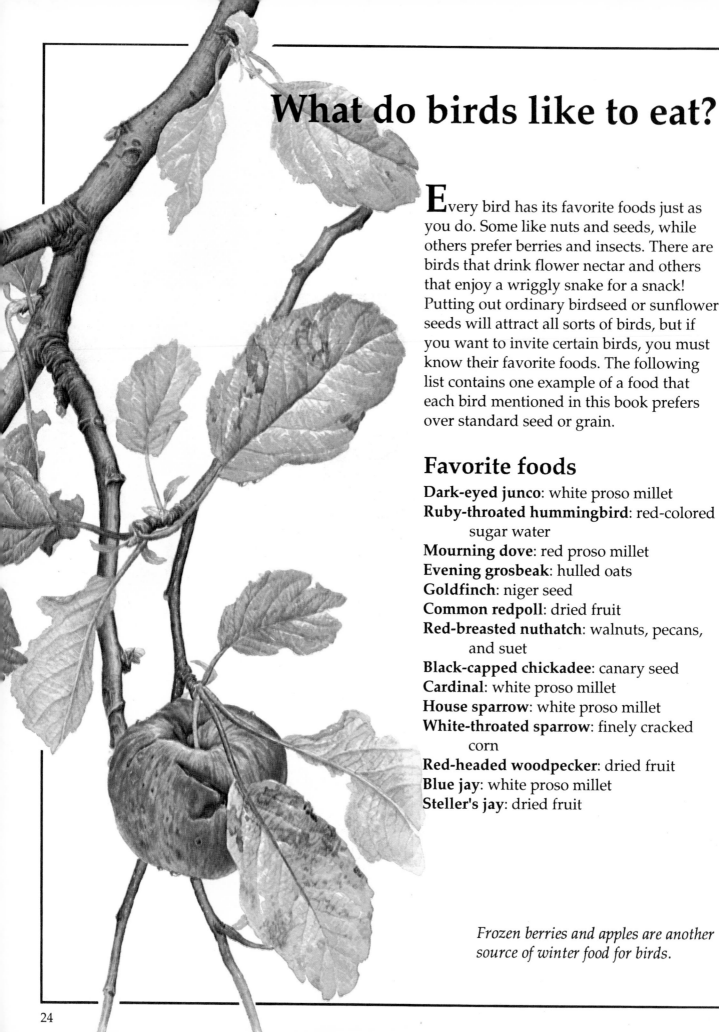

What do birds like to eat?

Every bird has its favorite foods just as you do. Some like nuts and seeds, while others prefer berries and insects. There are birds that drink flower nectar and others that enjoy a wriggly snake for a snack! Putting out ordinary birdseed or sunflower seeds will attract all sorts of birds, but if you want to invite certain birds, you must know their favorite foods. The following list contains one example of a food that each bird mentioned in this book prefers over standard seed or grain.

Favorite foods

Dark-eyed junco: white proso millet
Ruby-throated hummingbird: red-colored
    sugar water
Mourning dove: red proso millet
Evening grosbeak: hulled oats
Goldfinch: niger seed
Common redpoll: dried fruit
Red-breasted nuthatch: walnuts, pecans,
    and suet
Black-capped chickadee: canary seed
Cardinal: white proso millet
House sparrow: white proso millet
White-throated sparrow: finely cracked
    corn
Red-headed woodpecker: dried fruit
Blue jay: white proso millet
Steller's jay: dried fruit

*Frozen berries and apples are another
source of winter food for birds.*

A recipe for bird cake

You aren't the only one who likes cake. Birds will find the following cake recipe absolutely delicious! Take the cooled drippings from bacon or another kind of meat and mix them with birdseed, nuts, crumbs, dried fruit, or other bird favorites. This hardened mixture can be packed into a suet bag, onto a pine cone or a tree stump feeder, or into another type of feeder. Many birds will find this dessert a particularly satisfying winter treat.

Where to find birdseed

Most grocery stores carry standard birdseed or sunflower seeds. To find special birdseed, you will have to visit your local garden shop or pet store. Feeding birds does not, however, have to cost a lot of money. Bread or cheese crumbs, fat, stale pastry or cake, and even kitchen scraps such as bones are all excellent bird leftovers.

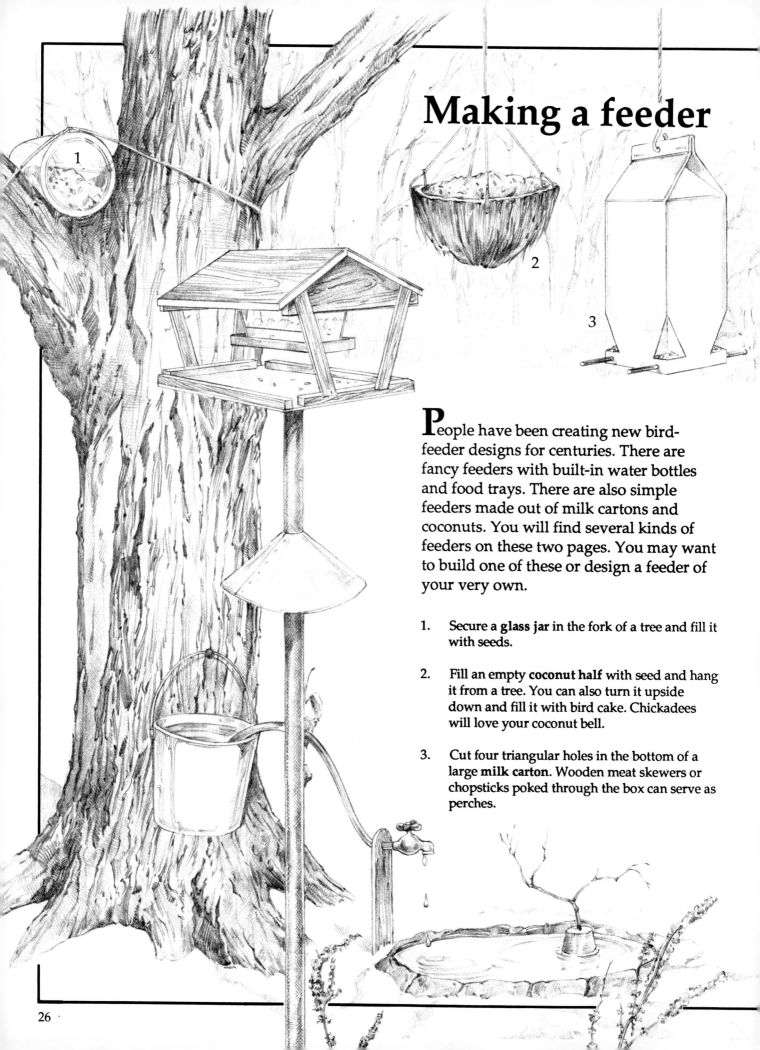

Making a feeder

People have been creating new bird-feeder designs for centuries. There are fancy feeders with built-in water bottles and food trays. There are also simple feeders made out of milk cartons and coconuts. You will find several kinds of feeders on these two pages. You may want to build one of these or design a feeder of your very own.

1. Secure **a glass jar** in the fork of a tree and fill it with seeds.

2. Fill an empty **coconut half** with seed and hang it from a tree. You can also turn it upside down and fill it with bird cake. Chickadees will love your coconut bell.

3. Cut four triangular holes in the bottom of a large **milk carton**. Wooden meat skewers or chopsticks poked through the box can serve as perches.

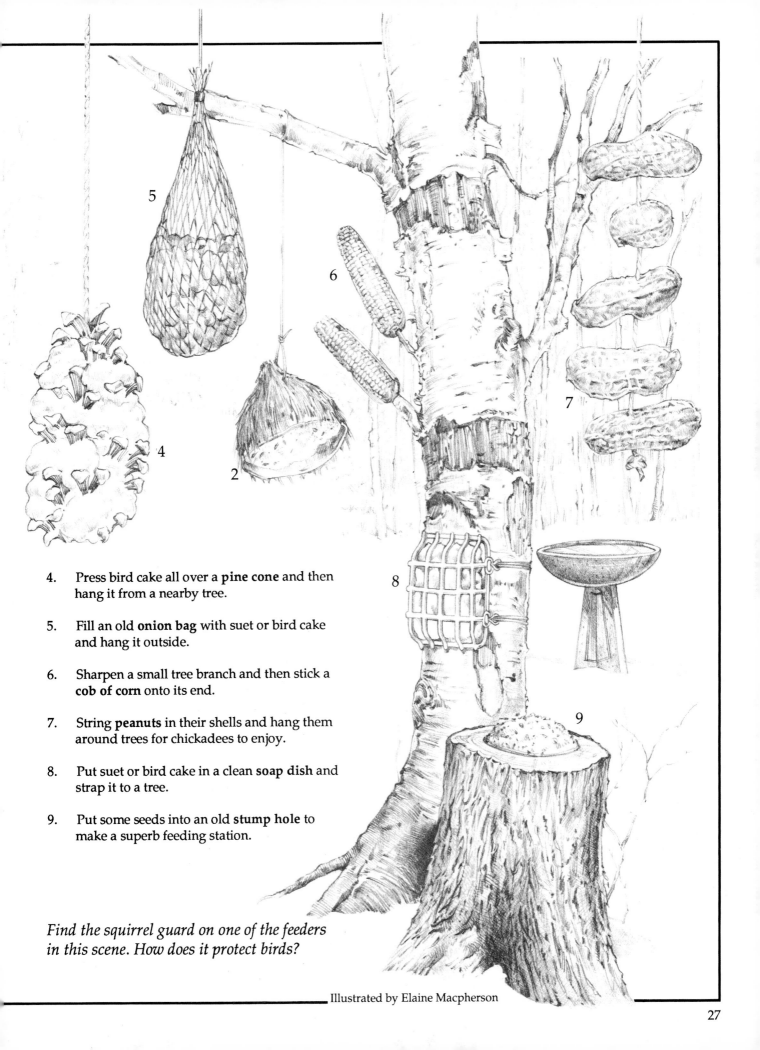

4. Press bird cake all over a **pine cone** and then hang it from a nearby tree.

5. Fill an old **onion bag** with suet or bird cake and hang it outside.

6. Sharpen a small tree branch and then stick a **cob of corn** onto its end.

7. String **peanuts** in their shells and hang them around trees for chickadees to enjoy.

8. Put suet or bird cake in a clean **soap dish** and strap it to a tree.

9. Put some seeds into an old **stump hole** to make a superb feeding station.

Find the squirrel guard on one of the feeders in this scene. How does it protect birds?

Illustrated by Elaine Macpherson

Protect your guests

Making a simple feeder may not be a difficult job, but protecting visiting birds could be. Birds often hit windows because they think that the reflection in the window is a passageway. If you put your feeder near a window, hang a mobile or windchime close by so that it breaks up the reflection. Clean the feeder regularly and throw away bad seed so that visiting birds will not get sick. If you or your neighbors have a cat, make sure it wears a bell on its collar. The sound of the bell will make it hard for the cat to sneak up on the birds at your feeder.

Squirrels, raccoons, and rats will not hurt the birds at your feeder, but these animals may still be unwelcome guests. Try to place your feeder away from jumping-off spots such as rooftops, and make sure you clean up spilled food.

Do all birds visit feeders?

Not all birds go to feeders. Some are afraid of other birds and some do not enjoy sharing their meals with company. Others may not like the food that you have put out. A cedar waxwing might be annoyed that you do not have any tasty insects or berries on your bird-feeder menu! A few fussy birds may even find the position or style of the feeder not to their liking!

Cedar waxwings prefer berries and insects to feeder food.

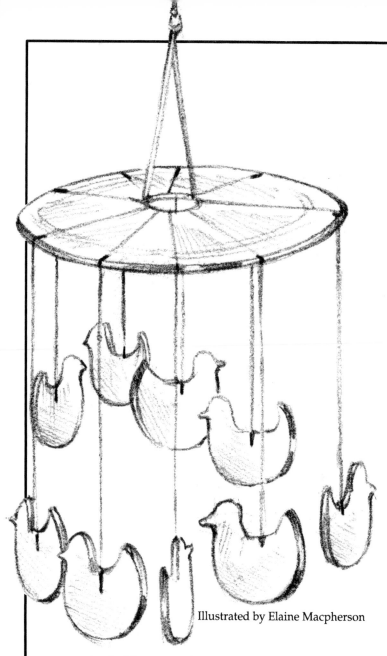

Illustrated by Elaine Macpherson

Adding a birdbath

You might see more birds at your feeder if you also build a birdbath. A birdbath does not need to be very deep—any shallow container will do. Make sure you place the bath above the ground on a table or a tree stump, so you don't expose your bird friends to danger. It might be helpful for you to know that birds are attracted to the sound of dripping or running water. If you can arrange to have a water tap dripping into your bath, you will attract even more birds. Birds also like having a perch at the birdbath so they can sit and preen while they are digesting their food.

Black-capped chickadee

When the snow is blowing and most birds are safely tucked away keeping warm, the hardy chickadee may be at your feeder. This small bird is a common sight all year round and is probably the one bird you will see most often. Keeping your feeder stocked with suet or sunflower seeds may attract a whole flock of these small birds. If you are patient and allow them to get used to you, you can even train them to eat seeds right out of your hand.

A gardener's delight

Black-capped chickadees appreciate feeder food, but they are also good at finding food on their own. In October they start storing their meals for the winter. They tuck nuts under loose tree bark or wrap them in old leaves. In the summer gardeners welcome chickadees because these small birds feed off the insects that damage trees, fruits, and vegetables.

Chickadee-dee-dee!

Black-capped chickadees are named after the black feathers on their heads and for their cheerful "chickadee" call. These birds do, however, make a lot of other sounds besides "chickadee." In late winter they make a noise that sounds like "feebee." This call usually means that chickadees are preparing to start families.

"Birds of a feather ..."

In the fall after chickadees have had their chicks, they form flocks of six to twelve birds. These flocks usually include a pair that has just had chicks, some single birds and, sometimes, a few young ones. Chickadees move in groups for protection. When one bird spies danger, it warns the others in its flock. If a flock member becomes separated from the rest, he or she just calls, "chickadee," and the rest of the group comes to its rescue. Being part of a flock also helps the birds find food. A flock can find the best feeding areas much faster than a single bird can.

Follow that food!

Woodpeckers, nuthatches, kinglets, and warblers often join flocks of chickadees for the winter months. These other birds know that chickadees are excellent food finders. Chickadees themselves sometimes follow one another to look for food. When one chickadee tries to hide a tasty morsel, another one follows and steals it!

Chickadees are so light they can perch on small branches when they are looking for food. They are often seen in evergreen trees, on weeds, and in groves of pussy willows.

Cardinal

Peetoo," says the angry cardinal. He is upset because another bird has just flown into his territory. A cardinal is not afraid to let other birds know that it is mad! It will even attack its own reflection in a window or in the polish of a shiny car, thinking that the reflection is an intruding bird!

Dining alone

Unlike most feeder birds, the cardinal tends to dine alone. It comes to the feeder early in the morning or late at night when there are fewer feathered companions around. If an impatient cardinal wants to shove another bird out of the way, it sticks its head forward, opens its mouth, and flaps its wings. Sunflower seeds and grain are the cardinal's favorite foods. Parent cardinals often bring their chicks to feeders, so listen for small "chips," and watch for beautiful red-feathered adults feeding their tiny offspring.

Courting cardinals

In the spring you might see a lot of puffy-chested male cardinals hopping around your feeder. These birds are looking for a mate. When a male wants to impress a female at mating time, he perks up his head feathers, puffs out his chest, and spreads his tail. Standing lopsided is another courting posture. A mating bird sticks one wing out and leans over. When he puts that wing down, the other one pops up. When a male cardinal really wants to get a female's attention, he offers her food.

In many species of birds the female is less colorful than the male. Which is the female cardinal?

Cup-sized nests

Cardinals make their nests in shrubs, evergreen trees, or in thick bunches of vines. Vines with large leaves are a favorite nesting place because the big leaves are good protection from rain and wintery storms. The cup-sized nests are built well above the ground.

Each cardinal couple can hatch three or four broods of chicks in a single year. Babies are carefully attended by both parents. Looking after newborn chicks is quite a task. These hungry babies demand to be fed every six minutes!

House sparrow

People usually think of house sparrows as the most common birds around. These birds live in cities and on farmlands all over the continent. Sometimes there are so many sparrows at a feeder that there isn't any landing room for other birds. These plentiful, tiny, brown birds haven't always been so common, though. Before 1850 there weren't any house sparrows in North America at all.

Introducing the sparrow!

When house sparrows were brought over from Europe, they quickly adapted to their new lives. These spunky birds learned to take over the nests of their other feathered friends and chase away birds as large as pigeons! Not only do sparrows steal nests, they also steal food. People have seen them

take a worm from a robin, a seed from the mouth of a grosbeak, and food from the mouth of another bird's chick. Being aggressive has helped the sparrow survive on a continent that is not its natural home.

A sparrow social

In the fall and winter large groups of one hundred or so sparrows gather to roost in the middle of the day. They stay together for an hour or two, preening and chirping loudly. Many believe that these daytime roosts take place so that sparrows can let one another know where the good feeding spots are.

A home for life

Unlike other birds that build new nests each year, sparrows keep the same nest throughout their lives. They also keep the same partners. The male sparrow picks a suitable spot and builds the nest. He then sings loudly to attract a mate. To keep bugs under control in their nests, sparrows use plants that are poisonous to certain insects.

Year-round brood

House sparrows raise up to four broods of chicks a year, whereas most birds raise only one or two. Although sparrows usually brood in the summer months, they are able to nest at any time. Sometimes a third sparrow stays with the parents to help with the chicks. This practise is unusual among birds.

White-throated sparrow

The white-throated sparrow is a little bird with a round body and a white chin patch under its beak. Some people think that adult white-throats look like fluffy baby birds. What makes them even more appealing is that they are often tame. If you spend time with them, they may feed from your hand or shoulder.

A scary color

Besides their white chin feathers, white-throated sparrows have another small patch of colored feathers under their beak and eyes. It is bright yellow and, for a reason that people do not understand, this yellow patch frightens other birds!

American or Canadian song?

Singing white-throats chirp one of the most familiar songs in the woods. Americans think these birds sing "Old Sam Peabody, Peabody, Peabody." Canadians think they are singing "Oh, Sweet Canada, Canada, Canada." It is for this very reason that many Canadians refer to this bird as the Canadian song sparrow and Americans refer to it as the poor Sam Peabody bird. What do you think the white-throated sparrow's song might really mean in bird language?

Impatient guests

You will find white-throats at your feeder both early and late in the day. They like to visit when there is less of a crowd and fewer predators around. If you are late filling up your feeder, these sparrows may dance around your window to remind you of your duty. When you come out with the seed, they might follow you from the door to the feeder as if to say, "Well! It's about time you fed us!"

White-throated sparrows eat mainly weed seeds, such as the milkweed, and some insects. They also eat leftover fruit in the winter.

Red-headed woodpecker

This bird looks as if someone grabbed it by its toes and dunked its head in red paint! A red-headed woodpecker's head is so bright compared to its black-and-white body that the color may startle you!

The red-headed woodpecker is a fairly large bird. The distance from the end of its beak to the tip of its tail is about the same as the width of this book. When these birds fly, they dip up and down like a small boat on a rough sea. They use a special rattling sound and chase after one another to protect their own food supplies. In order to spot this woodpecker, look around fence rows, orchards, and the edges of woods.

How much wood can a woodpecker peck?

Lots! Woodpeckers drill holes in trees to get at the insects and sap inside them. They also drill bigger holes for sleeping and nesting. You might think that all this drilling would give them terrible headaches! Yet, it is amazing how well adapted woodpeckers are for drilling. A woodpecker's skull is made of extra-thick bone. When a red-head raps like a jackhammer on a tree trunk, these thick bones help it withstand the pounding. There is also a narrow space between the outer membrane of the woodpecker's brain and the brain itself. This space helps absorb the shock that pecking produces. A woodpecker also has large neck muscles for added strength.

The sticky job of drilling

To help it grip the tree as it pecks, the woodpecker has two toes that point forward and two that face backward! Stiff tail feathers allow the bird to prop itself up against the trunk of a tree, the way you brace yourself for a tug-of-war by digging your feet into the ground. To help with drilling, the woodpecker has a very hard, sharp beak. A circle of bristly feathers surrounds its nostrils to keep sawdust out. Even the woodpecker's tongue is designed to help out with the job. It is long, sticky with saliva, and has barbs at the end. These barbs and sticky saliva help the woodpecker catch ants, lap up sap, and snag grubs that live in trees.

Nuts about nuts

Nuts are a favorite red-head food. Red-headed woodpeckers actually store nuts just as squirrels do! In fall and winter red-heads depend so much on acorns and beechnuts that their migration route follows the trees where these nuts grow. If there are lots of nuts in the north, northern red-heads don't have to migrate. However, every few years the nut crop cannot support the woodpecker population, and large numbers of red-heads fly south.

Blue jay

With a loud "jay-jay," and a flash of blue feathers, the blue jay arrives at your feeder. It often scares away other birds and scatters birdseed as it boldly lands. This bird is well known for its hearty appetite and for its ability to take food from any type of feeder. It will even make off with your sandwich if you let it get close enough!

Like its cousins the crow and the raven, the blue jay is a very intelligent bird. It can copy other bird calls and even imitate a human voice. People have reported seeing jays use twigs to get food out of a tight spot. These birds are curious, like to explore, and have good memories.

Stalking cats

When a cat, squirrel, or even a person, tries to approach a blue jay's nest, the jay becomes very upset. It swoops down on intruders, calling, "Ja-ay." Sometimes it might even tweak a person's hair or a cat's tail. Most other birds do not like the blue jay because it raids their nests, eats their chicks, and generally makes a nuisance of itself. Sometimes a gang of birds gets together and attacks an unsuspecting jay.

Although quarrelsome, blue jays can also be kind. Some flocks of jays have been known to care for old, worn-out blue jays. They feed and protect their old and injured friends.

The tree planters

Blue jays collect seeds and carry them in their crops until they find a good hiding place for them. They might shove an acorn underneath loose tree bark or lay pebbles and leaves on top of it on the ground. By doing this, jays have planted trees without knowing it. What is even more surprising is they accidentally plant trees at just the right distances apart!

Steller's jay

People living in the western regions of Canada and the United States are used to spotting the handsome Steller's jay at campsites and picnic grounds. This beautiful blue bird lives mostly in coniferous forests but can also be found in fruit orchards in more southern areas. Even though the Steller's jay is a close relative of the blue jay, it looks quite different. It has a sooty-black head and chest and sky-blue tail feathers. The rest of its body is deep blue, a much darker color than that of the blue jay. Its shiny plumage attracts and reflects light.

Not a fussy eater

Like its eastern cousin, the Steller's jay eats a great variety of foods and is one of the easiest birds to attract to your feeder. It enjoys suet, sunflower seeds, acorns, pine seeds, fruits, and small insects. The Steller's jay can be found at the feeder during the winter because it does not migrate. Like the blue jay, it is bold and noisy and often scares other birds away from the feeder. Its loud "shak shak" cry is even more harsh than the blue jay's cry.

Nesting time

Bird territories

Around breeding time, most birds settle in an area that becomes their own territory. There are several reasons why birds establish territories. One reason may simply be a desire to have a familiar home where food is easy to find. Birds that establish territories also want to protect their chicks and keep other birds away from their mates. Birds seldom fight over one another's territories. They sing and put on displays to let other birds know how far their territory reaches.

This oriole couple has just finished building a hanging nest.

Courting

When the mating season arrives, male birds become extremely entertaining. In order to attract the attention of the females, many males do dances, show off their flying styles, fluff up their feathers, and sing happy songs. Some will even begin building a nest, which the female usually throws out after mating occurs. Maybe the male builds this nest as a hint to the female that it is time for a family!

Nesting and eggs

After a mate has been found, the next step is to build a real nest. Nests come in various shapes and sizes. They are made from twigs, grasses, leaves, moss, pine needles, animal fur, and bird feathers, all glued together with mud. The female bird lays one egg per day until she has laid the right number. Afterwards either the female or the male sits on the eggs to keep them warm. Keeping the eggs warm is called **incubation**. During the incubation period, the feathers on the belly of the nesting bird drop out, leaving a bare patch of skin. The bird presses this warm patch of skin against the eggs in order to keep them at just the right temperature.

Finally, after twelve to fourteen days, a baby chick is ready to show itself. How does it get out? While still inside the shell, it grows an egg tooth on the top of its beak and develops a hatching muscle on the back of its neck. The egg tooth cracks through the shell, and the chick pokes its head out to say hello to the world.

The male eastern bluebird stays close by as the female incubates her eggs.

Brooding

Chicks are born wearing nothing but a soft coat of feathers called down! The parent birds keep them warm by sitting on them, just as they sat on the unhatched eggs. Keeping the chicks warm in this way is called **brooding**. During the brooding period, the chicks must be constantly fed.

Sometimes the parents take turns finding food. At other times the female stays with the chicks and the male finds food for the whole family! All this eating helps the chicks grow big and strong. Soon their adult feathers grow in, and they take off to brave the world on their own.

The color of eggs

Have you ever noticed that birds' eggs
come in different colors? Some are white,
some are blue, and some are speckled. The
color of the egg depends on the location
of the nest. White eggs are the easiest to
see. Birds that lay white eggs tend to build
nests in a tree hollow or an underground
burrow. Because these nests are hidden
away, the bright, white color of the eggs
does not signal predators. Birds that build
nests in more open places usually lay
darker, speckled eggs that blend in
with their surroundings. Birds that nest on
the ground often lay the darkest eggs of all
so they cannot be seen. The blue jay's eggs
are pale green or dull blue and spotted
with brown and gray. How might these
colors help camouflage the blue jay's eggs?

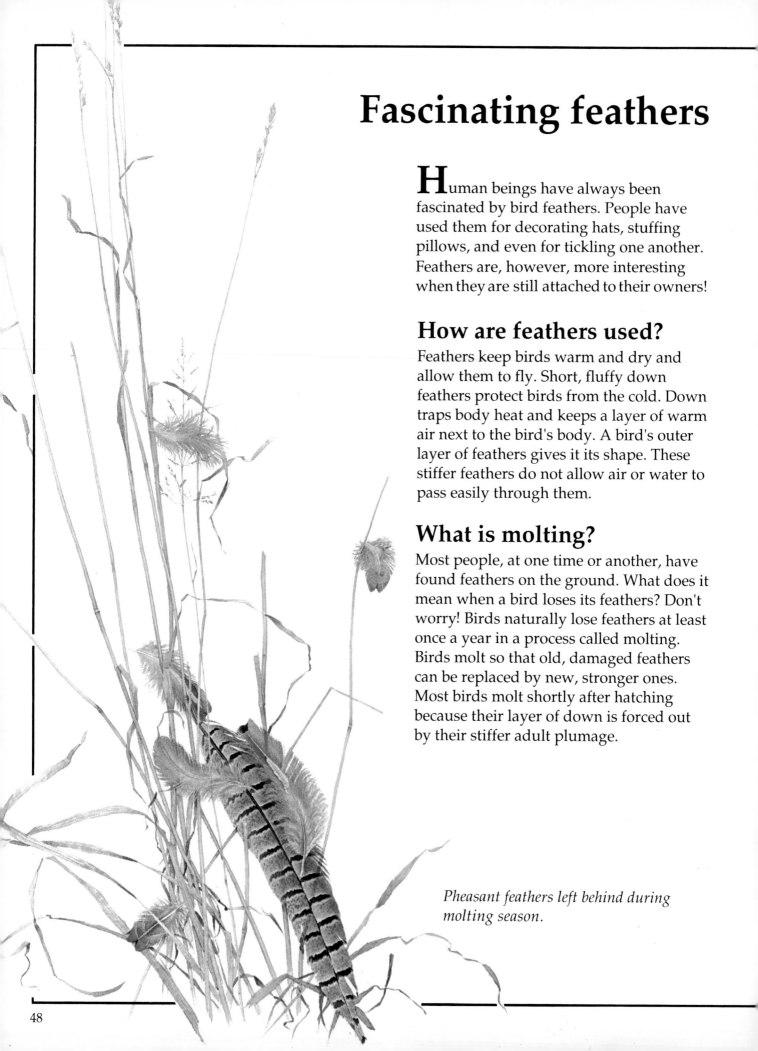

Fascinating feathers

Human beings have always been fascinated by bird feathers. People have used them for decorating hats, stuffing pillows, and even for tickling one another. Feathers are, however, more interesting when they are still attached to their owners!

How are feathers used?

Feathers keep birds warm and dry and allow them to fly. Short, fluffy down feathers protect birds from the cold. Down traps body heat and keeps a layer of warm air next to the bird's body. A bird's outer layer of feathers gives it its shape. These stiffer feathers do not allow air or water to pass easily through them.

What is molting?

Most people, at one time or another, have found feathers on the ground. What does it mean when a bird loses its feathers? Don't worry! Birds naturally lose feathers at least once a year in a process called molting. Birds molt so that old, damaged feathers can be replaced by new, stronger ones. Most birds molt shortly after hatching because their layer of down is forced out by their stiffer adult plumage.

Pheasant feathers left behind during molting season.

What do all the colors mean?

There is no simple way to explain the colors of birds. Colors often help birds blend in with their environment. Dark colors, such as black, help birds absorb sunlight to keep them warm. Birds of some species identify one another by their same bright colors. Birds even hope their bright colors will frighten other birds out of their territories! Can you think of some other good reasons why birds might have different colors?

Quills

For over a thousand years people depended on birds' feathers for writing! The feather pen, called a quill, was also a favorite tool of the artist. By using different sizes of quills, artists could draw both thin and thick lines. Quills are usually made from the largest wing feathers of geese, swans, and sometimes crows because these feathers are hollow and sturdy. First the feather must be dried, cleaned, and sharpened to a fine point. A small cut is made half a centimeter up into the tip. Then the quill is ready to be dipped into ink. Find a feather that a bird has lost and make your own quill pen!

A sturdy feather makes an excellent quill pen.

Staying neat and clean

When you see a bird picking at its fluffed-up feathers with its beak, it is **preening**. Preening is extremely important because it keeps a bird's feathers clean, waterproofed, and free of parasites.

When a bird preens, it works on one feather at a time. It grabs hold of the base of the feather with its bill and nibbles upwards to the tip. By doing this, the bird removes dirt, extra oil, and unwanted parasites. The bird then takes fresh oil from the oil gland located at the base of its tail and spreads it evenly over each feather. The oil prevents water from soaking into the bird's feathers. Preening also helps hook the **barbs**, or tiny branches, on a bird's feather back together. A preened bird can fly more easily than a bird with ruffled feathers.

Anting

A mysterious part of preening is a practise that is known as **anting**. For years bird watchers have noticed that many species of birds let ants crawl through their feathers. Sometimes a bird picks up ants in its beak and rubs them on its feathers. This is called **active anting**. At other times a bird will sit on top of an ant hill and allow the ants to crawl over its wings and tail. This is called **passive anting**. The reason for anting seems to be related to a substance called formic acid and oils that are on an ant's body. It is believed that these substances help kill parasites in the bird's feathers and may also soothe irritated skin after molting. The acid keeps bugs away, and the ant oils act as a soothing lotion!

Let's have a beer bath!

If there aren't any ants around, birds may "ant" with a variety of strange substances. Sometimes birds rub berries over their feathers. They have also been known to use beer, orange juice, coffee, and even soapsuds! Sounds pretty crazy, doesn't it? But birds have good reasons for doing this. All these things contain the same acidy substances found on the bodies of ants!

Mustard or vinegar?

Some blue jays have discovered that rubbing vinegar, mustard, soap, or hair tonic on their feathers seems to have the same effect as putting on lotion to stop itching. There are several people who have even reported seeing blue jays use lighted cigarettes to drive away mites.

Water, snow, sun, or dust?

How many different ways do you think birds bathe? Bird baths and ponds are definite favorites, but birds also bathe in snow, sunshine, and even in dust! On hot days birds splash around in water to cool down. They also tend to bathe before preening. In winter when water is not available, birds may use snow for cleansing. Some birds sunbathe to absorb heat from the sun. They do this in tree branches, on the warm ground, and even on rooftops. If you ever see a bird lying down with its wings spread out, its head to the side, and breathing heavily, it is probably sunbathing. Dust bathing is practised by pheasants, larks, wrens, and house sparrows. These birds dig small holes in the ground just big enough to hold them. Then they throw dust over their backs with their wings. Bird experts think that dust may get rid of parasites, remove extra oil in the feathers, and help birds retain heat.

Migration

In the fall you may have noticed honking geese flying south to escape winter. When the birds fly back in the spring, everyone feels that the warm weather is finally returning. Bird migrations such as this have gone on for thousands and thousands of years.

Why do birds migrate?

It is believed that birds are born with the urge to migrate. They seem to know by instinct the flight path to follow and where to find good feeding sites in the south. In the spring many birds migrate north to breed. The north is less crowded, there is plenty of food, and the longer days provide a lot of time to gather food for baby birds.

Do birds know where to fly?

Some birds cover huge distances each year. How do they find their way and not get lost? Migrating birds know their basic flight path by instinct, but they also have other methods of finding their way. It is believed that many birds use landmarks such as mountains, rivers, and islands to guide them. Other birds behave as if they have built-in magnets in their heads that help them tell direction! They use the earth's magnetic field to find their way. Birds may also respond to smells and noises on the ground. The wind, sun, and the position of the stars may also be tools used by migrating birds.

Do all birds migrate?

Not all birds that migrate do so every year. The urge to move south is stronger in some years and weaker in others. Birds migrate when the risk of bad winter weather is greater than the risk of migration. Migrations are often long, tiring journeys, and many birds do not survive. Even individual birds from within the same flock may not agree about whether to migrate or not. Some choose to stay, while others decide it is best to leave! The birds that do stay, however, are the ones that will depend on you for their winter food. So, get busy and stock up on bird-feeder food now!

Glen with his sons Christopher and Michael.

Glen Loates

Ever since Glen Loates was a child, his love of animals has led him to try capturing our natural world in drawings, paintings, and sculpture. As a boy he spent as much time as he could exploring neighborhood streams and woods. He started sketching interesting scenes during hikes and used these sketches to do more detailed illustrations.

Now, as a professional artist, Glen works in a light-filled studio in his own home. He has a natural history library and often borrows materials, such as animal pelts, from museums to help him make his paintings as realistic as possible. Glen also uses wildlife video tapes, clippings, and photographs from nature magazines as reference material for his work. Yet, no matter how much time Glen spends in the studio, he still thinks of the wilderness as his real working space.

A word from Glen

When I was a young boy just learning to draw, I was frustrated because I could not make my pictures realistic enough. Before long, though, I found out that I could greatly improve my sketches by doing them over and over. I took time to sketch every single day and, as if by by magic, my hands began to draw what my eyes were seeing.

If you are a budding nature artist, the best thing you can do is to draw as much as possible. Keep a daily sketchbook and hold onto both your good and bad drawings because they will help you see just how much your work has improved. If you start a collection of photographs and magazine clippings, you will have plenty of reference material to help you with your practise sketching—but don't just work with other people's pictures. Take as many field trips as possible and create your own impressions of nature.

Ruby-throated hummingbird sketches

While visiting Florida, Glen had a chance to observe many ruby-throated hummingbirds. He quickly sketched these tiny birds as they zipped from hibiscus flower to hibiscus flower. When he returned home, he completed a painting of the male and female hummingbirds using his Florida notes and sketches. (See page 13.)

To paint the brilliant colors of the male's shiny neck feathers, Glen used fluorescent inks and dyes. Unfortunately, this shiny effect only shows up on Glen's original painting and not on any printed copies of his work.

These are quick sketches of the ruby-throated hummingbird. Sketches help develop the artist's skill and may be used as reference material for finished paintings or sculptures.

Glossary

barb- A hooked, hairlike bristle. There are barbs on feathers and on red-headed woodpeckers' tongues.

beechnuts - The small nuts of the beech tree. Beech trees have light-gray bark and grow in cool climates.

brood - The young birds that hatch from a single set of eggs.

continent - One of the seven great areas of land on the earth. North America is a continent.

courtship - The beginning of mating season when a male and female get to know one another.

cranny - A small, narrow opening such as a crack.

flight path - The route a bird takes when it flies.

gizzard - The place where a bird's digestion begins. Birds do not chew their food. They use pieces of grit in their gizzards to grind food.

incubate - To keep eggs warm by sitting on them.

instinct - The natural drive to act a certain way. Birds migrate south by instinct.

intruder - An unwelcome visitor.

landmark - An object in the landscape that can be used as a guide.

magnetic field - A pulling force that surrounds the earth.

migrate - To move from one area to another during certain seasons. Many birds migrate south for the winter.

nectar - The sweet liquid in a flower.

parasite - An animal or plant that gets most of its food by living on or in a creature of a different species.

perch - What a bird holds onto with its claws in order to rest. A branch is a perch.

plumage - The feathers that cover a bird.

preen - When a bird uses its beak to clean and smooth its feathers.

proso millet - The seeds from millet, a type of grass.

quill - A large, stiff feather.

roost - The place where a bird rests.

roost - To rest on a branch.

saliva - The colorless liquid that is released by glands in the mouth.

skewer - A long, thin wooden or metal rod.

species - A distinct animal or plant group that shares similar characteristics and can produce offspring within its group.

suet - Uncooked animal fat that is used as bird food in bird feeders.

symphony - Beautiful music that has many parts.

territory - An area of land.

thistle - A prickly weed with purple or red flowers.

warble - A sound that goes up and down.

Answers to beak quiz on page 9
The blue jay eats fruit, seeds, insects, small animals, and reptiles.
The northern shrike eats birds, rodents, and a few insects.
The oriole eats insects, spiders, some fruits and seeds.

The cardinal eats hard-shelled seeds, cracked corn, fruit, and insects.
The red-breasted nuthatch eats, pine, spruce, and fir seeds, insects, and some nuts.

Index

3456789 BP Printed in Canada 7654321098

The
Big Field

A
Child's Year
Under the
Southern Cross

The
Big Field

A
Child's Year
Under the
Southern Cross

Anne Morddel

KWS
PUBLISHERS
CHICAGO ● LONDON

Second Edition © 2012 by Anne Morddel

Published by:
KWS Publishers
1516 North State Parkway
Chicago, Illinois 60610, U.S.A.

First Edition published in 2007 by Morddeleditions

ISBN 978-0-9826900-7-9

Printed in China

For the children of Paraná, and for mine.

My Mama and Papa work hard in the city
and they're always busy. That's why we live
on Granny's farm, Chloe and Baby and me.

Granny's farm is at the end of a long, twisty
road, by the great forest. She doesn't work the
farm much anymore. She has a few chickens
and not much else, now, and the big field she
always forgets to plow.

"That field has a story," my Granny says.
"It used to be part of the forest, but my grand-
daddy burned all the trees and planted coffee
and soybeans. My daddy did the same. I suppose
I should too," Granny says with her tiny smile.
"But somehow, I keep forgetting to plow."

JANUARY

I love the farm and I love the forest and I love the long summer days.

"Summer is the time to watch things," my Granny says.

We lie on our tummies and watch the spiders build their webs. Then we roll on our backs in the prickly grass and watch butterflies above us.

The nights are so warm, we have dinner outdoors. When it is dark and Chloe and Baby are asleep, Granny and I take a telescope each and lean back to watch the stars.

"First find the Southern Cross in the sky. It points south. If you can find that, you'll never be lost."

That's what my Granny says.

SUMMER

FEBRUARY

Early, early every day, "Before the heat knocks me flat," Granny takes her trug and crosses the big field to the forest, where she gathers all sorts of seeds.

I stay home and climb trees. The silk floss tree is the tallest, with pink flowers. But its trunk has sharp spikes, so you can't climb that! I climb the umbrella tree, where Granny and I built a bench on a branch.

On the ground below me, the leaf-cutter ants carry away bits of plants. Granny says it's their job to tidy up the whole forest.

High in my tree, I can see her come back from the forest with her trug full of seeds. When the sun goes down and it is cooler, we scatter the seeds all around the big field she always forgets to plow.

SUMMER

2005 AM

MARCH

Now it is so hot that Baby can't sleep.
Granny and I carry the cot outside
where a puff of wind in the trees
makes a soothing sound. But still Baby
cries and cries, until Granny says:

"I know what we'll try...ballerinas!"
We gather white tassel flowers from the
ingã tree and make a mobile for Baby to
see. It looks like a row of ballerinas twirling.
Finally, Baby is sleepy.

"The little bird of seven colors is hungry."
Granny hangs bananas for the birds and we
listen to the cicadas as loud as drums.
"Oh! This heat is making me numb," Granny
fans herself and sighs. Grand butterflies,
bluer than the sky, dance in the air like
falling hankies.

AUTUMN

A P R I L

"Yesterday-Today-Tomorrow is the name of this funny flower," Granny shows me. "Each flower opens a dark blue, then every day it is lighter until it is pure white."

Now is the time to harvest. I help Granny by climbing the trees and dropping oranges into the basket below. On a branch nearby, a trogan has perched and watches me with his round eye.

Chloe finds a big beetle to keep in a box. She talks to it the rest of the day. Granny is pleased that I found the first medallion tree seeds, long and bumpy.

"Longer than your arm, my sweet," she laughs. "And it grows to be a mighty tree with flowers of pure gold." She gives me a hug and picks up her trug and off we go to plant gold in the big field she always forgets to plow.

AUTUMN

2005 月三月

M A Y

Many leaves fall but most trees stay green. And the darkest flower I have ever seen blooms in the woods now. Strangely, the whole barn is covered with giant brown moths.

"This is the first time they have come out of the forest," says Granny. "I don't know why." She brushes them off of Chloe's dress and shoes.

The big seeds of the silk floss tree have started to fall and we collect them all. Granny pulls out the silky fluff.

"I'll make you a new quilted coat, my love," Granny says. "But be sure to leave some of those seeds on the ground for the parakeets. It's their favorite treat."

AUTUMN

JUNE

"Paraná, tra-la-la, Paraná pine," prattles Chloe. I'm trying to climb a Paraná pine, but it is very high. It has fat seed balls that come crashing down in winter. The monkeys eat the seeds raw, but we boil them with salt. On bonfire nights, Granny tells the tale of how the blue jay plants the Paraná pine trees.

"He takes as many seeds as he can and hides them all around, storing his food for winter. Each one he cannot find again grows into a pine. That tree will be his new home and will give him more seeds to eat."

Just then, Chloe starts to cry because her pet katydid has hopped away.

"Come child," Granny soothes. She pops a warm salty seed into Chloe's mouth. "Why don't you both help me toss the uncooked seeds into that big field I always forget to plow?"

WINTER

J U L Y

Every day is cold now. In the mornings the fog is so thick the forest seems to disappear. When I go out, it is scary because I can't even see our house.

"You know it's there because it's your home," Granny says. "Home is more than a house. It's like a nest or a den or an earth. It's the place you can find even if you are blinded by fog or fear. It's the place where you know you belong."

The oven-bird gives his harsh cry that echoes on and on in the fog. I hold on tightly to Granny's hand.

"That bird makes his house of mud and it looks just like an oven. Come! Would you like to play in the mud? Let's build our own mud house just for fun!"

WINTER

2005

AUGUST

No one likes August. It's dark and it's cold and the wind blows from the south so icy that it goes through your clothes. The lapwings scream and dive right at your throat if you go near their nests in the grass. I'd rather stay indoors.

"Nonsense!" Granny laughs. "With that wind your kite will soar! And see, I've finished your quilted silk floss coat. Now, bundle up and out we'll go. We'll stay away from the lapwings' nests and go down to where I saw some trees have begun to grow in the big field I always forget to plow.

WINTER

SEPTEMBER

The fog finally whispers away until one day spring is everywhere. My Granny says:

"When the ipê blossoms as bright and yellow as the sun, you know the cold is gone until next winter."

The thrush starts to sing and the scissor-birds bring their new families from the north. The grass is cool and the air is almost warm. I don't want to stay inside anymore.

I run outside and Chloe laughs to see me roll over and over down the hill.

SPRING

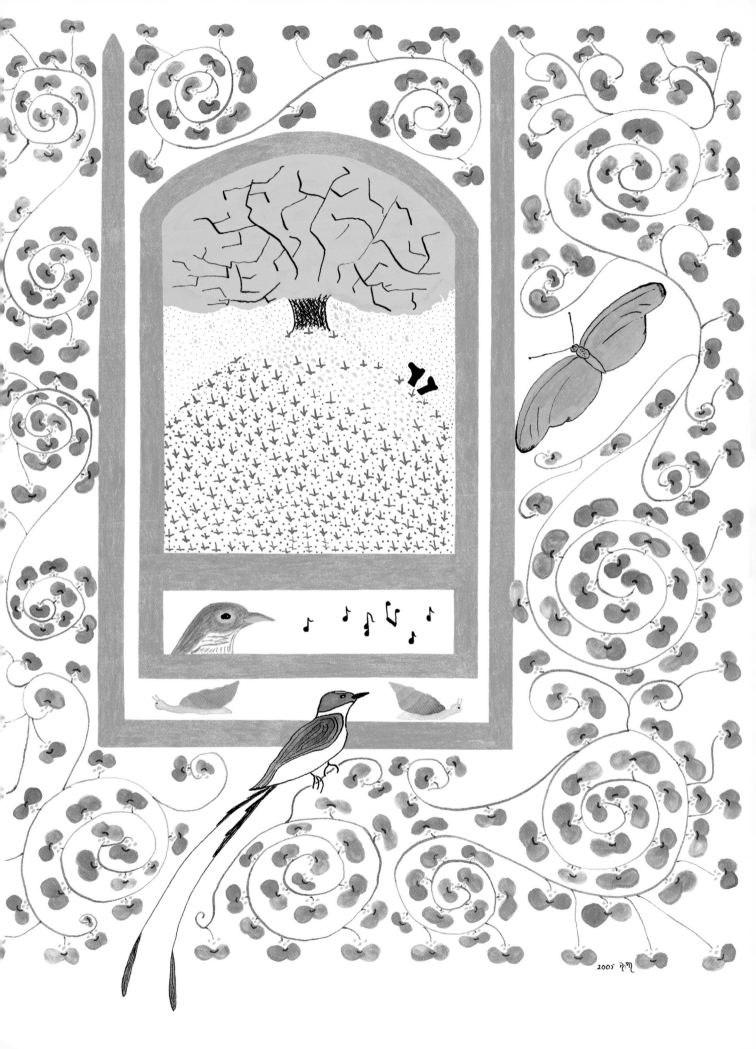

2005 小林

OCTOBER

Oh! We have rain and rain and rain, and even hail as well.

"Sometimes I think springtime is the season of mud," Granny mutters. Suddenly she smiles and points out the window. "Look! The swallows have come back! Right on time, too. They arrive with the rains every year to eat the termites that fly from their flooded mounds."

When the sun comes out we can go out and play. The storm has battered the blossoms from the tiger's claw tree and the ground is all orange. I lie flat and move my arms and legs to make an angel in the flowers. Suddenly, there is a big gong sounding in the forest!

"That fools everyone," Granny laughs. "It's the bell bird." She picks up her trug. "I hope my seeds will all grow to trees so that wonderful bird will return to the big field I always forget to plow."

SPRING

NOVEMBER

One day the rains stop coming so often and it starts to get really hot.

"Time to bring the chickens round the house!" Granny says. "They'll eat the nasty brown spiders that give such bad bites."

Pink dots dangle from everything high. They are Chloe's favorite flower. She carries one around all day and even takes it to bed. It never wilts.

"Those little flowers live on a particular air, between warmth and heat, just when spring turns to summer," Granny says, stroking Chloe's hair. We make platforms for more pink flowers to grow on.

In the garden, the medallion tree blossoms in gold and the primavera bush is covered in purple flowers.

"That's our warm weather sign. It will have flowers from now until the end of autumn. When the last purple flower falls, it will be cold again."

SPRING

2005

DECEMBER

It's summer again! The whole world is hot and green. The hummingbirds buzz. Toucans holler in the evening. Chickens come running when we rake leaves. They like to eat the stinging caterpillars that hide there.

The pitangas are ripe and this year I am big enough to eat them on my own. Granny still has to take out the seeds for Chloe so she won't choke. We save them all.

In the late light of the year's last night, we have a picnic by the waterfall. For many days we have been making little blue boats. Now, we set them afloat. Each has its own twinkling candle, and each has a seed, carrying New Year's wishes as they drift down the stream along the big field my Granny always forgets to plow.

SUMMER

Soon, I'll start school. I'll live with Mama and Papa in the city. But I'll come back to Granny's farm every weekend and every vacation that I can.

And we'll make oven-bird houses and ballerina mobiles and fly kites and float lights and make places for the pink flowers of spring to grow and...and...

"I know, child, I know." Granny hugs me close. "I don't want you to go, but you have work to do now." She wipes my tears and I wipe hers. "I'll make you a promise, my love: when you come back, you shall have my trug to fill with seeds and together we'll bring the forest back to the big field I always forget to plow."

THE
END

BUTTERFLIES AND MOTHS

 Brazilian Skipper   (*Calpodes ethlius*)

 Flame   (*Dryas julia*)

 Grecian Shoemaker   (*Catonephele numilia*)

 Helicon   (*Heliconius ethilla narcaea*)

 Lacewing   (*Actinote sp.*)

 Moth (*Hemiceras*)

 Orange-barred Giant Sulphur   (*Phoebis philea*)

 Orsis Bluewing   (*Myscelia orsis*)

BIRDS

 Azure Jay (*Cyanocorax caeruleus*)

 Bare-throated Bell-bird   (*Procnias nudicollis*)

 Blue-and-White Swallow   (*Notiochelidon cyanoleuca*)

 Scissor bird / Fork-tailed Flycatcher   (*Tyrannus savana*)

 Great Kiskadee   (*Pitangus sulphuratus*)

 Bird of Seven Colors / Green-headed Tanager   (*Tangara seledon*)

 Ovenbird   (*Furnarius rufus*)

Plain Parakeet   (*Brotogeris tirica*)

Red-breasted Toucan   (*Ramphastos dicolorus*)

Rufus-bellied Thrush (*Turdus rufiventris*)

Southern Lapwing   (*Vanellus chilensis*)

Swallow-tailed Hummingbird   (*Eupetomena macroura*)

Trogon   (*Trogon surruca*)

BUGS

Angular Wing Katydid (*Microcentrum*)

Brown Recluse Spider (*Lexosceles*)

Cicada (*Fidicina mannifera*)

Leaf-cutter Ant (*Atta sexdens*)

Lonomia Caterpillar   (*Lonomia obliqua*)

Millipede (*Diplopoda*)

Rhinoceros Beetle (*Oryctes nasicornis*)

Walking Stick (*Phasmatodea*)

Winged Termite (*Isoptera*)

TREES and PLANTS

Golden medallion tree   (*Cassia leptophylla*)

Ipê   (*Tabebuia chrysotricha*)

Paraná pine   (*Araucaria angustifolia*)

Pitanga (*Eugenia uniflora*)

Primavera / Bougainvillea   (*Bougainvillea spectabilis*)

Silk floss tree   (*Ceiba speciosa*)

Tiger's claw tree   (*Erythina falcata*)

Yesterday-Today-Tomorrow (*Brunfelsia pauciflora*)

Forthcoming Children's Titles from KWS Publishers

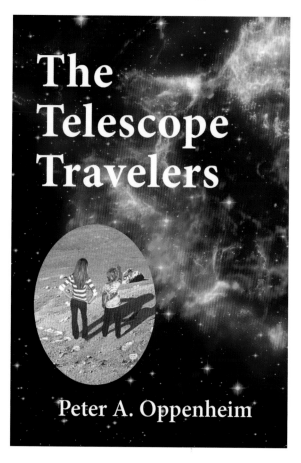

The Telescope Travelers

PETER A. OPPENHEIM

Eight-year-old Zack and eleven-year-old Taylor are an adventurous and intelligent brother-and-sister pair who lead a normal American suburban life with their parents. One day, while vacationing at the beach, they find a mysterious box buried in the sand that contains a telescope—but it's not just any telescope, as Zack and Taylor will quickly find out. This telescope will allow them to travel to worlds far beyond that of their comfortable suburban one—and will show them firsthand what other humans have only dreamed of seeing!

Where does this telescope come from? And who is the mysterious being who wants them to have it and to use it? Zack and Taylor take the reader on a series of adventures to see if they can find the answer to these questions, all the while experiencing a sort of space travel that no human has ever quite experienced before.

The Telescope Travelers will thrill children in the 7 to 12 age range—boys and girls alike—with stories of space travel and planetary adventures that take place beyond the scope of their own planet. This book is also an excellent introduction to science and astronomy for children who appreciate a little intrigue and excitement thrown in with their learning.

Enjoy the thrills that Zack and Taylor encounter with their unique telescope as they explore the moon and the rings of Saturn—and find a way to be home in time for dinner!

About the Author

Peter A. Oppenheim has been fascinated with astronomy and space travel since watching the first moon landing as a child on Long Island, New York. He is an avid astrophotographer who takes images of nebulae, galaxies and other astronomical wonders from his self-built observatory. His photographs have been featured in major magazines such as *Astronomy* and *Time Off*. Mr. Oppenheim has been an active volunteer in Project Astro Nova, which teams astronomers with teachers to bring hands-on astronomy to the classroom.

When he's not writing or attending NASA's Space Academy in Huntsville, Alabama, Mr. Oppenheim provides risk and crisis management services to large corporations. He resides in Prescott, Arizona.

Hardcover and e-Book • 6 x 9 • 60 pages • 13 color photos • ISBN: 978-1-937783-17-4 • August 2012 • $14.95

Forthcoming Children's Titles from KWS Publishers

There Were Dinosaurs Everywhere!: A *Rhyming Romp Through Dinosaur History*

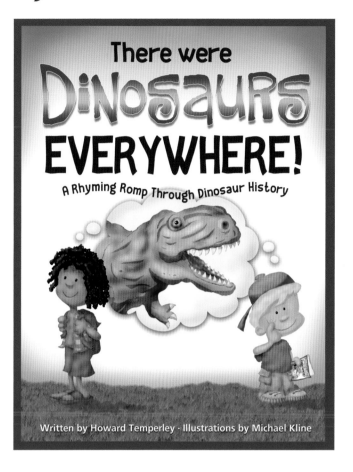

Howard Temperley
Illustrations by Michael Kline

The phenomenon of the dinosaur is one that continues to fascinate people of all ages. It is not hard to see why: these monstrous creatures dominated the earth in their day somewhat similarly to the way humans dominate the earth today. Certainly, the vast differences between dinosaurs and humans probably account for the enthrallment—we are amazed that such "mythical" creatures actually did exist.

There Were Dinosaurs Everywhere!: A Rhyming Romp Through Dinosaur History is a fun-filled history of the many species of dinosaurs, their eras, interesting facts about them, why the age of dinosaurs came to an end, and a dinosaur timeline—all told in an appealing verse form that children from ages 5 to 12 will find informative, funny and unforgettable.

This book contains much of the factual and historical information that a middle-school textbook on dinosaurs might contain, but the big difference between such textbooks and *There Were Dinosaurs Everywhere!* is that this is an instructional, educational book that no child (and perhaps many adults) will not want to put down.

Mr. Temperley's verse is captivating and catchy; Mr. Kline's illustrations are amusing and attractive. This is a unique addition to children's books on dinosaurs, and it is sure to stand out from the others—those that simply don't have the same flair for telling a very popular story.

About the Author

Howard Temperley lives in Norwich England, where until recently, he taught American History at the nearby University of East Anglia. He began writing humorous poems about dinosaurs for his two grandchildren, who showed them to classmates and teachers—with whom the verse proved to be quite popular. He was soon on his way to writing *There Were Dinosaurs Everywhere!* Although he has published several academic books and a memoir, this is his first children's book.

About the Illustrator

Michael Kline is fascinated by the way in which children view the world—including the adults who populate it. Add to that his gift for imbuing animals (often cats and dogs) with human thoughts and you have a man whose drawings bring words to life for people of all ages. Through his art in more than forty books and in *Kids Discover* magazine, children may be familiar with Mr. Kline's ability to illustrate facts with an appropriate dose of humor and imagination. Mr. Kline, who often visits classrooms to teach the art of creating cartoons, lives in Wichita, Kansas with his wife and children.

Hardcover • 8-½ x 11 • 80 pages • 86 color illustrations • ISBN: 978-1-937783-16-7 • August 2012 • $24.95

The Adviser's Guide to
HEALTH
CARₓE

Consulting with
Professional Practices

10785-356

Robert James Cimasi

MHA, ASA, CBA, AVA, CM&AA

Notice to Readers

The Adviser's Guide to Healthcare: Consulting with Professional Practices does not represent an official position of the American Institute of Certified Public Accountants, and it is distributed with the understanding that the author and publisher are not rendering, legal, accounting, or other professional services in the publication. This work offers a detailed treatment of basic characteristics related to various statutes and regulations that address topics within the healthcare professional practices industry. This book is intended to be an overview of the topics discussed within, and the author has made every attempt to verify the completeness and accuracy of the information herein. However, neither the author nor publisher can guarantee the applicability of the information found herein. If legal advice or other expert assistance is required, the services of a competent professional should be sought.

Publisher: Amy M. Stainken
Developmental Editor: Andrew Grow
Project Manager: Amy Sykes
Cover Design Direction: Clay Porter
Interior Designer: David McCradden

Dedication

Dedicated to my wife

Laura M. Baumstark, MBA, CAE

Acknowledgements

The assistance and support of a number of my HEALTH CAPITAL CONSULTANTS (HCC) colleagues were instrumental to the development and publication of this *Guide*. HCC's Vice President, Anne P. Sharamitaro, Esq., was central to the development of this project, both in conducting and directing the research for this book and in coordinating the efforts of all those who contributed to the project.

Todd A. Zigrang, MBA, MHA, FACHE, senior vice president, who has excelled for more than fifteen years in representing HCC throughout numerous healthcare professional practice and other client engagements, greatly assisted in contributing to this work.

HCC Senior Research Manager, Rachel L. Seiler, contributed significantly to this book and was tireless in her efforts and consistently innovative and enthusiastic throughout the research and writing phases of the project.

Kathryn A. Young, Esq.; Stephanie E. Gwillim, Esq.; Tim Alexander, MLS; and other members of HCC's library and research staff, as well as members of HCC's consulting and administrative support team, were of great help.

Also, many thanks to our professional colleagues who served as reviewers and commentators of the various drafts of this work along the way, including: David W. Ortbals, MD, FACP; William J. Hartel, DMD; and Timothy A. Wingert, OD, each of whom reviewed various chapters, as well as Richard D. Thorsen, CPA/ABV, CMEA, CVA, for his comments and contributing the *Foreword* to this *Guide*.

Finally, many thanks to Andrew J. Grow, Manager—Developmental Editing Services, at the AICPA, who served as my editor on this project. He deserves significant credit for his long suffering patience and persistent support.

Foreword

Whether we have been providing professional consulting services for many years, as I have, or we are relative newcomers to the field of consulting services, the current state of the healthcare environment certainly can tend to make us all feel a bit bewildered. The ongoing technological, economic, and political changes that are happening require all of us to arm ourselves with the knowledge and skills necessary to address these changes. Bob Cimasi's new, comprehensive, reference work is an essential tool if we are to be able to provide useful specialized advice to our clients.

This *Guide*, containing 18 chapters of up-to-date specialized information concerning every aspect of healthcare Professional Practices, is a monumental collection of detailed, useful information for CPAs, Business Valuators, Attorneys, Financial Planners, Health Care Executives, Administrators, and even for Physicians and Surgeons. It covers the waterfront of the types of entities providing healthcare services with specific attention to each medical and dental specialty.

In examining this vast range of entities and professionals, this *Guide* does not confine its presentations to highlights only. Rather, it delves deeply and precisely into the finer points of problems and opportunities confronting each of the specialized healthcare professional practice entities. A recurring theme throughout the book is to consider the delivery of healthcare professional services within the context of what Bob Cimasi terms "the four pillars of the healthcare industry, i.e., *regulatory, reimbursement, competition*, and *technology*."

As a CPA, business appraiser, and consultant who has practiced for 56 years, I believe that this monumental book should be in the library of every CPA firm, business valuation firm, legal firm, financial planner, and consultant who hopes to continue to serve clients in the healthcare field competently in these rapidly changing times. As I have learned as the father of a long-time practicing critical-care internist and hospitalist, I believe that the book also is a must for the libraries of professional physicians, surgeons, dentists, and administrators who are on the every-day firing lines trying to survive the sea of change in their respective professions. And before closing, I want to say some words about the author, Bob Cimasi. I have known Bob for many years, first as a participant in professional seminars and conferences in which he has been a presenter, and later on a more direct professional and personal basis. Throughout these years, I have been impressed with both his technical knowledge, and even more importantly, the unselfish and tireless sharing of his time, talent, and accumulated knowledge with his professional colleagues in the accounting, business valuation, and consulting professions. There are few people in the world that I have known who are of his caliber! This *Guide* confirms again what many of us know. Bob Cimasi is truly one-of-a-kind dedicated professional whose writings are worth reading.

Richard D. Thorsen, CPA/ABV, CMEA, CVA
May 2010
Past Member, Board of Directors and Vice President of the American Institute of CPAs (AICPA)

Preface

"Tho' much is taken, much abides." (Ulysses) Lord Alfred Tennyson, 1833

I was born in 1950, the fourth child in our family, and the first born in a hospital—my older brothers and sisters having been delivered in my grandmother's bed. In the small, upstate New York farming community where I was raised, doctor house calls were not unusual. When an injury or sudden illness required a response by emergency services, the dispatcher would sound the community sirens, signaling the volunteer firemen on duty to radio ahead from their emergency vehicle to the small, four-bed, rural hospital, which would then alert one of the three physicians in the community to rush to the hospital to provide emergency care. When our neighbors developed musculoskeletal conditions from working on the farms or in small manufacturing plants and machine shops, they would visit the town chiropractor who would perform manipulation and prescribe vitamins and various homeopathic remedies. The local dentist's services were in great demand with the prefluorination, widespread incidence of juvenile tooth decay. This was a time in U.S. history when *Marcus Welby* was not only a regular family television drama but was also a reasonable characterization of how healthcare services were perceived to be delivered by professional practices throughout much of the country.

During the sixty year period since 1950, the U.S. population has doubled from just more than 150 million to an estimated 300 million in 2010,[1] and the average life expectancy has increased from approximately 68 years to 78 years.[2] With the record number of births of the "baby boomer" generation from the late 1940s through the early 1960s, the proportion of the U.S. population over the age of 65 increased from 8.1 percent in 1950 to an estimated 13.2 percent in 2010.[3] This demographic shift is expected to continue, with the proportion of Americans over 65 expected to reach 20 percent of the total population by 2050—an estimated 360 percent increase over a single century.[4]

This increased life expectancy, and the subsequent "graying" of the U.S. population, with the accompanying rise in the incidence and prevalence of the diseases, conditions, and injuries for which the elderly are more at risk, is expected to continue driving demand for healthcare services, as well as a dynamic evolution in the demand for, the supply of, and the very nature of healthcare professional practices.[5]

Although age-related population trends are one of the key contributors to the changing demand for health services, other changes in the U.S. demographic and economic climate have significant bearing as well. The accelerated population shift from rural to urban areas during the last sixty years also may have influenced the increased incidence and prevalence of disease. Although the urbanization of the United

1   "Current Population Reports," Series P-25, Nos. 311, 917, 1095, National Population Estimates, U.S. Department of Commerce, Economics and Statistics Administration, Bureau of the Census, April 11, 2000, http://www.census.gov/population/estimates/nation/popclockest.txt (accessed 03/26/2010); "Current Population Reports: Population Projections of the United States by Age, Sex, Race, and Hispanic Origin: 1995 to 2050," Series P25-1130, U.S. Department of Commerce, Economics and Statistics Administration, Bureau of the Census, 1996, p. 1. "Table 1. Projections of the Population and Components of Change for the United States: 2010 to 2050 (NP2008-T1)," by U.S. Department of Commerce, Economics and Statistics Administration, Bureau of the Census, Population Division, August 14, 2008.

2   "United States Life Tables, 2003," by the U.S. Department of Health and Human Services, Centers for Disease Control and Prevention, National Center for Health Statistics, National Vital Statistics Report, Volume 54, Number 14, (April 19, 2006), p. 34; "International Data Base," United States Census Bureau, March 19, 2010, http://www.census.gov/ipc/www/idb/country.php (accessed 03/26/2010).

3   "Chapter 2—Age and Sex Composition," in "Demographic Trends in the 20th Century: Census 2000 Special Reports," by Frank Hobbs and Nicole Stoops, U.S. Department of Commerce, Economics and Statistics Administration, United States Census 2000, November 2002, CENSR-4, p. 56; "Table 3: Projections of the Population by Age, Race, and Hispanic Origin for the United States: 1995–2050—Principal Alternative Series," in "Current Population Reports: Population Projections of the United States by Age, Sex, Race, and Hispanic Origin: 1995 to 2050," Series P25-1130, U.S. Department of Commerce, Economics and Statistics Administration, Bureau of the Census, 1996, p. 90.

4   *Ibid.*

5   "The Impact of the Aging Population on the Health Workforce in the United States," by the National Center for Health Workforce Analysis, Bureau of Health Professions Health Resources and Services Administration, December 2005, p. 10; "Health, United States, 2008, With Special Feature on the Health of Young Adults," U.S. Department of Health and Human Services, National Center for Disease Statistics, March 2009, http://www.cdc.gov/nchs/data/hus/hus08.pdf#120 (accessed 09/11/2009), p. 4.

States was already under way in 1950, this shift continued to reshape the population distribution, with the urban population increasing from 64 percent of the U.S. population in 1950, to almost 80 percent in 2010.[6]

Additionally, the shift from an agrarian into an industrialized society, and once again into a service-driven economy, has affected the American lifestyle and related health trends.[7] The waning of family farms and rise of industrialized agriculture resulted in a shift in the U.S. diet. High-calorie commodities laden with fats, oils, and sugars, were mass produced at the expense of farming affordable, fresh, and nutritious produce.[8] With this increased availability, and, consequently, the consumption of high caloric-energy, came a decrease in energy expended, arising from the sedentary, high stress, and extended work day practices characteristic of many service industry sectors (for example, finance, legal, insurance and real estate, retail trade, and public utilities). The emergence and proliferation of automobile transportation, decreased emphasis on the family unit, and sedentary recreational habits led to a decrease in physical activity. These factors further fueled the impact of the fast food industry and processed food consumption on the health of the U.S. population, now plagued by chronic diseases for which obesity and poor diet are often major co-morbidities.[9]

The increased demand driven by these changes and other economic and demographic variables may have, in part, fueled the increase in healthcare expenditures from 5 percent of GDP in 1950, to more than 17 percent in 2010.[10] Increased spending also may be a consequence of the surge in technological and other medical advances in the healthcare industry, promulgated at the close of World War II and encouraged by the increase in federal and state funding for healthcare expenditures.[11] Since the adoption of Medicare in 1965, public (government) payors have come to fund more than half of all healthcare expenditures.[12]

Also, among the driving forces of U.S. healthcare industry trends that impact professional practices are the supply and distribution of various types and multiple levels of healthcare professionals who work within a dynamic framework of myriad competing interests in order to meet the growing needs of an aging and, in many ways, less healthy population. As a result of technological and medical advances, specialized medicine flourished across the healthcare workforce, growing as a significant trend in the 1950s.[13] In response to the past and present surge in demand, the physician population has increased from 219,997 in 1950 to 954,224 in 2009, and the number of physicians per 100,000 individuals has increased from 142.2 to 316.4.

Despite these growing workforce trends, it is expected that, with a disproportionate number of physicians retiring, an inadequate supply medical graduates, and the expected continuing growth in demand, the present shortage in supply of physician manpower will continue to worsen.[14] As a result, there has

---

6 "Table 1. Urban and Rural population: 1900–1990," by the U.S. Department of Commerce, Economics and Statistics Administration, Bureau of the Census, October 1995, http://www.census.gov/population/censusdata/urpop0090.txt (accessed 03/26/2010); U.S. Census Bureau 2010 Census Planning Data Base, U.S. Department of Commerce, Economics and Statistics Administration, Bureau of the Census, 2010, http://www.census.gov/procur/www/2010communications /tract%20level%20pdb%20with%20census%202000%20data%2001-19-07.pdf (accessed 03/26/2010).

7 "Obesity and the Economy: From Crisis to Opportunity," by Davis S. Ludwig, MD, PhD and Harold A. Pollack PhD, the Journal of the American Medical Association, Volume 301, Number 5, (February 4, 2009), p. 533; "The Role of Services in the Modern U.S. Economy," by Douglas B. Cleveland, Office of Service Industries, January 1999.

8 Ibid.

9 Ibid.

10 "Health Care Expenditures in the OECD," by the National Bureau of Economic Research, 2006, http://www.nber.org/aginghealth/winter06/w11833.html (accessed 03/26/2010); .

11 "Plunkett's Health Care Industry Trends and Statistics 2008 (Summary)," By Jack W. Plunkett, Plunkett Research Ltd., 2007, p. 3.

12 "Chapter 6—Health Care Personnel," and "Chapter 7—Financing Healthcare" in "Health Care USA: Understanding its Organization and Delivery," by Harry A. Sultz and Kristina M. Young, Jones and Bartlett Publishers, Sixth Edition (2009), p.196, 234–235.

13 "Chapter 7—Financing Healthcare" in "Health Care USA: Understanding its Organization and Delivery," by Harry A. Sultz and Kristina M. Young, Jones and Bartlett Publishers, Sixth Edition (2009), p. 231.

14 "Physician Characteristics and Distribution in the US 2010 Edition" American Medical Association, 2010, p. 458; "Table 201—Total and Active Physicians (MDs) and Physician-to Population Ratios, Selected Years: 1950-2000," in "Health Resources Statistics, 1965," by the U.S. Department of Health, Education, and Welfare, National Center for Health Statistics, PHS Pub. No. 1509, 1966.

been a further increase in diversification of the healthcare workforce, comprised of more than 13 million individuals, with fewer than one million being physicians.[15] The diversification, specialization, and collaboration of physician and nonphysician practitioners has increased, expanded, and enhanced to meet the compounding demand. This *Guide* addresses not just physician medical practices but discusses a comprehensive array of professional practice types, as well as the various practitioners that comprise the healthcare workforce, including allied health professionals, mid-level providers, and technicians and paraprofessionals, as well as complementary and alternative medical practitioners.

Although professional practice enterprises currently account for $447 billion of a $2.26 trillion healthcare market (19.8 percent), recent efforts at regulatory and reimbursement reform suggest that healthcare professional practices may be facing an unprecedented dramatic transition.[16] The evolution and increasing complexity of healthcare reimbursement, regulatory, competitive, and technological environments has made it more difficult for professionals to maintain revenue yield while avoiding running afoul of regulatory edicts.

A notable element of these challenges is an industry transition reflected in the recent increase in the number of hospital-employed physicians, and the dwindling of physician-ownership of private, independent practices. A growing number of young physicians, plagued by medical school debt and intent upon achieving a more comfortable work-life balance, are opting out of private, independent practice and pursing salaried employment by hospitals and health systems.

These trends have made it increasingly difficult for older independent practitioners to recruit junior partners, a struggle which, paired with the burden of rising costs, has led many physician-owners to sell their practices to hospitals and enter into salaried employment arrangements as well. This shift further away from the independent practice of medicine as a "cottage industry" in the United States may be viewed by patients as both a blessing and a burden of the changing healthcare delivery system. On one hand, the trend away from small, physician- or provider-owned, independent private practices holds the promise of improved quality and cost efficiency for the delivery of better and integrated medical care. Alternately, the "corporatization" of healthcare professional practices may result in a weakening of the independent physician- or provider-patient relationship, an intimacy and level of trust that was long a characteristic of the cottage industry healthcare delivery system of old.[17] Given these trends in healthcare professional practices, it may not be far-fetched to believe that "Marcus Welby is dead!" (see chapter 2 of *Professional Practices*).

These dramatic and ongoing changes, as well as the sheer size and complexity of the healthcare delivery system, have provided new opportunities in healthcare consultancy. Responding to the expanding market in the current era of reform, many financial and management consulting firms have extended their service line to include healthcare advisory services. Accounting firms, which traditionally have served as primary business and financial advisors for their clients, also have steadily increased the scope of their healthcare professional practice advisory services.

The persistent volatility of the healthcare industry landscape can be difficult to navigate. To be effective in offering services to healthcare professional practice clients, consulting professionals should possess an understanding of the history and background of professional practice enterprises, as well as the market mechanisms at work in the current healthcare environment—in particular, how those forces

---

15 *Ibid.*
16 "Plunkett's Health Care Industry Trends and Statistics 2008 (Summary)," By Jack W. Plunkett, Plunkett Research Ltd., 2007, p. 44.
17 "More Doctors Giving Up Private Practices," by Gardiner Harris, New York Times, March 25, 2010; "The Social Transformation of American Medicine," by Paul Starr, Basic Books Inc. 1982, p. ix.

interact to shape the future direction of professional practices in the healthcare delivery system under pending legislative reform.

Although consultancy for healthcare professional practices may present an attractive business development opportunity for consultants, it is not an area that lends itself to ad hoc, generic advisory services. In light of the increasingly complex, diverse, and ever-changing scope and volume of information that contributes to a comprehensive understanding of the healthcare industry, consulting professionals who possess a more general background and expertise and pursue providing services to healthcare professional practices may endeavor to become better informed to avoid being viewed, in some regard, as jacks of all trades and masters of none.

This three book set is designed to serve as a reference guide for those seeking a more in-depth knowledge of the healthcare marketplace; a working and applied understanding of the forces that affect the industry within which healthcare providers operate; and a primer regarding how consulting services may be offered to these enterprises specifically, healthcare professional practices, in an ever-changing reimbursement, regulatory, competitive, and technological healthcare environment. Such industry-specific knowledge should serve as a catalyst for these consulting professionals to better serve their existing clients and expand their services for potential new engagements.

This *Guide* may also prove useful to the licensed healthcare professionals who own independent practices, as well as their professional advisors, managers, and administrators. Providing these stakeholders with in-depth background information and a context within which to view professional practice enterprises as part of a dynamic healthcare marketplace may enhance their ability to assist their organizations in surviving and thriving in the future.

With the first publication of this *Guide*, we earnestly solicit reader comments, criticisms, and suggestions for improvements in future editions.

Sincerely,

Robert James Cimasi, MHA, ASA, CBA, AVA, CM&AA
HEALTH CAPITAL CONSULTANTS
Saint Louis, Missouri
November, 2010

Table of Contents

About the Author

Robert James Cimasi, MHA, ASA, CBA, AVA, CM&AA

Robert James Cimasi is President of Health Capital Consultants (HCC), a nationally recognized health-care financial and economic consulting firm. With more than twenty-five years of experience in serving healthcare clients in forty-nine states. Mr. Cimasi's professional focus is on the financial and economic aspects of healthcare organizations including the valuation of enterprises, assets, and services; litigation support and expert testimony; business intermediary and capital formation services for healthcare industry transactions; certificate-of-need; and other regulatory and policy planning consulting.

Mr. Cimasi holds a Masters in Health Administration from the University of Maryland, the Accredited Senior Appraiser (ASA) designation in Business Valuation, as well as the Certified Business Appraiser (CBA), Accredited Valuation Analyst (AVA), and the Certified Merger & Acquisition Advisor (CM&AA). He is a nationally known speaker on healthcare industry topics and has served as conference faculty or presenter for such organizations as the American Society of Appraisers, the American Institute of Certified Public Accountants, the Institute of Business Appraisers, the National Association of Certified Valuation Analysts, the American College of Healthcare Executives, the National Society of Certified Healthcare Business Consultants, Academy Health, Healthcare Financial Management Association, the American Association of Ambulatory Surgery Centers, Physician Hospitals of America, the Health Industry Group Purchasing Association, and the National Litigation Support Services Association, as well as numerous other national and state healthcare industry associations, professional societies, trade groups, companies, and organizations. He has been certified and has served as an expert witness on cases in numerous federal and state venues, and he has provided testimony before federal and state legislative committees. In 2006, Mr. Cimasi was honored with the prestigious Shannon Pratt Award in Business Valuation conferred by the Institute of Business Appraisers.

Mr. Cimasi is the author of *A Guide to Consulting Services for Emerging Healthcare Organizations* (John Wiley & Sons, 1999), *The Valuation of Healthcare Entities in a Changing Regulatory and Reimbursement Environment* (IBA Course 1011 text—1999), and *An Exciting Insight Into the Health Care Industry and Medical Practice Valuation* (AICPA course text 1997, rev. 2006). He has authored chapters on healthcare valuation in *The Handbook of Business Valuation* (John Wiley & Sons), *Valuing Professional Practices and Licenses: A Guide for the Matrimonial Practitioner, 3rd ed., 1999* (Aspen Law & Business), and *Valuing Specific Assets in Divorce* (Aspen Law & Business) and has been a contributor to *The Guide to Business Valuations* (Practitioners Publishing Company), *Physician's Managed Care Success Manual: Strategic Options, Alliances, and Contracting Issues* (Mosby), and numerous other chapters. He has written published articles in peer review journals, frequently presented research papers and case studies before national conferences, and is often quoted by healthcare industry professional publications and the general media. Mr. Cimasi's latest book, *The U.S. Healthcare Certificate of Need Sourcebook*, was published in 2005 by Beard Books.

Introduction

These papers, advocating a more active participation in public affairs by physicians than has been the custom in this country, are reprinted with the belief that such broader activity on the part of my colleagues will help to free the State from many present evils. A good doctor must be educated, honest, sensible and brave. Nothing more is needed in its citizens to make a state great.

John B. Roberts, 1908

THE FOUR PILLARS OF THE HEALTHCARE INDUSTRY

When developing an understanding of the forces and stakeholders that have the potential to drive healthcare markets, it is useful to examine professional practice enterprises as they relate to the "four pillars" of the healthcare industry: reimbursement, regulatory, competition, and technology (see the following figure I-1). These four elements shape the professional practice and provider dynamic, while serving as a framework for analyzing the viability, efficiency, efficacy, and productivity of healthcare enterprises. The four pillars, discussed briefly in this introduction, are discussed at length in chapters 2-5 in *An Era of Reform*.

Figure I-1: Four Pillars of Healthcare Enterprises

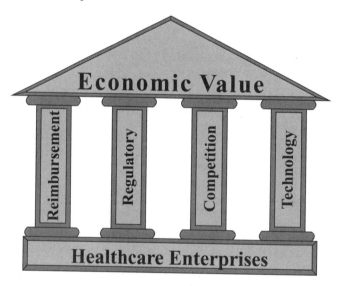

REIMBURSEMENT

Chapter 2 of *An Era of Reform* provides an overview of current and future trends in healthcare reimbursement. With healthcare reform on the horizon, it is vital for providers to maintain an applied understanding of healthcare payment sources (for example, Medicare, Medicaid, State Children's Health Insurance Program, etc.), revenue and billing procedures (for example, the resource-based relative value scale payment system, relative value units and their components, Current Procedural Terminology codes, etc.), and payment plans (for example, fee-for-service plans, performance-based payment plans, and consumer driven health plans).

As healthcare expenditures rise, proponents of reform advocate for both a reduction in service costs and increases in quality of care. To achieve these goals, the industry variously has moved toward managed care, pay-for-performance programs, gainsharing arrangements, and patient-centered models of medical practice (for example, boutique medicine, the medical home model, etc.). In addition, reimbursement for physician services has become a highly contested issue; repeated annual congressional overrides of reductions to physician payment rates for services under the sustainable growth rate system have created a large gap in current healthcare spending and target (sustainable) expenditures. To combat these rising costs, for example, the high expenditures for imaging services, billing codes have, during the past decade, been "bundled." Bundling has been utilized to reduce the overall payment for certain interrelated services by billing for them under one, combined code, rather than under independent codes. The emergence of bundled codes, among other trends, is evidence of the rapidly changing reimbursement environment within the U.S. healthcare delivery system.

REGULATORY

The U.S. healthcare industry is governed by a network of ever-changing state and federal regulations, relating to both physician and nonphysician professionals. Chapter 3 of *An Era of Reform* contains a detailed overview of the general provisions that apply to the various practitioners and providers in the healthcare industry.

Various key regulatory issues may influence the healthcare climate. For example, in recent years, there has been increased government scrutiny of regulatory violations of fraud and abuse laws, particularly as the violations relate to acquisition and compensation transactions between hospitals and physicians. Failure to comply with valuation standards for physician and executive compensation arrangements (for example, fair market value and commercial reasonableness) may result in liability under the False Claims Act, the antikickback statute, and the Stark law. Chapter 3 of *An Era of Reform* includes a discussion of these concepts and regulations along with the definitions, applications, implications, and trends of additional federal and state healthcare laws and regulations (for example, Certificate of Need programs).

COMPETITION

Additionally, rapid changes in the healthcare competitive market may be attributed to the ever-increasing demand for care from the aging baby boomer population and to the continuous development of new technologies, the latter which may enhance the quality and efficiency of the healthcare delivery system. In recent years, there has been a rapid growth in the number of limited-service providers, or "niche providers," such as specialty and surgical hospitals (for example, orthopedic and heart hospitals), which are sometimes referred to as "focused factories."[1] As a result of this trend toward specialization, concern has been raised that the medical care offered by niche providers may have a negative impact on the profitability of general acute care hospitals, which traditionally have provided specialty and primary care to patients. Similarly, there has been a movement toward increasing the scope and volume of mid-level provider-issued care, resulting in additional market competition for physicians.

The changing demographics of the patient population (that is, the baby boomer population) and the physician workforce also may have a lasting impact on the healthcare competitive environment. There has been an increase in concern related to the shortage of physician manpower and the limited number of available residency slots that restrict physician entry into the healthcare market. Among the most notable concerns is the perceived shortage of primary care physicians; with many medical students opting for careers in higher-paying medical specialties, primary care physicians are pressed more than ever to meet patient demand for services. Additionally, women and minorities make up a much higher percentage of the physician workforce than they have in the past (in most specialties), effectively diversifying the traditionally Caucasian male physician demographic. Although they provide patients with more choices for care, they also are presenting challenges related to the demands of achieving a practice—lifestyle balance.

These issues and numerous others, such as healthcare and insurance reform, shape the unique and dynamic healthcare competitive environment. Chapter 4 of *An Era of Reform* includes a more detailed examination of these issues within the context of Porter's five forces of competition.

TECHNOLOGY

Significant technological advances during the past few decades have had a notable impact on the U.S. healthcare delivery system. Electronic health record technologies gradually have been integrated into medical records maintenance systems, replacing traditional paper files. Similarly, Computerized physician order entry has streamlined the process of ordering prescriptions and minimized error caused by handwritten orders. Although these new electronic approaches to healthcare delivery are saving employers money, physician unwillingness to adopt these new technologies has impeded their widespread emergence into the healthcare market. Regardless, new and improved management technology is slowly becoming an important facet of the healthcare industry.

Progress in clinical technology also has flourished in recent years, including highly controversial practices such as stem cell research. However, one of the various genres of medical services that may have drawn the most attention is *imaging*; services that utilize the technology, such as the various types of magnetic resonance imaging, computed tomography (for example, positron emission tomography-computed tomography, single photon emission computed tomography, and picture archiving and communications systems), and teleradiology services, have become a staple in modern diagnostic radiology practice.

Oncologists and surgeons also have seen major advancements in the treatment and detection of cancer and in minimally invasive or noninvasive surgery, respectively. For oncologists, radiation therapy methods are improving continuously, and their use of innovative alternative and supporting technologies, such as image-guided radiation therapy, which is used during intensity-modulated radiation therapy; gamma knives; and stereotactic radiosurgery, is increasing. The use of robotics has become a rapidly advancing trend, and surgeons with robotics experience are sought after for their skills. Robotic technologies have been used for urologic, gynecologic, and cardiothoracic procedures, among others. Although expensive, robotic technology minimizes the degree of invasiveness, shortens recovery time, and improves patient outcomes.

These advancements in medical technology have helped to revolutionize modern medicine. The cost of implementing and maintaining these new devices and procedures, however, may counterbalance efforts to control healthcare expenditures. The future of healthcare may well depend on a compromise between the advancement of medical technological capabilities and the cost of supporting those technologies that allows practitioners to provide the best quality care possible. Chapter 5 of *An Era of Reform* includes a more detailed discussion of the impact of technology on healthcare practices.

STRUCTURE OF THIS *GUIDE*

This *Guide* serves as a resource for consulting professionals who provide services to professional practices and related healthcare providers. It is divided into three books:

1. *An Era of Reform*, consisting of six chapters, begins with an abridged history of healthcare, from the origins of medicine to the transformation of modern healthcare in the twentieth and twenty-first centuries (chapter 1). The next several chapters (chapters 2–5) provide a more comprehensive look at the reimbursement, regulatory, competitive, and technological environments as they

apply to healthcare practice. The last chapter (chapter 6) provides an overview of the healthcare environment and related healthcare reform bills, at the time of the submission of this *Guide*.

2. *Professional Practices*, consisting of eight chapters, discusses the myriad of practice structures (chapter 1), medical specialties, and professionals seen in healthcare to date. This discussion includes emerging models of healthcare enterprises, physicians, mid-level providers, technicians and paraprofessionals, allied health professionals, alternative medicine practitioners, and a new paradigm for professional practices (chapters 2–8, respectively), as well as information regarding the scope of subspecialties, types of providers, and practitioners of each service type.

3. *Consulting with Professional Practices*, consisting of four chapters, provides a descriptive overview for consultants advising professional practice clients on matters related to healthcare consulting (chapter 1); benchmarking strategies related to healthcare and valuation (chapter 2); compensation and income distribution (chapter 3); and financial valuation of healthcare enterprises, assets, and services (chapter 4). The information provided in these chapters should supply the reader with the tools necessary to translate healthcare consulting theory into practice.

It should be noted that this book and second book of this *Guide* focus on the professional practice component of the U.S. healthcare delivery system and do not directly address other healthcare sectors, including inpatient (for example, hospitals), outpatient and ambulatory (for example, ambulatory surgery centers and diagnostic imaging centers), long term care (for example, nursing homes and hospice), and home health sectors. However, many of the concepts and much of the content in this book and second book of this *Guide* may be applicable to consulting projects in these other healthcare sectors, as well.

READER TOOLS: SIDEBARS, TABLES, AND FIGURES

To enhance the utility of this *Guide* as a navigable source for readers of various backgrounds, certain tools have been developed and appear throughout:

1. **Sidebars.** These supplemental features have been integrated into the content of each chapter and have been grouped as follows:

    a. **Key terms.** Key terms are important words used in text that may need to be defined for the reader. This tool can be found at the beginning of each chapter and serves to identify those terms that appear within the text of corresponding chapters as well as in the glossary at the end of this book. Key terms may be discussed, or, at least, mentioned in multiple chapters.

    b. **Key concepts.** Similar to key terms, key concepts are the important concepts mentioned in text that may require further elaboration or emphasis and a list of key concepts can be found at the beginning of each chapter. This tool serves a bimodal role, to further stress important ideas discussed in the chapter and to further discuss ideas that may have only been mentioned in passing.

    c. **Key sources.** This feature points to significant sources, both used within this *Guide* and fundamental to the chapter content. These sources serve as chapter-specific bibliographies, and, therefore, may be found in multiple chapters. Key sources can be found at the end of each chapter.

    d. **Associations.** A brief list of topic-relevant associations provides the reader with contact information for associations referenced within a chapter. A list of related associations can be found at the end of each chapter.

e. **Factoids.** These are brief, related facts of interest either mentioned in text or supplemental to a topic discussed in a particular chapter that help build a contextual framework for the reader that may aid in explaining the material. You will find factoids located close to the content that they address within each chapter.

2. **Tables.** Tables are used to display benchmark data, to demonstrate numerical trends, and to draw comparisons. They are referenced in text, but they may be used to display extra information not discussed in the content of the chapter.

3. **Figures.** Pictorial and graphical depictions have been used to complement the text and enhance the reader's comprehension of the material. These figures are referenced and discussed in text.

PROFESSIONAL PRACTICE TAXONOMY

Healthcare reform is driven by complex, polar, and potentially conflicting market factors, such as increased spending; a growing and graying demographic; workforce shortages and inefficiencies; problematic chronic and acute health indicators; and shortcomings in the delivery of efficient, quality care. The subsequent chapters detail these issues, their implications, and the reform initiatives proposed to delicately counterbalance the U.S. healthcare delivery system on the nation's scale of justice. However, before delving into the complexities of healthcare reimbursement, regulation, competition, and technology, the dynamic healthcare provider workforce should be addressed.

Provider versatility has been growing and changing to complement an evolving healthcare industry.[2] The diverse healthcare workforce is instrumental to improving efficacy, quality of care, financial efficiency, patient satisfaction, workforce productivity, and professional satisfaction.[3] In order to capitalize on this potential, institutions adopt models that strategically allocate physician and nonphysician manpower resources on the basis of scope and skill set—ensuring that the right care is provided by the right provider at the right time and place."[4] Implementation models are characterized by (1) the site of service (for example, hospital, clinic, or community), (2) the guidelines that regulate provider practice and compensation within an intraprofessional care model, (3) the system by which scope of practice is defined for each provider classification, (4) the degree to which providers are liable for their professional actions, and (5) the degree to which they model efficacy and efficiency.[5]

The intraprofessional care models that have been implemented most successfully stem from several provider taxonomies, which were intended to mirror the complex relationships within the existing healthcare workforce. The most influential provider taxonomies (detailed in tables I-1[A-D] and I-2) are each based on a different system of classification that focuses on a portion of the industry dynamic and include those developed by (1) the Human Resources and Services Administration, which utilizes a four-tiered hierarchal system and aggregates specific occupations based on the degree of training and type of services provided (table I-1A); (2) the American Medical Association, which classifies professionals based on the specialized area of medical practice under which they provide their services (table I-1B); and (3) the Centers for Medicare and Medicaid Services, which categorizes professionals based on how they bill these professionals for services (table I-1C). Although these taxonomies are based on key structural considerations, they each neglect certain industry facets, and discrepancies arise due to the limitations that this unilateral rationale presents. The models used to enhance the delivery of intraprofessional care face similar limitations, as institutions typically focus on only one, highly customized model, foregoing a more industrywide perspective by neglecting models that represent the other industry sectors.[6]

Alternately, multiple models can be synthesized to represent an industrywide, intrapersonal dynamic.[7] Elements from three models, the physician extender model, the triage model, and the parallel model, were used to derive the taxonomical system for classifying healthcare professionals that is utilized in this *Guide* (detailed in tables I-1D and I-2).

Traditionally, all nonphysician clinicians are referred to as "allied health professionals."[8] However, advances in technology and capability paired with the change in healthcare demand during the course of medical history have rendered this system of classification far too rudimentary for the diversity that the workforce now holds. As the healthcare industry continues to change and market demand for primary, preventative, and rehabilitative care increases, the varying degrees of responsibility, expertise, and autonomy afforded to the increasingly diverse nonphysician healthcare workforce is reassessed and the scope of practice continues to expand.[9] By creating a taxonomy based on these three representative models, allied health professionals may be partitioned into appropriate substrata of nonphysician providers, because they would function within the ideal intraprofessional workforce dynamic.

Under the physician extender model, the scope of nonphysician professional practice lies entirely within the scope of physician practice.[10] These *physician extenders* (hereinafter "technicians and paraprofessionals") supplement physician care, either as highly technical or technological support or as manpower support.[11] Specifically, one subset of the professionals defined within this model is trained in a highly specialized technical or technological field and provides services that physicians rely upon but are incapable of providing independently. The other subset of professionals, physician extenders, provides routine medical and administrative services to relieve physicians of a portion of their workload, allowing them to focus on more difficult and complex tasks. From an official standpoint, these professionals may or may not be licensed or certified (depending on which subset of the provider population they belong to or which role they tend to fill most appropriately).

The original rationale behind the classification of "mid-level providers," as defined for the purposes of this *Guide*, derives from the *triage model*.[12] Under this model, nonphysician professionals are trained to provide a specific subset of physician services, and they traditionally serve as a source of physician relief by providing triage care and enhancing patient throughput.[13] Historically, these providers could only practice under direct or indirect supervision of a physician.[14] As demand increased, namely for the provision primary care services, the autonomy of mid-level providers increased.[15] To date, these professionals are relied upon for the provision of specialized services that are incident to physician services but also exercise a certain measure of independence, because they can autonomously provide a specific scope of services in lieu of physicians.[16] The services which mid-level providers are authorized to provide in lieu of physicians typically are limited to a portion of primary care practice healthcare services, and, consistent with the triage model, complex cases are handed off to physicians, because they may fall outside that predetermined scope of service.[17]

The *parallel model* lies on the opposite end of the spectrum. Under this model, the scope of the allied health professional practice is separate, distinct, and, essentially, parallel to the scope of physician practice.[18] These allied health professionals are nonphysician practioners who practice independently and offer services that, despite some overlap with physician care, are largely outside the scope of physician practices.[19] Although allied health professionals (as defined in this *Guide*) and physicians sometimes may compete due to shared patient populations and practice objectives, the specific services they provide typically have distinct differences.

Table I-1A: Healthcare Professional Practices Provider Taxonomies
Organization: Bureau of Labor Statistics   **Classification System:** A six-digit hierarchal structure resulting in four levels of aggregation (categories): Category 1=Major Group, Category 2=Minor Group, Category 3=Broad Occupation, Category 4=Detailed Occupation.

Category	Definition	Subcategories
Healthcare Practitioners and Technical Occupations	Major Occupational Group A—Professional occupations concerns with the study, application, and/or administration of medical practices or theories. Some occupations are concerned with interpreting, informing, expressing, or promoting ideas, products, etc. by written, artistic, sound, or physical medium. This category also includes technical occupations, involved in carrying out technical and technological functions in health. May perform research, development, testing, and related activities. May operate technical equipment and systems.	**Health Diagnosing Occupations**

Subcategories (continued):

Health Diagnosing Occupations

Chiropractors

Dentists

Dentists, General	Prosthodontists
Oral and Maxillofacial Surgeons	Dentists, All Other Specialties
Orthodontists	

Optometrists

Physicians and Surgeons

Podiatrists

Veterinarians

Health Assessment and Treating Occupations

Dietitians and Nutritionists

Pharmacists

Physician Assistants

Therapists

Occupational Therapist	Respiratory Therapists
Physical Therapist	Speech-Language Pathologist
Radiation Therapists	Exercise Physiologists
Recreational Therapists	Therapists, All Other

Registered Nurses

Nurse Anesthetists

Nurse Midwives

Nurse Practitioners

Miscellaneous Health Diagnosing/Treating Practitioners

Health Technologists and Technicians

Clinical Laboratory Technologists/Technicians

Medical and Clinical Laboratory Technologists	Medical and Clinical Laboratory Technicians

Dental Hygienists

Diagnostic Related Technologists and Technicians

Cardiovascular Technologists and Technicians	Radiologic Technologists
Diagnostic Medical Sonographers	Magnetic Resonance Imaging Technologists
Nuclear Medicine Technologists	

Table I-1A: Healthcare Professional Practices Provider Taxonomies *(continued)*
Organization: Bureau of Labor Statistics   **Classification System:** A six-digit hierarchal structure resulting in four levels of aggregation (categories): Category 1=Major Group, Category 2=Minor Group, Category 3=Broad Occupation, Category 4=Detailed Occupation.

Category	Definition	Subcategories	
Healthcare Practitioners and Technical Occupations *(continued)*		*Emergency Medical Technicians/Paramedics*	
		Health Practitioner Support Technologists/Technicians	
		Dietetic Technicians	Surgical Technicians
		Pharmacy Technicians	Veterinary Technicians
		Psychiatric Technicians	Ophthalmic Medical Technicians
		Respiratory Technicians	
		Licensed Practical and Licensed Vocational Nurses	
		Medical Records and Health Information Technicians	
		Opticians, Dispensing	
		Miscellaneous Health Technologists/Technicians	
		Orthotists and Prosthetists	Other
		Hearing Aid Specialists	
		Other Healthcare Practitioners/Technical Occupations	
		Occupational Health and Safety Specialists/Technicians	
		Occupational Health and Safety Specialists	Occupational Health and Safety Technicians
		Miscellaneous Health Practitioners/Technical Workers	
		Athletic Trainers	Other
Healthcare Support Occupations	Major Occupational Group K - Occupations concerned with other health care services for children and adults, mainly cater to the provision of support services.	**Nursing, Psychiatric, and Home Health Aides**	
		Home Health Aides	Nursing Assistants
		Psychiatric Aides	Orderlies
		Occupational Therapy/Physical Therapist Assistants/Aides	
		Occupational Therapy	
		Occupational Therapy Assistants	Occupational Therapy Aides
		Physical Therapy	
		Physical Therapy Assistants	Physical Therapy Aides
		Other Healthcare Support Occupations	
		Massage Therapists	
		Miscellaneous Healthcare Support Occupations	
		Dental Assistants	Medical Equipment Preparers
		Medical Assistants	

Notes:
* "Chapter 6. Occupation and Industry Classification Systems," in "Nursing Aides, Home Health Aides, and Related Health Care Occupations—National and Local Workforce Shortages and Associated Data Needs" by the U.S. Department of Health and Human Services, Health Resources and Services Administration, 2009, http://bhpr.hrsa.gov/ healthworkforce/reports/nursing/nurseaides/chap6.htm.
** "2010 Standard Occupational Classification," by the Bureau of Labor Statistics, January 2009, p. 16-19.
† "MOG—Level Definitions," in "Occupational Classification System Manual," by the U.S. Bureau of Labor Statistics, National Compensation Survey, http://www.bls.gov/ncs/ ocs/ocsm/comMOGADEF.htm#mogaanchor (accessed 01/04/09).

Table I-1B: Healthcare Professional Practices Provider Taxonomies
Organization: Centers for Medicare and Medicaid   **Classification System:** Based on System for Billing for Services

Category	Definition	Subcategories	
Physician	As stated in Section 1861(r) SSA to include the professionals listed here	**N/A**	
		MDs[*]	Doctor of Optometry[*]
		DOs[*]	Chiropractor[*]
		Doctor of Dental Surgery/Dental Medicine[*]	Interns and Residents[*]
		Doctor of Podiatric Medicine[*]	
Allied Health Providers	As stated in 42USC sec. 295p to include those professionals who: (A) who has received a certificate, an associate's degree, a bachelor's degree, a master's degree, a doctoral degree, or post baccalaureate training, in a science relating to health care; (B) who shares in the responsibility for the delivery of health care services or related services, including: (i) services relating to the identification, evaluation, and prevention of disease and disorders; (ii) dietary and nutrition services; (iii) health promotion services; (iv) rehabilitation services; or (v) health systems management services; and (C) who has not received a degree of doctor of medicine, a degree of doctor of osteopathy, a degree of doctor of dentistry or an equivalent degree, a degree of doctor of veterinary medicine or an equivalent degree, a degree of doctor of optometry or an equivalent degree, a degree of doctor of podiatric medicine or an equivalent degree, a degree of bachelor of science in pharmacy or an equivalent degree, a degree of doctor of pharmacy or an equivalent degree, a graduate degree in public health or an equivalent degree, a degree of doctor of chiropractic or an equivalent degree, a graduate degree in health administration or an equivalent degree, a doctoral degree in clinical psychology or an equivalent degree, or a degree in social work or an equivalent degree or a degree in counseling or an equivalent degree.	**Mid-Level Provider—also known as: Non-Physician Practitioner/Physician Extender—Health professionals who may deliver covered Medicare services if the services are incident to a physician's service or if there is specific authorization in the law**	
		Physician Assistant/Advanced Practice Nurses	
		Physician Assistant[*,**,†]	Certified Registered Nurse Anesthetists[*,**,†]
		Nurse Practitioners[*,**,†]	Certified Nurse Midwives[*,**,†]
		Other	
		Qualified Clinical Psychologists[*,**,†]	Respiratory Therapy Workers[††,‡,‡‡,§]
		Clinical Social Workers[*,**,†]	Speech Pathologist/Audiologists[††,‡,‡‡,§]
		Dieticians/Dietetic Technicians[*,**,†,††,‡,‡‡,§]	Dietetic Assistants[††,‡,‡‡,§]
		Dental Hygienists/Assts/Lab Techs[††,‡,‡‡,§]	Genetic Assistants[††,‡,‡‡,§]
		EMT/Paramedic[††,‡,‡‡,§]	Operating Room Technicians[††,‡,‡‡,§]
		Health Information Admin/Tech[††,‡,‡‡,§]	Ophthalmic/Optometric Medical Assistants[††,‡,‡‡,§]
		Occupational Therapists[††,‡,‡‡,§]	Medical Transcriptionists[††,‡,‡‡,§]
		Orthotists and Prosthetists[††,‡,‡‡,§]	Vocational Rehab Counselors[††,‡,‡‡,§]
		Physical Therapists[††,‡,‡‡,§]	Other Rehabilitation Workers[††,‡,‡‡,§]
		Radiologic Service Workers[††,‡,‡‡,§]	Other Social and Mental Health Workers[††,‡,‡‡,§]

Notes:
* "Physicians" in "The Public Health and Welfare," United States Code Title 42 1395x(r).
** "Ratio of Physician to Physician Extenders (Resolution 303, I-97)," by Kay K. Hanley, MD, December 1998, CMS Report 10-1-98.
† " 'Incident to' Services," MLN Matters, SE0441.
†† "Definitions, Federal Health Insurance for the Aged and Disabled, Center for Medicare and Medicaid Services, Department of Health and Human Services" 42 CFR 405.400.
‡ "Chapter 6A: Definitions, General Provisions, Health Professions Education, Public Health Service, The Public Health and Welfare," United States Code Title 42 p.295.
‡‡ "Civil Remedies Decision CR1961," by the Departmental Appeals Board, Department of Health and Human Services, June 16, 2009, p. 3.
§ "Interdisciplinary, Community-Based Linkages, Title VII, Part D, Public Health Service Act," by the Advisory Committee on Interdisciplinary, Community-Based Linkages, 2006, Fifth Annual report to the Secretary of the U.S. Department of Health and Human Services and to the Congress.

Table I-1C: Healthcare Professional Practices Provider Taxonomies

Organization: American Medical Association   **Classification System:** As utilized in the Health Care Careers Directory 2009-2010

Category	Definition	Subcategories	
Physician	There are two types of physicians: MD—Doctor of Medicine—and DO-Doctor of Osteopathic medicine … Both MDs and DOs may legally use all accepted methods of treatment, including drugs and surgery.	**N/A**	
		MDs*	DOs*
Optometry		Optometrist*,**	
Complementary and Alternative Medicine		Chiropractic*,**	
Dentistry		Dentist*,**	
Pharmacy		Pharmacist*,**	
Podiatry	"Specialize in diagnosing and treating disorders, diseases, and injuries of the foot, ankle, and lower leg"	**N/A**	
		Podiatrist*,**	
Veterinary Medicine	Provide healthcare professional and support services for the care of pets, livestock, and zoo, sporting, and laboratory animals	**N/A**	
		Veterinarian*,**	
Nursing		Registered Nurses*,**	Licensed Vocational Nurses**
		Licensed Practical Nurses**	
		Mid-Level Provider - also known as: Non-Physician Practitioner/ Physician Extender - Health professionals who may deliver covered Medicare services if the services are incident to a physician's service or if there is specific authorization in the law	
		Advanced Practice Nurses	
		Nurse Practitioners†,††,‡	Certified Nurse Midwives†,††,‡
		Certified Registered Nurse Anesthetists†,††,‡	
Psychology		*Clinical Psychologists*	
		Clinical Psychologists†,††,‡	
Allied Health Professional	"Participate in the delivery of health care, diagnostic, and rehabilitation services, therapeutic treatments, or related services," and excludes "the MODVOPP professions: medicine (allopathic), osteopathic medicine, dentistry, veterinary medicine, optometry, podiatry, and pharmacy—as well as chiropractic, clinical psychology, any level of nursing education, and graduate degrees in public health or health administration."	*Physician Assistant*	
		Physician Assistant†,††,‡	Dieticians/Dietetic Technicians†,††,‡
		Clinical Social Workers†,††,‡	
		Dietetics	
		Dietitian/Nutritionist*,**	Dietetic Technician*,**
		Dentistry and Related Fields	
		Dentist*,**	Dental Hygienist*,**
		Dental Assistant*,**	Dental Lab Technician*,**
		Communication Sciences	
		Audiologist*,**	Speech-Language Pathologist*,**
		Complementary and Alternative Medicine	
		Massage Therapist*,**	
		Counseling	
		Counselor*,**	Rehabilitation Counselor*,**
		Genetic Counselor*,**	
		Expressive/Creative Art Therapies	
		Art Therapist*,**	Music Therapist*,**
		Dance/Movement Therapist*,**	

Table I-1C: Healthcare Professional Practices Provider Taxonomies *(continued)*

Organization: American Medical Association   **Classification System:** As utilized in the Health Care Careers Directory 2009-2010

Category	Definition	Subcategories	
Allied Health Professional *(continued)*		**Health Information and Communication**	
		Cancer Registrar[*][**]	Medical Coder[*][**]
		Health Information Administrator[*][**]	Medical Librarian[*][**]
		Health Information Technician[*][**]	Medical Transcriptionist[*][**]
		Laboratory Science	
		Blood Bank Technology-Specialist[*][**]	Clinical Laboratory Technician/ Medical Laboratory Technician[*][**]
		Clinical Assistant[*][**]	Cytogenetic Technologist[*][**]
		Clinical Laboratory Scientist/Medical Technologist[*][**]	Cytotechnologist[*][**]
		Medical Imaging	
		Diagnostic Molecular Sonographer[*][**]	Magnetic Resonance Technologist[*][**]
		Histotechnician[*][**]	Medical Dosimetrist[*][**]
		Histotechnologist[*][**]	Nuclear Medicine Technologist[*][**]
		Pathologists' Assistant[*][**]	Radiation Therapist[*][**]
		Phlebotomist[*][**]	Radiographer[*][**]
		Diagnostic Medical Sonographer[*][**]	Registered Radiologist Assistant[*][**]
		Vision-Related Professions	
		Ophthalmic Assistant/Technician/ Technologist[*][**]	Orthoptist[*][**]
		Ophthalmic Dispensing Optician[*][**]	Teacher of the Visually Impaired[*][**]
		Optometrist[*][**]	Vision Rehabilitation Therapist[*][**]
		Orientation and Mobility Specialist[*][**]	
		Therapy and Rehabilitation	
		Occupational Therapist[*][**]	Physical Therapist Assistant[*][**]
		Occupational Therapy Assistant[*][**]	Therapeutic Recreation Specialist[*][**]
		Physical Therapist[*][**]	
		Other	
		Anesthesiologist Assistant[*][**]	Nursing Aides, Orderlies, Attendants[*][**]
		Anesthesia Technologist/Technician[*][**]	Occupational Health and Safety Technician[*][**]
		Athletic Trainer[*][**]	Orthotists and Prosthetists[*][**]
		Cardiovascular Technician/Technologist[*][**]	Orthotics and Prosthetics Technicians[*][**]
		Electroneurodiagnostic Technologist[*][**]	Perfusionist[*][**]
		Emergency Medical Technician-Paramedic[*][**]	Pharmacy Technician[*][**]
		Exercise Science (Personal Fitness Trainer, Exercise Physiologist, and Exercise Science Professional)[*][**]	Polysomnographic Technologist[*][**]
		Home Health, Personal Care, and Psychiatric Aides[*][**]	Psychiatric Aides/Technicians[*][**]
		Kinesiotherapist[*][**]	Respiratory Therapist[*][**]
		Medical Assistant[*][**]	Respiratory Therapy Technicians[*][**]
		Medical Equipment Preparer[*][**]	Surgical Assistant[*][**]
		Medical Illustrator[*][**]	Surgical Technologist[*][**]

Notes:

*   "Health Care Careers Directory 2009-2010," by the American Medical Association, p. iii-iv.

** "Coming Together, Moving Apart: A History of the Term Allied Health in Education, Accreditation, and Practice," by Fred G. Donini-Lenhoff, MA, Journal of Allied Health, Spring 2008, Volume 37, Number 1, p. 46-49

†   "Physicians" in "The Public Health and Welfare," United States Code Title 42 1395x(r).

†† "Ratio of Physician to Physician Extenders (Resolution 303,I-97)," by Kay K. Hanley, MD, December 1998, CMS Report 10-I-98.

‡   "'Incident to' Services," MLN Matters, SE0441.

Table I-1D: Healthcare Professional Practices Provider Taxonomies

Organization: Health Capital Consultants　　**Classification System:** N/A

Category	Definition	Subcategories	
Physicians	Doctors of allopathic or osteopathic medicine. Both allopathic and osteopathic physicians may specialize in many of the same areas, though the process required to achieve specialization certifications occasionally differs between the two forms of medicine.	**N/A**	
		MDs	DOs
Allied Health Professionals	Non-physician providers of health services who provide primary healthcare services. Allied health professionals may work with physicians, mid-level providers, paraprofessionals and technicians, but they are professionally licensed to work autonomously in the provision of services.	**N/A**	
		Dentists	Psychologists
		Optometrists	Podiatrists
		Chiropractors	
Midlevel Providers	Non-physician providers who may or may not provide healthcare services independently of a superior licensed provider. Depending on state licensing criteria, mid-level provides (e.g. nurse practitioners, physicians' assistants, dental hygienists) may work independently in the provision of services, or may need to be supervised by a licensed physician or allied health professional.	**Clinical Service Providers**	
		Therapists	
		Physical	Audiologists/Speech
		Occupational	
		Physician Assistants	
		Physician Assistant	
		Registered Nurses	
		Registered Nurses	
		APRNS	
		Certified Registered Nurse Anesthetists	Dieticians & Nutritionists
		Nurse Practitioners	Nurse Midwives
		Technical Service Providers	
		Dental Hygientists	Opticians
		Dental Assistants	Dental Assistants
Technicians & Paraprofessionals	Non-physician providers who may never provide healthcare services independently of a supervising licensed provider. This category of provider is divided between licensed and unlicensed paraprofessionals.	**Assistants**	
		Social and Human Service Assistants	Physical Therapist Assistants
		Anesthesiologists Assistants	Dental Assistants
		Occupational Therapist Assistants	Medical Assistants
		Aides	
		Personal Care Aides	Psychiatric Aides
		Home Health Aides	Physical Therapist Aides
		Nursing Aides, Orderlies, Attendants	Pharmacy Aides
		Therapists	
		Radiation Therapists	Respiratory Therapists

Table I-1D: Healthcare Professional Practices Provider Taxonomies *(continued)*

Organization: Health Capital Consultants   **Classification System:** N/A

Category	Definition	Subcategories
Technicians & Paraprofessionals *(continued)*		**Technologists**
		Medical and Clinical Laboratory Technologists / Nuclear Medicine
		Cardiovascular / Surgical
		Radiologic
		Technicians
		Cardiovascular / Psychiatric
		Medical and Clinical Laboratory / Respiratory Therapy
		Radiologic / Medical Records and Health Information
		Emergency Medical / Occupational Health and Safety
		Dietetic / Orthotics and Prosthetics
		Pharmacy
		Nurses
		Licensed Vocational Nurses / Licensed Practical Nurses
		Other
		Medical Dosimetrist / Medical Equipment Preparers
		Diagnostic Medical Sonographers / Medical Transcriptionists
		Athletic Trainers
Alternative Medicine Providers	Providers who may or may not be physicians, but who practice forms of therapy and treatment outside the mainstream practice of medicine, e.g. homeopathic medicine. Alternative medicine practitioners may provide primary or secondary care, and are generally licensed to work independently of supervision by another licensed provider.	**Whole Medical Systems**
		Eastern Whole Medical Systems
		Traditional Chinese Medicine / Ayurvedic Medicine
		Western Whole Medical Systems
		Homeopathic / Naturopathic
		Mind-Body Medicine
		Aromatherapy / Mental Healing
		Cognitive Behavioral Theory / Expressive/Creative Arts Therapy
		Meditation & Prayer
		Biologically Based Practices
		Dietary Supplements / Herbal Remedies
		Manipulative & Body-Based Practices
		Massage Therapy / Chiropractic Medicine
		Energy Medicine
		Biofield Therapy / Reiki
		Bioelectromagnetic-Based Therapy / Therapeutic Touch

Table I-2: Healthcare Professional Practices Provider Taxonomies Comparison Chart

Profession	Health Capital Consultants	BLS[1, 2, 3]	CMS[4, 5, 6, 7, 8, 9, 10, 11, 12]	AMA[11, 12, 13, 14, 15]
Chiropractors	Allied Health	Health Diagnosing Occupations	Physician	Complementary and Alternative Medicine
Dentists	Allied Health	Health Diagnosing Occupations	Physician	Dentistry and Related Fields
Psychologists	Allied Health	Social Scientists and Urban Planners	Mid-Level Provider*	Mid-Level Provider*
Podiatrists	Allied Health	Health Diagnosing Occupations	Physician	Podiatrists
Optometrists	Allied Health	Health Diagnosing Occupations	Physician	Optometry
Aromatherapy	Alternative Medicine	Other Health Diagnosing/Treating Practitioners	Auxiliary personnel—not covered for therapy services	Allied Health
Ayuredic Medicine	Alternative Medicine	Miscellaneous Health Diagnosing/Treating Practitioners	Auxiliary personnel—not covered for therapy services	Allied Health
Bioelectromagnetic-Based Therapy	Alternative Medicine	Other Health Diagnosing/Treating Practitioners	Complementary and Alternative Medicine	Allied Health
Biofield Therapy	Alternative Medicine	Other Health Diagnosing/Treating Practitioners	Complementary and Alternative Medicine	Allied Health
Cognitive Behavioral Theory	Alternative Medicine	Other Health Diagnosing/Treating Practitioners	Auxiliary personnel—not covered for therapy services	Allied Health
Dietary Supplements	Alternative Medicine	Other Health Diagnosing/Treating Practitioners	Auxiliary personnel—not covered for medical services	Allied Health
Expressive Creative Arts Therapy	Alternative Medicine	Other Health Diagnosing/Treating Practitioners	Complementary and Alternative Medicine	Allied Health
Herbal Remedies	Alternative Medicine	Other Health Diagnosing/Treating Practitioners	Auxiliary personnel—not covered for medical services	Allied Health
Homeopathic	Alternative Medicine	Miscellaneous Health Diagnosing/Treating Practitioners	Auxiliary personnel—not covered for medical services	Allied Health
Massage Therapy	Alternative Medicine	Other Health Diagnosing/Treating Practitioners	Auxiliary personnel—not covered for therapy services	Allied Health
Meditation & Prayer	Alternative Medicine	Other Health Diagnosing/Treating Practitioners	Complementary and Alternative Medicine	Allied Health
Mental Healing	Alternative Medicine	Other Health Diagnosing/Treating Practitioners	Auxiliary personnel—not covered for medical services	Allied Health
Naturopathic	Alternative Medicine	Miscellaneous Health Diagnosing/Treating Practitioners	Auxiliary personnel—not covered for medical services	Allied Health
Reiki	Alternative Medicine	Other Health Diagnosing/Treating Practitioners	Auxiliary personnel—not covered for medical services	Allied Health
Therapeutic Touch	Alternative Medicine	Other Health Diagnosing/Treating Practitioners	Complementary and Alternative Medicine	Allied Health
Traditional Chinese Medicine	Alternative Medicine	Other Health Diagnosing/Treating Practitioners	Auxiliary personnel—not covered for medical services	Allied Health
Prosthetists & Orthotists	Mid-Level	Health Technologists and Technicians	Allied Health—Professionals/Qualified Auxiliary Personnel	Allied Health

(continued)

Table I-2: Healthcare Professional Practices Provider Taxonomies Comparison Chart *(continued)*

Profession	Health Capital Consultants	BLS[1, 2, 3]	CMS[4, 5, 6, 7, 8, 9, 10, 11, 12]	AMA[11, 12, 13, 14, 15]
Audiologists/Speech-Language Pathologists	Mid-Level	Health Assessment and Treating Occupations	Allied Health—Professionals/Qualified Auxiliary Therapy Personnel	Allied Health
Dental Hygienists	Mid-Level	Health Technologists and Technicians	Allied Health—Professionals/Qualified Auxiliary Personnel	Allied Health
Dieticians & Nutritionists	Mid-Level	Health Assessment and Treating Occupations	Allied Health—Professionals/Qualified Auxiliary Personnel	Allied Health
Certified Registered Nurse Anesthetists	Mid-Level	Health Assessment and Treating Occupations	Mid-Level Provider*	Mid-Level Provider*
Nurse Midwives	Mid-Level	Health Assessment and Treating Occupations	Mid-Level Provider*	Mid-Level Provider*
Nurse Practitioners	Mid-Level	Health Assessment and Treating Occupations	Mid-Level Provider*	Mid-Level Provider*
Physician Assistants	Mid-Level	Health Assessment and Treating Occupations	Mid-Level Provider*	Mid-Level Provider*
Registered Nurses	Mid-Level	Health Assessment and Treating Occupations	Allied Health—Professionals/Qualified Auxiliary Personnel	Nursing
Pharmacists	Mid-Level	Health Assessment and Treating Occupations	Pharmacists	Pharmacy
Occupational Therapists	Mid-Level	Health Assessment and Treating Occupations	Allied Health—Professionals/Qualified Auxiliary Therapy Personnel	Allied Health
Physical Therapists	Mid-Level	Health Assessment and Treating Occupations	Allied Health—Professionals/Qualified Auxiliary Therapy Personnel	Allied Health
Opticians	Mid-Level	Health Assessment and Treating Occupations	Allied Health—Professionals/Qualified Auxiliary Personnel	Allied Health
DOs	Physician	Health Diagnosing Occupations	Physician	Physician
MDs	Physician	Health Diagnosing Occupations	Physician	Physician
Anesthesiologist Assistants	Technicians and Paraprofessionals	Other Healthcare Support Occupations	Allied Health—Professionals/Qualified Auxiliary Personnel	Allied Health
Athletic Trainers	Technicians and Paraprofessionals	Other Healthcare Practitioners/Technical Occupations	Allied Health—Auxiliary Personnel—not covered for therapy services	Allied Health
Cardiovascular Technicians	Technicians and Paraprofessionals	Health Technologists and Technicians	Allied Health—Professionals/Qualified Auxiliary Personnel	Allied Health
Cardiovascular Technologists	Technicians and Paraprofessionals	Health Technologists and Technicians	Allied Health—Professionals/Qualified Auxiliary Personnel	Allied Health
Emergency Medical Technicians	Technicians and Paraprofessionals	Health Technologists and Technicians	Allied Health—Professionals/Qualified Auxiliary Personnel	Allied Health
Home Health Aides	Technicians and Paraprofessionals	Nursing, Psychiatric, and Home Health Aides	Allied Health—Professionals/Qualified Auxiliary Personnel	Allied Health

Table I-2: Healthcare Professional Practices Provider Taxonomies Comparison Chart *(continued)*

Profession	Health Capital Consultants	BLS[1, 2, 3]	CMS[4, 5, 6, 7, 8, 9, 10, 11, 12]	AMA[11, 12, 13, 14, 15]
Medical Assistants	Technicians and Paraprofessionals	Other Healthcare Support Occupations	Allied Health—Professionals/ Qualified Auxiliary Personnel	Allied Health
Medical Equipment Preparers	Technicians and Paraprofessionals	Other Healthcare Support Occupations	Allied Health—Professionals/ Qualified Auxiliary Personnel	Allied Health
Nursing Aides, Orderlies, Attendants	Technicians and Paraprofessionals	Nursing, Psychiatric, and Home Health Aides	Allied Health—Professionals/ Qualified Auxiliary Personnel	Allied Health
Occupational Health and Safety Technicians	Technicians and Paraprofessionals	Health Technologists and Technicians	Allied Health—Professionals/ Qualified Auxiliary Personnel	Allied Health
Orthotics and Prosthetics Technicians	Technicians and Paraprofessionals	Health Technologists and Technicians	Allied Health—Professionals/ Qualified Auxiliary Personnel	Allied Health
Personal Care Aides	Technicians and Paraprofessionals	Nursing, Psychiatric, and Home Health Aides	Allied Health—Professionals/ Qualified Auxiliary Personnel	Allied Health
Psychiatric Aides	Technicians and Paraprofessionals	Nursing, Psychiatric, and Home Health Aides	Allied Health—Professionals/ Qualified Auxiliary Personnel	Allied Health
Psychiatric Technicians	Technicians and Paraprofessionals	Health Technologists and Technicians	Allied Health—Professionals/ Qualified Auxiliary Personnel	Allied Health
Respiratory Therapists	Technicians and Paraprofessionals	Health Assessment and Treating Occupations	Allied Health—Professionals/ Qualified Auxiliary Personnel	Allied Health
Respiratory Therapy Technicians	Technicians and Paraprofessionals	Health Technologists and Technicians	Allied Health—Professionals/ Qualified Auxiliary Personnel	Allied Health
Surgical Technologists	Technicians and Paraprofessionals	Health Technologists and Technicians	Allied Health—Professionals/ Qualified Auxiliary Personnel	Allied Health
Social and Human Service Assistants	Technicians and Paraprofessionals	Other Healthcare Support Occupations	Clinical Social Workers are Mid-Level Providers*; others are Allied Health—Professionals/Qualified Auxiliary Personnel	Allied Health
Dental Assistants	Technicians and Paraprofessionals	Other Healthcare Support Occupations	Allied Health—Professionals/ Qualified Auxiliary Personnel	Allied Health
Dietetic Technicians	Technicians and Paraprofessionals	Health Technologists and Technicians	Allied Health—Professionals/ Qualified Auxiliary Personnel	Allied Health
Medical Records and Health Information Technicians	Technicians and Paraprofessionals	Health Technologists and Technicians	Allied Health—Professionals/ Qualified Auxiliary Personnel	Allied Health
Medical Transcriptionists	Technicians and Paraprofessionals	Other Healthcare Support Occupations	Allied Health—Professionals/ Qualified Auxiliary Personnel	Allied Health
Medical and Clinical Laboratory Technicians	Technicians and Paraprofessionals	Health Technologists and Technicians	Allied Health—Professionals/ Qualified Auxiliary Personnel	Allied Health
Medical and Clinical Laboratory Technologists	Technicians and Paraprofessionals	Health Technologists and Technicians	Allied Health—Professionals/ Qualified Auxiliary Personnel	Allied Health
Diagnostic Medical Sonographers	Technicians and Paraprofessionals	Health Technologists and Technicians	Allied Health—Professionals/ Qualified Auxiliary Personnel	Allied Health
Medical Dosimetrist	Technicians and Paraprofessionals	Health Technologists and Technicians	Allied Health—Professionals/ Qualified Auxiliary Personnel	Allied Health

(continued)

Table I-2: Healthcare Professional Practices Provider Taxonomies Comparison Chart *(continued)*

Profession	Health Capital Consultants	BLS[1, 2, 3]	CMS[4, 5, 6, 7, 8, 9, 10, 11, 12]	AMA[11, 12, 13, 14, 15]
Nuclear Medicine Technologists	Technicians and Paraprofessionals	Health Technologists and Technicians	Allied Health—Professionals/ Qualified Auxiliary Personnel	Allied Health
Radiation Therapists	Technicians and Paraprofessionals	Health Assessment and Treating Occupations	Allied Health—Professionals/ Qualified Auxiliary Personnel	Allied Health
Radiologic Technicians	Technicians and Paraprofessionals	Health Technologists and Technicians	Allied Health—Professionals/ Qualified Auxiliary Personnel	Allied Health
Radiologic Technologists	Technicians and Paraprofessionals	Health Technologists and Technicians	Allied Health—Professionals/ Qualified Auxiliary Personnel	Allied Health
Licensed Practical Nurses	Technicians and Paraprofessionals	Health Technologists and Technicians	Allied Health—Professionals/ Qualified Auxiliary Personnel	Nursing
Licensed Vocational Nurses	Technicians and Paraprofessionals	Health Technologists and Technicians	Allied Health—Professionals/ Qualified Auxiliary Personnel	Nursing
Pharmacy Aides	Technicians and Paraprofessionals	Other Healthcare Support Occupations	Allied Health—Professionals/ Qualified Auxiliary Personnel	Pharmacy
Pharmacy Technicians	Technicians and Paraprofessionals	Health Technologists and Technicians	Allied Health—Professionals/ Qualified Auxiliary Personnel	Pharmacy
Occupational Therapist Assistants	Technicians and Paraprofessionals	Occupational Therapy/Physical Therapist Assistants/Aides	Allied Health—Professionals/ Qualified Auxiliary Personnel	Allied Health
Physical Therapist Aides	Technicians and Paraprofessionals	Occupational Therapy/Physical Therapist Assistants/Aids	Allied Health—Professionals/ Qualified Auxiliary Personnel	Allied Health
Physical Therapist Assistants	Technicians and Paraprofessionals	Occupational Therapy/Physical Therapist Assistants/Aids	Allied Health—Professionals/ Qualified Auxiliary Personnel	Allied Health

Notes

1 "Chapter 6. Occupation and Industry Classification Systems," in "Nursing Aides, Home Health Aides, and Related Health Care Occupations—National and Local Workforce Shortages and Associated Data Needs" by the "U.S. Department of Health and Human Services, Health Resources and Services Administration, 2009, http://bhpr.hrsa.gov/healthworkforce/reports/nursing/nurseaides/chapt6.htm."

2 "2010 Standard Occupational Classification," by the Bureau of Labor Statistics, January 2009, p. 16-19.

3 "MOG—Level Definitions," in "Occupational Classification System Manual," by the U.S. Bureau of Labor Statistics, National Compensation Survey, http://www.bls.gov/ncs/ocs/ocsm/comMOGADEF.htm#mogaanchor (accessed 01/04/09).

4 "Definitions, Federal Health Insurance for the Aged and Disabled, Center for Medicare and Medicaid services, Department of Health and Human Services" 42 CFR 405.400.

5 "Chapter 6A: Definitions, General Provisions, Health Professions Education, Public Health Service, The Public Health and Welfare," United States Code Title 42 295p.

6 "CR1961," by the Departmental Appeals Board, Civil Remedies Division, Department of Health and Human Services, June 16, 2009, p. 3.

7 "Interdisciplinary, Community-Based Linkages, Title VII, Part D, Public Health Service Act," by the Advisory Committee on Interdisciplinary, Community-Based Linkages, 2005, Fifth Annual report to the Secretary of the U.S. Department of Health and Human Services and to the Congress.

8 "Chapter 15—Covered Medical and Other Health Services," in: "Medicare Benefit Policy Manual," Centers for Medicare and Medicaid Services, Rev. 109, August 7, 2009.

9 "Chapter 5—Definitions," in "Medicare General Information, Eligibility, and Entitlement," Centers for Medicare and Medicaid Services, Rev. 58, March 6, 2009.

10 "Medicare National Coverage Determinations," by the Department of Health and Human Services, Centers for Medicare and Medicaid, Transmittal 2 (Pub. 100-03), October 17, 2003.

11 "Physicians" in "The Public Health and Welfare," United States Code Title 42 1395x(r).

12 "Incident to' Services," MLN Matters, SE0441.

13 "Health Care Careers Directory 2009–2010," by the American Medical Association, p. iii-iv.

14 "Coming Together, Moving Apart: A History of the Term Allied Health in Education, Accreditation, and Practice," by Fred G. Donini-Lenhoff, MA, Journal of Allied Health, Spring 2008, Volume 37, Number 1, p. 46–49.

15 "Ratio of Physician to Physician Extenders (Resolution 303,I-97)," by Kay K. Hanley, MD, December 1998, CMS Report 10-I-98.

* also known as: Non-Physician Practitioner/Physician Extender.

This *Guide* distinguishes among five general types of health professionals. The trifurcation of non-physician practitioners in mainstream medicine, as described previously, serves as the rationale behind allied health professionals, mid-level providers, and technicians and paraprofessionals, as they are defined herein. In addition to the physician and nonphysician professionals who practice conventional medicine, a class of professionals exists that provides complementary and alternative medical services that, to date, is treated as a parallel (sometimes intertwined) but unconventional subset of the healthcare workforce. In brief, the five taxonomical categories of professional providers, as they are discussed in this *Guide*, are defined as:

1. *Physicians*—Doctors of allopathic or osteopathic medicine. Both allopathic and osteopathic physicians may specialize in many of the same areas, though the process required to achieve specialization certifications occasionally differs between the two forms of medicine.

2. *Allied health professionals*—Nonphysician providers of health services who provide primary healthcare services. Allied health professionals may work with physicians, mid-level providers, and paraprofessionals and technicians, but they are professionally licensed to work autonomously in the provision of services. This *Guide* discusses five distinct allied health professions: dentists, optometrists, chiropractors, psychologists, and podiatrists.

3. *Mid-level providers*—Nonphysician providers who may or may not provide healthcare services independently of a superior licensed provider but are, by in large, moving into increasingly autonomous practice types. These professionals typically provide primary care services in lieu of physicians. Depending on state licensing criteria, mid-level providers (such as nurse practitioners, physicians' assistants, and dental hygienists) may work independently in the provision of services. Mid-level providers are further divided between clinical service providers and technical service providers.

4. *Technicians and paraprofessionals*—Nonphysician providers who may never provide healthcare services independently of a supervising licensed provider. These individuals either serve to alleviate a manpower deficit or to contribute to the technological sophistication, efficiency, and quality of physician services; in either case, their scope of practice is contingent upon the scope of their physician's practice and nonexistent otherwise. On the basis of these two types of physician extenders, this category of provider is divided between licensed and unlicensed technicians and paraprofessionals.

5. *Alternative medicine practitioners*—Providers who may or may not be physicians but who practice forms of therapy and treatment outside the mainstream practice of medicine, for example, homeopathic medicine. Alternative medicine practitioners may provide primary or secondary care, and they generally are licensed to work independently of supervision by another licensed provider.

Endnotes

1   "Specialty Hospitals, Ambulatory Surgery Centers, and General Hospitals: Charting a Wise Public Policy Course," by David Shactman, Health Affairs, Volume 24, Number 1, (May/June 2005), p. 869; "The Attack on Ancillary Service Providers at the Federal and State Level," by Robert Cimasi MHA, ASA, CBA, AVA, CM&AA, CMP, Orthopedic Clinics of America, Volume 39, Issue 1, (January 2008), p. 118.

2   "Coming Together, Moving Apart: A History of the Term *Allied Health* in Education, Accreditation, and Practice," by Fred G. Donini-Lenhoff, Journal of Allied Health, Volume 37, Number 1, (Volume 37), p. 47; "Interprofessional Healthcare: A Common Taxonomy to Assist with Understanding," by Alice B. Aiken, PT, PhD and Mary Ann McColl, PhD, Journal of Allied Health, Volume 38, Number 3 (Fall 2009), p. e-92.

3   *Ibid.*

4   "Interprofessional Healthcare: A Common Taxonomy to Assist with Understanding," by Alice B. Aiken, PT, PhD and Mary Ann McColl, PhD, Journal of Allied Health, Volume 38, Number 3 (Fall 2009), p. e-92.

5   *Ibid.*

6   *Ibid.*

7   "Interprofessional Healthcare: A Common Taxonomy to Assist with Understanding," by Alice B. Aiken, PT, PhD and Mary Ann McColl, PhD, Journal of Allied Health, Volume 38, Number 3 (Fall 2009), p. e-92-e-93.

8   "Interprofessional Healthcare: A Common Taxonomy to Assist with Understanding," by Alice B. Aiken, PT, PhD and Mary Ann McColl, PhD, Journal of Allied Health, Volume 38, Number 3 (Fall 2009), p. e-92.

9   "The Impact of Nonphysician Clinicians: Do They Improve the Quality and Cost-Effectiveness of Health Care Services?" by Miranda Laurant; Mirjam Harmsen, Hub Wollersheim, Richard Grol, Marjan Faber, and Bonnie Sibald, Medical Care Research and Review, Volume 66, Number 6, (December 2009), p. 36S.

10   "Interprofessional Healthcare: A Common Taxonomy to Assist with Understanding," by Alice B. Aiken, PT, PhD and Mary Ann McColl, PhD, Journal of Allied Health, Volume 38, Number 3 (Fall 2009), p. e-93.

11   *Ibid.*

12   "Interprofessional Healthcare: A Common Taxonomy to Assist with Understanding," by Alice B. Aiken, PT, PhD and Mary Ann McColl, PhD, Journal of Allied Health, Volume 38, Number 3 (Fall 2009), p. e-94.

13   *Ibid.*

14   *Ibid.*

15   *Ibid.*

16   "Special Issues in Physician Compensation," in "Physician Compensation Plans: State-of-the-Art Strategies," by Bruce A. Johnson, JD, MPA and Deborah Walker Keegan, PhD, FACMPE, Medical Group Management Association, 2006, p. 193-194.

17   "Special Issues in Physician Compensation," in "Physician Compensation Plans: State-of-the-Art Strategies," by Bruce A. Johnson, JD, MPA and Deborah Walker Keegan, PhD, FACMPE, Medical Group Management Association, 2006, p. 193-194; "Interprofessional Healthcare: A Common Taxonomy to Assist with Understanding," by Alice B. Aiken, PT, PhD and Mary Ann McColl, PhD, Journal of Allied Health, Volume 38, Number 3 (Fall 2009), p. e-94-e-95.

18   "Interprofessional Healthcare: A Common Taxonomy to Assist with Understanding," by Alice B. Aiken, PT, PhD and Mary Ann McColl, PhD, Journal of Allied Health, Volume 38, Number 3 (Fall 2009), p. e-94-e-95.

19   *Ibid.*

Healthcare Consulting

It has long been observed that in towns and villages the doctor and his family associate with the best people and are usually among the best educated and the most prosperous citizens. It is not meant by this statement that doctors as a rule become rich, because doctors do not make large sums of money. The income of medical men does not compare with that which can be made by men in commercial life, who can employ a multitude of clerks and hands to increase the profits from business. A doctor has to do everything himself, and cannot delegate much of his work to an assistant with advantage. For this and other reasons a doctor is not likely to be a wealthy citizen. It is, however, true that physicians are, as a rule, not only the best educated and most influential citizens; but are prosperous up to the point of comfort, even if they are not to be numbered among the unusually rich. Association, therefore, with the medical men and their families in one's neighborhood is sure to bring congenial friends and companions.

John B. Roberts, 1908

KEY TERMS

- Audit
- Benchmarking
- Charge Description Master
- Charting
- Clients
- Coding
- Complex or Compound
- Corporate Compliance Services
- Employee Retirement and Income Security Act
- Fee Arrangements
- Forecasting
- Management Advisory Services
- Organizational Development
- Practice Management
- Presentation
- Prospects
- Qualified Domestic Relations Orders (QDRO)
- Risk Management
- Strategic Initiatives
- Summarization
- Suspects
- Tactical Plans
- Targets
- "Tick and Tie"
- Valuation
- Vision

Key Concept	Definition	Citation
Modalities of Consulting Activity	(1) continuity services, (2) annuity services, and (3) episodic services	"Organizational Change and Development," by Karl E. Weick and Robert E. Quinn, Annual Review of Psychology, Vol. 50, (1999), p. 367–82.
Three Types of Financial Statement Preparation	(1) financial statement compilation, (2) financial statement review, and (3) financial statement audit	"Proposed Statements on Standards for Accounting and Review Services," by the AICPA Accounting and Review Services Committee, April 28, 2009, p. 17.
401(k) Safe Harbor Notices and Internal Revenue Service or NCDR Notice of Change to Director's Rules Letters	A written notice provided by an employer participating in a 401(k) safe harbor plan to employees similarly involved of the employees rights and obligations under the plan, the safe harbor method in use and how eligible employees can make electors, as well as other plans involved. There are also timing and content requirements.	"401(k) Resource *Guide*—Plan A Sponsors—401(k) Plan Overview" United States Internal Revenue Service, www.irs.gov/retirement/sponsor/article/0,,id=151800,00.html (accessed December 16, 2009).
Stages of the Engagement Process	(1) Suspect Stage; (2) Prospect Stage; (3) Target Stage; and, (4) Client Stage	n/a
The Phases of a Consulting Engagement	(1) proposal, (2) research, (3) analysis, and (4) presentation	n/a
Types of Research	(1) specific and (2) general (as defined in chapter 2, *Benchmarking*)	n/a
Analysis Tools Used in an Engagement	(1) summarization, (2) benchmarking, (3) forecasting, and (4) complex or compound	n/a
The Records Management and Archiving Process	(1) identification, (2) classification, (3) storage, and (4) retrieval	n/a
Certified Public Accountant (CPA)	A CPA is a financial advisor who has taken 150 semester hours of college coursework, has passed the Uniform CPA Examination, and has gained licensure from the state in which he or she practices.	"Becoming A CPA," The American Institute of Certified Public Accountants, www.aicpa.org/Becoming+a+CPA/CPA+Candidates+and+Students/Becoming+A+CPA.htm#Become_A_CPA (accessed December 16, 2009).
Accredited in Business Valuation (ABV)	ABV designation is awarded to CPAs who demonstrate (1) AICPA membership and good standing, (2) valid and unrevoked CPA certification, (3) a passing score on the ABV examination, (4) payment of the $350 credentialing fee, and (5) meet recertification requirements.	"Mission and Objectives of the ABV Program," by the AICPA, 2010, http://fvs.aicpa.org/Memberships/Mission+and+Objectives+of+the+ABV+Credential+Program.htm (accessed March 18, 2010); "A Guide to the AICPA Accredited in Business Valuation Credential," by the AICPA, 2010, http://fvs.aicpa.org/NR/rdonlyres/6F13D4DC-97EF-4F0F-88B2-42F3562D3A63/0/ABV_application_kitfinal_012710.pdf (accessed March 18, 2010).
Certified Business Valuator (CBV)	At least two years of experience are required to be an accredited member and a minimum of five years of appraisal experience is necessary before consideration for Accredited Senior Appraiser status.	"Accreditation" American Society of Appraisers, www.appraisers.org/ ASAAccredditation /ASAAccredditation.aspx (accessed October 2, 2009).
Accredited by the Institute of Business Appraisers (AIBA)	AIBA certification requires a four-year college degree; successful completion of IBA course 8002, the eight-day workshop in valuing closely held businesses; or the journeyman level designation in business valuing. All applicants must also complete IBA's course 1010, a sixteen-hour curriculum for report writing.	"Accredited by IBA (AIBA)," The Institute of Business Appraisers, www.go-iba.org/overview.html (accessed March 19, 2010).
Certified Business Appraiser (CBA)	To obtain CBA certification, the applicant must hold a four-year college degree or equivalent; must have completed at least ninety classroom hours of upper level course work, at least twenty-four of which were courses provided by the IBA; and must have completed a six-hour, proctored, CBA written exam covering the theory and practice of business accreditation.	"Certified Business Appraiser," The Institute of Business Appraisers, www.go-iba.org/overview.html (accessed March 19, 2010).

Key Concept	Definition	Citation
Business Valuator Accredited in Litigation (BVAL)	BVAL certification is designed to recognize experienced business appraisers who demonstrate their ability to competently present expert testimony which supports their objective conclusion of value, and requires completion of five days of IBA course 7001, sixteen Certified Physician Executive (CPE) hours, passage of a four-hour written exam, demonstration at testimony clinics, a business appraisal-related designation, and references of trial performance from at least two attorneys.	"Business Valuator Accreditation for Litigation (BVAL)," The Institute of Business Appraisers, www.go-iba.org/overview. html (accessed March 19, 2010).
Accredited in Business Appraisal Review (ABAR)	ABAR is a new certification that is designed to provide a level of quality assurance to stakeholders in the business appraisal process. It is contingent upon good standing, two professional and personal references, possession of a business appraisal designation, completion of a four-year university degree program, completion of IBA course 1044, and submission of an appraisal review.	"Business Appraisal Review Accreditation Workshop (ABAR)," The Institute of Business Appraisers, www.go-iba.org/ overview.html (accessed March 19, 2010).
Certified Valuation Analysts (CVA)	CVA certification is available to licensed CPAs [in good standing with the National Association of Certified Valuation Analysts (NACVA)] with references and at least two years of CPA experience, who pass a two-part exam and can attend an optional five-day training session is decided to have a level of expertise deemed credible by NACVA.	"Qualification for the CVA: Certified Valuation Analyst Designation" National Association of Certified Valuation Analysts, www.nacva.com/certifications/C_cva.asp (accessed November 20, 2009).
Accredited Valuation Analysts (AVA)	AVAs may hold any business degree, but they must have verified substantial business valuation (shown by two years of full-time experience, performance of ten or more business valuations, or demonstration of substantial knowledge of business valuation theory, methods and practice) with three personal and three business references. AVAs must pass a two-part exam, the second half of which is a standardized case study mimicking the performance of a complete business valuation. In addition, applicants must be members in good standing with NACVA.	"Qualifications for the AVA: Accredited Valuation Analyst Designation" National Association of Certified Valuation Analysts, www.nacva.com/certifications/C_ava.asp (accessed November 20, 2009).
Certified Forensic Financial Analyst (CFFA)	Credentialed through the Financial Forensics Institute, (a subsidiary of NACVA), CFFAs are specialists one of five areas: financial litigation, forensic accounting; business fraud deterrence, detection, and investigation; business and intellectual property damages; and matrimonial litigation support. Applicants must possess a previous credential, varying levels of experience depending on specialization, one business and two profession references, and a passing grade on a two-part exam.	"CFFA Credentialing Criteria" National Association of Certified Valuation Analysts, www.nacva.com/CTI/CFFAprerequisites. asp (accessed November 20, 2009).
Chartered Financial Analyst (CFA)	An member of the CFA (requires four or more years of qualified work experience) with a bachelor's degree or four years of education (or combination) who has passed all three of the CFA exams testing competence and integrity in managing portfolios and analyzing investments may become a charter holder with the CFA Institute.	"CFA Institute—Work Experience," Chartered Financial Analyst Institute, www.cfainstitute.org/cfaprog/charterholder/ membership/work_experience.html (accessed November 16, 2009); "Become a CFA Charterholder," Chartered Financial Analyst Institute, www.cfainstitute.org/cfaprog/charterholder/ index.html (accessed December 17, 2009); "Four Steps to Enroll and Register in the CFA Program," Chartered Financial Analyst Institute, www.cfainstitute.org/cfaprog/register/ index.html (accessed December 17, 2009).

(continued)

(continued)

Key Concept	Definition	Citation
Certified Merger & Acquisition Advisor Certification (CM&AA)	CM&AAs have maintained the Alliance of Merger & Acquisition Advisors' (AM&AA's) standards of professional excellence through the completion of thirty-six hours of AM&AA courses (five-day online curriculum) and a comprehensive exam covering the areas of the private capital marketplace, the dynamics of a merger and acquisition (M&A) engagement, corporate M&A development, business valuation and M&A standards, M&A tax issues, legal issues, and acquisition and growth financing.	"AM&AA: Alliance of Merger & Acquisition Advisors" Brochure, Alliance of Merger and Acquisition Advisors, www.amaaonline.com/files/amaabro09.pdf (accessed October 2, 2009).
Certified Physician Executive (CPE)	Certification is open to candidates who (1) graduate from an approved medical program (either through the Liaison Committee on Medical Education, American Osteopathic Association, or Educational Commission for Foreign Medical Graduates), (2) hold a valid license, (3) have three years of experience, (4) hold board certification in a medical specialty area, (5) complete 150 hours of management education and a graduate management degree (in areas including business, medical management, science, health administration, or public health), (6) have one year of medical management experience, and (7) provide a letter of recommendation confirming management experience. Referred to as diplomates.	"CPE Eligibility," by the Certifying Commission in Medical Management, 2009, www.ccmm.org/tutorialeligibility.aspx (accessed March 23, 2010).
Fellow of American College of Physician Executives (FACPE)	Open to diplomates with board certification in medical management (CPE) who have maintained American College of Physician Executives (ACPE) membership for five consecutive years and demonstrate that their expertise is of regional or national stature.	"Fellowship," by the American College of Physician Executives, 2009, www.acpe.org/Membership/professionalrecognition/fellowship.aspx (accessed March 23, 2010).
Distinguished Fellow of ACPE	Fellows awarded the highest distinction due to their exceptional and continued contribution to the field of medical management. These physician executives are nominated by their peers.	"Distinguished Fellowship," by the American College of Physician Executives, 2009, www.acpe.org/Membership/professionalrecognition/distinguishedfellow.aspx (accessed March 23, 2010).
Vanguard	A new ACPE classification open to members that are board certified in medical management (CPE), hold fellowship or distinguished fellowship status, and have earned an advanced degree in management through ACPE's graduate degree program.	"Vanguard," by the American College of Physician Executives, 2009, www.acpe.org/Membership/professionalrecognition/vanguard.aspx (accessed March 23, 2010).
Certified Healthcare Financial Professional (CHFP)	CHFP applicants must successfully complete the Healthcare Financial Management Association (HFMA) Core Certification Exam as well as one of four specialty exams in accounting and finance, patient financial services, financial management of physician practices, or managed care. The requirements also include: (1) two years total as a regular or advanced HFMA member, (2) sixty semester hours of college coursework from an accredited institution or sixty professional development contact hours, (3) references from a current elected HFMA chapter officer and the candidate's CEO or supervisor, and (4) timely submission of a conforming CHFP application within twelve months of successfully completing the two required exams.	"Earning the Certified Healthcare Financial Professional Designation" Healthcare Financial Management Association, www.hfma.org/certification/chfp/ (accessed March 22, 2010).
Fellow of the Healthcare Financial Management Association (FHFMA)	This certification is only available to those who have already received the CHFP designation and have (1) five years total as a regular or advanced HFMA member; (2) a bachelor's degree or 120 semester hours from an accredited college or university, (3) a reference from an FHFMA or current elected HFMA chapter officer, and (4) volunteer activity in healthcare finance within three years of applying for the FHFMA designation.	"About HFMA's Certification Programs," Healthcare Financial Management Association, www.hfma.org/certification/ (accessed March 22, 2010); "Fellow of HFMA (FHFMA) Requirements," Healthcare Financial Management Association, www.hfma.org/certification/fhfma/ (accessed March 22, 2010).

Key Concept	Definition	Citation
Fellow of the American Association of Healthcare Consultants	Fellows are full-time consultants who have met the standards set by the credentialing and standards committee, including having at least a bachelor's degree and a minimum of three years of experience in their respective consulting field, performing acceptably in an interview meant to evaluate skills, passing objective testing, and being in compliance with the organizations code of ethics.	"The AAHC Credential" American Association of Healthcare Consultants, www.aahc.net/c3.htm (accessed November 20, 2009); "Membership Criteria" American Association of Healthcare Consultants, www.aahc.net/c7.htm (accessed November 20, 2009).
Certified Healthcare Business Consultant (CHBC)	National Society of Certified Healthcare Business Consultants (NSCHBC) members may become a CHBC by passing a NSCHBC examination, demonstrating an understanding of the "total healthcare business environment—both practice and financial management."	"Certification," National Society of Certified Healthcare Business Consultants, www.ichbc.org/certification/index.cfm (accessed November 3, 2009); "Membership," National Society of Certified Healthcare Business Consultants, www.nschbe.org/membership/index.cfm (accessed December 17, 2009).
Certified Coding Specialist (CCS)	A CCS categorizes medical data from patient records, mainly in hospital settings and exhibits a practitioner's tested data quality, integrity skills and ability, and a high level of coding proficiency. CCS candidates must have earned a high school diploma or have an equivalent educational background, and although not required, at least three years of on-the-job experience.	"Certified Coding Specialist (CCS)," American Health Information Management Association, ahima.org/certifications/ccs (accessed March 19, 2010).
Certified Coding Association (CCA)	The CCA designation is often viewed as a starting point for a person entering a coder career, and it demonstrates competency in the health information field and a commitment to the coding profession. CCA examination candidates must have a high school diploma or equivalent, and although not required, at least six months of coding experience.	"Certification Candidate Guide," American Health Information Management Association, http://ahima.org/certifications/ccs (accessed March 19, 2010).
Certified in Healthcare Privacy and Security (CHPS)	This certification demonstrates a concentration on the privacy and security aspects of health information management and signifies competence in the design, implementation, and administration of comprehensive security and privacy programs in various healthcare organizations.	"Certification Candidate Guide," American Health Information Management Association, http://ahima.org/certifications/ccs (accessed March 19, 2010).
Certified Health Data Analyst (CHDA)	The CHDA-certified practitioner demonstrates broad organizational knowledge and communication skills with individuals and groups at multiple levels, due to training in obtaining, managing, examining, understanding, and transforming data into accurate, relevant information.	"Certification Candidate Guide," American Health Information Management Association, http://ahima.org/certifications/ccs (accessed March 19, 2010).
Certified Medical Planner (CMP)	Certification is given after completion of a one-year online course of curriculum and a passing grade on the CMP certification examination, which is designed to test knowledge on managerial and financial issues specific to medical practices.	"Course Overview," Medical Business Advisors, Inc., www.medicalbusinessadvisors.com/institute-cmp-course.asp (accessed November 3, 2009); "Guide to Certified Medical Planner Certification" Medical Business Advisors, Inc., www.medicalbusinessadvisors.com/institute-cmp-guide.asp (accessed November 3, 2009).
Professional, Academy for Healthcare Management (PAHM)	Certification is given by the AHM after completion of the course "Healthcare Management: An Introduction," which covers the basics of health insurance plans, healthcare providers, as well as operational, regulatory, legislative, and ethical issues.	"Professional, Academy for Healthcare Management" America's Health Insurance Plans, www.ahip.org/ciepd/options/pahm.html (accessed November 23, 2009).
Fellow, Academy for Healthcare Management (FAHM)	Advanced certification is gained through completion of the introductory course as well as completion of additional coursework in governance and regulation, health plan finance and risk management, network management, and medical management.	"Fellow, Academy for Healthcare Management" America's Health Insurance Plans, www.ahip.org/ciepd/options/fahm.html (accessed November 23, 2009).

Overview

Rapidly changing regulations, reimbursement issues, competitive forces, and technological advancements have created opportunities for those seeking to provide consulting services to healthcare professional practices. Despite the 2009 economic downturn, the healthcare consulting industry earned approximately $34.1 billion in 2008, with revenues expected to grow with a compounded annual growth rate of 5.3 percent through 2012.[1]

As the healthcare industry has evolved during the past several decades, demand has increased for consulting services related to assisting healthcare professional practices in navigating complicated industry obstacles, such as reduced reimbursement for physician's professional services, increased competition, costs associated with technological advancements, as well as regulatory pitfalls. This increased need for healthcare consulting services has been met by professionals who have entered the consulting arena from a diverse array of professional backgrounds, including, for example, accounting, finance and economics, insurance, law, health administration, medicine, nursing, academics, and public health.

Although healthcare consulting requires a large body of specialized knowledge, healthcare professional practices are also businesses and are subject to many of the same regulations and market forces as businesses in nonhealthcare industries. (Although no longer the case, a well-known adage in the healthcare profession is that one should refrain from considering a professional practice as a *business*, or anything other than as a *learned profession*, at risk of offending the physician owner.) As a result, similar consulting methods and, therefore, processes related to nonhealthcare businesses are applicable to healthcare professional practices. This chapter will discuss various opportunities for healthcare consulting, as well as the general principles and processes that are useful in many consulting engagements.

Consulting Activities

Modality of Consulting Activity

Consulting services may be offered through several different modalities, that is, on a continuous basis, annually, or episodically on a case-by-case basis. Typically, the nature and scope of the required service determines the modality of the consulting activity, for example, management consultation often requires continuous monitoring, and tax issue consultation typically requires attention only once a year. Healthcare consultants also will find an array of discrete engagements based on one-time needs of professional practice clients, for example, implementation of an electronic health records (EHRs) system or the valuation of a practice upon its dissolution. A description of the different areas and modalities in which consulting services may be offered is set forth in figure 1-1.

Figure 1-1: Categorization of Healthcare Counsulting Services

Areas of Consulting Services	Description	Type		Modality
Accounting and Tax Related Services	Similar to other nonhealthcare professional practices, healthcare consultants assist their healthcare practice clients through financial statement auditing processes and tax filings.	Bookkeeping or Financial Accounting		Continuity
		Financial Statement Preparation, Auditing Services, or Assurance Services		Continuity
		Tax Services		Annuity
		Management or Cost Accounting		Continuity
Revenue Cycle Services	Assist healthcare professional practices to navigate reimbursement and regulatory parameters to properly code and charge for services rendered and then to obtain payment through the claims resolution and collection process.	Coding and Charting		Annuity or Eplsodic
		Billing and Claims Resolution		Continuity
		Reimbursement Yield Enhancement		Episodic
Regulatory Related Services	Assist healthcare professionals to avoid running afoul of strict regulatory restrictions, in addition to aiding in the acquisition and maintenance of accreditations, certifications, and licenses.	Corporate Compliance Audit		Episodic
		Risk Management		Episodic
		Accreditation, Certification, or Licensing	Provider Accredication, Certification, or Licensing	Episodic
			Certification of Need	
Structure and Governance and Organizational Structure Consulting	Assist in practice start-up activities, such as staffing and marketing, as well as the development of a practice mission to ensure staff buy-in.	Practice Start-Up Services		Episodic
		Organizational Development Services		Episodic
		Physician Compensation and Income Distribution		Episodic
Operational Management Consulting	Consultation on basic business and practice management, as well as implementation and management of healthcare information technology.	Supply-Side or Purchasing Consulting		Episodic
		Insurance Consultating		Episodic
		Practice Operational Management Services		Continuity
		Information Systems or Information Technology Services		Episodic
		Facilities Assessment		Episodic
		Operational Throughput		Episodic
		Turnaround or Management Restructuring Services		Episodic
Transition Planning	Provide expertise to clients regarding the physician successorship, retirement planning, and valuation of a practice upon sale, liquidation, merger, and so forth.	Financial or Investment Planning and Retirement Services		Annuity or Episodic
		Successorship or Exit Planning		Episodic
		Valuation Services		Episodic
		Intermediary Services		Episodic
Strategic Planning and Business Development	Assist clients in strategic planning activities in an effort to maintain profitable business structures in the midst of constantly changing regulatory and reimbursement environments.	Marketing Analysis		Episodic
		Feasibility Analysis		Episodic
		Service Line Analysis		Episodic
Litigation Support	Use of consulting expertise to support legal counsel in their litigation engagements by providing healthcare consulting services or expert witness testimony.	Expert Witness		Episodic
		Nontestifying		Annuity or Episodic

Continuity Services

Consulting services that typically are provided on an ongoing basis are commonly referred to as **continuity services**. Many types of continuity services exist, including

(1) financial statement auditing services for both regular business services and compliance with specific healthcare related laws and regulations,

(2) assistance with the practice's billing and claims resolution process,

(3) cost **management advisory services** for healthcare professionals without substantial business experience, and

(4) operational management services for healthcare professionals looking for more in-depth assistance in managing their practices.

> Examples of services provided on a continuing or annual basis: auditing services, coding and charting audits, financial planning and retirement services, management advisory services, practice management services, and tax services.

This type of consulting generally provides a source of recurring work and a stable stream of income for the healthcare consultant.

Annuity Services

In contrast to continuity services, healthcare consultants also may assist their professional practice clients on an annual basis by providing *annuity services*. Although annuity services may not provide the constant stream of work that continuity services do, annuity services still often represent a relatively regular income stream for a healthcare consulting practice, particularly when positive client rapport generates a long-term relationship between the healthcare consultant and the professional practice. Services that typically are provided on an annual basis include:

(1) Coding and charting audits and process review

(2) Financial statement auditing

(3) Tax filing services

(4) Financial planning and retirement services both for the practice as a whole and for the healthcare professionals associated with the practice (note that these services are also often requested by clients to be provided on an episodic basis)

Episodic Services

In addition to services provided on a continuing or annual basis, healthcare consulting services also may be provided on an **episodic**, or discrete, engagement basis. Each episodic project will have separate deliverables and timetables, and they often will have a different engagement agreement detailing the terms of each. Although episodic engagements may not provide the regular revenue stream that continuity and annuity services do, these engagements are extremely important to a healthcare consultant because they are often the means by which the consultant may build rapport with a particular client, thereby providing a valuable source of both future work and referrals, for the purpose of expanding the consultant's client base. The following services typically are provided on an episodic basis:

(1) Providing corporate compliance and risk management audit services for a wide variety of legal and regulatory issues

(2) Advising the practice on revenue cycle issues related to reimbursement yield enhancement

(3) Assisting with the practice's accreditation, certification, and licensure

(4) Implementing information systems or information technology projects or hardware or software upgrades

(5) Providing practice start-up and organizational development services

(6) Advising for physician compensation and income distribution services

(7) Providing turnaround or management restructuring services

(8) Providing transition planning services, for example, successorship planning, intermediary, and valuation services

(9) Providing strategic planning services, that is, marketing, feasibility, and service line analysis

(10) Providing litigation support services

> Examples of services provided on an episodic basis: corporate compliance and risk management, technology implementation, organizational development, restructuring services, and valuation services.

CONSULTING PROFESSIONALS

Consulting professionals from diverse educational and experiential backgrounds offer unique skills and perspectives from their respective areas of expertise to their professional practice client. Although not an exhaustive list, healthcare consultants include professionals such as certified public accountants (CPAs), management consultants, transactional consultants, insurance professionals, legal consultants, investment professionals, computer technologists, coding professionals, and valuation professionals, among others. Depending on the given professional's credentials and expertise, various niche markets exist within the larger healthcare consulting arena, thereby allowing professionals with experience in other industry sectors to enter healthcare related consulting submarkets.

BUSINESS AND FINANCIAL CONSULTING SERVICES

"Do your duty and then collect your money" is the physician's motto. "Be sure of your money before you deliver the goods" is the perfectly proper motto of the business man. John B. Roberts, 1908

As previously mentioned, healthcare consultants provide a wide variety of business-related consulting services to healthcare professional practices. Because business advisory services are expected to grow faster through 2012 than all other healthcare consulting service lines, understanding the basic principles related to business and financial consulting in the healthcare sector is an important step in order to successfully enter this subfield of the healthcare consulting market.[2]

Accounting and Tax Related Services

Financial Statement Preparation and Auditing Services

Three types of financial statement preparation are applicable to professional practices:

(1) *Financial statement compilation* is used to present information, that is, the representation of management (owners), without undertaking to express any assurance on the financial statements.[3]

(2) *Financial statement review* is used to express limited assurance that there are no material modifications that should be made to the financial statements in order for the statements to be in conformity with GAAP.[4]

(3) ***Financial statement audit*** is an expression of an opinion on the fairness with which the practice presents, in all material respects, financial position, results of operations, and its cash flows in conformity with GAAP.[5]

Compilation of unaudited financial statements is defined under the Statements on Standards for Accounting Review Services Section 110.01-03 as

> *A compilation of one or more specified elements, accounts, or items of a financial statement is limited to presenting financial information that is the representation of management (owners) without undertaking to express any assurance on that information. (The accountant might consider it necessary to perform other accounting services to compile the financial information). Examples of specified elements, accounts, or items of a financial statement that an accountant may compile include schedules of rentals, royalties, profit participation, or provision for income taxes.[6]*

Financial statement review services typically include, "… through the performance of inquiry and analytical procedures, a reasonable basis for expressing limited assurance that there are no material modifications that should be made to the financial statements in order for the statements to be in conformity with generally accepted accounting principles."[7]

Although most nonhealthcare professional practices do not audit their financial statements, healthcare professional practices and enterprises may be required to comply with the same, if not more stringent, requirements for financial and accounting auditing as do other nonhealthcare businesses, and auditing the financial statements of healthcare enterprises is often necessary for ensuring government compliance, as well as to assist the professional practice in its future financial and management decisions. Healthcare professional practices also may desire independent audits of their corporate compliance or risk management programs or a review of previous auditing work that has been performed.

Tax Services

Consulting opportunities exist for providing tax-related services for healthcare professional practices and other related enterprises. Healthcare professional practices may require a consultant for such services as preparation of state and federal tax forms and filings, year-end tax projections, and audit support.

Additionally, nonprofit healthcare enterprises may seek consulting services to assist them in fulfilling additional government fiscal requirements and reporting standards. Further, because healthcare professional practices may be organized in a variety of ways, each with its own unique tax implications, opportunities for tax consulting services exist when these different legal organizations merge, set up joint ventures, or create other operating arrangements.[8]

MANAGEMENT OR COST ACCOUNTING

In an industry in which cost is increasingly becoming a necessary consideration in many decisions affecting a professional practice, implementation of a cost accounting system that enables management to properly understand the costs associated with the practice through a breakdown, at the level of the diagnostic or treatment procedure performed, can often assist administrators with the following tasks: negotiating with payors who reimburse on a case basis, planning service expansions more strategically, and improving the processes for monitoring physician efficiency by providing data on individual treatment protocols.[9] Various ways of conceptualizing cost exist (for example, direct variable costs, direct fixed costs, indirect overhead costs, and so forth), and healthcare consultants, particularly those with accounting experience, may offer their expertise in implementing appropriate cost accounting systems and in utilizing those systems to identify cost-saving opportunities. By understanding various elements comprising the practice's cost data, healthcare professional practices are better able to implement effective management accounting systems by considering both financial and operational information in order to more effectively focus the practice on achieving specified objectives.[10]

RELEVANCE OF THIS GUIDE

Although auditing, tax, and management or cost accounting services primarily will often utilize the accounting skills of a consultant, basic knowledge of the healthcare industry as a whole is an important component in the provision of these services, because the consultant should maintain a contextual understanding of the subject enterprise, the source of provided data and information, and how the data is being generated. Chapter 3 of *An Era of Reform* addresses tax law as well as audits of corporate compliance and risk management programs. Additionally, chapter 2 of *An Era of Reform* may be a useful reference for management or cost accounting services, because it details a professional practice's revenue cycle and breaks down reimbursement and policy implications by payor.

REVENUE CYCLE SERVICES

Optimization of the revenue cycle is important to the success of any healthcare professional practice, whether a solo-practitioner practice, a group practice, or a hospital-based practice. The revenue cycle has many elements that should be understood thoroughly (both as discrete elements as well as in the aggregate) in order to avoid a potential loss in revenue. Consultants may provide assistance to healthcare professionals who may be too focused on a single part of the revenue cycle to effectively address other aspects with a comprehensive understanding of the entire revenue cycle. The more familiar a healthcare consultant is with the specifics of the revenue cycle, including, but not limited to, coding and charting procedures, charge capture, reimbursement policies, billing procedures, and claim resolution methods, the better prepared he or she will be to assist clients.

CODING AND CHARTING

Healthcare is reimbursed through a system that begins with charting the diagnostic and treatment services provided to each patient. This information is then converted to a system of codes that are billed to payors and patients at a predetermined rate. Significant unrecognized revenue can exist when patient services are being charted or coded improperly. Accordingly, consulting opportunities related to reviewing **coding** policies and **charting** guidelines ensure that practitioners are being reimbursed the full and correct payment amount for the services they provide. Additionally, as further described in **Corporate Compliance** or **Risk Management Services**, healthcare consultants may conduct audits of past medical records to ensure that sufficient documentation supporting the coded amounts exists (for example, ensuring that "bundled" procedure codes are not reported individually) and that no over- or under-payments are being made to the practice.[11]

REIMBURSEMENT YIELD ENHANCEMENT

Effective charge capture and payment collection involves not only proper coding procedures but also an understanding of how providers are reimbursed by different payors. Chargemaster consulting is a process by which a consultant can assist healthcare professional practice clients to ensure their code lists are up-to-date and being utilized properly. By analyzing the **charge description master (CDM)**, or a professional practice's charging mechanism, healthcare consultants can help practice administrators identify services for which the practice receives less reimbursement than the procedures cost to deliver, as well as assist the practice in revising its CDM to appropriately recover all costs associated with each service, thereby maximizing cash flow to the practice.[12]

Additionally, consultants can aid their healthcare professional practice clients by effectively communicating the intricacies of payor reimbursement models and the payment rates under those models for particular procedure codes, which may allow the clients to enhance their reimbursement yield through optimization of their fee structures based on up-to-date reimbursement rates.[13]

BILLING AND CLAIMS RESOLUTION

Proper submission of claims to payors is an integral step in the revenue cycle and may determine whether a practice will receive reimbursement for services rendered to a patient. Claim submission is governed by individual payor requirements, which vary substantially from payor to payor and presents numerous openings for claim denial if not accurately followed. Many times, claim denial can be traced back to errors committed by the practice, such as failure to verify insurance coverage prior to service, failure of the primary care physician to send a referral to the payor, failure to verify coverage for particular services, failure to use updated and proper coding and charting procedures, errors in charge capture or charge entry, or a combination of these.[14] Understanding payor reimbursement guidelines (such as Medicare's *National Coverage Determinations* is the primary means by which to avoid claim denial, and consultants can assist healthcare professionals by explaining the different reimbursement policies used by Medicare, Medicaid, and various private and commercial payors. Additionally, when reviewing Medicare claims, it is important to differentiate between claims decisions made by the primary payor and those made by local intermediaries, which use their own medical review policies.[15]

In the event that a denied claim is appealable, healthcare consultants can assist professional practices by being well-versed in appeals processes, as the potential pitfalls, and effective strategies for streamlining the process.[16] Additionally, an analysis of the grounds given for payor denial of a claim may be a useful tool for re-engineering the practice's revenue cycle to avoid future denials.[17]

RELEVANCE OF THIS *GUIDE*

As previously mentioned, chapter 2 and chapter 3 of *An Era of Reform* provide an overview of reimbursement and regulatory considerations which healthcare consultants generally should be aware of in order to effectively counsel their professional practice clients on matters related to the revenue cycle, such as, proper charting and coding requirements and regulations regarding the bundling of procedure codes. Because reimbursement schemes and regulatory structures are constantly changing, healthcare consultants should keep abreast of pronouncements from various federal and state governing bodies, namely, the Centers for Medicare and Medicaid Services (CMS), that is, Medicare and Medicaid, as well as commercial and private payors. For example, consultants assisting healthcare professional practices in their billings and claims resolution processes may wish to review updated payor guidelines, for example, Medicare's National Coverage Determinations.

REGULATORY RELATED SERVICES

CORPORATE COMPLIANCE OR RISK MANAGEMENT SERVICES

Healthcare providers are under constant scrutiny from regulatory agencies at the local, state, and federal level, as well as from private organizations such as insurers or payors and investment groups. Improperly maintained and managed policies and procedures can lead to heavy fines, revocation or suspension of licenses or certifications, mandatory reporting, exclusion from state and federal reimbursement programs, and potential criminal penalties. Accordingly, a healthcare provider's **corporate compliance program** requires continuous monitoring and updating. Healthcare consultants may assist professional practices with this task by providing **risk assessments** and, in turn, development and implementation of a compliance program, which may include training programs, policy and procedure manuals, and auditing support.[18]

ACCREDITATION OR CERTIFICATION CONSULTING

The healthcare industry is laden with complicated accreditation, certification, and licensing requirements for healthcare professional practices. A provider's failure to meet certain of these requirements may result in the practice facing certain restrictions regarding the provision of patient services, for example, if required by the particular state in which a healthcare practice operates, a provider may be restricted from operating a computed tomography scanner in his or her office without first obtaining a Certificate of Need (see chapters 3 and 4 of *An Era of Reform*). Additionally, certain payors may refuse to reimburse providers who are not certified or accredited. Healthcare consultants can assist in this arena by understanding how state certification and licensing requirements, as well as other accreditation requirements, may affect their healthcare professional clients and assist them in appropriately meeting these requirements.

RELEVANCE OF THIS *GUIDE*

Chapter 3 of *An Era of Reform* gives a brief overview of federal and state laws and regulations related to corporate compliance, as well as of licensing and accreditation requirements. Chapters 3, 4, 5, and 6 of *Professional Practices* provide more details related to the licensing standards for physician professionals, allied health professionals, mid-level providers, and technicians and paraprofessionals, respectively, while chapters 1 and 2 of *Professional Practices* and chapter 3 of this book discuss the implications of laws applicable to each of the various business structures that healthcare professional practices may choose to employ. However, it also may be useful to consult additional sources of information, such as state licensing and certification standards, up-to-date news and literature, and existing and proposed actions of relevant federal and state authoritative agencies.

Structure and Governance Consulting

Practice Start-Up Services

Healthcare providers are not required to have any business or management training, therefore, numerous opportunities exist for consulting professionals to assist healthcare professionals with practice start-up services. Such opportunities include advising the professional practice client on matters related to obtaining insurance; selecting, setting up, staffing, and maintaining an office; marketing the practice to the public and other professionals; complying with local, state, and federal regulations; and developing procedures for day-to-day operational management and accounting practices, among many other issues. Further, should two or more providers seek to integrate their practices into an independent practice association or another type of integrated provider entity, healthcare consultants may provide market research and analysis to determine if the integration would disparately affect competition in a particular service area (that is, raise antitrust concerns) and may work with each practice's legal counsel to structure the integration in a legally permissible manner.

Organizational Development Services

Organizational development in the healthcare professional practice setting often involves assisting a professional practice in development of a mission and vision, ensuring staff acceptance of these principles, and structuring each segment of the professional practice to fit within the principles upheld by the practice mission and vision.[19] This type of consulting typically requires identification of core competencies of the organization and alignment of the practice's business strategy to complement them.[20]

Physician Compensation and Income Distribution

Development of physician compensation and income distribution plans involves identification of the appropriate methods by which to compensate the practice's physicians for their professional services based on practice revenues and expenses. As discussed in depth in chapter 3, *Compensation and Income Distribution*, physician compensation plans may

(1) contribute to the incentive and performance feedback system,

(2) assist in driving performance to achieve goals, and

(3) facilitate more effective identification and communication of an organization's values, dynamic, productivity objectives, and performance expectations.[21]

Several *internal indicators*, or practice characteristics, are suggestive of the success (or failure) of an existing compensation plan: (1) practitioner perceptions, (2) practice productivity, (3) financial standing, and (4) the current level of compensation.[22] Although the mechanical details of the compensation development process may vary due to the diverse array of practice types and provider arrangements, the healthcare consultant may assist the practice with an evaluation of the existing compensation system, financial modeling of alternative plans, and contribute to the proposal of alternative plans to the practice's physicians.

RELEVANCE OF THIS *GUIDE*

Several chapters contained in this *Guide* may be particularly useful for a healthcare consultant providing advisory services related to business structure and governance:

- Chapter 2 of *An Era of Reform*, which discusses reimbursement and the healthcare revenue cycle;
- Chapter 3 of *An Era of Reform*, which highlights legal issues relevant to the healthcare professional practice;
- Chapter 4 of *An Era of Reform*, which discusses the competitive trends in healthcare as they may affect decisions related to changes in business structure and governance;
- Chapter 5 of *An Era of Reform*, which discusses developments in clinical, as well as practice management technology;
- Chapter 1 of *Professional Practices*, which describes the basic structure of the professional practice;
- Chapter 2 of *Professional Practices*, which outlines the characteristics of integrated provider groups and other emerging trends;
- Chapters 3 through 7 of *Professional Practices*, as they relate to the type or types of professionals that characterize the subject practice;
- Chapter 3, *Compensation and Income Distribution*, which describes compensation and benefits issues related to healthcare professionals; and
- Chapter 4, *Financial Valuation of Enterprises, Assets and Services*, which more thoroughly outlines the valuation process of provider compensation agreements, particularly as they are regulated by state and federal fraud and abuse laws.

OPERATIONAL MANAGEMENT CONSULTING

PRACTICE MANAGEMENT SERVICES

Practice management consulting involves a breakdown of the day-to-day management of the healthcare professional practice and analysis of the existing processes in order to identify areas needing improvement. This type of consulting service is fairly broad in nature and is related to other consulting topics for example, coding and charting, auditing, corporate compliance, information systems and information technology, tax and accounting services, and organizational development, among others.

INFORMATION SYSTEMS AND INFORMATION TECHNOLOGY SERVICES

At the time of publication, information technology (IT) consulting and integration engagements represented half of the healthcare consulting marketplace.[23] This subsector is ideal for consultants with experience in information systems, especially those specific to the healthcare industry.

Numerous advances in healthcare information technology have been made in recent years, and legislation is incentivizing practitioners to move toward the use of advanced technology, such as EHRs, in order to reduce errors, streamline the healthcare delivery process, and reduce associated costs (see chapter 5 of *An Era of Reform* for further discussion regarding the implementation of EHRs). Privacy regulations, such as those found in the Health Insurance Portability and Accountability Act of 1996 and the Red Flags Rule, also regulate the secure storage and transmission of private health or other identifying data, requiring some special equipment and programming or reprogramming of old equipment.

Consultants can provide an array of services in this arena, including the implementation of information security systems; installation and configuration of medical enterprise resource planning systems; assistance in the transition to EHRs, telemedicine and e-prescribing; assisting with maintenance of the organization's data network; and development of a website or other advanced marketing tools.[24]

FACILITIES ASSESSMENT

Numerous factors can be considered when planning a new facility or for the expansion of an existing facility, which requires knowledge of general business and architectural concepts, as well as knowledge of the healthcare industry. First, it is necessary to understand the patient market so that a facility can make any necessary adjustments to properly accommodate the needs of those patients. Second, the facility should be assessed with regard to location, the use of space within the facility, and the physical condition of the structure itself. Important factors in this analysis include the visibility and accessibility of the facility, zoning restrictions limiting the ability to expand, the impact of the location on the practice's ability to grow, how easily traffic moves through the interior space of the facility, the proximity of facility entrances to patient parking areas, the positioning of furniture and equipment to make the most efficient use of the space, occupancy costs of the facility, facility security, and whether the appearance of the facility projects an image that indicates a high quality of care, among many others.[25]

OPERATIONAL THROUGHPUT

The number of patients passing through a healthcare professional practice is often crucial to the future viability of the practice. Many times, however, healthcare professional practices do not move patients through efficiently, thereby resulting in a reduction in revenue to the practice. Healthcare consultants can provide valuable assistance to healthcare practices by assessing a facility's existing throughput with an analysis of patient flow, patient safety, customer (patient) satisfaction, staffing ratios, triage practices, exam room capacity vis-à-vis utilization, and so forth.[26] Healthcare consultants with a background in medicine most likely will be particularly adept at assisting clients in optimizing operational throughput due to their understanding of how the various factors previously indicated are likely to affect patient flow through the practice.

INSURANCE CONSULTING

Numerous opportunities for legal liability exist for healthcare professional practice providers. As with other nonhealthcare businesses, healthcare professional practices typically maintain insurance against loss of property due to fire, theft, or other similar occurrence, as well as insurance to cover loss of income due to a provider's disability caused by sickness or accident.[27] Also, similar to other businesses, healthcare professional practices should typically obtain premises liability insurance, some sort of employee health insurance plan, and employee fidelity bonds.[28] Perhaps most important for healthcare providers, however, is maintaining professional liability, or medical malpractice, insurance, the cost of which varies from provider to provider but often can be very expensive.[29]

Healthcare consultants, particularly those with experience in the insurance industry, may provide invaluable services assisting physicians and other healthcare providers in understanding how to protect themselves from both professional liability as well as loss to their professional practice. As many types of insurance, particularly professional liability or malpractice insurance, can be costly, the healthcare consultant also can help the healthcare professional develop an insurance coverage scheme best tailored to the physician or practice's specialty, the services provided, location, and potential for liability.[30] Further, as insurance providers change their policies to reflect changes in laws governing malpractice claim awards, healthcare professional practices may seek the services of a consultant to assist them in keeping abreast of policies and trends applicable to healthcare provider professional liability insurance.

TURNAROUND OR MANAGEMENT RESTRUCTURING SERVICES

In the evolving regulatory, reimbursement, competitive, and technology environments, as well as in the economic environment, many healthcare professional practices may find it difficult to maintain profit levels due to excessive debt, both personally (for example, education) and professionally (for example, due to decreased reimbursement, the increasing complexity of the regulatory environment, and changes to the practice patient base). Healthcare consultants may assist professional practices by providing services such as a billing process assessment, collections evaluation, fee schedule review, benchmarking exercise for office efficiency, and proposal for reducing office expenditures and employee outsourcing, among many others.

RELEVANCE OF THIS *GUIDE*

Because many areas of the professional practice business are being scrutinized for inefficiencies and possible improvements, the following chapters in this *Guide* should prove useful to a healthcare consultant who is identifying potential areas of concern, as well as developing resolutions to address these concerns:

- Chapter 2 of *An Era of Reform*
- Chapter 3 of *An Era of Reform*
- Chapter 4 of *An Era of Reform*
- Chapter 5 of *An Era of Reform* (see section that discusses trends in practice management technology)
- Chapter 1 of *Professional Practices*
- Chapter 2 of *Professional Practices*

TRANSITION PLANNING SERVICES

FINANCIAL PLANNING AND RETIREMENT SERVICES

Healthcare professional practices deal with many of the same financial planning and retirement planning issues as other businesses. Additionally, care must be taken to ensure retirement planning complies with the provisions of the *Employee Retirement and Income Security Act*. Consulting opportunities exist for healthcare consultants to

- review or design plans,
- work with a professional practice concerning these plans adoption or alteration,
- prepare tax filings in relation to these plans,

- project contributions midyear,
- conduct allocations or accountings for plans,
- coordinate **qualified domestic relations orders**,
- maintain disbursements or loans from retirement plans,
- generate 401(k) safe harbor notices and Internal Revenue Service or Notice of Change to Director's Rules letters, and
- generate summary annual reports.[31]

SUCCESSORSHIP PLANNING SERVICES

As described in chapter 3 of *Professional Practices*, the majority (approximately 56 percent) of the physician workforce is over the age of fifty-five, indicating a reasonable likelihood that a large number of physicians will be exiting the profession within the next decade.[32] Coupled with the fact that physician perspectives on work-life balance have shifted in recent years, leading to different workload expectations, this data emphasizes the importance of strong succession plans so that a practice can continue after the departure of one of its physicians.[33] Healthcare consultants may advise the practice on issues related to physician retirement and the resulting effect on the practice's operating expenses and revenue, as well as how the shareholder or partnership or employment agreement should be restructured to accommodate a physician who is contemplating only partial retirement.[34] More generally, a succession plan may seek advisory services regarding restructuring the practice, income distribution, on-call responsibilities, and recruitment activities.

In the case of a solo practitioner, no practice exists to absorb the patients of the retiring physician, and, therefore, retiring solo practitioners typically must find a successor to take over their practice. In this circumstance, the healthcare consultant may assist the practice in performing market research to locate interested buyers or other practices who may want to merge.[35]

VALUATION SERVICES

Besides physician succession, other events such as purchases, sales, liquidations, dissolutions, and the settling of claims of a healthcare professional practice, are governed by regulations requiring them to be valued at the thresholds of fair market value and commercial reasonableness during the transaction process. The requirement of an appropriate practice **valuation** in these situations provides opportunities for healthcare consultants with backgrounds in finance, accounting, appraisal, or even general business. These opportunities include assignments for practice valuation, identification of potential buyers based on market research, negotiation of transaction terms, collaboration with legal counsel to prepare documents related to the transaction, completion of a due diligence overview, and provision of assistance with financing arrangements, among other things. Knowledge of the healthcare industry is critical to an appropriate valuation of such transactions, because the value of a healthcare enterprise depends on several factors exclusive to the healthcare industry, and healthcare consultants who understand these factors may subsequently capitalize on these opportunities.

INTERMEDIARY SERVICES

Due to the rampant and consistent change in the environment in which healthcare professional practices operate, many enterprises are forced to examine the manner in which they deliver their services and search for more efficient ways to treat patients. For many professional practices, consolidation, merger, strategic alliance, and, in some cases, timely divestiture can be the keys to survival. In such cases, the healthcare consultant can provide valuable services serving as an intermediary between the client and its legal and financial advisors by conducting market research and feasibility analyses, developing potential strategies for the future of the client practice, structuring governance and operation of newly created enterprises, and presenting new potential ownership strategies.

RELEVANCE OF THIS *GUIDE*

For the purpose of providing transition planning services to healthcare professional practices, it will be useful to have a general understanding of the unique characteristics attributable to the subject practice (chapter 3 of *Professional Practices*), in addition to having knowledge of how the competitive marketplace (chapter 4 of *An Era of Reform*), reimbursement and regulatory environments (chapters 2 and 3 of *An Era of Reform*), and technological developments (chapter 5 of *An Era of Reform*) affect a practice. Understanding how to appropriately structure both the practice itself (chapters 1 and 2 of *Professional Practices*) and physician compensation plans (chapter 3, *Compensation and Income Distribution*) will be necessary whenever a physician decides to reduce his or her workload or retire. Finally, chapter 4, *Financial Valuation of Enterprises, Assets, and Services*, will be a useful tool for understanding how to value a healthcare professional practice.

STRATEGIC PLANNING AND BUSINESS DEVELOPMENT

MARKETING ANALYSIS

The marketing of healthcare services is distinct from marketing in other industries because often the purchaser of healthcare services is not the actual consumer, that is, third-party payors typically pay for services rendered to patients, who pay for little to none of the cost of the service. As such, patients are attracted to healthcare professional practices based for other reasons, for example, perceived quality of care, convenience, and reputation, rather than as the result of a cost-benefit analysis. Further, under many employer-based insurance programs, physicians are chosen in conjunction with an insurance plan, because they come together as a package in a managed care plan. Therefore, marketing activity is aimed primarily at the employer, and secondly, to the patient.[36] Healthcare consultants with a background in business and marketing, coupled with an understanding of the healthcare marketplace, can assist healthcare professionals in creating a marketing scheme aimed at the appropriate audience.

FEASIBILITY ANALYSIS

A feasibility analysis is useful when determining whether to open a practice, develop a new service line, or expand a practice, service line, or facility. Healthcare consultants can provide invaluable market research required for an accurate and comprehensive feasibility study. Further, consulting professionals with the appropriate experience may actually develop the feasibility analysis by studying the (proposed) enterprise or service line, assessing the competitive marketplace for the enterprise, analyzing the data, and developing a report for a client's consideration.

SERVICE LINE ANALYSIS

The healthcare industry is strongly influenced by market forces (that is, the four pillars: reimbursement, regulatory, competition, and technology), which can be used to evaluate the future profitability and success of the service line(s) a practice provides. The consultant, by compiling existing and projected industry data (using the four pillars framework) can assess the service line(s) provided by a healthcare practice and compile data that demonstrates industrywide and regional trends specific to those service line(s). These trends allow the consultant and client to analyze the scope, supply and demand, provider demographics, reimbursement and regulatory environments, and market competition relevant to each service line, in order determine the resulting effect of these forces on the relevant subject service line.

RELEVANCE OF THIS *GUIDE*

Services in strategic planning and business development may be enhanced by developing an understanding the healthcare competitive marketplace, which is addressed in chapter 4 of *An Era of Reform*. Typically, the success of a healthcare professional practice's marketing efforts will heavily depend on having an accurate and complete understanding of the practice's "products" or services, which are discussed in chapters 3 through 7 of *Professional Practices*. Further, chapter 2, *Benchmarking* discusses the different modes of benchmarking, which can be a useful research tool for consulting professionals who wish to conduct market research for a feasibility analysis. Finally, in order to properly evaluate a particular service line, a healthcare consultant should have a working understanding of the driving forces of the healthcare industry, with particular attention paid to the four pillars, discussed in chapters 2 through 5 of *An Era of Reform*.

LITIGATION SUPPORT SERVICES

Many of the consulting services described previously also can be utilized by a healthcare consultant when providing litigation support services. In this role, the healthcare consultant may solely provide consulting services to assist legal counsel throughout the litigation engagement with preparation of opposing expert deposition and trial questions. Additionally, the healthcare consultant may be engaged to provide expert witness testimony services during the deposition and trial. The expertise of the consultant will typically determine the scope of his or her expert opinion and may include such topics as the value of a practice, industry standards of care and corporate compliance, typical revenue cycle procedures and billing practices, and so forth.

A consultant must meet various qualifications to qualify as an expert witness in a court of law, based both on Federal Rule of Evidence 702 and the United States Supreme Court opinions rendered in the *William Daubert v. Merrell Dow Pharmaceuticals, Inc.* and *Kumho Tire Company et al. v. Patrick Carmichael*, etc., et al. cases.[37] Federal Rule of Evidence 702 states:

> *If scientific, technical, or other specialized knowledge will assist the trier of fact to understand the evidence or to determine a fact in issue, a witness qualified as an expert by knowledge, skill, experience, training, or education, may testify thereto in the form of an opinion or otherwise, if (1) the testimony is based upon sufficient facts or data, (2) the testimony is the product of reliable principles and methods, and (3) the witness has applied the principles and methods reliably to the facts of the case.*[38]

To determine whether expert testimony is the "product of reliable principles and methods" and, therefore, admissible, the *Daubert* court determined that courts must verify whether the theory or technique

(1)   can be and has been tested,

(2)   has been subjected to peer review or publication,

(3)   has

    a.   a high known or potential rate of error and

    b.   standards controlling the technique's operation, and

(4)   enjoys general acceptance within a relevant scientific community.[39]

Six years later, the Supreme Court decided *Kumho Tire*, clearly stating that *Daubert* was to be applied to nonscientific testimony as well. However, given that the gatekeeping obligation in *Daubert*, as it relates to nonscientific testimony situations, may never "fit" the enumerated factors, the *Kumho Tire* decision encouraged judges to be "flexible" when determining admissibility.[40]

Although most state courts typically follow the Federal Rule of Evidence 702 related to expert witness testimony, some states have imposed additional requirements, for example, restrictions on expert testimony in medical malpractice cases, prohibiting expert testimony by physicians who dedicate too much of their time to testifying as experts in personal injury cases.[41]

CONSULTING METHODS

CONSULTING SKILLS

Two classes of skill sets are useful for effective healthcare professional practice consulting: strategic and organizational.

> Two classes of skills are required in consulting: strategic and organizational.

STRATEGIC

Strategic thinking requires a sound understanding of general business principles as well as specialized knowledge of the healthcare market. This knowledge can be derived from both research (both specific and general, discussed further in *Research* and chapter 4, *Gathering Necessary Data*) and experience (for example, education, professional experience, training, and so forth). An accurate understanding of the depth of this experience is crucial to a consultant's decision to accept engagements relating to specialized topics.

ORGANIZATIONAL

The process of organizing and planning for each aspect of the engagement is important to the consulting engagement. The tools presented in this chapter, along with an understanding of a few sound principles, can serve as a basis for such a process.

BUSINESS DEVELOPMENT FOR CONSULTING SERVICES

Consultants in the field of healthcare professional practice consulting face competition from established consulting firms as well as other new entrants to the field. In order to identify potential clients for consulting engagements, organizations must have a pre-engagement plan for dealing with healthcare professional practices. These may range from informal efforts to well-designed, extensive client "recruitment" programs. Regardless of the scope, the efficacy of these programs depends upon the quality of their planning and design. Ideally, such a program would involve the evaluation of potential clients using a selection process, discussed in the following sections.

THE ENGAGEMENT CHECKLIST

(1) Evaluate whether to accept the engagement.

    a. Identify all parties to prospective engagement, for example, client, subject company or practice, company or practice owners, or hospital affiliations.

    b. Perform a conflict search to disclose any potential conflicts to client and obtain permission or agreement before proceeding.

    c. Perform a capabilities, resources, and skill sets assessment.

    d. Prepare a schedule and timetable review.

(2) Develop an estimate of required chargeable hours and fees.

    a. Fee indicators include the number of FTE providers, number of locations, and gross revenues.

    b. Consider the complexity of legal structure and the availability and sufficiency of data.

    c. Define the purpose, scope, and format of report.

(3) Prepare and submit to client a proposal letter and engagement agreement with schedule of professional fees.

    a. Determine the fee basis (for example, straight hourly, hourly with cap, or flat fee).

    b. Set forth required retainer and expense requirements.

    c. Send two original agreements. The agreement letter should include instructions for the client to sign both originals and return both to consultant.

(4) Submit a preliminary request for documents and information in the proposal package as appropriate.

(5) Obtain a signed engagement agreement and retainer from client.

    a. Sign both originals after they are returned from client with client's signature.

    b. Receive one original (with both signatures) for client's records; the other will be kept in consultant's secured records.

(6) Develop a detailed work program.

    a. Assign tasks to appropriate staff based on skill sets, experience, and availability.

    b. Complete a preliminary budget.

    c. Identify project milestones and estimated date of completion schedule in conformity with client needs and expectations.

    d. Discuss with client; set up telephone conferences if necessary and appropriate.

(7) Collect and analyze the data appropriate for the engagement methods to be used.

    a. General data includes economic, demographic, industry, specialty, managed care environment, utilization demand, and physician or population ratios.

    b. Specific data (obtained from subject company) includes financial statements, tax returns, inventory list, staff listing, and other relevant data.

    c. Discuss appropriate means to obtain data with client (for example, directly from subject company, from accountant(s), and attorney(s), and so forth).

(8) File all documents in project binder(s) separated by numbered indices.

    a. Prepare a table of contents detailing contents of binder(s) according to the numbering system.

    b. Reserve the first section for correspondence and the second section for copies of client agreements (signed), copies of any invoices sent, and any work in progress details.

(9) Follow up with client or subject company regarding documents still needed, if necessary.

    a. Make copies before writing, particularly if marking or writing on data and documents is necessary during the engagement process. Never write on original client documents, because they may have to be returned to the client at the end of the engagement.

    b. Consider obtaining a representation letter regarding accuracy and validity of data submitted to consultant by client, if appropriate and possible.

(10) Instruct staff members to use the consulting and analysis methods selected under the supervision of an experienced consultant or supervisor.

(11) Complete trend analysis and comparison to industry norms.

(12) Perform ratio analysis of subject company and compare those ratios with industry or specialty ratios. Describe and analyze these comparisons in the narrative report.

(13) Prepare narrative to document and communicate to reader of the report all work performed and conclusions reached, in a manner that will allow the reader to replicate consultant's work.

(14) Prepare a final discussion draft of the report.

    a. Update general industry and specific sources of documents used (located near the end of report).

    b. Attach copies of subject company financial data utilized at the appendix of the narrative report.

(15) Perform a detailed review of the work papers and final discussion draft of the report.

(16) Obtain an independent internal review of the work papers and report draft.

(17) Resolve any internal professional disagreements relative to methodologies employed.

(18) Prepare a "**tick and tie**" report, correct any errors.

(19) Discuss engagement findings and final report draft with client.

    a. Request that client disclose any errors of omission or commission that may have been discovered in client's review of the final discussion draft of the report.

(20) Determine that all review points and open items have been cleared.

(21) Prepare and bind the final report in multiple originals according to client agreement.

(22) Sign and apply embossed certification seal, if applicable, to the multiple original reports on both the transmittal letter and certification pages.

(23) File all work papers, data sources, and other engagement-related documents for secured filing.

(24) Prepare and submit final billing for engagement to client.

(25) Conduct a post-engagement review to evaluate staff performance and quality of final work product.

The Engagement Process

Suspect Stage

The **Suspect** stage, which is very broad in scope, is the process by which potential clients are identified and information is collected to create **Prospects** for the consulting organization. The Suspect stage begins with determining the minimum preliminary criteria required by the organization to become a Prospect. This includes factors such as whether the practice is inside a feasible geographic area for which perform an engagement, the size and complexity of the practice in comparison to other clients a consultant has been able to deal with successfully, and possible consulting needs of the organization that would match with any special expertise of the consulting organization. A database is then created identifying all possible candidate professional practices with contact information and basic market research for each of them. Information needed to convert the Suspects into Prospects is gathered from each identified practice (for example, size of practice, location(s), specialty(s), services, ownership, financial status, and so forth). This information can be obtained through public means (for example, directories, electronic databases, publications, and so forth) or from the individual professional practices themselves. This information is then organized in a format from which to screen the Suspects and determine if they qualify for the Prospect stage (for example, datasheets, tables, and so forth).

Prospect Stage

Although it is acknowledged that the consideration of specific professional practices necessarily involves a level of subjective evaluation, it is advantageous to develop a methodology to enhance the objective aspects of the consideration and selection process of specific professional practices to be approached for client engagements. The criteria chosen for this process, although not exhaustive of all significant aspects of a professional practice, reflects significant consideration of a reasonable and manageable scope of comparative factors. Representative selection criteria may include the following:

(1) Location or proximity of practice

(2) Number and complexity of relationships with other practices or hospitals

(3) Healthcare professional or practice reputation

(4) Known consulting needs of the professional practice

(5) Past or pending legal or professional action against the professional practice

(6) Managed care payor relationships and insurance plan participation

(7) Current stage in the professional practice lifecycle

(8) Receptiveness of healthcare professionals to consulting conclusions

(9) Practice size and patient volume

(10) Professional practice financial viability

Following the consideration and selection of specific professional practices as Prospects, preliminary proposals may be prepared on a case-by-case basis, and these professional practices now can be considered Targets.

TARGET STAGE

The practices that qualify as **Targets**, given the criteria in the selection rating system matrix, are then surveyed (in depth) to

(1) verify and gauge their level of interest in a consulting engagement;

(2) measure the professional practice's compatibility with the consultant's organization regarding consulting needs and philosophy;

(3) determine the extent of the consulting engagement that the professional practice requires at this point;

(4) determine the reasons and rationale for their consulting engagement;

(5) discern the current areas of consensus, disagreement about the consulting engagement inside the practice, or both; and

(6) discuss the emphasis of each member's participation in, and ownership of, steps of the consulting process.

The surveyed Prospects that meet all of the qualifications become Target practices. Due diligence and an analysis of any preliminary data received are then performed to prepare for turning the Targets into **Clients**.

CLIENT STAGE

The Client stage of the process is the point at which the planning process and negotiated detail are memorialized by representatives of the client and consulting organization. Depending on the type of consultation, the Client stage could be limited to developing an engagement agreement. Some of the tools utilized in this stage include follow-up requests for production of documents, site visits, interviews, and confidentiality agreements.

VISION, STRATEGIC INITIATIVES, AND TACTICAL PLANS

An effective way of organizing the strategic planning process is by using the hierarchy (1) vision, (2) strategic initiatives, and (3) tactical plans. It is important not to confuse the scope and definition of these terms:

- **Vision** answers "why" and is long term. A client first must define or confirm their vision; the resulting vision statement answers the long-term question: "Why are we in business?"

- **Strategic initiatives** answer "what" and "who." Strategic initiatives are intermediate and generally are objectives that, if met, would satisfy the vision of the organization.

- **Tactical plans** answer "how," "when," and "where." Tactical plans are short term and ever changing. The details of the organization's strategy must be addressed by defining tactical plans. Tactical plans describe how, when, and where the strategic initiatives will be met.

THE PHASES OF THE CONSULTING ENGAGEMENT

The purpose of consulting work is the provision of an opinion. The consulting process consists of four basic phases: proposal, research, analysis, and presentation.

> The purpose of consulting work is the provision of opinion.

PROPOSAL

The first phase, *proposal*, involves business development activities culminating in the delivery of a proposal for specific consulting work. Business development is beyond the scope of this *Guide*, but numerous considerations exist that pertain to the development of a proposal and acceptance of an engagement that weigh heavily on the successful outcome of the project. A consulting pre-engagement acceptance form can lead a consultant through many of the questions that must be addressed before accepting an engagement, including the self-assessment of expertise, available resources (personnel and financial), any conflicts of interest, and many other issues.

RESEARCH

Once the consultant accepts an engagement, the next phase, *research*, involves compiling the necessary data to complete the assignment. The *specific research* consists of gathering information from the subject healthcare professional practice, including financial, business, operational, staffing, and other information. The other portion of this phase is the performance of *general research* using materials that are available through published governmental and private sources and may include information on topics such as the healthcare market, local economic conditions, competitors, healthcare facilities, managed care organizations, benchmarking statistics, reimbursement trends, specialty or industry trends, supply of practitioners and facilities, and many other relevant topics (also discussed in chapter 2, *Overview* and chapter 4, *Gathering Necessary Data*).

ANALYSIS

The third phase of an engagement, *analysis*, involves summarizing and interpreting the information gathered in the research phase and comparing the specific research with the general research. This analysis can range anywhere from providing simple summaries of the compiled research to an in-depth financial analysis. Consultants should understand a number of standard tools for analysis.

Summarization

This includes tables, matrices, abstracts, and so forth, that are designed to allow for the distillation of a body of information into one or more of its essential characteristics. These tools provide readers with an overview or comparison of information.

Benchmarking

Benchmarking refers to the comparison of specific research data on the subject with industry norms. This may be as simple as a variance analysis on a single characteristic such as physician compensation, or as complex as an analysis involving numerous variables and incorporated within another, larger analysis. See chapter 2, *Benchmarking* for further discussion of the purpose of benchmarking and the various types and techniques utilized in healthcare valuation and analysis.

Forecasting

Forecasting generally involves trend analysis and produces a prediction of values or performance. Financial pro formas, budgets, demand analysis, and space or staffing forecasts are all examples of this type of analysis. Several sections in chapter 4, *Financial Valuation of Enterprises, Assets and Services* detail forecasting approaches for professional practice valuations.

Complex or Compound

This is a type of multifaceted analysis that may incorporate several different tools to synthesize an overall conclusion. A large proportion of consulting analysis falls into this category. The following is an example of valuation engagement deliverables that would require a **complex** or **compound analysis**.

(1) Space allocation

    a. Estimate of bed utilization based on average daily census

    b. Location of services

(2) Payor source evaluation

    a. Breakdown of payors

    b. Self-pay mission alignment

(3) Information systems needs assessment

(4) Financial statements

    a. Income and cash flow

    b. Projected volume utilization or current utilization

(5) Staffing ratios and management structure

    a. Staffing needs based on volume by discipline

      b. Management structure

      c. Efficiency of shift length

(6) Risk assessment

      a. Strengths and weaknesses

      b. Potential risks of a joint venture or merger

(7) Compliance assessment or gap analysis

      a. Compliance Review and Corrective Actions

      b. File Integrity Monitoring, medical record, or billing audit

(8) Organizational development

      a. Philosophies or vision

PRESENTATION

The final phase of a consulting engagement, **presentation**, involves the reporting of results to clients or other parties. Though presentation is the final phase, presentation aspects, such as progress reports, updates, interim reports, and other intermediate communications, will occur throughout the engagement. These reports may occur in a variety of formats, including business correspondence, oral presentations, and written reports. Generally, final reports should be formal, written in a technical style, and include the results of all analysis, as well as the opinion and recommendations of the consultant.

RECORD MANAGEMENT, MEMORIALIZING, AND ARCHIVING

The organization of any project requires diligence and planning in the maintenance of project and business records. The first portion of this duty for the consultant involves memorializing events, discussions, correspondence, decisions, and records. The process includes the creation and retention of agendas and minutes for all meetings, results, or summaries of all appropriate decisions, options, lists, and other documents. Memorializing information serves a number of functions, most notably legal concerns for both the client and consultant, and provides a complete history of events related to the project as well as evidence for facilitating dispute resolution.

The records management and archiving process consists of four consecutive functions: identification, classification, storage, and retrieval. These steps provide a framework for the design and maintenance of a records management system. Numerous document tracking systems and software are available for these purposes. Beyond the obvious reasons for careful design and upkeep of records management systems—such as internal project management capability—numerous legal and ethical concerns require the diligent preservation of client business records.

THE ENGAGEMENT PROCESS

Each consulting engagement will include specific project tasks and steps; however, most engagements will typically include certain standard procedures, as discussed below.

PROFESSIONAL FEES

It is important to discuss options for arranging professional fees and to understand how different types of engagements require different **fee arrangements**. Countless factors can affect the amount of time and resources an engagement requires and, therefore, have an impact on its profitability for the consultant. Fee options range from flat fees, by which payment is fixed regardless of the amount of work performed, to hourly rates, by which consultants are compensated based on their time spent on the project. Consultants must learn what factors can affect the amount of time spent on various engagement types and contract using the appropriate fee arrangements. Fee levels will depend on the consultant's internal costs as well as the value that their work and experience can command in the market. Six common types of professional fee arrangements in consulting are shown in figure 1-2.

Figure 1-2: Fee Option Discussion Matrix

	Fee Option 1	Fee Option 2	Fee Option 3	Fee Option 4	Fee Option 5	Fee Option 6
Hourly Rate	X	X	X	X	X	
Retainer	X	X	X	X		
No Cap	X				X	
10 Percent Cap Over Estimate		X	X	X		
Estimate at Client Expense		X				
Estimate at Limited Client Expense			X			
Estimate at Consultant Expense				X		
Flat Fee						X

HEALTHCARE CONSULTING ORGANIZATIONS AND ASSOCIATIONS

Numerous professional associations and organizations are related to the different types of healthcare consulting professionals. The following sections provide a brief overview of some of the most commonly recognized organizations and associations.

BUSINESS AND FINANCIAL CONSULTING GROUPS

AMERICAN INSTITUTE OF CERTIFIED PUBLIC ACCOUNTANTS (AICPA)

The American Institute of Certified Public Accountants (AICPA) is a national professional organization for all CPAs, whose mission it is to work with state CPA organizations to provide its members with information, resources, and leadership "that enable them to provide valuable services in the highest professional manner to benefit the public as well as employers and clients."[42] The AICPA and its predecessor organizations date as far back to 1887 and was merged into its present form in 1936, at which time, the AICPA agreed to restrict its membership to CPAs only.[43] The AICPA provides national representation for the promotion of AICPA members' interests before governments and regulatory bodies and seeks to provide the highest level of uniform certification and licensing standards in pursuit of promoting and protecting the CPA designation, as well as promoting public awareness and reliance in the integrity, objectivity, competency, and professionalism of CPAs. Further, the AICPA provides recruitment and educational services, in addition to setting performance standards for the profession.[44] As of August 2009, the AICPA's membership was comprised of approximately 342,490 "regular" members, including 10,253 members in consulting, 7,818 members in education, 11,682 members in government, 134,941 members in business and industry, 2,187 members in law, 149,395 members in public accounting, 23,523 retired members, and 2,691 members who designated themselves in the "other" category.[45]

Certified Public Accountants

CPAs are professionals with a background in accounting who have met certain education and experience requirements, including passing the Uniform CPA Exam.[46] Generally, CPAs are financial advisors who assist individuals, businesses, and other organizations in developing and achieving financial goals. CPAs include both chief financial officers of major corporations and accounting advisors to small local businesses.[47] Services provided by CPAs may include such public accounting activities as auditing, assurance services, environmental accounting, forensic accounting, information technology services, international accounting, consulting services, personal financial planning, and tax advisory services.[48] As indicated previously, the CPA credential requires certain educational requirements, including 150 semester hours of college coursework in accounting, as well as passing the Uniform CPA Exam.[49]

Accredited in Business Valuation (ABV)

The Accredited in Business Valuation (ABV) credential is designated to CPAs who are experts in the field of business valuation.[50] Four types of ABV exam candidates exist: new entrants not previously certified by any other credentialing organization (required to sit for an eight-hour examination); candidates previously certified either as Certified Valuation Analysts (CVA) by the National Association of Certified Valuation Analysts, Certified Business Appraisers (CBA) by the Institute of Business Appraisers, or Chartered Financial Analysts (CFA) by the CFA Institute; registrants that previously enrolled for the exam but did not schedule to sit for the exam during the year that they registered; and individuals who are retaking the exam because they did not pass on previous attempts.[51] Requirements for ABV certification include: (1) AICPA membership and good standing, (2) valid and unrevoked CPA certification, (3) a passing score on the ABV examination, and (4) payment of the $350 credentialing fee.[52] Recertification requirements must be met every three years and include (1) AICPA membership and good standing, (2) valid and unrevoked CPA certification, (3) completion of at least sixty hours of related lifelong learning during the preceding three years, and (4) electronic submission of intent to maintain compliance with all recertification requirements.[53] Although not a strict requirement, the AICPA suggests that candidates only sit for the exam after having completed at least six business valuation engagements.[54]

AMERICAN SOCIETY OF APPRAISERS (ASA)

The American Society of Appraisers (ASA) is a global organization of appraisal professionals and others involved in the appraisal profession. Originating in 1936 and incorporating in 1952, ASA is the oldest appraisal organization and the only organization that represents all appraisal specialties.[55] The ASA publishes a code of ethics and principles of appraisal practice as well as a set of standards for business valuation.[56] They also are a sponsor of the Appraisal Foundation and work together with the foundation to create and update the Uniform Standards of Professional Appraisal Practice, the standard criteria that professional appraisers must follow.[57]

Certified Business Valuator (CBV)

Appraisers can be accredited in a variety of appraisal specialties such as appraisal review and management, business valuation, gems and jewelry, machinery and technical specialties, personal property, and real property.[58] At least two years of experience are required to be an Accredited Member and a minimum of five years appraisal experience is necessary before consideration for Accredited Senior Appraiser status.[59] This must be supported by an appropriate experience log.[60] Accreditation also requires either a four-year college degree or double its equivalent in additional work experience.[61] Additionally, applicants are required to have an appraisal report or reports issued within the last two years that should support the experience reported on the application.[62]

Institute of Business Appraisers (IBA)

Established in 1978, the Institute of Business Appraisers (IBA) is the oldest professional society devoted solely to the appraisal of closely held businesses.[63] The IBA offers education to group members and the general public through seminars, media, workshops, and conferences. The IBA also offers business appraisal education, industry research, and business appraisal certifications including the following: (1) Accredited by IBA (AIBA), (2) CBA, (3) Business Valuator Accredited in Litigation (BVAL), and (4) Accredited in Business Appraisal Review (ABAR). See the following sections for detailed discussion of each of these certifications.

Accredited by IBA

Receipt of an AIBA certification requires a four-year college degree; successful completion of IBA course 8002, the eight-day workshop in valuing closely held businesses; or possession of a journeyman level designation in business valuing.[64] All applicants must also complete IBA's course 1010, a sixteen-hour curriculum for report writing.[65] Additionally, applicants must provide proper references, be a member in good standing with the IBA, pass a comprehensive written examination, and submit a demonstrative report.[66]

Certified Business Appraiser

The CBA certification is a professional designation that signifies a level of competence attained by accomplished business appraisers and grants its recipients special respect and esteem among other appraisers, the courts, and the business appraisal community at large.[67] To obtain CBA certification, an applicant must hold a four-year college degree or equivalent; must have completed at least ninety classroom hours of upper level course work, at least twenty-four of which were courses provided by the IBA; and must have completed a six-hour, proctored, CBA written exam covering the theory and practice of business accreditation.[68] Ten thousand hours of active experience as a business appraiser is accepted in lieu of the ninety-hour classroom requirement.[69] Finally, the applicant must submit two demonstration reports that illustrate a high level of skill, knowledge, and judgment as a business appraiser.[70]

Business Valuator Accredited in Litigation

The BVAL certification is designed to recognize experienced business appraisers who demonstrate their ability to competently present expert testimony that supports their objective conclusion of value.[71] The BVAL designation requires completion of five days of IBA course 7001, sixteen Certified Physician Executive (CPE) hours, passage of a four-hour written exam, demonstration at testimony clinics, a business appraisal-related designation, and references of trial performance from at least two attorneys.[72]

Accredited in Business Appraisal Review

The ABAR is a new certification that is designed to provide a level of quality assurance to stakeholders in the business appraisal process.[73] The designation requires IBA members in good standing to submit two professional and personal references, hold a business appraisal designation, hold a four-year university degree, complete IBA course 1044, and submit an appraisal review.

National Association of Certified Valuation Analysts (NACVA)

The National Association of Certified Valuation Analysts (NACVA), established in 1990, is an organization of more than 6,500 members who support practitioners of business asset valuation, intangible asset valuation, and financial forensic services with training and certification for valuation professionals.[74] They provide training courses through the Consultants Training Institute, offer software support for valuation in the form of their ValuSource software, and publish KeyValueData research for their members to view and analyze the details of healthcare transactions.[75] Membership requires at least thirty-six hours of continuing professional education every three years in the areas of accounting, tax, or financial analysis.[76]

Certified Valuation Analysts

CVAs are trained to provide valuation services professionally, competently, and consistent with industry standards at a level of expertise deemed credible by NACVA.[77] In order to obtain this certification, applicants must be a licensed CPA with at least two years of CPA experience and pass a two-part exam including a valuation case study. Applicants also can attend an optional five-day training session.[78]

Accredited Valuation Analyst (AVA)

Accredited valuation analysts (AVAs) also are trained to provide valuation services to the consulting community and their clients with similar standards to which the CVA is held.[79] Unlike CVAs, they can hold any business degree, but they must have had two or more years of business valuation or related experience, performed ten or more business valuations, or have been able to demonstrate substantial knowledge of business valuation theory, methods, and practice.[80] Similar to CVAs, they also must complete a two-part exam, the second half of which is a standardized case study mimicking the performance of a complete business valuation.[81]

Certified Forensic Financial Analyst (CFFA)

The certified forensic financial analyst (CFFA) is a specialist in areas such as financial litigation, forensic accounting, business and intellectual property damages, fraud prevention and detection, or matrimonial litigation support.[82] CFFAs must have certain educational and experiential requirements differing for each of the previously mentioned specialties.[83]

CFA Institute

The CFA Institute is an international, nonprofit association of more than 96,000 investment professionals and 136 professional societies focusing on offering educational opportunities and promoting ethical standards among its members.[84] Its mission is to "lead the investment profession globally by setting the highest standards of ethics, education, and professional excellence."[85] It maintains the Global Body of Investment Knowledge, which it uses to educate its members on all aspects of the investment industry.[86] It also offers certification as a Chartered Financial Analyst (CFA) and a Certificate in Investment Performance Measurement (CIPM).[87]

Chartered Financial Analyst

A CFA is an investment professional who has passed all three of the CFA exams testing his or her competence and integrity in managing portfolios and analyzing investments and fulfilled other experiential requirements.[88] To enter the examination program requires a bachelor's degree or a combined four years of education and relevant professional work experience.[89] To become a charterholder, an applicant must participate in an assigned curriculum, take the three levels of the CFA exam sequentially, and have acquired four years of relevant investment industry work experience.[90] More than 83,000 members of the CFA Institute are charterholders.[91] The CFA Institute also offers the CIPM, which covers investment performance measurement, attribution, evaluation, standards, and professional ethics in the international arena.[92]

ALLIANCE OF MERGER AND ACQUISITION ADVISORS (AM&AA)

The Alliance of Merger and Acquisition Advisors (AM&AA) was founded in 1998 and is a collection of CPAs, attorneys, and other corporate financial advisors who combine their knowledge and experience to better serve the special needs of middle-market clients.[93] They provide business research tools and a variety of opportunities for collaboration between members as well as continuing education and credentialing programs.[94]

Certified Merger and Acquisition Advisor (CM&AA)

The Certified Merger and Acquisition Advisor certification is meant to maintain the AM&AA's standards of professional excellence and serve as a benchmark for professional achievement within the corporate financial advisory and transactional services industry.[95] This involves training and assessment in the areas of the private capital marketplace, merger and acquisition (M&A) engagements, corporate M&A development, business valuation and M&A standard practices, tax issues, legal issues, and growth and acquisition financing.[96]

HEALTHCARE CONSULTING GROUPS

AMERICAN COLLEGE OF PHYSICIAN EXECUTIVES (ACPE)

The American College of Physician Executives (ACPE) is an organization that assists physicians who hold or aspire toward executive positions in their healthcare professional practices.[97] With more than 10,000 members, the ACPE is one of the leading societies for the support of physician executives.[98] The ACPE offers a number of opportunities for professional advancement, with designations including (1) CPE, (2) fellow, (3) distinguished fellow, and (4) vanguard.[99]

Certified Physician Executive (CPE)

The CPE designation represents "a superior level of excellence in medical management, with the education, expertise, and demonstrated skills to effectively lead health care organizations in today's challenging markets."[100] Board certification is issued by the Certifying Commission in Medical Management, which requires that candidates (1) graduate from an approved medical program (either through the Liaison Committee on Medical Education, American Osteopathic Association, or Educational Commission for Foreign Medical Graduates), (2) hold a valid license, (3) have three years of experience, (4) hold board certification in a medical specialty area, (5) complete 150 hours of management education, or a graduate management degree (in areas of business, medical management, science, health administration, or public health), (6) have one year of medical management experience, and (7) provide a letter of recommendation confirming management experience.[101] Physicians who receive the CPE designation are referred to as *diplomates*.[102]

Fellow of ACPE (FACPE)

To become a fellow of ACPE (FACPE), diplomates with board certification in medical management (CPE) must maintain ACPE membership for five consecutive years and demonstrate that their expertise is of regional or national stature.[103] They must also provide two letters of recommendation: one from a current ACPE fellow as a nomination for fellowship and another from a person who holds a leadership role within the physician's organization of employment who can attest to the applicant's standing in the field of medical management.[104] Applicants also must demonstrate superior involvement in the field of medical management, for example, through published articles, books, or papers; teaching; research; service; or a combination of these.[105] They must be actively involved in ACPE, and they must provide an up-to-date curriculum vitae, an up-to-date resume, and a narrative describing their accomplishments in the field of medical management.[106]

Distinguished Fellow of ACPE

Distinguished fellows are fellows awarded the highest distinction due to their exceptional and continued contribution to the field of medical management.[107] No application process exists, because candidates for distinguished fellowship are nominated by their peers.[108]

Vanguard

Vanguard membership is a new ACPE classification that recognizes members who demonstrate dedication to their performance in medical management and, therefore, remain at the forefront of healthcare leadership.[109] These ACPE members are board certified in medical management, hold fellowship or distinguished fellowship status, and have earned an advanced degree in management through ACPE's graduate degree program.[110]

Medical Group Management Association (MGMA)

The Medical Group Management Association (MGMA), consisting of 22,500 members and more than 13,700 organizations representing almost 275,000 physicians, seeks to improve the performance of medical group practice organizations and the professionals they employ.[111] It began as the National Association of Clinical Managers in 1926 and changed its name to the Medical Group Management Association in 1963 to highlight the continued expansion in the diversity of management roles found in group practices.[112]

Healthcare Consulting Group

The MGMA Healthcare Consulting Group, founded in 1970, was formed to provide consulting services to healthcare professionals and organizations.[113] The group, with each member averaging more than twenty-seven years of healthcare consulting experience, can consult group practices and professionals in the areas of academic practice consulting, compensation planning, conflict resolution, recruitment, valuations and appraisals, benchmarking financial and operational efficiency, organizational governance, information technology, integrated delivery systems, management, organizational and business development, revenue cycle analysis, and many others.[114]

HEALTHCARE FINANCIAL MANAGEMENT ASSOCIATION (HFMA)

The Healthcare Financial Management Association (HFMA) is an organization for healthcare financial management executives and other leaders in the healthcare field.[115] The HFMA assists these professionals by (1) providing education and analysis, (2) developing coalitions with other healthcare associations to accurately represent the healthcare finance profession, (3) educating key decision makers on the important aspects of maintaining fiscally sound healthcare organizations, and (4) working with stakeholders to improve the healthcare industry by overcoming deficiencies in knowledge, best practices, and standards.[116] The HFMA's vision is: "To be the indispensable resource for healthcare finance."[117] The HFMA offers two certification levels, described in the following sections.

Certified Healthcare Financial Professional (CHFP)

The Certified Healthcare Financial Professional (CHFP) requires the success completion of the HFMA core certification exam as well as one of four specialty exams in accounting and finance, patient financial services, financial management of physician practices, or managed care.[118] The requirements also include: (1) two years total as a regular or advanced HFMA member, (2) sixty semester hours of college coursework from an accredited institution or sixty professional development contact hours, (3) references from a current elected HFMA chapter officer and the applicant's CEO or supervisor, and (4) timely submission of a conforming CHFP application within twelve months of successfully completing the two required exams.[119]

Fellow of the Healthcare Financial Management Association (FHFMA)

The HFMA's second certification level is the Fellow of the Healthcare Financial Management Association (FHFMA). This certification is only available to those who have already received the CHFP designation, and it represents exemplary educational achievement, experience, and volunteer service to the healthcare finance industry.[120] To qualify, an applicant must have (1) five years total as a regular or advanced HFMA member, (2) a bachelor's degree or 120 semester hours from an accredited college or university, (3) a reference from an FHFMA or current elected HFMA chapter officer, and (4) volunteer activity in healthcare finance within three years of applying for the FHFMA designation.[121]

AMERICAN ASSOCIATION OF HEALTHCARE CONSULTANTS (AAHC)

The American Association of Healthcare Consultants (AAHC), founded in 1949, is a professional society for healthcare consultants.[122] Its mission includes advancing the profession of healthcare consulting by attracting qualified healthcare consultants and advisors and promoting them to prospective clients. The AAHC also conducts some educational and research initiatives, and it promotes collaboration and networking between healthcare consultants and other professionals. Additionally, it develops and maintains professional standards and a code of ethics for healthcare consultants in order to evaluate individual members.[123]

Fellow of the American Association of Healthcare Consultants (FAAHC)

To become a certified as a Fellow of the American Association of Healthcare Consultants (FAAHC), a consultant must pass the standards set by the credentialing and standards committee.[124] This involves having at least a bachelor's degree, a minimum of three years of experience in his or her respective consulting field, perform acceptably in an interview meant to evaluate skills, objective testing of the consultant's knowledge, compliance with the organizations code of ethics, and a demonstration of no conflicts of interests in his or her consulting services.[125] The applicant must be a full-time consultant or be available for healthcare consulting for at least 1,000 hours a year.[126]

NATIONAL SOCIETY OF CERTIFIED HEALTHCARE BUSINESS CONSULTANTS

The National Society of Certified Healthcare Business Consultants was founded in 2006 as a combination of the Institute of Certified Healthcare Business Consultants, the National Association of Healthcare Consultants, and the Society of Medical Dental Management Consultants.[127] The society now fulfills the combined missions of its parent organizations including the advancement the field of healthcare consulting, the establishment of standards of qualifications and ethics for consultants, and the sponsorship of a certification program for its members.[128] It also promotes its members to the healthcare industry and facilitates the sharing of management techniques and individual skills and provides a wide variety of educational programs and other benefits to its members.[129]

Certified Healthcare Business Consultant (CHBC)

A certified healthcare business consultant (CHBC) must pass an examination showing proficiency in business planning and organization, coding and billing practices, legal liability and compliance, employment issues, marketing and quality control, and financial aspects, including accounting, valuation, financial planning, and tax issues.[130] These diverse areas are tested to ensure that the CHBC has a broad understanding of the healthcare business environment.[131]

AMERICAN HEALTH INFORMATION MANAGEMENT ASSOCIATION (AHIMA)

The American Health Information Management Association (AHIMA) dates back to 1928 when the American College of Surgeons established the Association of Record Librarians of North America to "elevate the standards of clinical records in hospitals and other medical institutions."[132] In 1938, the association changed its name to the American Association of Medical Record Librarians and moved forward with the creation of standards and regulations that established its members as medical records experts. In 1970, it became the American Medical Record Association before becoming AHIMA in 1991. The association now works toward addressing issues such as implementation of EHRs in addition to working toward adopting and implementing clinical coding systems per *International Statistical Classification of Diseases and Related Health Problems*, Tenth Edition (ICD-10).[133]

The Commission on Certification for Health Informatics and Information Management is the AHIMA commission responsible for ensuring the competency of professionals providing health information management services.[134]

Certified Coding Specialist (CCS)

A certified coding specialist (CCS) categorizes medical data from patient records, mainly in hospital settings.[135] The CCS responsibilities include reviewing patient records and applying proper numeric codes for each diagnosis, maintaining expertise in the ICD-9-CM and Current Procedural Terminology coding systems, and possessing knowledge about medical terminology, disease processes, and pharmacology.[136] The CCS credential exhibits a practitioner's tested data quality and integrity skills and ability and a high level of coding proficiency.[137] CCS candidates must have earned a high school diploma or have an equivalent educational background, and although not required, at least three years of on-the-job experience.[138]

Certified Coding Associate (CCA)

The Certified Coding Associate (CCA) designation is often viewed as a starting point for a person entering a coder career, and it demonstrates competency in the health information field and a commitment to the coding profession.[139] CCA examination candidates must have a high school diploma or equivalent, and although not required, at least six months of coding experience.[140]

Certified in Healthcare Privacy and Security (CHPS)

The Certified in Healthcare Privacy and Security (CHPS) designation signifies competence in the design, implementation, and administration of comprehensive security and privacy programs in various healthcare organizations.[141] This certification demonstrates a concentration on the privacy and security aspects of health information management.

Certified Health Data Analyst (CHDA)

The Certified Health Data Analysis (CHDA) designation provides recognition of mastery and expertise in health data analysis.[142] This certification gives practitioners the knowledge to obtain, manage, examine, understand, and transform data into accurate, relevant information.[143] The CHDA-certified practitioner demonstrates broad organizational knowledge and communication skills with individuals and groups at multiple levels.[144]

ACADEMY OF HEALTHCARE MANAGEMENT

Founded in 1997 by America's Health Insurance Plans and Blue Cross Blue Shield Association, the Academy for Healthcare Management works to provide online education for healthcare, business, or insurance professionals seeking education on the health insurance plan industry.[145]

Professional, Academy for Healthcare Management

The first level of the academy's certifications is the designation of Professional, Academy for Healthcare Management.[146] This certification requires completion of a course covering the basics of health insurance plans, healthcare providers, as well as operational, regulatory, legislative, and ethical issues.[147]

Fellow, Academy for Healthcare Management (FAHM)

The academy's more advanced certification, Fellow, Academy for Healthcare Management, completes the introductory course mentioned previously as well as additional coursework in governance and regulation, health plan finance and risk management, network management, and medical management.[148]

THE INSTITUTE OF MEDICAL BUSINESS ADVISORS (IMBA)

The Institute of Medical Business Advisors (IMBA) is an organization devoted to furthering the nation's healthcare professionals by connecting financial and business consultants with medical professionals to help build wealth and assist institutional management in the performance of fiduciary responsibilities.[149] They also seek to empower clients and members by educating them about financial planning and the latest management trends and engage members of both the healthcare and financial communities to increase understanding and communication between the two.[150] They offer services in the areas of asset and wealth management, financial planning, medical practice management, valuations and appraisals, and healthcare information technology.[151]

Certified Medical Planner (CMP)

To become a Certified Medical Planner (CMP), a practitioner must complete a one-year online course of curriculum covering issues in healthcare such as legal compliance, human resources, information technology, reimbursement and insurance issues, cost management, contracting, unions, and other business and financial issues unique to the practice of medicine.[152] These courses are meant to complement an applicant's already existing investment, accounting, law, brokerage, or financial services, with the last quarter of coursework customized to better apply to their sector of the healthcare industry.[153]

Conclusion

This synopsis of the modalities of healthcare professional practice consultancy, the corresponding services that may be provided, the process of business development for consultants seeking to provide such services, and the various organizations and associations that represent professionals in healthcare consulting may be used, in conjunction with the other chapters in this *Guide*, to assist in understanding subject enterprises (for example, professional practices) within the context of the healthcare market. This *Guide* should not be considered comprehensive or universal in its scope or applicability but as a basic framework and preliminary working knowledge which may direct more focused, specific, and time-sensitive research on the issues that are pertinent to a particular client's practice in order to further tailor and bolster the credibility of consulting services rendered.

In the evolving regulatory, research, competitive, and technology environments of the healthcare industry, the knowledge required of a healthcare consultant may stem from a broad range of educational and experiential backgrounds. Additionally, the wealth of certification and additional educational opportunities for consultants in the healthcare field will contribute to the growing field of healthcare consulting. Note that given the highly regulated nature of the healthcare industry, consultants, although unable to offer a legal opinion, should be versed in the most up-to-date regulatory guidelines, and they may, in this respect, be likely to work closely with healthcare attorneys. As new consulting opportunities arise in lieu of the ever-increasing regulatory scrutiny regarding healthcare enterprise transactions and employment arrangements, this type of collaboration is likely to become more and more commonplace.

Overall, within the context of the four pillars, of the various modalities and types of healthcare consulting activities discussed previously, three key areas will undergo significant growth (both in quantity and type of consulting engagements): competition and income distribution, benchmarking, and financial valuation, each of which is discussed in further detail in the subsequent chapters in this third book of the *Guide*.

Key Sources

Key Source	Description	Citation	Hyperlink
2009 Current Procedural Coding Expert	A tool and procedural guide for Medicare coding and reimbursement.	"Current Procedural Coding Expert: CPT Codes with Medicare Essentials Enhanced for Accuracy," Ingenix, 2008.	n/a
Internal Revenue Service (IRS)	The IRS is a bureau of the United States Department of the Treasury that acts as a tax administrator for the government with full authority to administer and enforce the internal revenue laws.	"The Agency, Its Mission and Statutory Authority," Internal Revenue Service, www.irs.gov/irs/article/0,,id=98141,00.html (accessed December 16, 2009).	www.irs.gov
Centers for Medicare and Medicaid Services (CMS)	CMS administers the Medicare, Medicaid, and Children's Health Insurance Program programs. CMS is responsible for setting reimbursement rates under Medicare and Medicaid. The CMS website contains important information for beneficiaries of these programs, as well as for guidelines for providers.	www.cms.hhs.gov	www.cms.hhs.gov

Associations

Type of Association	Professional Association	Description	Citation	Hyperlink	Contact Information
National Professional Organization	American Institute of Certified Public Accountants (AICPA)	AICPA works with state Certified Public Accountants (CPAs) organizations to provide its members with information, resources, and leadership "that enable them to provide valuable services in the highest professional manner to benefit the public as well as employers and clients."	"AICPA Mission," The American Institute of Certified Public Accountants, www.aicpa.org/About+the+AICPA/AICPA+Mission/(accessed November 2, 2009); "Where to Turn," The American Institute of Certified Public Accountants, www.aicpa.org/download/about/Where_to_Turn.pdf (accessed December 18, 2009).	www.aicpa.org	**American Institute of Certified Public Accountants** 1211 Avenue of the Americas New York, NY 10036 Phone: 888-777-707 Fax: 800-362-5066 E-mail: service@aicpa.org

(continued)

(continued)

Type of Association	Professional Association	Description	Citation	Hyperlink	Contact Information
International Professional Organization	American Society of Appraisers (ASA)	The oldest appraisal organization, the ASA is the only professional valuation organization representing all appraisal specialties. ASA helped create the Appraisal Foundation and follows the Uniform Standards of Professional Appraisal Practice, the criteria followed by professional appraisers. In addition, the ASA educates and accredits and helps the public and professionals locate ASA accredited appraisers.	"ASA Home," American Society of Appraisers, www.appraisers.org/ASAHome.aspx (accessed October 2, 2009): "About Us" American Society of Appraisers," www.appraisers.org/AboutUs/AboutUs.aspx (accessed December 18, 2009).	www.appraisers.org/ASAHome.aspx	**American Society of Appraisers** 555 Herndon Parkway, Suite 125 Herndon, VA 20170 Phone: 800-ASA-VALU and 800-272-8258 Fax: 703-742-8471 E-mail: asainfo@appraisers.org
Independent Nonprofit Association	Institute of Business Appraisers (IBA)	Established in 1978, the IBA is the oldest professional society devoted solely to the appraisal of closely held businesses.	"Company Profile," The Institute of Business Appraisers, www.go-iba.org/overview.html (accessed March 19, 2010).	www.go-iba.org	**The Institute of Business Appraisers** PO Box 17410 Plantation, FL 33318 Phone: 954-584-1144 Fax: 954-584-1184 E-mail: hgiba@go-iba.org
Professional Association	National Association of Certified Valuation Analysts (NACVA)	NACVA provides training through the Consultants Training Institute division, offering Certified Valuation Analyst and Accredited Valuation Analyst certifications and more than ten new courses a year. An alliance with ValuSource software allows NACVA to develop valuation software, and an alliance with KeyValueData offers extensive research support for members.	"Why you Should Join—NACVA," National Association of Certified Valuation Analysts, www.nacva.com/n_join.asp (accessed October 2, 2009); "NACVA," National Association of Certified Valuation Analysts, www.nacva.com/Contact/contactus.asp (accessed December 18, 2009).	www.nacva.com	**National Association of Certified Valuation Analysts** 1111 Brickyard Road, Suite 200 Salt Lake City, UT 84106-5401 Phone: 801-486-0600 Fax: 801-486-7500 E-mail: nacva1@nava.com
International, Nonprofit Association	Certified Financial Analyst Institute (CFA)	CFA has accrued a "global body of investing knowledge," that it uses to educate investment professionals with the "highest standards of ethics, education, and professional excellence." The institute offers the self-study graduate level CFA Program and the Certificate in Investment Performance Measurement program.	"CFA Institute—Overview," Chartered Financial Analyst Institute, www.cfainstitute.org (accessed October 2, 2009); "About Us: CFA Institute Worldwide," Certified Financial Analyst Institute, www.cfainstitute.org/aboutus/worldwide/index.html (accessed December 18, 2009).	www.cfainstitute.org	**Certified Financial Analyst Institute** USA Main Office 560 Ray C. Hunt Drive Charlottesville, VA 22903 Phone: 424-951-5499 E-mail: info@cfainstitute.org

Type of Association	Professional Association	Description	Citation	Hyperlink	Contact Information
National Nonprofit Organization	Appraisal Foundation	A combination of the ASA and eight other appraisal societies to create an uniform criteria for professional appraisers, the Uniform Standards of Professional Appraisal Practice. The foundation is recognized by the U.S Congress as a source of appraisal standards and qualification.	"ASA Professional Standards," American Society of Appraisers, www.appraisers.org/Professional Standards.aspx, (accessed November 20, 2009); "Contact Us" The Appraisal Foundation, www.netforumon demand.com/eWeb/Dynamic Page.aspx?Site= TAF&WebCode= contact (accessed December 18, 2009).aspx?Site= TAF&WebCode= contact (accessed December 18, 2009).	www.appraisers.org/Professional Standards.aspx	**The Appraisal Foundation** 1155 15th Street, NW, Suite 1111 Washington, DC 20005 Phone: 202-347-7722 Fax: 202-347-7727 E-mail: info@ appraisalfoundation.org
Professional Association	The Alliance of Merger & Acquisition Advisors (AM&AA)	The AM&AA is a collection of CPAs, attorneys, and other corporate financial advisors who combine their knowledge and experience to better serve the special needs of middle-market clients. AM&AA also offers continuing education to members in the form of conferences, programs, and the Certified Merger & Acquisition Advisor credential, as well as, access to OneSource, a Web-based business and financial resource.	"AM&AA: Alliance of Merger & Acquisition Advisors," Brochure, Alliance of Merger and Acquisition Advisors, www.amaaonline.com/files/amaabro09.pdf (accessed October 2, 2009).	www.amaaonline.com	**Alliance of Merger & Acquisition Advisors** 200 E. Randolph Street, 24th Floor Chicago, IL 60601 Phone: (877) 844-2535 Fax: (312) 729-9800
National Organization	The American College of Physician Executives (ACPE)	The ACPE is an organization aimed at assisting physicians who hold or aspire toward executive positions in their healthcare professional practices.	"The Story: American College of Physician Executives," by the American College of Physician Executives, 2009, www.acpe.org/Footer/AboutACPE.aspx (accessed March 23, 2010).	www.acpe.org	**The American College of Physician Executives** 400 N. Ashley Drive Suite 400 Tampa, FL 33602 Phone: (800) 562-8088 Fax: (813) 287-8993 E-mail: acpe@acpe.org

(continued)

(continued)

Type of Association	Professional Association	Description	Citation	Hyperlink	Contact Information
Professional Association	Medical Group Management Association (MGMA)	MGMA strives to improve the performance of medical group practice organizations and the professionals they employ through the American College of Medical Practice Executives, the standard-setting certification division of the MGMA.	"About the MGMA," Medical Group Management Association, mgma.com/about/ (accessed November 23, 2009); "About the American College of Medical Practice Executives (ACMPE)," Medical Group Management Association, www.mgma.com/about/default.aspx?id=242 (accessed December 19, 2009); "Contact Us," Medical Group Management Association, www.mgma.com/about/default.aspx?id=74 (accessed December 18, 2009).	www.mgma.com	**Medical Group Management Association** 104 Inverness Terrace East Englewood, CO 80112 Phone: 303-799-1111 Toll Free Phone: 877-ASK-MGMA, (877-275-6462) E-mail: support@mgma.com
Professional Association	Healthcare Financial Management Association (HFMA)	The HFMA is an organization for healthcare financial management executives and other leaders in the healthcare field. HFMA assists these professionals by (1) providing education and analysis, (2) developing coalitions with other healthcare associations to accurately represent the healthcare finance profession, (3) educating key decision makers on the important aspects of maintaining fiscally sound healthcare organizations, and (4) working with stakeholders to improve the healthcare industry by overcoming deficiencies in knowledge, best practices, and standards.	"About HFMA," Healthcare Financial Management Association, www.hfma.org/about/ (accessed March 22, 2010).	www.hfma.org	**Healthcare Financial Management Association** 2 Westbrook Corporate Center, Suite 700 Westchester, IL 60154 Phone: 708-531-9600 Fax: 708-531-0032
Professional Association	American Association of Healthcare Consultants (AAHC)	The AAHC creates a forum for qualified healthcare consultants and advisors and promotes them to prospective clients and recognizes their individual achievement. It also develops and maintain professional standards and a code of ethics for healthcare consultants in order to evaluate individual members.	"Mission and Purpose," American Association of Healthcare Consultants, www.aahc.net/c1.htm (accessed November 20, 2009).	www.aahc.net	**American Association of Healthcare Consultants** 5938 N. Drake Ave. Chicago, IL 60659 Phone: 888-350-2242 E-mail: info@aahcmail.org

Type of Association	Professional Association	Description	Citation	Hyperlink	Contact Information
Professional Association	National Society of Certified Healthcare Business Consultants (NSCHBC)	Founded in 2006 as a combination of the Institute of Certified Healthcare Business Consultants, the National Association of Healthcare Consultants, and the Society of Medical Dental Management Consultants, the NSCHBC's goal is to create a strong bond for the members of the three former organizations.	"History of the NSCHBC," National Society of Certified Healthcare Business Consultants, www.ichbc.org/about/history.cfm (accessed October 2, 2009); "NSCHBC" National Society of Certified Healthcare Business Consultants, www.ichbc.org/contact.cfm (accessed December 18, 2009).	www.ichbc.org	**National Association of Certified Healthcare Business Consultants** 12100 Sunset Hills Road, Suite 130 Reston, CA 20190 Phone: 703-234-4099 Fax: 703-435-4390 E-mail: info@nschbc.org
Professional Association	American Health Information Management Association (AHIMA)	The AHIMA works toward addressing such issues as implementation of electronic health records in addition to working toward adopting and implementing clinical coding systems as per *International Statistical Classification of Diseases and Related Health Problems, Tenth Edition.*	"AHIMA History," American Health Information Management Association, www.ahima.org (accessed March 19, 2010).	www.ahima.org	**American Health Information Management Association** 233 N. Michigan Avenue, 21st Floor Chicago, IL 60601-5809 Phone: 312-233-1100 Fax: 312-233-1090 E-mail: info@ahima.org
Professional Association	Institute of Medical Business Advisors (iMBA)	The iMBA virtually connects financial professionals and business consultants with medical professionals to help build wealth and assist institutional management in the performance of fiduciary responsibilities. They also educate members with online courses, newsletters, CD-ROMs, subscription services, and textbooks.	"iMBA Introduction," Medical Business Advisors, Inc., www.medicalbusinessadvisors.com/aboutus-overview.asp (accessed November 3, 2009); "iMBA FAQs/Contact Us" Medical Business Advisors, Inc., www.medicalbusinessadvisors.com/contactus.asp (accessed December 18, 2009).	www.medicalbusinessadvisors.com	**Institute, Medical Business Advisors, Inc.** Peachtree Plantation West, Suite 5901 Wilbanks Drive Norcross, GA 30092 Phone: 770-448-0769 Fax: 775-361-8831 E-mail: marcinkoadvisors@msn.com

(continued)

(continued)

Type of Association	Professional Association	Description	Citation	Hyperlink	Contact Information
Consulting Company	MGMA Healthcare Consulting Group (MGMA HGC)	Associated with the MGMA, the MGMA HCG provides consulting services to healthcare professionals and organizations.	"About MGMA Healthcare Consulting Group," Medical Group Management Association, 2009, www.mgma.com/solutions/landing.aspx?cid=17702&id1=17596&id2=1&id3=17590&id4l=17598&id4r=17602&mid=17596 (accessed December 2, 2009); "Contact Us" Medical Group Management Association, www.mgma.com/about/default.aspx?id=74 (accessed December 18, 2009).	www.mgma.com	**Medical Group Management Association** 104 Inverness Terrace East Englewood, CO 80112 Phone: 303-799-1111 Toll Free Phone: 877-ASK-MGMA, (877-275-6462) E-mail: support@mgma.com
National Organization	Academy for Healthcare Management (AHM)	Through an alliance between America's Health Insurance Plans and the Blue Cross Blue Shield Association, the AHM provides online education for healthcare, business, or insurance professionals seeking education on the health insurance plan industry.	"About the Academy for Healthcare Management," America's Health Insurance Plans, www.ahip.org/ciepd/ahm/ (accessed July 27, 2009); "Contact Us" America's Health Insurance Plans, www.ahip.org/ciepd/contact.html (accessed December 2, 2009).	www.ahip.org/ahm	**America's Health Insurance Plans Center for Insurance Education and Professional Development** Phone: 800-509-4422 Fax: 202-861-6354 E-mail: info@ AHIPinsuranceEducation.org

Endnotes

1   "Consulting Industry Overview" Plunkett Research, Ltd, 2009, http://www.plunkettresearch.com/Industries/Consulting/ConsultingStatistics/tabid/177/Default.aspx (Accessed 01/04/09). ; "Healthcare Consulting Marketplace 2009-2012: Opportunities in Life Sciences, Provider, Payer, and Government Markets" By Kelly Matthews and Derek Smith, Kennedy Consulting Research & Advisory, BNA Subsidiaries, Inc., 2009, p. 2.

2   "Healthcare Consulting Marketplace 2009-2012: Opportunities in Life Sciences, Provider, Payer, and Government Markets" By Kelly Matthews and Derek Smith, Kennedy Consulting Research & Advisory, BNA Subsidiaries, Inc., 2009, p. 4.

3   "Compilation and Review of Financial Statements" The American Institute of Certified Public Accountants, December 1978, http://www.aicpa.org/download/members/div/auditstd/AR-00100.PDF (Accessed 03/18/10).

4   Ibid.

5   "Responsibilities and Functions of the Independent Auditor" The American Institute of Certified Public Accountants, November 1972, https://www.aicpa.org/download/members/div/auditstd/AU-00110.PDF (Accessed 3/18/10).

6   "Statements on Standards for Accounting and Review Services" Section 110.01-03 (July 2005), www.aicpa.org.

7   "Compilation and Review of Financial Statements" The American Institute of Certified Public Accountants, December 1978, http://www.aicpa.org/download/members/div/auditstd/AR-00100.PDF (Accessed 03/18/10).1423

8   "Tax Services" Healthcare Management Consultants, http://www.healthcaremgmt.comt/tax.html (Accessed 7/28/09).

9   "Issues in Cost Accounting for Health Care Organizations," By Steven A. Finkler, Aspen Publishers, Inc. (1994), p. 6.

10 "Management Accounting" By Anthony A. Atkinson, Robert S. Kaplan, and S. Mark Young, Fourth Edition, Upper Saddle River, NJ: Pearson Prentice Hall, (2004), p. 3.

11 "Dermatology Coding Services" DermResources, http://www.dermresources.com/coding.html (Accessed 07/28/09).

12 "Charge Master Consulting" T.T. Mitchell Consulting, Inc., http://www.ttmitchellconsulting.com/chargemaster.html (Accessed 01/08/10).

13 "Financial Management of the Medical Practice" By Max Reiboldt, Second Edition, The Coker Group, American Medical Association, 2002, p. 17-18.

14 "The Physician Billing Process: Avoiding Potholes in the Road to Getting Paid" By Deborah L. Walker, Sara M. Larch, and Elizabeth W. Woodcock, Englewood, CO: Medical Group Management Association, 2004, p. 114.

15 "The Physician Billing Process: Avoiding Potholes in the Road to Getting Paid" By Deborah L. Walker, Sara M. Larch, and Elizabeth W. Woodcock, Englewood, CO: Medical Group Management Association, 2004, p. 118.

16 Ibid.

17 "The Physician Billing Process: Avoiding Potholes in the Road to Getting Paid" By Deborah L. Walker, Sara M. Larch, and Elizabeth W. Woodcock, Englewood, CO: Medical Group Management Association, 2004, p. 120.

18 "Healthcare Management Corporate Compliance" The Rehmann Group, 2009, http://www.rehmann.com/pdfs/SellSheets/hc_compliance.pdf (Accessed 5/27/10).

19 "Organizational Development: An Overview" Organizational Development Consulting & Training, http://www.orgdct.com/overview.htm (Accessed 11/25/09).

20 "Total Performance Organization Development" Organization Development Consultants, Inc., 2009, http://www.od-consultants.com/hpod.htm (Accessed 11/25/09).

21 " Physician Compensation: Models for Aligning Financial Goals and Incentives" By Kenneth M. Hekman, New York, NY: McGraw-Hill, 2000, p.156-157; "Physician Compensation Plans: State-of-the-Art Strategies" By Bruce A. Johnson and Deborah Walker Keegan, New York, NY: Medical Group Management Association, 2006, p. 9-10.

22 "Physician Compensation Plans: State-of-the-Art Strategies" By Bruce A. Johnson and Deborah Walker Keegan, New York, NY: Medical Group Management Association, 2006, p. 10.

23 "Healthcare Consulting Marketplace 2009-2012: Opportunities in Life Sciences, Provider, Payer, and Government Markets" By Kelly Matthews and Derek Smith, Kennedy Consulting Research & Advisory, BNA Subsidiaries, Inc., 2009, p. 3.

24 "iMBA Healthcare Information Technology" Medical Business Advisors, Inc. 2009, http://www.medicalbusinessadvisors.com/services-information.asp (Accessed 11/03/09).

25 "Developing Ambulatory Healthcare Facilities: For Medical Groups, Hospitals, and Integrated Delivery Systems: A Practical Guidebook" Marshall Erdman and Associates, Inc., Madison, WI: Marshall Erdman and Associate, Inc. (January 1996) p. 67.

26 "Emergency Department Throughput Evaluation" Quorum Health Resources, http://www.qhr.com/consulting/clinical_operations/emergency_department_throughput_evaluation/ (Accessed 1/14/10).

27 "The Business Side of Medical Practice" By The American Medical Association, Milwaukee, WI: American Medical Association (1989) p. 45.

28 "The Business Side of Medical Practice" By The American Medical Association, Milwaukee, WI: American Medical Association (1989) p. 48-52.

29 "The Business Side of Medical Practice" By The American Medical Association, Milwaukee, WI: American Medical Association (1989) p. 46-47.

30 "The Business Side of Medical Practice" By The American Medical Association, Milwaukee, WI: American Medical Association (1989) p. 47.

31 "Retirement Plan Administration" Healthcare Management Consultants, http://www.healthcaremgmt.com/rpa.html (Accessed 5/27/10).

32 "Physicians Need To Do More To Boost Their Retirement Plan Growth" By Kathleen McKee, Medical Economics, Vol. 82, No. 16 (August 19, 2005), p. 55; "Financial Survey: Retirement Plans Are Lagging" By Kathleen McKee, Medical Economics, Vol. 82, No. 16 (August 19, 2005), p [?]; "Physician Characteristics and Distribution in the US" By Derrick R. Smart, 2009 Edition, Chicago, IL: American Medical Association 2009, p. 1.

33 "Succession Planning and the Physician Practice: Is Your Practice Prepared?" By Jon-David Deeson, The Journal of Medical Practice Management, Vol. 22, No. 6 (May/June 2007), p. 323-324.

34 Ibid.

35 "Taking Down Your Shingle: Developing and Implementing an Exit Strategy" By Vasilios J. Kalogredis and Neil H. Baum, The Journal of Medical Practice Management, Vol. 22, No. 6 (May/June 2007), p. 359.

36 "Healthcare Marketing in Transition: Practical Answers to Pressing Questions" By Terrence J. Rynne, Chicago, IL: Irwin Professional Publishing (1995), p. xi.

37 "William Daubert v. Merrell Dow Pharmaceuticals, Inc." 509 U.S. 579 (1993).579

38 "Testimony By Experts" Fed. R. Evid. 702 (December 1, 2006).

39 "William Daubert v. Merrell Dow Pharmaceuticals, Inc." 509 U.S. 579 (1993).592-594

40 "Kumho Tire Company, LTD v. Patrick Carmichael et al" 526 U.S. 137, 141 (1999).141

41 "University of Maryland Medical System Corporation v. Rebecca Marie Waldt et al" 983 A.2d 112 (Md.Ct.App 2009); "Maryland High Court Validates Rule Setting Minimum Requirements for Expert Witnesses" By Amy Lynn Sorrel, American Medical News, November 26, 2009, http://www.ama-assn.org/amednews/2009/11/23/prsk1126.htm (Accessed 01/14/10).

42 "AICPA Mission" The American Institute of Certified Public Accountants, 2009, http://www.aicpa.org/About+the+AICPA/AICPA+Mission/ (Accessed 11/02/09).

43 "History of the AICPA" The American Institute of Certified Public Accountants, http://www.aicpa.org/About/MissionandHistory/Pages/History%20of%20the%20AICPA.aspx (Accessed 11/02/2009).

44 "AICPA Mission" The American Institute of Certified Public Accountants, 2009, http://www.aicpa.org/About+the+AICPA/AICPA+Mission/ (Accessed 11/02/09).

45 "Membership Figures" The American Institute of Certified Public Accountants, 2009, http://www.aicpa.org (Accessed 11/2/09).

46 "Becoming a CPA" The American Institute of Certified Public Accountants, 2009, http://www.aicpa.org/Becoming+a+CPA/CPA+Candidates+and+Students/Becoming+A+CPA.htm#Become_A_CPA (Accessed 11/02/09).

47 Ibid.

48 "Career Paths" The American Institute of Certified Public Accountants, http://www.aicpa.org/Becoming+a+CPA/CPA+Candidates+and+Students/Career+Paths.htm (Accessed 11/02/09).

49 "Becoming a CPA" The American Institute of Certified Public Accountants, 2009, http://www.aicpa.org/Becoming+a+CPA/CPA+Candidates+and+Students/Becoming+A+CPA.htm#Become_A_CPA (Accessed 11/02/09).

50 "Mission and Objectives of the ABV Program" The American Institute of Certified Public Accountants, 2010, http://fvs.aicpa.org/Memberships/Mission+and+Objectives+of+the+ABV+Credential+Program.htm (Accessed 03/18/10).

51 "The ABV Examination" Tthe American Institute of Certified Public Accountants, 2010, http://fvs.aicpa.org/Community/The+ABV+Examination.htm (Accessed 03/18/10).

52 "A Guide to the AICPA" The AICPA, 2010, http://fvs.aicpa.org/NR/rdonlyres/6F13D4DC-97EF-4F0F-88B2-42F3562D3A63/0/ABV_application_kitfinal_012710.pdf (Accessed 03/18/10).

53 Ibid.

54 "The ABV Examination" Tthe American Institute of Certified Public Accountants, 2010, http://fvs.aicpa.org/Community/The+ABV+Examination.htm (Accessed 03/18/10).

55 "ASA Home" American Society of Appraisers, http://www.appraisers.org/ASAHome.aspx (Accessed 10/2/09).

56 "ASA Professional Standards" American Society of Appraisers, http://www.appraisers.org/ProfessionalStandards.aspx (Accessed 11/20/09).

57 Ibid.

58 "Accreditation" American Society of Appraisers, 2009, http://www.appraisers.org/ASAAccredditation/ASAAccredditation.aspx (Accessed 10/02/09).

59 Ibid.

60 "Business Valuation Guide to Professional Accreditation" American Society of Appraisers, July 1, 2009, http://www.appraisers.org/Files/Accred-Reaccred/BVAccredGuide.pdf (Accessed 05/26/10).7

61 "Accreditation" American Society of Appraisers, 2009, http://www.appraisers.org/ASAAccredditation/ASAAccredditation.aspx (Accessed 10/02/09).

62 Ibid.

63 "Company Profile" The Institute of Business Appraisers, http://www.go-iba.org/overview.html (Accessed 03/19/10).

64 "Accredited by IBA (AIBA)" The Institute of Business Appraisers, 2009, http://www.go-iba.org/overview.html (Accessed 3/19/10).

65 Ibid.

66 Ibid.

67 "Certified Business Appraiser" The Institute of Business Appraisers, 2010, http://www.go-iba.org/professional-certifications/certified-business-appraiser.html (Accessed 03/19/10).

68 Ibid.

69 Ibid.

70 Ibid.

71 "Business Valuator Accredited for Litigation (BVAL)" The Institute of Business Appraisers, http://www.go-iba.org/professional-certifications/business-valuator-accredited-for-litigation.html (Accessed 03/19/10).

72 Ibid.

73 "Business Appraisal Review Accreditation Workshop (ABAR)" The Institute of Business Appraisers, http://www.go-iba.org/professional-certifications/accredited-in-business-appraisal-review.html (Accessed 03/19/10).

74 "Join US: The National Association of Certified Valuation Analysts (NACVA)" National Association of Certified Valuation Analysts, 2009, http://www.nacva.com/n_join.asp (Accessed 10/02/09).

75 Ibid.

76 Ibid.

77 "Why Certify?" National Association of Certified Valuation Analysts, http://www.nacva.com/certifications/ (Accessed 10/2/09).

78 "Qualifications for the CVA- Certified Valuation Analyst Designation" National Association of Certified Valuation Analysts, http://www.nacva.com/certifications/C_cva.asp (Accessed 11/20/2009).

79 "Why Certify?" National Association of Certified Valuation Analysts, http://www.nacva.com/certifications/ (Accessed 10/2/09).

80 "Qualifications for the AVA: Accredited Valuation Analyst Designation" National Association of Certified Valuation Analysts, http://www.nacva.com/certifications/C_ava.asp (Accessed 11/20/09).

81 Ibid.

82 "CFFA Credentialing Criteria" National Association of Certified Valuation Analysts, 2009, http://www.nacva.com/CTI/CFFAprerequisites.asp (Accessed 11/20/09).

83 Ibid.

84 Ibid.

85 "Our Mission, Vision, and Strategic Objectives" Chartered Financial Analyst Institute, http://www.cfainstitute.org/aboutus/overview/mission.html (Accessed 11/2/2009).

86 "CFA Institute—Overview" Chartered Financial Analyst Institute, 2009, http://cfainstitute.org/cfaprog/overview/index.html (Accessed 10/02/09).

87 Ibid.

88 Ibid.

89 Ibid.

90 "CFA Institute—Work Experience" Chartered Financial Analyst Institute, 2009, http://www.cfainstitute.org/cfaprog/charterholder/membership/work_experience.html (Accessed 11/16/09).

91 "CFA Institute—Overview" Chartered Financial Analyst Institute, 2009, http://cfainstitute.org/cfaprog/overview/index.html (Accessed 10/02/09).

92 Ibid.

93 "Alliance of Merger & Acquisition Advisors" Alliance of Merger and Acquisition Advisors, 2009, http://www.amaaonline.com/files/amaabro09.pdf (Accessed 10/02/09).

94 Ibid.

95 Ibid.

96 Ibid.

97 "The Story: American College of Physician Executives" The American College of Physician Executives, 2009, http://www.acpe.org/Footer/AboutACPE.aspx (Accessed 03/23/10).

98 "Media Kit" The American College of Physician Executives, 2009, http://www.acpe.org/Footer/MediaKit.aspx (Accessed 03/23/10).

99 "Issues in Cost Accounting for Health Care Organizations" By Steven A. Finkler, Gaithersburg, MD: Aspen Publishers, Inc. (1994), p.6; "Professional Advancement" By The American College of Physician Executives, 2009, http://www.acpe.org/Membership/professionalrecognition/index.aspx?expand=memproreq2 (Accessed 03/23/10).

100 "Certified Physician Executive (CPE)" The American College of Physician Executives, 2009, http://www.acpe.org/Membership/professionalrecognition/certifiedexe.aspx (Accessed 03/23/10).

101 "CPE Eligibility" The Certifying Commission in Medical Management, 2009, http://www.ccmm.org/tutorialeligibility.aspx (Accessed 03/23/10).

102 "Diplomate" The American College of Physician Executives, 2009, http://www.acpe.org/Membership/professionalrecognition/diplomate.aspx (Accessed 03/23/10).

103 "Fellowship" The American College of Physician Executives, 2009, http://www.acpe.org/Membership/professionalrecognition/fellowship.aspx (Accessed 03/23/10).

104 "Requirements for Fellowship" By The American College of Physician Executives, 2009, http://www.acpe.org/Membership/professionalrecognition/Fellowship_Requirements.aspx (Accessed 03/23/10).

105 *Ibid.*

106 *Ibid.*

107 "Distinguished Fellow" The American College of Physician Executives, 2009, http://www.acpe.org/Membership/professionalrecognition/distinguishedfellow.aspx (Accessed 03/23/10).

108 *Ibid.*

109 "Vanguard" The American College of Physician Executives, 2009, http://www.acpe.org/Membership/professionalrecognition/vanguard.aspx (Accessed 03/23/10).

110 *Ibid.*

111 "About the MGMA" Medical Group Management Association, 2009, http://mgma.com/about/ (Accessed 11/23/09).

112 *Ibid.*

113 "Why the MGMA Health Care Consulting Group is the Right Choice for You" Medical Group Management Association, 2009, http://www.mgma.com/solutions/landing.aspx?cid=17702&id1=17596&id2=1&id3=17590&id4l=17598&id4r=17602&mid=17596 (Accessed 12/02/09).

114 "Health Care Consulting Group" Medical Group Management Association, http://www.mgma.com/WorkArea/linkit.aspx?LinkIdentifier=id&ItemID=5580 (Accessed 11/23/09).

115 "About HFMA" Healthcare Financial Management Association, http://www.hfma.org/about/ (Accessed 03/22/10).

116 *Ibid.*

117 *Ibid.*

118 "About HFMA's Certification Programs" Healthcare Financial Management Association, http://www.hfma.org/certification/ (Accessed 03/22/10).

119 "Earning the Certified Healthcare Financial Professional Designation" Healthcare Financial Management Association, 2010, http://www.hfma.org/Education-and-Events/Certification/CHFP/Earning-the-Certified-Healthcare-Financial-Professional-Designation/ (Accessed 05/27/10).

120 "About HFMA's Certification Programs" Healthcare Financial Management Association, http://www.hfma.org/certification/ (Accessed 03/22/10).

121 "Earning the Fellow of HFMA Designation" Healthcare Financial Management Association, 2010, http://www.hfma.org/Education-and-Events/Certification/FHFMA/Earning-the-Fellow-of-HFMA-Designation/ (Accessed 03/22/10).

122 "Mission and Purpose" American Association of Healthcare Consultants, 2009, http://www.aahc.net/c1.htm (Accessed 11/20/09).

123 *Ibid.*

124 "The AAHC Credential" American Association of Healthcare Consultants, http://www.aahc.net/c3.htm (Accessed 11/20/09).

125 "Membership Criteria" American Association of Healthcare Consultants, 2009, http://www.aahc.net/c7.htm (Accessed 11/20/09); "The AAHC Credential" American Association of Healthcare Consultants, http://www.aahc.net/c3.htm (Accessed 11/20/09).

126 "Membership Criteria" American Association of Healthcare Consultants, 2009, http://www.aahc.net/c7.htm (Accessed 11/20/09).

127 "History of the NSCHBC" National Society of Certified Healthcare Business Consultants, 2009, http://www.ichbc.org/about/history.cfm (Accessed 10/02/09).

128 *Ibid.*

129 *Ibid.*

130 "Certification" National Society of Certified Healthcare Business Consultants, 2009, http://www.ichbc.org/certification/index.cfm (Accessed 11/03/09).

131 *Ibid.*

132 "AHIMA History" American Health Information Management Association, 2010, http://www.ahima.org/about/history.aspx (Accessed 05/26/10).

133 *Ibid.*

134 "About CCHIIM" American Health Information Management Association, http://ahima.org/certification (Accessed 03/19/10).

135 "Certified Coding Specialist (CCS)" American Health Information Management Association, 2010, http://ahima.org/certifications/ccs.aspx (Accessed 03/19/10).

136 *Ibid.*

137 *Ibid.*

138 *Ibid.*

139 "Certification Candidate Guide" American Health Information Management Association, http://ahima.org/certifications/ccs (Accessed 03/19/10).

140 *Ibid.*

141 *Ibid.*

142 *Ibid.*

143 *Ibid.*

144 *Ibid.*

145 "About the Academy for Healthcare Management" America's Health Insurance Plans, 2009, http://www.ahip.org/ciepd/ahm/ (Accessed 07/27/09).

146 "Professional, Academy for Healthcare Management" America's Health Insurance Plans, http://www.ahip.org/ciepd/options/pahm.html (Accessed 11/23/09).

147 *Ibid.*

148 "Fellow, Academy for Healthcare Management" America's Health Insurance Plans, http://www.ahip.org/ciepd/options/fahm.html (Accessed 11/23/2009).

149 "iMBA Introduction" Medical Business Advisors, Inc., 2009, http://www.medicalbusinessadvisors.com/aboutus-overview.asp (Accessed 11/3/09).

150 *Ibid.*

151 *Ibid.*

152 "Become a Certified Medical Planner Professional" Medical Business Advisors, Inc., http://www.medicalbusinessadvisors.com/institute-cmp-guide.asp (Accessed 11/03/09); "Course Overview" Medical Business Advisors, Inc., 2009, http://www.medicalbusinessadvisors.com/institute-cmp-course.asp (Accessed 11/03/09).

153 "Become a Certified Medical Planner Professional" Medical Business Advisors, Inc., http://www.medicalbusinessadvisors.com/institute-cmp-guide.asp (Accessed 11/03/09).

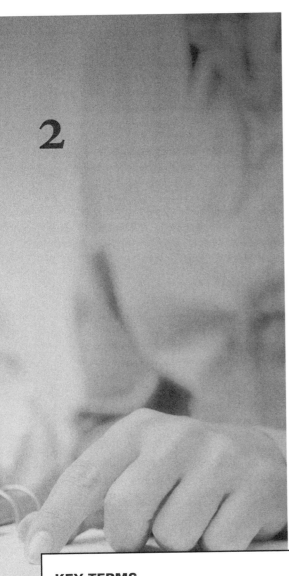

2

Benchmarking

The fruit of healing grows on the tree of understanding. Without diagnosis, there is no rational treatment. Examination comes first, then judgment, and then one can give help.

Carl Gerhardt, 1873

KEY TERMS

- Activity Ratio
- Benchmarking
- Benchmarking to Industry Norms
- Clinical Benchmarking
- Clinical Quality Indicators
- Collaborative Benchmarking
- Competitive Benchmarking
- Competitor Benchmarking
- Disease-Specific Indicators
- Economic Benchmarking
- External Benchmarking
- Financial Benchmarking
- Financial Ratio Analysis
- Functional Benchmarking
- Functional Indicators
- General Research
- Generic Benchmarking
- Generic Indicators
- Global Benchmarking
- Historical Subject Benchmarking
- Industry Benchmarking
- Institutional Quality Indicators
- Internal Benchmarking
- Leverage Ratio
- Liquidity Ratio
- Operational Benchmarking
- Performance Benchmarking
- Process Benchmarking
- Profitability
- Service Quality Indicators
- Specific Research
- Strategic Benchmarking
- The Joint Commission

Key Concept	Definition	Citation
Generations of Benchmarking	The idea that benchmarking is a developing science, and types of benchmarking were redefined over the years based on shifts in industry and the gradual progression and recognition of best practices. The five generations of benchmarking are: (1) reverse engineering, (2) competitive benchmarking, (3) process benchmarking, (4) strategic benchmarking, and (5) global benchmarking.	"Strategic Benchmarking: How to Rate Your Company's Performance Against the World's Best," by Gregory H. Watson, John Wiley & Sons, Inc., 1993, p. 5–8.
Common Sizing	"Common size ratios are used to compare financial statements of different-size companies, or of the same company over different periods." This provides insight into how different companies compare.	"Common Size Financial Statements", by NetMBA.com (2007), www.netmba.com/finance/statements/common-size/ (accessed August 13, 2009).
Clinical Research Utilization	A subset of clinical benchmarking concerned with the amount of resources used by a healthcare entity and the impact of resource use on quality of care.	"Financial and Clinical Benchmarking: The Strategic Use of Data," by HFMA, HCIA, Inc., 1997, p. 58.

OVERVIEW

Although many elements contribute to the success or failure of a healthcare professional practice, the most significant is the practice's ability to adapt within the rapidly changing healthcare marketplace. Management entities that respond to market changes efficiently and effectively may find that timely and informed decision-making can facilitate the temperate acclimation of their practices. These informed decisions are bolstered by two types of research: general and specific (see also chapter 4, *Gathering Necessary Data*). **General research** is not specifically related to the organization, practice, business, or enterprise of interest and may be comprised of such elements as industry conditions, demographics, compensation trends, transactions, and industry-specific trends. **Specific research** concerns only the organization of interest and typically is obtained from that organization. General research typically is gathered to provide a perspective for evaluating the specific data using a number of instruments and methods, which may include *benchmarking*, "a technique or a tool for performance improvement and good quality practice by striving to be the best."[1]

HISTORY OF BENCHMARKING IN HEALTHCARE

Benchmarking was first employed by Xerox in 1979 as a method of finding and implementing best practices in order to reach new goals and pursue continuous improvement. Benchmarking techniques have been adopted by various industry sectors, including healthcare, and are generally used to compare business processes, products, or both against the "best" reported industry standards. Since the 1990s, projected trends have suggested continued growth in the use of benchmarking strategies by healthcare organizations.[2] For healthcare entities, many benchmarking methods have been tailored to provide practices with a foundation for quality improvement and total quality management (TQM), which will be discussed in more detail in this chapter.[3] The use of benchmarking to enhance the quality and efficiency of business processes and outcomes is expected to continue to increase as a result of current economic conditions and efforts to curb healthcare spending while improving the overall standard of care in the United States.[4]

Pursuant to this, it is important to recognize that healthcare expenditures in the United States are notoriously high compared to other nations and that healthcare costs continue to grow.[5] The Centers for

Medicare and Medicaid Services (CMS) has projected that national health expenditures (NHEs), with an estimated 6.1 percent increase in 2008, can be expected to increase by 6.2 percent annually through 2018.[6] Traditionally, healthcare spending has been largely attributed to the cost of personal healthcare, such as hospital costs and payment for professional services (for example, physician or clinical services).[7] The continuous growth of NHE in recent decades has prompted the introduction of several cost reduction initiatives, for example, managed care and prospective payment systems, in an effort to curb the amount of money spent on healthcare each year.[8] Anticipating a continued rise in healthcare spending during the next decade, CMS suggested drastic cuts to physician payments in its proposed 2010 physician fee schedule in an effort to contain healthcare expenditures to a sustainable target amount.[9] Physicians are expected to receive a 21.5 percent reduction in payments for services in 2010, with estimated further reductions of 5 to 6.5 percent in subsequent years, until a target level of spending is reached.[10] Despite these reductions, as of 2010, the President Barack Obama's administration feels that healthcare reform should also aim to improve healthcare quality and efficiency.[11] Therefore, the healthcare industry must rely on benchmarking techniques to reach these goals within the confines of a "sustainable" budget.

The following sections will provide a brief overview of benchmarking as it applies to the healthcare industry and an introduction to generally accepted types of benchmarking (*Types of Benchmarking*) and the benchmarking process (*The Benchmarking Process*). Subsequent sections will provide a more detailed look at the theory and application of some benchmarking types (for example, operational, financial, clinical, and economic benchmarking) that may be of specific use for the valuation of healthcare professional practices.

PURPOSE OF BENCHMARKING

Benchmarking is used to establish an understanding of the operational, clinical, and financial performance of healthcare professional practices. Benchmarking techniques also can be utilized to illustrate the degree to which an organization varies from comparable healthcare industry norms, in addition to providing vital information regarding trends in the organization's internal operational performance and financial status. Correct use of benchmarking may reveal a practice's operational and clinical strengths and weaknesses. In this manner, the process of benchmarking can be used, not only in identifying performance ineptitudes and anomalies in costs, levels of productivity, and financial ratios, but also in discovering their underlying causes. Once the driving factors for aberration from the norm are determined, they should be further investigated and assessed for potential weaknesses and risk factors, as well as for potential strengths they pose for the organization going forward. This benchmarking process is not only essential for internal managers seeking to adjust business methods to optimize performance, but it is also an invaluable tool for valuators, financial analysts, and accountants.

Benchmarking within the healthcare sector serves several purposes:

1. Offering insight into practice and practitioner performance as it relates to the rest of the market (for example, allowing organizations to find where they "rank" among competitors and as a means for continuous quality improvement);

2. Objectively evaluating performance indicators on practice and practitioner levels;

3. Indicating variability, extreme outliers, and prospects;

4. Identifying areas that require further attention and possible remediation (for example, redistributing resources and staff and increasing operating room utilization);

5. Promoting improvement (for example, improving average length of stay (ALOS) and other clinical efficiency measures); and

6. Providing practices with a value-metric system to determine if they comply with legal standards for fair market value and commercial reasonableness.[12]

Although certain applications may have a foothold in clinical or operational benchmarking, several of these benchmarking measures, or metrics, are applicable to financial benchmarking, as well (for example, by improving practice performance). Generally accepted types of benchmarking are not necessarily mutually exclusive of each other, and they should not be used as such. In healthcare, for example, benchmarking must not be used solely to improve financial performance, because this may result in a reduction of quality. Although inherent trade-offs exist between cost reduction and quality, benchmarking practices must account for both; this requires a valuator to be knowledgeable of and comfortable with several types of benchmarking in order to apply the correct techniques to a healthcare professional practice.

Benchmarking in Financial Valuation

Financial analysts, lenders, bond agencies, and valuators regularly utilize benchmarking methods to assist in the assessment of an organization's risk by identifying and quantifying the relative strengths and weaknesses of the organization of interest against competitors within the same industry. The application of benchmarking analysis results to the valuation of a given organization may commonly include the following elements:

1. Adjustment of operating expense, capital items, and capital structure to industry norms (when valuing control position)

2. Adjustment of a discount rate or cost of equity as indicated based on market analysis (business-specific risk premium)

3. Selection of the appropriate financial ratios (for example, price/earnings, price/revenue, price/EBITDA, and so forth) for the purpose of the valuation

4. Selection of the appropriate discounts and premiums, based on the level of value sought (for example, discount for lack of marketability, control premium, minority discount, and so forth)

It is essential for a management or valuation firm to know what benchmarking is and how to utilize it to answer some of the tougher questions posed by clients. It is also important to choose the right benchmark for a client. For example, it would be inappropriate to compare every fund with the S&P 500 or NASDAQ, funds made up exclusively of stock offers from larger companies. Choosing the right benchmark for a particular situation allows an independent valuator to make an unbiased judgment of performance.[13]

Compensation Benchmarking

Benchmarking, as part of compensation plan development, serves such purposes as

1. determining where a particular practice stands, in comparison to similar practices, in terms of overhead spending, staffing and staff distribution, supply expenditures, and so forth;

2. identifying problematic areas of operation in which a practice may wish to improve efficiency;

3. comparing physician-specific rates of compensation for fairness;

4. comparing physician-specific rates of production;

5. comparing physician-specific rates of compensation to rates of production and determine if appropriate correlation exists; and

6. ensuring that practices comply with Stark law and antikickback laws and rules, as well (when applicable) laws placed on tax-exempt organizations.[14]

Commonly accepted sources for physician compensation benchmarking data are listed in *Sources of Healthcare Executive Compensation Data*. Additionally, see chapter 3, *Practitioner Benchmarking* for additional discussion of benchmarking as it relates to physician compensation and income distribution plans.

THE BENCHMARKING PROCESS

Practices utilize both external and internal benchmarking methods (see also *Types of Benchmarking*), that is, they compare key practice and practitioner performance indicators against industry standards while evaluating practitioners against their peers within the practice.[15]

Internal benchmarking is considered the first step in a benchmarking process, and it is often carried out on a smaller scale than the other types of benchmarking, which fall under the umbrella of external benchmarking processes, discussed in *Types of Benchmarking*.

The general procedure of external benchmarking, applied across all types, involves

1. identifying sources of benchmark data;

2. determining how the data collected by these sources was defined;

3. collecting practice data that is comparable to the benchmark data, as it is defined by the source;

4. conducting a gap analysis to identify areas for improvement; and

5. repeating these steps routinely and frequently[16]

Generally speaking, benchmarking is performed on two levels: one that focuses on organization-wide indicators and another that focuses on the practitioner.[17]

TYPES OF BENCHMARKING

Throughout the 1980s and 1990s, several different benchmarking models evolved. The concept of "generations of benchmarking," proposed by Gregory Watson (1998), illustrates benchmarking as a developing science, because types of benchmarking were redefined over the years based on shifts in industry and the gradual progression and recognition of best practices.[18] Some of the first benchmarking types and categories were formerly introduced by Robert C. Camp in the late 1980s, and they are still widely respected.[19] However, over the years, several different classification schemes for benchmarking have been developed, some more complex than others. G. Anand and Rambabu Kodali (2008) provide an extensive listing of classification schemes and benchmarking types that have been introduced to formal literature over the years.[20] Despite the lack of consensus regarding a universal classification scheme, benchmarking models can most easily be distinguished as subgroups identified by (1) *who* is being compared against, (2) *what* they are meant to benchmark, and (3) the *purpose* for the relationship between the entities being compared.[21] Sik Wah Fong, Eddie W.L. Cheng, and Danny C.K. Ho (1998) were responsible for the first classification scheme based on these three broadly defined categories.[22]

The following five models, internal benchmarking and four types of external benchmarking, are based on *whom* an organization decides to compare processes or products with; they are used to define the general process of benchmarking (see *The Benchmarking Process*), as it is outlined in this chapter.

Internal benchmarking often involves the comparison of different subdivisions or analogous products within one organization. Although this type of benchmarking is limited by the relative success of internal company processes compared to industry best practices, because comparison is limited to within-company projects and processes, internal benchmarking often bypasses difficulties of cultural or definitional problems inherent in comparisons between two different businesses. In addition, specific information on company processes can be easily obtained for different projects.[23]

Four types of **external benchmarking** include:

1. **Competitor benchmarking** (analogous to what Robert C. Camp refers to as "competitive benchmarking") is a type of external benchmarking used for comparing work processes with those of that industry's best competitor to determine new target performance levels.[24] This method allows an organization to develop a clear understanding of its direct competition and to compare its own processes to industry best practices.

2. **Industry benchmarking** is a type of external benchmarking process used to compare an organization with its competitors, but it differs from competitive benchmarking in that it utilizes both direct competitors as well as its industry noncompetitors.

3. **Generic benchmarking**, also known as "generic process benchmarking" or "best-in-class benchmarking," was developed as a byproduct of TQM processes. This type of benchmarking focuses on the identification and comparison of key business processes to those of the leading competitor(s). Due to the nonspecific nature of many of these processes, generic benchmarking may be conducted with comparative organizations regardless of industry or market differences.[25]

4. **Global benchmarking** is a more recent phenomenon that expands the boundaries of who can constitute a comparison organization and is based on geographic location. As with any form of external benchmarking, but more noticeably so in global benchmarking, cultural and definition differences must be taken into account.

In addition to the five basic types of benchmarking based on *who* the subject entity is being compared to, benchmarking also may be classified based on *what* elements are being compared, including the following four classifications:

1. **Process benchmarking** focuses on the identification of particular key business processes or operational characteristics that require improvement. This relies on the establishment of some *standard of performance* and is notable in that the metrics utilized for this type of benchmarking do not necessarily include outcomes, but rather the underlying functional and procedural traits of an organization that can affect outcomes.[26]

2. **Functional benchmarking** is related to process benchmarking, and it is used to compare two or more organizations via comparison of specific business functions.[27] Similar to generic bench-

marking, functional benchmarking does not require comparison organizations to be direct competitors, nor are they necessarily within the same industry.[28]

3. **Performance benchmarking** utilizes outcome or output characteristics as benchmarking metrics (for example, price, speed, and reliability) in contrast to process benchmarking.[29]

4. **Strategic benchmarking** is based on the same concept as process benchmarking, and it is a form of external benchmarking dependent upon identification of characteristics underlying the observed successful (or unsuccessful) outcomes. However, strategic benchmarking compares the strategies and decisions that precede business performance instead of focusing on specific processes. Results of this type of benchmarking can dramatically change downstream business processes, as opposed to slight alterations to a specific operation.[30]

Fong et al. classifies two additional types of benchmarking based on the *purpose* for analyzing the relationship between the two entities of comparison:

1. **Competitive benchmarking**, not to be confused with competitor benchmarking, is used for the purpose of gaining a measurable advantage over others (that is, competitors).[31]

2. **Collaborative benchmarking** is benchmarking for the development of an atmosphere that facilitates learning and the sharing of knowledge.[32] This type of benchmarking appeals to healthcare organizations for the support it lends to the ideals of collaboration, mutual benefit, and continuous improvement for all partners.[33]

It is helpful to know the generally accepted basic benchmarking types, because much overlap often exists between different types of benchmarking, due to the nature of the process and the lack of universal classification schemes for benchmarking types.[34] In practice, it is often found that the combination of two or more generic types of benchmarking can be beneficial, for example, the combination of functional or generic benchmarking with process benchmarking,[35] and, accordingly, it is important to have an understanding of the fundamental benchmarking types.

> In practice, it is often found that the combination of two or more generic types of benchmarking can be beneficial.

"Industrial Benchmarking for Competitive Advantage," by Bjørn Andersen, Human Systems Management, Vol. 18 (1999), p. 289.

In addition to the generic types of benchmarking described previously, there exist several types not mentioned in this *Guide*, many of which were created for industry-specific purposes. In particular, four additional types of benchmarking may be used to represent benchmarking applications that are of specific significance within the healthcare industry: (1) operational, (2) financial, (3) economic, and (4) clinical. Each model has a unique application within the healthcare industry and will be discussed in further detail in subsequent sections.

OPERATIONAL BENCHMARKING

Operational benchmarking is used to target noncentral work or business processes for improvement.[36] It is conceptually similar to both process and performance benchmarking, but it is generally classified by the *application of the results*, as opposed to *what* is being compared.[37] Operational benchmarking studies tend to be smaller in scope than other types of benchmarking, but, like many other types of benchmarking, they are limited by the degree to which the definitions and performance measures used by comparing entities differ.[38] Common sizing is a technique used to reduce the variations in measures caused by differences (for example, definition issues) between the organizations or processes being compared.[39]

IMPORTANCE OF COMMON SIZING

Common sizing is a technique used to alter financial operating data prior to certain types of benchmarking analysis and may be useful for any type of benchmarking that requires the comparison of entities that differ on some level (for example, scope of respective benchmarking measurements, definitions, and business processes). This is done by expressing the data for differing entities in relative (that is, comparable) terms.[40] For example, common sizing is often used to compare financial statements of the same company over different periods of time (for example, historical subject benchmarking) or of several companies of differing sizes (for example, benchmarking to industry norms). The latter type may be used for benchmarking an organization to another in its industry, to industry averages, or to the best performing agency in its industry.[41]

In common sizing, the item of interest is expressed as a ratio over some reference amount, which creates a benchmarking measure of less variation than the unaltered original value. Some examples of common size measures utilized in healthcare include

1. percent of revenue or per unit produced, for example, relative value unit (RVU);

2. per provider, for example, physician;

3. per capacity measurement, for example, per square foot; or

4. other standard units of comparison.

As with any data, differences in how data is collected, stored, and analyzed over time or between different organizations may complicate the use of it at a later time. Accordingly, appropriate adjustments must be made to account for such differences and provide an accurate and reliable dataset for benchmarking.

BENCHMARKING MEASURES AND METRICS (PERFORMANCE INDICATORS)

Performance indicators vary by the type of benchmarking utilized, as well as by industry. Models for assessing benchmarking data will not be discussed in this section, because the section is intended to provide the reader with a basic idea of types of benchmarking indicators that are typically used in practice. Given the various methods of defining and classifying benchmarking, performance indicators may apply to several benchmarking types. This discussion of benchmarking metrics (interchangeably referred to as "indicators" or "measures") will be revisited in subsequent sections; indicators of financial status, as well as clinical resource utilization and quality performance, will be discussed further, as well.

Choosing performance indicators that are appropriate to a particular practice depends on several factors. The initial considerations for choosing organization benchmarks typically include, "whether the function or activity is needed at all, and if it is, to what extent and for what purpose."[42] An appropriate benchmark for a particular practice should encompass the qualities generally attributed to effective benchmarks, such as those listed in figure 2-1.

Figure 2-1: Necessary Qualities of Effective Benchmarks[*]

1. Forward-looking } Chosen benchmarks must account for present and future conditions of the enterprise of interest

2. Holistic
3. Participative
4. Stakeholder-driven
5. Quality-focused } Benchmarks must include needs of all partners and stakeholders involved, including any necessary focus on a particular stakeholder, if appropriate

6. Clear communication of goals and objectives
7. Identification of best practices and results
8. Ability to be utilized to achieve best practice(s)
9. Part of continuous improvement measures
10. Internal and competitive excellence } No benchmarking project should sacrifice quality for efficient or cost, and must maintain an acceptable level of quality and utility

[*] "Benchmarking Strategies: A Tool for Profit Improvement," by Rob Reider, John Wiley & Sons, Inc., 2000, p. 17–18.

In addition to the ten qualities mentioned previously, data for the ideal benchmarking indicators will be readily available, easily collected, comparable to data from other organizations, and will have an appropriate analysis method identified. It is considered advantageous for an organization to select benchmarking measures that are similar or comparable to data from other organizations (for example, by adapting generic measures utilized by noncompetitors or by simulating measures previously published by similar entities), for the purposes of facilitating an easy comparison.[43] To this end, for the past two decades, The Joint Commission, formerly known as the **Joint Commission on Accreditation of Healthcare Organizations**, has been developing a system of hospital accreditation that relies on a universal system of performance metrics.[44] Beginning in 1987, the Joint Commission introduced the idea of accreditation through a flexible performance measurement system.[45] Under what eventually became known as the *ORYX* initiative, hospitals could choose from hundreds of different metrics in order to apply for accreditation.[46] This system, although an improvement, it presented difficulties when comparing data across hospitals that had chosen different performance measures.[47] As a result, an initial core measurement set was pilot tested in 1999, which eventually was fragmented into four core measurement sets, implemented in May 2001: (1) Acute Myocardial Infarction Core Measure Set, (2) Heart Failure Core Measure Set, (3) Community Acquired Pneumonia Core Measure Set, and (4) Pregnancy and Related Conditions Core Measure Set.[48] For the past six years, the Joint Commission and CMS have worked together to align their similar measurement systems for these four core areas, resulting in the *Specifications Manual for National Hospital Inpatient Quality Measures*.[49] This manual is one of several resources for benchmarking metrics and data; additional sources will be discussed in *Sources of Benchmarking Data*.

> Data for the ideal benchmarking indicators will be readily available, easily collected, comparable to data from other organizations, and will have an appropriate analysis method identified.

"Benchmarking Strategies: A Tool for Profit Improvement," by Rob Reider, John Wiley & Sons, Inc., 2000, p. 17–19.

FINANCIAL BENCHMARKING

Financial benchmarking can assist healthcare managers and professional advisors in understanding the operational and financial status of their organization or practice. The general process of financial benchmarking analysis may include three elements: (1) historical subject benchmarking, (2) benchmarking to industry norms, and (3) financial ratio analysis.

HISTORICAL SUBJECT BENCHMARKING

Historical subject benchmarking compares a healthcare organization's most recent performance with its reported past performance in order to examine performance over time, identify changes in performance within the organization (for example, extraordinary and nonrecurring events), and to predict future performance. As a form of internal benchmarking, historical subject benchmarking avoids issues such as differences in data collection and use of measurement tools and benchmarking metrics that often cause problems in comparing two different organizations. However, it is necessary to common size data in order to account for company differences over time that may skew results.[50]

BENCHMARKING TO INDUSTRY NORMS

Benchmarking to industry norms, analogous to Fong and colleagues' concept of *industry benchmarking*, involves comparing internal company-specific data to survey data from other organizations within the same industry.[51] This method of benchmarking provides the basis for comparing the subject entity to similar entities, with the purpose of identifying its relative strengths, weaknesses, and related measures of risk.

The process of benchmarking against industry averages or norms will typically involve the following steps:

1. Identify and select appropriate surveys to use as a benchmark, that is, to compare with data from the organization of interest. This involves answering the question, "In which survey would this organization most likely be included?"

2. If appropriate, recategorize and adjust the organization's revenue and expense accounts to optimize data compatibility with the selected survey's structure and definitions (for example, common sizing).

3. Calculate and articulate observed differences of organization from the industry averages and norms, expressed either in terms of variance in ratio, dollar unit amounts, or percentages of variation.

Benchmarking Productivity

Clinical productivity may be measured in a variety of ways, including an analysis of Current Procedural Terminology code history by provider, collections, or generated relative value unit (RVU) or work relative value unit (wRVU) history.

FINANCIAL RATIO ANALYSIS

Financial ratio analysis typically involves the calculation of ratios that are financial and operational measures representative of the financial status of an enterprise. These ratios are evaluated in terms of their relative comparison to generally established industry norms, which may be expressed as positive or negative trends for that industry sector. The ratios selected may function as several different measures of operating performance or financial condition of the subject entity.

Common types of financial indicators that are measured by ratio analysis include:

1. *Liquidity*—**Liquidity ratios** measure the ability of an organization to meet cash obligations as they become due, that is, to support operational goals. Ratios above the industry mean generally indicate that the organization is in an advantageous position to better support immediate goals. The *current ratio*, which quantifies the relationship between assets and liabilities, is an indicator of an organization's ability to meet short-term obligations. Managers use this measure to determine how quickly assets are converted into cash.

2. *Activity*—**Activity ratios**, also called *efficiency ratios*, indicate how efficiently the organization utilizes its resources or assets, including cash, accounts receivable, salaries, inventories, properties, plants, and equipment. Lower ratios may indicate an inefficient use of those assets.

3. *Leverage*—**Leverage ratios**, measured as the ratio of long-term debt to net fixed assets, are used to illustrate the proportion of funds, or capital, provided by shareholders (owners) and creditors to aid analysts in assessing the appropriateness of an organization's current level of debt. When this ratio falls equal to or below the industry norm, the organization typically is not considered to be at significant risk.

4. *Profitability*—Indicates the overall net effect of managerial efficiency of the enterprise. To determine the **profitability** of the enterprise for benchmarking purposes, the analyst should first review and make adjustments to the owner(s) compensation, if appropriate. Adjustments for the market value of the "replacement cost" of the professional services provided by the owner are particularly important in the valuation of professional medical practices for the purpose of arriving at an "economic level" of profit.

The selection of financial ratios for analysis and comparison to the organization's performance requires careful attention to the homogeneity of data. Benchmarking of intra-organizational data (that is, internal benchmarking) typically proves to be less variable across several different measurement periods. However, the use of data from external facilities for comparison may introduce variation in measurement methodology and procedure. In the latter case, use of a standard chart of accounts for the organization or recasting the organization's data to a standard format can effectively facilitate an appropriate comparison of the organization's operating performance and financial status data to survey results.

ECONOMIC BENCHMARKING

Generally speaking, **economic benchmarking** may be used as a substitute for research in market forces, which falls under the umbrella of general research (see *Overview*). More specifically, it is understood as a comparison of business operation efficiency based on economic principles or as it affects a particular market.[52] One study hypothesized that economic benchmarking can be used to (1) improve the average performance of a given entity within the marketplace, (2) improve the performance of poorly performing organizations more than others above a certain threshold of performance, or (3) reduce the gaps in performance between organizations.[53]

The client base and earnings of a healthcare organization are associated with the demographics of the area in which the entity operates. For example, the value of an existing practice with an established patient population would typically be negatively affected by high population growth and turnover rates, making it easier for a new practice to establish itself and become equally profitable.[54] In contrast, the value of an existing practice will increase with a stable population base.[55] A rising population rate also may promote economic growth and increase the cost of services within a typical market.[56]

The age distribution of a patient population is also an important factor in market demand for certain medical specialties. Practitioners of geriatric medicine, ophthalmology, and orthopedics are generally dependent upon an aging population, whereas a younger population will increase demand for practitioners of pediatrics, obstetrics and gynecology, and neonatology. The aging baby boomer population has increased demand for the former range of specialties.

Economic benchmarking provides a guideline by which consultants can compare the efficiency, needs of, and demands on healthcare organizations, while accounting for market forces. As a segment of what can be considered general research, economic benchmarking is generally utilized to provide basic information regarding where a given organization stands with regard to its effectiveness, efficiency, or both within the competitive market.[57] This provides a foundation for further studies of organization-specific studies for the purpose of benchmarking an organization's operational and clinical performance and financial status to improve its efficiency and function within the marketplace.

ECONOMIC BENCHMARKING INDICATORS AND SOURCES

A variety of local and national sources provide basic economic data. Some of the more common economic indicators include unemployment, labor statistics, inflation, new housing starts, household income, inflation rates, interest rates, gross national product, the Composite Index of Leading Economic Indicators, return rates for government securities, and financial market data and indexes, among others. Data on these indicators, and more, can be found in a variety of places at both the national and local levels.

Some common sources of national economic data include the U.S. Bureau of Labor Statistics (www.bls.gov); "The National Economic Review," published quarterly by Mercer; the "Survey of Current Business," published monthly by the U.S. Department of Commerce; the federal and individual branches of the Federal Reserve Bank; U.S. Department of the Commerce's Bureau of the Census (www.census.gov); the Economic and Statistics Administration; and the Bureau of Economic Analysis, along with other governmental, business, and investment company data; journals; and Internet sources. Potential sources of local or smaller scale economic benchmarking data include local chambers of commerce and Claritas (www.claritas.com); IHS Health Group (formerly known as Medical Data International) and U.S. Lifeline's "The MAX" Reference service (www.uslifeline.com) both focus on local healthcare trends.[58]

CLINICAL BENCHMARKING

Clinical benchmarking, initially a subset of industry benchmarking, addresses several aspects of clinical care, including the continuous development and maintenance of quality healthcare, how best practice supports the attainment of targeted patient-focused outcomes, the compilation of all generally accepted evidenced-based benchmarks for best practices, an evaluation of the involvement of practitioners and multidisciplinary effort across levels of care in benchmarking activities, and the dissemination of best practices.[59]

Clinical benchmarking is typically utilized with the expectation that a given organization is aiming to improve the quality of clinical care; obtain, maintain, or both a particular standard of excellence; or increase the number of practices or processes that are founded in evidence-based practice.[60] The impact of successful clinical benchmarking can include the continuous utilization of best practices and innovative progression in quality of care, but the application of findings is directly dependent upon the practitioner(s) involvement and investment in the benchmarking process.[61]

> The application of clinical benchmarking results is directly dependent upon the practitioner(s) involvement and investment in the benchmarking process.

"Sharing the Evidence: Clinical Practice Benchmarking to Improve Continuously the Quality of Care," by Judith Ellis, Journal of Advanced Nursing, Vol. 32, No. 1 (2000), p. 220.

METRICS IN CLINICAL BENCHMARKING

Because clinical benchmarking practices were adapted from industry benchmarking, many of the same types of performance indicators are utilized, though they are adapted to clinical practices as opposed to industry- or business-related processes. The applicability of a given metric is dependent upon the needs of the organization, department, purpose of the benchmarking study, and other factors. A few of the more commonly used benchmarking indicators, for example, clinical resource utilization and types of quality indicators, are discussed in more detail in the following sections.

Measuring Clinical Resource Utilization

Clinical resource utilization, an issue that is becoming more important with the upswing in healthcare quality initiatives, includes concerns regarding the amount of resources used by a healthcare entity and the impact of resource utilization practices on quality of care.[62] The importance of measuring and benchmarking utilization rates is reflected in current and proposed legislation regarding physician payments for imaging services; due to recent concern regarding increasing imaging expenditures, some governmental organizations, such as the Congressional Budget Office, have proposed increasing the utilization of machines for imaging services as one type of cost-reduction initiative.[63]

Inpatient diagnosis-related groups (DRGs) are considered helpful benchmarks for utilization rates, and they can be collected from standard claim forms for physician payment.[64] Additionally, because submission of DRGs is regulated by the Health Care Industry Association's International Classification of Clinical Services coding system, hospital-specific codes are converted to a universal system, standardizing patient-level data from different hospitals for easy comparison.[65] Additional useful benchmarking indicators for measuring clinical resource utilization include measurements for ALOS, pharmaceutical units or pharmacy cost, laboratory units per cost, imaging units per cost, and average routine charges, for example, room and board costs per case per day, total ancillary costs, operating room costs, anesthesia costs, and medical or surgical supply costs, which are often designated as ratios (that is, per case or per day).[66]

Measuring Quality

For the past few decades, providers and patients of the U.S. healthcare system have voiced concern regarding the effect(s) that healthcare reform will have on quality of care.[67] With an agenda focused on increasing quality while decreasing healthcare expenditures and cost, balancing the interests of patients, physicians, *and* employers remains a challenge. Subsequently, quantifying quality of care is perceived to be difficult, because the many industry stakeholders may define the concept of "quality" differently. As such, there exists a variety of ways to measure quality of healthcare. In this section, three types of quality indicators will be described: (1) institutional quality indicators, (2) service quality indicators, and (3) clinical quality indicators.

Institutional quality indicators are benchmarking metrics used to determine how well a provider adheres to regulatory standards set by accreditation agencies, associations, and other regulatory bodies.[68] Traditionally, institutional quality is determined by measuring outcomes, but several organizations continue to utilize measures of compliance to quantify adherence to regulatory measures.[69] Examples of organizations requiring hospital compliance with quality targets include the Joint Commission, the College of American Pathologists for laboratory operations, the Occupational Safety and Health Administration for workplace safety, and the National Council for Quality Assessment for measuring quality of health plans.[70]

Methods of collecting data on quality vary by hospital, health system, or state. For example, some states require hospitals to fill out "hospital scorecards," which may be used to measure anything from clinical outcomes of various specialties (for example, in obstetrics, Cesarean delivery rate or post-delivery complication rate) to hospital throughput data (for example, number of cases or ALOS).[71] This data may be used in a variety of ways at the discretion of the provider; examples include use for consumer marketing of services or to obtain additional health maintenance organization contracts.[72]

Service quality indicators are used to measure customer satisfaction regarding the healthcare services provided.[73] This is, in some ways, the most direct method by which to gauge performance and success of an organization's customer service goals, but because many organizations tailor satisfaction surveys to the particular services provided, data may not be comparable across organizations. Regular assessment of customer satisfaction may be useful for improving long-term quality outcomes of a healthcare entity, but it is often impractical as a short-term or immediate outcome measure due to the variable time interval between survey collection and implementation of desired changes.[74] The American Medical Group Association (AMGA) provides three different annual quality surveys that allow participating organizations to compare their data to industry peers across the nation. These include the (1) Patient Satisfaction Benchmarking Program, (2) Provider Satisfaction Benchmarking Program, and (3) Employee Satisfaction and Engagement Benchmarking Program.[75]

Lastly, there exist several hundred **clinical quality indicators**, which may be useful in measuring any clinical outcome or patient treatment. Some of the most commonly used indicators include:

1. **Generic indicators**, such as morbidity and mortality or readmission, which are measures based on a rate of occurrence within the patient population;

2. **Disease-specific indicators**, which are used to classify patients with regard to either a specific diagnosis or procedure (with varying degrees of specificity), for example, the number of patients undergoing an elective surgery; and

3. **Functional indicators**, which are outcomes used as a proxy for patient quality of life or overall population health, and may include, for example, patient functional performance following a procedure.[76]

All clinical quality indicators are examples of measurements of output quality or a determination of whether the quality standard was met as a result clinical care or treatment.[77]

Table 2-1: Types of Compensation and Production Survey Criteria

Types of Revenue Data	AMA[*,**,†]	AMGA[*,†]	MGMA[*,†]	NSCHBC[†]
Accounts Receivable			X	X
Collections	X	X	X	X
Compensation	X	X	X	X
Gross Charges		X	X	X
Compensation Criteria				
Demographic Classification			X	X
Employment Status	X		X	
Gender			X	
Geographic Section	X	X	X	
Group Type	X	X	X	
Hours Worked per Week			X	
Medical Specialty	X	X	X	X
Method of Compensation	X		X	
Percent of Capitation Revenue			X	
Size of Practice	X	X	X	X
Weeks Worked per Year			X	
Years in Specialty			X	
Gross Charges Criteria				
Employment Status			X	
Gender			X	
Geographic Section	X		X	X
Group Type			X	X
Hours Worked per Week	X		X	
Medical Specialty	X	X	X	X
Method of Compensation			X	
Percent of Capitation Revenue			X	
Size of Practice	X		X	
Weeks Worked per Year	X		X	
Years in Specialty			X	

*   Survey includes cost data.
** Survey includes expense data.
†   AMA: American Medical Association; AMGA: American Medical Group Association; MGMA: Medical Group Management Association; NSCHBC: National Society of Certified Healthcare Business Consultants [formerly known as National Association of Healthcare Consultants (NAHC)].

SOURCES OF BENCHMARKING DATA

Healthcare industry survey benchmarking data may be obtained from several publicly available sources; this data enables an analyst to compare the financial, operational, and clinical performance data for a particular healthcare entity to peer group (industry-specific) data. The most current possible survey data should always be utilized, but it should be noted that survey data publication delays of a year or more are not uncommon. In the rapidly changing healthcare reimbursement and regulatory environment, there are often significant annual changes, so utilizing data from different years due to publication delays may affect the efficacy and applicability of the analysis.

Table 2-2: Criteria of Surveys Including Cost and Expense Benchmarking Data

Types of Expense Data	AMA*,**,†	AMGA*,†	MGMA*,†	NSCHBC†
Accounting			X	
Administrative Costs			X	X
Advertising			X	X
Automobile				X
Business Professional Fees				X
Dues and Education				X
Equipment		X	X	X
Insurance	X	X	X	X
Laboratory			X	X
Occupancy Costs		X	X	X
Other Expenses		X	X	X
Professional Promotion		X	X	X
Staffing Costs		X	X	X
Supplies		X	X	X
Taxes				X
Telephone				X
Staffing Criteria				
Administrative Support			X	X
Clinical Laboratory			X	X
Housekeeping, Maintenance, Security		X	X	X
Information Technology		X	X	
Licensed Practical Nurses		X	X	
Medical Assistants, Nurses Aides		X	X	X
Other Medical Support	X		X	X
Radiology and Imaging			X	
Registered Nurses		X	X	
Retirement		X		X
Utilization Data				
Total Relative Value Units			X	
Work Relative Value Units		X	X	

* Survey includes cost data.
** Survey includes expense data.
† AMA: American Medical Association; AMGA: American Medical Group Association; MGMA: Medical Group Management Association; NSCHBC: National Society of Certified Healthcare Business Consultants [formerly known as National Association of Healthcare Consultants (NAHC)]

There exists a wide variety of national and regional sources of published data available for the comparison of the financial, clinical, economic, and operational performance of healthcare enterprises with the historical performance of industry peers. The surveys presented in the next few sections represent some of the more widely known and generally accepted sources in the industry.

BENCHMARKING SURVEYS WITH COMPENSATION AND EXPENSE DATA

See tables 2-1 and 2-2 to identify several criteria provided in the various compensation and production surveys described in this section.

AMERICAN MEDICAL ASSOCIATION (AMA) SURVEYS

The American Medical Association (AMA) maintains the most comprehensive database of information on physicians in the United States, with information on more than 940,000 physicians and residents and 77,000 medical students.[78] Started in 1906, the AMA "Physician Masterfile," which contains information on physician education, training, and professional certification information, is updated annually through the Physicians' Professional Activities questionnaire and the collection and validation efforts of AMA's Division of Survey and Data Resources.[79] The following AMA surveys publish data related to the demographics of the U.S. physician workforce:

> "Physician Characteristics and Distribution in the U.S." is an annual survey based on a variety of demographic information from the Physician Masterfile dating back to 1963. It includes detailed information regarding trends, distribution, and professional and individual characteristics of the physician workforce.[80]

"Physician Socioeconomic Statistics," published from 2000 to 2003, was a result of the merger between two AMA annuals: "Socioeconomic Characteristics of Medical Practice" and "Physician Marketplace Statistics."[81] Data has compiled from a random sampling of physicians from the Physician Masterfile into what is known as the Socioeconomic Monitoring System, which includes physician age profiles, practice statistics, utilization, physician fees, professional expenses, physician compensation, revenue distribution by payor, and managed care contracts, among other categories.[82]

GROUP PRACTICE ASSOCIATIONS COMPENSATION AND PRODUCTION SURVEYS

The AMGA, formerly known as the American Group Practice Association, has conducted the "Medical Group Compensation and Financial Survey" (known as the "Medical Group Compensation and Productivity Survey" until 2004) for twenty-two years. This annual survey is co-sponsored by RSM McGladrey, Inc., which is responsible for the independent collection and compilation of survey data.[83] Compensation and production data are provided for medical specialties by size of group, geographic region, and whether the group is single or multispecialty.[84]

The Medical Group Management Association's (MGMA) "Physician Compensation and Production Survey" is one of the largest in the United States with approximately 2,000 group practices responding as of the 2009 edition.[85] Data is provided on compensation and production for 125 specialties.[86] The survey data are also published on CD by John Wiley & Sons ValueSource; the additional details available in this media provide better benchmarking capabilities.[87]

MEDICAL PRACTICE EXPENSE SURVEYS

MGMA's "Cost Survey" is one of the best known surveys of group practice income and expense data, having been published, in some form, since 1955. It obtained more than 1,600 respondents, combined, for the 2008 surveys: "Cost Survey for Single Specialty Practices" and "Cost Survey for Multispecialty Practices."[88] Data is provided for a detailed listing of expense categories and is also calculated as a percentage of revenue and per full-time equivalent (FTE) physician, FTE provider, patient, square foot, and RVU.[89] The survey provides information on multispecialty practices by performance ranking, geographic region, legal organization, size of practice, and percent of capitated revenue.[90] Detailed income and expense data is provided for single specialty practice in more than fifty different specialties and subspecialties.[91]

The "Medical Group Financial Operations Survey" was created through a partnership between RSM McGladrey and the AMGA and provides benchmark data on support staff and physician salaries, physician salaries, staffing profiles and benefits, and other financial indicators.[92] Data is reported as a percent of managed care revenues, per FTE physician, and per square foot and is subdivided by specialty mix, capitation level, and geographic region with detailed summaries of single specialty practices in several specialties.[93]

"Statistics: Medical and Dental Income and Expense Averages," is an annual survey produced by the National Society of Certified Healthcare Business Consultants, formerly known as the National Association of Healthcare Consultants (NAHC), and the Academy of Dental CPAs. It has been published annually for a number of years and the "2008 Report Based on 2007 Data" included detailed income and expense data from more than 2,200 practices and 4,600 physicians in sixty specialties.[94]

Table 2-3: Various Financial Benchmarking Criteria

Collections Criteria	AMA[*,**,†]	AMGA[*,†]	MGMA[*,†]	NSCHBC[†]
Adjusted Fee for Service Collection (%)			X	
Fee for Service Collect (%)			X	X
Accounting Criteria				
Accounts Receivable			X	X
Assets			X	
Current Assets			X	
Current Liabilities			X	
Liabilities			X	
Working Capital			X	
Dues and Education Criteria				
Conventions or Seminars				X
Dues or Journals				X
Insurance Criteria				
Business				X
Malpractice	X		X	X
Occupancy Cost Criteria				
Building Depreciation				X
Building Interest				X
Janitorial				X
Rent				X
Utilities				X
Supplies Criteria				
Clerical				X
Clinical			X	X
Taxes Criteria				
Income				
Payroll				X
Other				X
Total Relative Value Unit (RVU) Criteria				
Group Type			X	
Hospital Ownership			X	
Percent of Capitation Revenue			X	
Physician Compensation per Total RVU			X	
Physician Compensation per Total RVU by Group Type			X	
Work Relative Value Unit (wRVU) Criteria				
Group Type			X	
Hospital Ownership			X	
Percent of Capitation Revenue			X	
Physician Compensation per Physician wRVU		X	X	
Physician Compensation per Physician wRVU by Group Type		X	X	

*   Survey includes cost data.
** Survey includes expense data.
†   AMA: American Medical Association; AMGA: American Medical Group Association; MGMA: Medical Group Management Association; NSCHBC: National Society of Certified Healthcare Business Consultants [formerly known as National Association of Healthcare Consultants (NAHC)].

BENCHMARKING SURVEYS BY CRITERIA

Table 2-3 illustrates a variety of available financial benchmarking data. Each category of data (for example, revenue, expense, and utilization) is further divided into subcategories, for a more in-depth look into potential benchmarking metrics by criteria.

BENCHMARKING DATA SOURCES FOR HEALTH SERVICE SECTOR ENTITIES

Several sources of available data for the various entities in the healthcare industry exist. See tables 2-4, 2-5, 2-6, and 2-7 for some representative samples of generally accepted compensation and transaction surveys and resources for differing healthcare organizations and enterprises.

Table 2-4: Healthcare Support Service Businesses

Survey Title	Publisher	Frequency	URL
HEALTH INSURERS			
HMO Aggregates and Averages	AM Best Co	Annual	www.ambest.com
HMO/PPO Directory	Medical Economics Publishing	Annual	www.greyhouse.com/hmo_ppo.htm
HMO-PPO/Medicare-Medicaid Digest	Aventis Pharmaceuticals	Annual	www.managedcaredigest.com
The InterStudy Competitive Edge	InterStudy Publications	Semiannual	http://home.healthleaders-interstudy.com/index.php?p=competitive-edge
PULSE	The Sherlock Company	Monthly	www.sherlockco.com
BILLING COMPANIES			
Medical Billing Salary and Statistics Survey	Medical Association of Billers	Annual	www.physicianswebsites.com/
CONSULTANTS			
Compensation & Recruiting Trends in Management Consulting	Kennedy Information, Inc.	Annual	www.kennedyinfo.com

Table 2-5: Select Surveys Containing Healthcare Entity Transaction Data

Name of Survey	Source (Name of Association/Publisher)	Website
The Health Care M&A Report	Levin Associates	www.levinassociates.com
Pratts Stats	BVR	http://bvmarketdata.com/
Bizcomps	BVR	http://bvmarketdata.com/
Goodwill Registry	Health Care Group	www.thehealthcaregroup.com/c-5-goodwill-registry-online.aspx
Mergerstat Review	FactSet Mergerstat, LLC	https://www.mergerstat.com/newsite/bookstore.asp
IBA Database	IBA	www.vswebapp.com/
Done Deals	NVST, Inc.	www.donedeals.com
SDC Platinum	Thomson Reuters	http://thomsonreuters.com/products_services/financial/financial_products/deal_making/investment_banking/sdc

(continued)

Survey Title	Publisher	Frequency
PHYSICIAN GROUP PRACTICES (MULTI- AND SINGLE-SPECIALTY)		
Cost Survey	MGMA	Annual
Cost Survey for Single-Specialty Practices	MGMA	Annual
Cost Survey for Multispecialty Practices	MGMA	Annual
Cost Survey for Cardiovascular or Thoracic Surgery and Cardiology	MGMA	Annual
Cost Survey for Orthopedic Practices	MGMA	Annual
Medical Group Compensation and Financial Survey	American Medical Group Association	Annual
Cost Survey for Obstetrics and Gynecology Practices	MGMA	Annual
Cost Survey for Anesthesia Practices	MGMA	Annual

Table 2-7: Other Allied Health Providers

Survey Title	Publisher	Frequency	URL	Notes
DENTISTRY				
The Survey of Dental Practice	American Dental Association Bureau of Economic and Behavioral Research	Annual (in four parts)	www.ada.org	—
Statistics: Medical and Dental Income and Expense Averages	National Society of Certified Healthcare Business Consultants, and the Academy of Dental CPAs	Annual	www.ichbc.org/statistics/index.cfm	—
CHIROPRACTIC				
Statistics: Medical and Dental Income and Expense Averages	National Society of Certified Healthcare Business Consultants, and the Academy of Dental CPAs	Annual	www.ichbc.org/statistics/index.cfm	—
OPTOMETRY				
Caring for the Eyes of America	American Optometric Association	Annual	www.aoa.org	—
PSYCHOLOGY				
National Association of Psychiatric of Psychiatric Health Systems (NAPHS) Annual Survey	National Association of Psychiatric of Psychiatric Health Systems	Annual	www.naphs.org	—
Statistics: Medical and Dental Income and Expense Averages	National Society of Certified Healthcare Business Consultants, and the Academy of Dental CPAs	Annual	www.ichbc.org/statistics/index.cfm	—
PHYSICAL THERAPY				
APTA Research Services	American Physical Therapy Association	—	www.apta.org	APTA conducts a number of annual member research surveys about patients, utilization, compensation, and other issues.
Statistics: Medical and Dental Income and Expense Averages	National Society of Certified Healthcare Business Consultants, and the Academy of Dental CPAs	Annual	www.ichbc.org/statistics/index.cfm	—

Website	Notes
www.mgma.com	—
www.mgma.com	—
www.mgma.com	—
www.mgma.com	—
www.mgma.com	—
https://ecommerce.amga.org/iMISpublic/Core/Orders/product.aspx?catid=3&prodid=1489	—
www.mgma.com	—
www.mgma.com	—

SOURCES OF PHYSICIAN COMPENSATION DATA

Table 2-8 lists generally accepted industry sources for physician compensation data (including clinical and on-call compensation).

Table 2-8: Physician Compensation Surveys

Name of Survey	Source (Name of Association/Publisher)	Website
Medical Group Compensation and Financial Survey	American Medical Group Association	https://ecommerce.amga.org/iMISpublic/Core/Orders/product.aspx?catid=3&prodid=1489
Physician Compensation and Production Survey	Medical Group Management Association (MGMA)	www5.mgma.com/ecom/Default.aspx?tabid=138&action=INVProductDetails&args=4610&kc=SUR10WE00
Hospital Salary and Benefits Report	Hospital & Healthcare Compensation Service; John R. Zabka Associates, Inc.	www.hhcsinc.com/hcsreports.htm
Physician Salary Survey Report	Hospital & Healthcare Compensation Service; John R. Zabka Associates, Inc.	www.hhcsinc.com/hcsreports.htm
Physician Compensation Survey Results	National Foundation for Trauma Care	—
Physician On-Call Pay Survey Report	Sullivan Cotter and Associates, Inc.	www.sullivancotter.com/surveys/purchase.php
Physician Compensation and Productivity Survey Report	Sullivan Cotter and Associates, Inc.	www.sullivancotter.com/surveys/purchase.php
Physician Compensation Report	Hay Group	www.haygrouppaynet.com.
Physician Placement Starting Salary Survey	MGMA	www5.mgma.com/ecom/Default.aspx?tabid=138&action=INVProductDetails&args=4609&kc=SUR10WE00
Academic Practice Compensation and Production Survey for Faculty and Management	MGMA	www5.mgma.com/ecom/Default.aspx?tabid=138&action=INVProductDetails&args=4588&kc=SUR10WE00
ASC Employee Salary and Benefits Survey	Federated Ambulatory Surgery Association	https://members.ascassociation.org/eweb/DynamicPage.aspx?Site=ASC&WebKey=e1b0a66d-f0d3-4894-a342-77d419ae716b
Northwest Health Care Industry Salary Survey	Milliman	http://salarysurveys.milliman.com/industry_surveys/healthcare_surveys/northwest_healthcare_salary/
Emergency Medicine Salary Survey	Daniel Stern & Associates	www.danielstern.com
Allied Health & Physician Compensation & Benefits Survey	Warren Surveys, a division of DeMarco & Associates	www.demarowarren.com/brochures.shtml
Staff Salary Survey	The Health Care Group	http://thehealthcaregroup.com/p-18-staff-salary-survey.aspx

(continued)

(continued)

Name of Survey	Source (Name of Association/Publisher)	Website
Modern Healthcare Physician Compensation Review	Merritt Hawkins and Associates	www.merritthawkins.com/pdf/2005_Modern_Healthcare_Physician_Compensation_Review.pdf
Physician Compensation Survey	MD Network Research	www.md-network.com/survey.htm
Medical Directorship and On-Call Compensation Survey	MGMA	www5.mgma.com/ecom/Default.aspx?tabid=138&action=INVProductDetails&args=4623&kc=SUR10WE00
Survey of Health Care Clinical & Professional Personnel Compensation	Watson Wyatt Data Services	www.wwds.com/OurProducts/ProductDetail.asp?ProductID=18011&CatID=1
All Health Care Salary Survey	Abbott, Langer Association	www.abbott-langer.com/index.cfm?title=All-Health-Care-Salary-Survey&fuseaction=SRSurveys.Salary-Survey&SurveyID=6&participate=0&JF=N&AL=N&CountryId=193
Healthcare Associations and Disciplines Salary Survey	Abbott, Langer Association	www.abbott-langer.com/index.cfm?SurveyList&fuseaction=products.main
Health Care Services Salary Survey	Abbott, Langer Association	www.abbott-langer.com/index.cfm?SurveyList&fuseaction=products.main
Hospital Salary Survey	Abbott, Langer Association	www.abbott-langer.com/index.cfm?SurveyList&fuseaction=products.main
Mental Health Hospitals and Services Salary Survey	Abbott, Langer Association	www.abbott-langer.com/index.cfm?SurveyList&fuseaction=products.main
2009 Review of Physician and CRNA Recruiting Incentives	Merritt Hawkins and Associates	www.merritthawkins.com/pdf/mha2009incentivesurvey.pdf

SOURCES OF HEALTHCARE EXECUTIVE COMPENSATION DATA

Many surveys and other sources of healthcare executive and administrative or management compensation data exist. The following table, table 2-9, lists several of the most prominent.

Table 2-9: Executive Compensation Surveys

Name of Survey	Source	Website
Health Care Executive Compensation Survey	Clark Consulting (Healthcare Group)	For a copy of the survey, send an e-mail inquiry to surveys.healthcaregroup@clarkconsulting.com
Management Compensation Survey	Medical Group Management Association (MGMA)	www5.mgma.com/ecom/Default.aspx?tabid=138&action=INVProductDetails&args=4611&kc=SUR10WE00
Hospital Salary & Benefits Report	Hospital & Healthcare Compensation Service; John R. Zabka Associates, Inc.	www.hhcsinc.com/hcsreports.htm
Physician Executive Compensation Survey	The American College of Physician Executives	www.acpe.org/membersonly/compensationsurvey/index.aspx?theme=c
Survey Report on Hospital & Health Care Management Compensation	Watson Wyatt Data Services	www.wwds.com/OurProducts/ProductDetail.asp?ProductID=20911&OT=
Integrated Health Networks Compensation Survey	William M. Mercer, Inc.	
2008 Executive Pay in the Medical Device Industry	Top 5 Data Services, Inc.	www.top5.com/compensation/2009md.php
2008 Executive Pay in the Biopharmaceutical Industry	Top 5 Data Services, Inc.	www.top5.com/compensation/2009bp.php
ERI Electronic Compensation Survey	Economic Research Institute	www.erieri.com/index.cfm?fuseaction=Home.Product Matrix
Top Management & Executive	Abbott, Langer & Associates / Salaries Review	
Academic Practice Compensation and Production Survey for Faculty and Management	MGMA	www5.mgma.com/ecom/Default.aspx?tabid=138&action=INVProductDetails&args=4588&kc=SUR10WE00
2009 Compensation Survey Salaries & Benefits of Healthcare IT Professionals	Vendome Group	www.vendomegrp.com/index.asp?PageAction=VIEWPROD&ProdID=6147

Name of Survey	Source	Website
Multi-facility Corporate Compensation Report	Hospital & Healthcare Compensation Service	www.hhcsinc.com/hcsreports.htm
SIRS Executive Compensation Survey	ORC Worldwide	www.orcworldwide.com/compensation/sirs/medical devices.php#
Upper Midwest Exempt, Nonexempt & Executive Compensation	Stanton Group	www.stanton-group.com/services/documents/2009 SurveyCatalogHiRes.pdf
LOMA Executive Compensation Survey	LOMA	www.loma.org/compexec.asp
Culpepper Executive Compensation Survey	Culpepper	www.culpepper.com/info/cs/durveys/Executive/default/ asp
MEDTECH Equity & Executive Compensation Survey	MEDTECH	www.remedycomp.com/pages/download/surveys/ Remedy_MEDTECH_Executive_Equity_Compensation_ Survey.pdf
Northwest Health Care Executive Compensation Survey	Milliman	http://salarysurveys.milliman.com/industry_surveys/ healthcare_surveys/northwest_healthcare_ executive_compensation/
Board of Directors Compensation Survey	Milliman	http://salarysurveys.milliman.com/regional_surveys/ northwest_surveys_general/northwest_board_of_ directors/
Northwest Management and Professional Salary Survey	Milliman	http://salarysurveys.milliman.com/regional_surveys/ northwest_surveys_general/northwest_management_ and_professional/
CEO Compensation Survey and Trends	Mercer Human Resource Consulting	www.mercer.com/referencecontent.htm?idContent= 1089750
US IHN Module 1—Health Plan Executives	Mercer Human Resource Consulting	www.mercer.com/shoplisting.htm?geographyId=2080300 00&subTopicId=140200031&submit=Go
US IHN Module 4A—Healthcare Provider System Executives and Management	Mercer Human Resource Consulting	www.mercer.com/shoplisting.htm?geographyId=2080300 00&subTopicId=140200031&submit=Go
US IHN Module 4B—Healthcare Provider Faculty Executives and Management	Mercer Human Resource Consulting	www.mercer.com/shoplisting.htm?geographyId=2080300 00&subTopicId=140200031&submit=Go
US IHN Module 4C—Combo Healthcare Provider Executives and Management	Mercer Human Resource Consulting	www.mercer.com/shoplisting.htm?geographyId=2080300 00&subTopicId=140200031&submit=Go
Medical Directorship and On-Call Compensation Survey	Medical Group Management Association	www5.mgma.com/ecom/Default.aspx?tabid=138&action =INVProductDetails&args=4623&kc=SUR10WE00
Survey of Manager and Executive Compensation in Hospital and Health Systems	Sullivan Cotter and Associates, Inc.	www.sullivancotter.com/surveys/purchase.php
Medical Group Executive Compensation Survey	Sullivan Cotter and Associates, Inc.	www.sullivancotter.com/surveys/purchase.php
MCHC Senior Executive Compensation and Benefits Survey of Chicago-Area Healthcare Organizations	Sullivan Cotter and Associates, Inc.	www.sullivancotter.com/surveys/purchase.php
Survey of Health Care Clinical & Professional Personnel Compensation	Watson Wyatt Data Services	www.wwds.com/OurProducts/ProductDetail. asp?ProductID=18011&CatID=1
Survey of Health Care Executive & Management Personnel Compensation	Watson Wyatt Data Services	www.wwds.com/OurProducts/ProductDetail. asp?ProductID=17011&CatID=1
All Health Care Salary Survey	Abbott, Langer Association	www.abbott-langer.com/index.cfm?title=All-Health-Care-Salary-Survey&fuseaction=SRSurveys.Salary-Survey& SurveyID=6&participate=0&JF=N&AL=N&CountryId=193

CONCLUSION

Whether healthcare reform efforts as of 2010 continue to gain momentum or deteriorate with time, the demand for a uniform standard for benchmarking of healthcare practices that includes quality, performance, productivity, utilization, and compensation measures seems to be increasing. Benchmarking will be used progressively more by healthcare organizations in order to facilitate reductions in healthcare expenditures while simultaneously improving products and service quality.

> Benchmarking will be used progressively more by healthcare organizations in order to facilitate reductions in expenditures while simultaneously improving products and service quality.

"An Introduction to Benchmarking in Healthcare," by Harold R. Benson, Radiology Management (Fall 1994), p. 35.

From a management perspective, the use of benchmarking as a performance indicator will become increasingly important in healthcare as quality assurance and effectiveness research becomes more pronounced through pay for performance initiatives and increasingly stringent fraud and abuse laws. From a valuation standpoint, as the Internal Revenue Service initiates its 2010 payroll audits, confirming fair market value of compensation for executives, physicians, and other practitioners through benchmarking data will become progressively more important, especially for nonprofit hospitals wishing to retain their tax exempt status.[95] Additionally, if healthcare spending continues to rise, consumers and regulators will continue to view providers with increasing scrutiny, further emphasizing the importance of standardizing comparative measures to benchmark utility and productivity of healthcare provider practices.

The wide range in benchmarking processes, indicators, and categorization schemes will necessarily delay the implementation of a uniform system of reporting, but as the use and reputability of entities, such as the Joint Commission, continue to grow, healthcare industry benchmarking processes, and the necessary oversight and regulation of the benchmarking process, will continue to improve.

🔑 Key Sources

Key Source	Description	Citation	Hyperlink
"Benchmarking the Benchmarking Models," by G. Anand and Rambabu Kodali, Benchmarking: An International Journal, Vol. 15, No. 3 (2008)	Provides an extensive listing of classification schemes and benchmarking types that have been published in peer-reviewed literature.	"Benchmarking the Benchmarking Models," by G. Anand and Rambabu Kodali, Benchmarking: An International Journal, Vol. 15, No. 3 (2008), p. 260–61.	n/a
"Benchmarking Strategies: A Tool for Profit Improvement," by Rob Reider, published by John Wiley & Sons, Inc., 2000	Provides guidelines for how to identify the correct performance indicator or organizational benchmarking.	"Benchmarking Strategies: A Tool for Profit Improvement," by Rob Reider, published by John Wiley & Sons, Inc., 2000, p. 17–19.	n/a
U.S. Bureau of Labor Statistics	Source of national economic data, for example, labor and unemployment statistics.	"Home Page," Bureau of Labor Statistics, www.bls.gov (accessed December 9, 2009).	www.bls.gov
"The National Economic Review," by Mercer Capital	Source of national economic data, updated quarterly, that includes several economic indicators of interest, for example, employment, housing, income, gross domestic product, interest rates, and so forth.	"National Economic Review." Mercer Capital, www.mercercapital.com/index.cfm?action=page&id=163 (accessed December 9, 2009).	www.mercercapital.com/index.cfm?action=page&id=163

Key Source	Description	Citation	Hyperlink
"Survey of Current Business," by the U.S. Department of Commerce	Resource for national economic business data	"Survey of Current Business Online," Bureau of Economic Analysis, www.bea.gov/scb/ (accessed December 9, 2009).	www.bea.gov/scb/
U.S. Department of the Commerce's Bureau of the Census	Resource for national economic business data	"Census Bureau Home Page," Census Bureau, www.census.gov, (accessed December 9, 2009).	www.census.gov
Economic and Statistics Administration	Resource for national economic data.	"Latest Economic Indicators," Economics and Statistics Administration, www.esa.doc.gov/ (accessed December 9, 2009).	www.esa.doc.gov/
U.S. Bureau of Economic Analysis	Resource for national economic data.	"Bureau of Economics Home Page," Bureau of Economic Analysis, www.bea.gov/ (accessed December 9, 2009).	www.bea.gov/
Claritas	Nielsen Claritas is "the nation's leading provider of syndicated surveys and databases of consumer behavior."	"Nielsen Claritas: Overview," Nielsen Claritas, www.claritas.com (accessed December 9, 2009).	www.claritas.com
"The MAX" Reference Service by U.S. Lifeline	Resource for local healthcare trends.	"Welcome to the U.S. Lifeline Website," U.S. Lifeline, www.uslifeline.com (accessed December 9, 2009).	www.uslifeline.com
"Physician Masterfile," by American Medical Association	Data, updated annually, regarding physician education, training, and professional certification information, which is used to update various American Medical Association (AMA) surveys.	"AMA Physician Masterfile," American Medical Association, www.ama-assn.org/ (accessed December 9, 2009).	www.ama-assn.org/
"Physician Characteristics and Distribution in the U.S.," by American Medical Association	Annual survey providing physician demographic information, based on the AMA Physician Masterfile.	"Physician Characteristics and Distribution in the US," Derek R. Smart, et. Al., American Medical Association, 2008, https://catalog.ama-assn.org/Catalog/product/product_detail.jsp;jsessionid=IBTFFVC20WB5DLA0MRPVX5Q?productId=prod1500004&page=rightnav (accessed December 9, 2009).	https://catalog.ama-assn.org/Catalog/product/product_detail.jsp;jsessionid=IBTFFVC20WB5DLA0MRPVX5Q?productId=prod1500004&page=rightnav
"Medical Group Compensation and Productivity Survey," by American Medical Group Association	Annual survey providing compensation and production data for medical specialties.	"AMGA 2009 Medical Group Compensation and Financial Survey," American Group Management Association, www.rsmmcgladrey.com/Health-Care/AMGA-2009-Medical-Group-Compensation-and-Financial-Survey?itemid=178&mid=178 (accessed December 9, 2009).	www.rsmmcgladrey.com/Health-Care/AMGA-2009-Medical-Group-Compensation-and-Financial-Survey?itemid=178&mid=178
"Physician Compensation and Production Survey," by Medical Group Management Association	Annual survey providing information on the "critical relationship between compensation and productivity for providers."	"Physician Compensation and Production Survey CD: 2009 Interactive Report Based on 2008 Data," Medical Group Management Association, MGMA, 2009.	www5.mgma.com/ecom/Default.aspx?tabid=138&action=INVProductDetails&args=4612
"Cost Survey," by Medical Group Management Association	Annual survey currently published by type of practice, providing data for various medical expense data.	"Cost Survey," Medical Group Management Association, MGMA, 2004.	www.mgma.com/article.aspx?id=29008
"Statistics: Medical and Dental Income and Expense Averages," by National Society of Certified Healthcare Business Consultants	Annual survey providing income and expense data for various medical and dental practitioners and practices.	"Practice Statistics," National Society of Certified Healthcare Business Consultants, www.ichbc.org/statistics/index.cfm, (accessed December 9, 2009).	www.ichbc.org/statistics/index.cfm

⚑ Associations

Type of Association	Professional Association	Description	Citation	Hyperlink	Contact Information
National	Medical Group Management Association (MGMA)	"The mission of MGMA is to continually improve the performance of medical group practice professionals and the organizations they represent."	"About the Medical Group Management Association," Medical Group Management Association, www.mgma.com/about/ (accessed March 18, 2010).	www.mgma.com	**Medical Group Management Association** 104 Inverness Terrace East Englewood, CO 80112-5306 Phone: 303-799-1111 or 877-ASK-MGMA (877-275-6462) E-mail: support@mgma.com
National	American Group Management Association (AMGA)	"The American Medical Group Association improves health care for patients by supporting multispecialty medical groups and other organized systems of care."	"Overview," American Group Management Association www.amga.org/AboutAMGA/index_aboutAMGA.asp (accessed March 18, 2010).	www.amga.org	**American Group Management Association** 1422 Duke Street Alexandria, VA 22314 Phone: 703-838-0033 Fax: 703-548-1890
National	American Medical Association (AMA)	The AMA "promote[s] the art and science of medicine and the betterment of public health."	"About AMA," American Medical Association, www.ama-assn.org/ama/pub/about-ama.shtml (accessed March 18, 2010).	www.ama-assn.org	**American Medical Association** 515 N. State Street Chicago, IL 60654 Phone: 800-621-8335

Type of Association	Professional Association	Description	Citation	Hyperlink	Contact Information
National	National Society of Certified Healthcare Business Consultants (NSCHBC)	"The NSCHBC is a national organization dedicated to serving the needs of consultants who provide ethical, confidential and professional advice to the healthcare industry."	"Welcome to the National Society of Certified Healthcare Business Consultants Website," National Society of Certified Healthcare Business Consultant, http://nschbc.com/ (accessed March 18, 2010).	www.ichbc.org/	**National Society of Certified Healthcare Business Consultants** 12100 Sunset Hills Road, Suite 130 Reston, VA 20190 Phone: 703-234-4099 Fax: 703-435-4390 E-mail: info@nschbc.org
National	American Hospital Association (AHA)	The AHA "is the national organization that represents and serves all types of hospitals, health care networks, and their patients and communities."	"About the American Hospital Association," American Hospital Association, www.aha.org/aha/about/index.html (accessed March 18, 2010).	www.aha.org	**American Hospital Association** 155 N. Wacker Dr. Chicago, IL 60606 Phone: 312-422-3000

Endnotes

1 "Benchmarking: A General Reading for Management Practitioners" By Sik Wah Fong, Eddie W.L. Cheng, and Danny C.K. Ho, Management Decision, Vol. 36, No. 6 (1998), p. 407.

2 "An Introduction to Benchmarking in Health Care" By Harold R. Benson, Radiology Management, (Fall 1994), p. 35; "Benchmarking Applied to Health Care" By Robert C. Camp and Arthur G. Tweet, Journal of Quality Improvement, Vol. 20, No. 5 (May 1994), p. 229-238.

3 *Ibid.*

4 *Ibid.*

5 "Trends in Health Care Costs and Spending" Kaiser Family Foundation, March 2009, http://www.kff.org/insurance/upload/7692_02.pdf (Accessed 05/26/10).

6 "National Health Expenditure Projections 2008-2018: Forecast Summary and Selected Tables" The Centers for Medicare and Medicaid Services, 2009, http://www.cms.gov/NationalHealthExpendData/downloads/proj2008.pdf (Accessed 05/26/10).

7 "National Health Expenditure Projections 2008-2018: Forecast Summary and Selected Tables" The Centers for Medicare and Medicaid Services, 2009, http://www.cms.gov/NationalHealthExpendData/downloads/proj2008.pdf (Accessed 05/26/10); "Trends in Health Care Costs and Spending" Kaiser Family Foundation, March 2009, http://www.kff.org/insurance/upload/7692_02.pdf (Accessed 05/26/10).

8 "An Introduction to Benchmarking in Health Care" By Harold R. Benson, Radiology Management, (Fall 1994), p. 35.

9 "Medicare Program; Payment Policies Under the Physician Fee Schedule and Other Revisions to Part B for CY 2010" The Centers for Medicare & Medicaid Services, July 1, 2009,http://www.cms.gov/LongTermCareHospitalPPS/Downloads/cms-1485-p.pdf (Accessed 05/26/10) p. 655.

10 *Ibid.*

11 "Medicare Program; Payment Policies Under the Physician Fee Schedule and Other Revisions to Part B for CY 2010" The Centers for Medicare & Medicaid Services, July 1, 2009,http://www.cms.gov/LongTermCareHospitalPPS/Downloads/cms-1485-p.pdf (Accessed 05/26/10) p. 656.

12 "Financial and Clinical Benchmarking: The Strategic Use of Data" Healthcare Financial Management Association and HCIA, Inc.: Baltimore, MD 1997, p. 76-77; "Measuring Clinical Care: A Guide for Physician Executives" By Stephen C. Schoenbaum, Tampa, FL: American College of Physician Executives, 1995, p. 57; "Physician Compensation Arrangements: Management and Legal Trends" By Daniel K. Zismer, Gaithersburg, MD: Aspen Publishers, Inc., 1999, p. 108-115; "Physician Compensation Plans: State-of-the-Art Strategies" By Bruce A. Johnson and Deborah Walker Keegan, Englewood, CO: Medical Group Management Association, 2006, p. 110-11.

13 "Picking the Right Benchmark" By John S. Battaglia, Jr. and Richard C. Musar, Journal of Accountancy, (August 2000), p. 63-64.

14 "Physician Compensation Plans: State-of-the-Art Strategies" By Bruce A. Johnson and Deborah Walker Keegan, Englewood, CO: Medical Group Management Association, 2006, p. 110-112.

15 "Physician Compensation Plans: State-of-the-Art Strategies" By Bruce A. Johnson and Deborah Walker Keegan, Englewood, CO: Medical Group Management Association, 2006, p. 112.

16 "Physician Compensation Plans: State-of-the-Art Strategies" By Bruce A. Johnson and Deborah Walker Keegan, Englewood, CO: Medical Group Management Association, 2006, p. 110-113; "Physician Compensation: Models for Aligning Financial Goals and Incentives" By Kenneth M. Hekman, Medical Group Management Association, 2000, p. 118-119; "Physician's Compensation: Measurement, Benchmarking, and Implementation" By Lucy R. Carter and Sara S. Lankford, New York, NY: John Wiley & Sons, Inc., 2000, p. 60-61.

17 "Measuring Clinical Care: A Guide for Physician Executives" By Stephen C. Schoenbaum, Tampa, FL: American College of Physician Executives, 1995, p. 51, 57;

"Physician Compensation Plans: State-of-the-Art Strategies" By Bruce A. Johnson and Deborah Walker Keegan, New York, NY: Medical Group Management Association, 2006, p. 31-32; "Physician's Compensation: Measurement, Benchmarking, and Implementation" By Lucy R. Carter and Sara S. Lankford, New York, NY: John Wiley & Sons, Inc., 2000, p. 20-21.

18 "Strategic Benchmarking: How to Rate Your Company's Performance Against the World's Best" By Gregory H. Watson, New York, NY: John Wiley & Sons, Inc., 1993, p. 5-8.

19 "Benchmarking Applied to Health Care" By Robert C. Camp and Arthur G. Tweet, Journal of Quality Improvement, Vol. 20, No. 5 (May 1994), p. 230-231; "Benchmarking: The Search for Industry Best Practices That Lead to Superior Performance" By Robert C. Camp, Milwaukee, WI: ASQC Quality Press, 1989, p. 60-65.

20 "Benchmarking the Benchmarking Models" By G. Anand and Rambabu Kodali, Benchmarking: An International Journal, Vol. 15, No. 3 (2008), p. 262-265.

21 "Benchmarking: A General Reading for Management Practitioners" By Sik Wah Fong, Eddie W.L. Cheng, and Danny C.K. Ho, Management Decision, Vol. 36, No. 6 (1998), p. 410.

22 "Benchmarking: A General Reading for Management Practitioners" By Sik Wah Fong, Eddie W.L. Cheng, and Danny C.K. Ho, Management Decision, Vol. 36, No. 6 (1998), p. 409-411.

23 "Benchmarking the Management of Projects: A Review of Current Thinking" By Elizabeth Barber, International Journal of Project Management, Vol. 22 (2004), p. 302-303.

24 "Benchmarking Applied to Health Care" By Robert C. Camp and Arthur G. Tweet, Journal of Quality Improvement, Vol. 20, No. 5 (May 1994), p. 231.

25 "Benchmarking Applied to Health Care" By Robert C. Camp and Arthur G. Tweet, Journal of Quality Improvement, Vol. 20, No. 5 (May 1994), p. 231; "Industrial Benchmarking for Competitive Advantage" By Bjørn Andersen, Human Systems Management, Vol. 18 (1999), p. 288.

26 "How Process Benchmarking Supports Corporate Strategy" By Gregory H. Watson, Strategy & Leadership, Vol. 21, No. 1 (Jan/Feb 1993), p. 13; "Beyond Outcomes: Benchmarking in Behavioral Healthcare" By Paul M. Lefkovitz, Behavioral Healthcare Tomorrow (February 2004), p. 34.

27 "Benchmarking: A General Reading for Management Practitioners" By Sik Wah Fong, Eddie W.L. Cheng, and Danny C.K. Ho, Management Decision, Vol. 36, No. 6 (1998), p. 410-411.

28 "Benchmarking Applied to Health Care" By Robert C. Camp and Arthur G. Tweet, Journal of Quality Improvement, Vol. 20, No. 5 (May 1994), p. 231; "Benchmarking: The Search for Industry Best Practices That Lead to Superior Performance" By Robert C. Camp, Milwaukee, WI: ASQC Quality Press, 1989, p. 63.

29 "Benchmarking: A General Reading for Management Practitioners" By Sik Wah Fong, Eddie W.L. Cheng, and Danny C.K. Ho, Management Decision, Vol. 36, No. 6 (1998), p. 410-411; "Industrial Benchmarking for Competitive Advantage" By Bjørn Andersen, Human Systems Management, Vol. 18 (1999), p. 288.

30 "Benchmarking the Management of Projects: A Review of Current Thinking" By Elizabeth Barber, International Journal of Project Management, Vol. 22 (2004), p. 303; "Strategic Benchmarking: How to Rate Your Company's Performance Against the World's Best" By Gregory H. Watson, New York, NY: John Wiley & Sons, Inc., 1993, p. 8.

31 "Benchmarking: A General Reading for Management Practitioners" By Sik Wah Fong, Eddie W.L. Cheng, and Danny C.K. Ho, Management Decision, Vol. 36, No. 6 (1998), p. 410-411.

32 *Ibid.*

33 "Collaborative Benchmarking in Health Care" By Doug Mosel and Bob Gift, Journal on Quality Improvement, Vol. 20, No. 5 (1994), p. 242.

34 "Benchmarking the Benchmarking Models" By G. Anand and Rambabu Kodali, Benchmarking: An International Journal, Vol. 15, No. 3 (2008), p.260, 262-265.

35 "Industrial Benchmarking for Competitive Advantage" By Bjørn Andersen, Human Systems Management, Vol. 18 (1999), p. 289.

36 "A Perspective on Benchmarking" By Gregory H. Watson, Benchmarking for Quality Management & Technology, Vol. 1, No. 1 (1994), p. 6.

37 Ibid.

38 Ibid.

39 "Principles of Financial & Managerial Accounting" By Carl S. Warren and Philip E. Fess, 3rd Edition, Cincinnati, Ohio: South-Western Publishing Co., 1992, p. 1169.

40 Ibid.

41 Ibid.

42 "Benchmarking Strategies: A Tool for Profit Improvement" By Rob Reider, New York, NY: John Wiley & Sons, Inc., 2000, p. 17.

43 "The Benchmarking Book" By Michael J. Spendolini, American Management Association: New York, NY, 1992, p. 58-59.

44 "A Comprehensive Review of Development and Testing for National Implementation of Hospital Core Measures" The Joint Commission, http://www.jointcommission.org/NR/rdonlyres/48DFC95A-9C05-4A44-AB05-1769D5253014/0/AComprehensive ReviewofDevelopmentforCoreMeasures.pdf (Accessed 08/24/09), p. 1-3.

45 "A Comprehensive Review of Development and Testing for National Implementation of Hospital Core Measures" The Joint Commission, http://www.jointcommission.org/NR/rdonlyres/48DFC95A-9C05-4A44-AB05-1769D5253014/0/AComprehensive ReviewofDevelopmentforCoreMeasures.pdf (Accessed 08/24/09), p. 2.

46 Ibid.

47 Ibid.

48 "Introduction: The History of CMS/The Joint Commission Measure Alignment" CMS and The Joint Commission, 2009, p. i.

49 Ibid.

50 "Common Size Financial Statements" NetMBA, 2007, http://www.netmba.com/finance/statements/common-size/ (Accessed 8/13/09).

51 "Benchmarking: A General Reading for Management Practitioners" By Sik Wah Fong, Eddie W.L. Cheng, and Danny C.K. Ho, Management Decision, Vol. 36, No. 6 (1998), p. 410.

52 "Economic Benchmarking and its Applications" By Virendra Ajodhia, Konstantin Petrov, and Gian Carlo Scarsi, Bonn, Federal Republic of Germany: KEMA Consultanting, http://www.infraday.tu-berlin.de/fileadmin/documents/infraday/2005/papers/Petrov_et_al_Benchmarking_and_its_applications.pdf (Accessed 5/25/10), p. 1.

53 "In Search of a Benchmarking Theory for the Public Sector" By Jan van Helden and Sandra Tillema, Financial Accountability & Management, Vol. 2, No. 3 (August 2005), p. 341.

54 "Research for Valuations: The Theory and Practice of Industry Data Gathering" By Anne P. Sharamitaro, National Association of Certified Valuation Analysts: St. Louis, MO, January 26, 2007, p. 29.

55 Ibid.

56 Ibid.

57 "In Search of a Benchmarking Theory for the Public Sector" By Jan van Helden and Sandra Tillema, Financial Accountability & Management, Vol. 2, No. 3 (August 2005), p. 339.

58 "Research for Valuations: The Theory and Practice of Industry Data Gathering" By Anne P. Sharamitaro, National Association of Certified Valuation Analysts: St. Louis, MO, January 26, 2007, p. 27-30.

59 "Sharing the Evidence: Clinical Practice Benchmarking to Improve Continuously the Quality of Care" By Judith Ellis, Journal of Advanced Nursing, Vol. 32, No. 1 (2000), p. 216.

60 "Sharing the Evidence: Clinical Practice Benchmarking to Improve Continuously the Quality of Care" By Judith Ellis, Journal of Advanced Nursing, Vol. 32, No. 1 (2000), p. 216-218.

61 "Sharing the Evidence: Clinical Practice Benchmarking to Improve Continuously the Quality of Care" By Judith Ellis, Journal of Advanced Nursing, Vol. 32, No. 1 (2000), p. 220.

62 "Financial and Clinical Benchmarking: The Strategic Use of Data" Healthcare Financial Management Association and HCIA, Inc.: Baltimore, MD 1997 p. 58.

63 "Budget Options Volume I: Health Care" Congressional Budget Office, Congress of the United States, December 2008 p. 117-118.

64 "Financial and Clinical Benchmarking: The Strategic Use of Data" Healthcare Financial Management Association and HCIA, Inc.: Baltimore, MD 1997, p. 59-61.

65 Ibid.

66 "Financial and Clinical Benchmarking: The Strategic Use of Data" Healthcare Financial Management Association and HCIA, Inc.: Baltimore, MD 1997, p. 60.

67 "Benchmarking Quality Under U.S. Health Care Reform: The Next Generation" By Daniel Lorence, Quality Progress, April 1994, p. 103-107.

68 "Financial and Clinical Benchmarking: The Strategic Use of Data" Healthcare Financial Management Association and HCIA, Inc.: Baltimore, MD 1997, p. 47.

69 Ibid.

70 "Financial and Clinical Benchmarking: The Strategic Use of Data" Healthcare Financial Management Association and HCIA, Inc.: Baltimore, MD 1997, p. 47-48.

71 "Financial and Clinical Benchmarking: The Strategic Use of Data" Healthcare Financial Management Association and HCIA, Inc.: Baltimore, MD 1997, p. 49.

72 "Financial and Clinical Benchmarking: The Strategic Use of Data" Healthcare Financial Management Association and HCIA, Inc.: Baltimore, MD 1997, p. 49-50.

73 "Financial and Clinical Benchmarking: The Strategic Use of Data" Healthcare Financial Management Association and HCIA, Inc.: Baltimore, MD 1997, p. 50.

74 "Financial and Clinical Benchmarking: The Strategic Use of Data" Healthcare Financial Management Association and HCIA, Inc.: Baltimore, MD 1997, p. 50-51.

75 "Benchmarking" American Medical Group Association, http://www.amga.org/Research/benchmarking_research.asp (Accessed 09/15/09).

76 "Financial and Clinical Benchmarking: The Strategic Use of Data" Healthcare Financial Management Association and HCIA, Inc.: Baltimore, MD 1997, p. 57.

77 "The Guide to Benchmarking in Healthcare: Practical Lessons From the Field" By Arthur G. Tweet and Karol Gavin-Marciano, New York, NY: Quality Resources, 1998, p. 25.

78 "AMA Physician Masterfile" American Medical Association, 2009, http://www.ama-assn.org/ama/pub/about-ama/physician-data-resources/physician-masterfile.shtml (Accessed 08/03/09).

79 Ibid.

80 "Physician Characteristics and Distribution in the U.S.: 2008 Edition" By Derek R. Smart and Jayme Sellers, American Medical Association, 2008, p. iii-iv.

81 "Physician Socioeconomic Statistics: Profiles for Detailed Specialties, Selected States, and Practice Arrangements" By John D. Wassenaar and Sara L. Thran, 2003 Edition, American Medical Association, 2003, p. 1.

82 Ibid.

83 "2008 Medical Group Compensation and Financial Survey" American Medical Group Association and RSM McGladrey, Inc.: Alexandria, VA. 2008, p. 1; "American Medical Group Association 2009 Medical Group Compensation and Financial Survey: 2009 Report Based on 2008 Data Survey Methodology" AMGA and RSM McGladrey, Inc., 2009, http://www.amga.org/Publications/ECommerce/Comp%20 Survey/2009Methodology.pdf (Accessed 09/03/09), p. 1.

84 "2008 Medical Group Compensation and Financial Survey" American Medical Group Association and RSM McGladrey, Inc.: Alexandria, VA. 2008, p. 1, 3.

85 "Physician Compensation and Production Survey: 2009 Report Based on 2008 Data" Medical Group Management Association, 2009, p. xii.

86 Ibid.

87 "Physician Compensation and Production Survey: 2009 Report Based on 2008 Data" Medical Group Management Association, 2009, p. 6.

88 "Cost Survey for Multispecialty Practices: 2008 Report Based on 2007 Data" Medical Group Management Association, 2008, p.14; "Cost Survey for Multispecialty Practices: 2008 Report Based on 2007 Data" Medical Group Management Association, 2008, p. 17.

89 "Cost Survey for Multispecialty Practices: 2008 Report Based on 2007 Data" Medical Group Management Association, 2008, p. 14-16; "Cost Survey for Multispecialty Practices: 2008 Report Based on 2007 Data" Medical Group Management Association, 2008, p. 18-19.

90 "Cost Survey for Multispecialty Practices: 2008 Report Based on 2007 Data" Medical Group Management Association, 2008, p. 17-19.

91 "Cost Survey for Multispecialty Practices: 2008 Report Based on 2007 Data" Medical Group Management Association, 2008, p. 14-16.

92 "2002 Medical Group Financial Operations Survey" American Medical Group Association and RSM McGladrey: Inc.: Alexandria, VA, 2002, p. 3.

93 "2002 Medical Group Financial Operations Survey" American Medical Group Association and RSM McGladrey: Inc.: Alexandria, VA, 2002, p. 3, 5.

94 "Practice Statistics" National Society of Certified Healthcare Business Consultants, September 15, 2009, http://www.ichbc.org/statistics/index.cfm (Accessed 12/9/09).

95 "An Introduction to I.R.C. 4958 (Intermediate Sanctions)" By Lawrence M. Brauer et al., Internal Revenue Service (2002), http://apps.irs.gov/pub/irs-tege/eotopich02.pdf (Accessed 12/28/09), p. 275-276; "Enforcement Efforts Take Aim at Executive Compensation of Tax-Exempt Health Care Entities" By Candace L. Quinn and Jeffrey D. Mamorsky, 18 Health Law Reporter 1640, (December 17, 2009) Accessed at http://news.bna.com/hlln/display/batch_print_display.adp (Accessed 12/28/09).

Compensation and Income Distribution

No slur is meant to be cast on the merchant, tradesman or promoter, who endeavors to increase his capital or his earnings in honest business enterprises; no intention exists to deprive the doctor of his right to earn his living by collecting proper compensation for his professional services.

John B. Roberts, 1908

KEY TERMS

- Buy-in
- Compensation Planning Committee
- Consultants
- Foregone Compensation Formula
- Internal Revenue Code
- Physician Compensation Plan
- Practice Profiling

	Definition	Citation
	A verse from Rudyard Kipling's *The Elephant's Child*: I KEEP six honest serving-men They taught me all I knew; Their names are *What* and *Why* and *When* and *How* and *Where* and *Who*	"The Elephant's Child," in "Just so Stories," by Rudyard Kipling and J.M. Gleeson, Doubleday and Company, Inc., 1902, p. 65.
Role of Physician Compensation Plans	(1) Contribute to the incentive and performance feedback system, (2) assist in driving performance to achieve goals, and (3) facilitate more effective identification and communication of an organization's values, dynamic, productivity objectives, and performance expectations.	"Implementation of Physician Compensation Programs," in "Physician Compensation: Models for Aligning Financial Goals and Incentives," by Kenneth M. Hekman, Medical Group Management Association, 2000, p. 153–57; "Do You Need a New Compensation Plan?" in "Physician Compensation Plans: State-of-the-Art Strategies," by Bruce A. Johnson, JD, MPA, and Deborah Walker Keegan, PhD, FACMPE, Medical Group Management Association, 2006, p. 9.
Components of Practitioner Compensation	(1) base salary, (2) incentive pay, and (3) benefits	"Tax Considerations for Physician Compensation Arrangements," in "Physician's Compensation: Measurement, Benchmarking, and Implementation," by Lucy R. Carter, CPA, and Sara S. Lankford, CPA, John Wiley & Sons, Inc., 2000, p. 62.
Indicators of Compensation Plan Success or Failure	(1) internal indicators (practice characteristics) and (2) external indicators (industry trends, namely, the four pillars)	"Do You Need a New Compensation Plan?" in "Physician Compensation Plans: State-of-the-Art Strategies," by Bruce A. Johnson, JD, MPA, and Deborah Walker Keegan, PhD, FACMPE, Medical Group Management Association, 2006, p. 9.
Internal Indicators of the Efficacy of a Compensation Plan	(1) practitioner perceptions, (2) practice productivity, (3) financial standing, and (4) the current level of compensation	"Do You Need a New Compensation Plan?" in "Physician Compensation Plans: State-of-the-Art Strategies," by Bruce A. Johnson, JD, MPA, and Deborah Walker Keegan, PhD, FACMPE, Medical Group Management Association, 2006, p. 10.
Three Types of Practices, as a Result of Where They Fall on the Spectra of Tendencies Related to Internal Indicators	(1) practices that must seek an alternative compensation plan, (2) practices that adopt a dynamic compensation plan, and (3) practices that fall somewhere in between	"Do You Need a New Compensation Plan?" in "Physician Compensation Plans: State-of-the-Art Strategies," by Bruce A. Johnson, JD, MPA, and Deborah Walker Keegan, PhD, FACMPE, Medical Group Management Association, 2006, pp. 9–10.
Fraud and Abuse Regulation	(1) Stark law, (2) False Claims Act, (3) antikickback statute, and (4) Internal Revenue Service Governance of Compensation	"Regulatory Considerations in Physician Compensation Arrangements," in "Physician's Compensation: Measurement, Benchmarking, and Implementation," by Lucy R. Carter, CPA and Sara S. Lankford, CPA, John Wiley & Sons, Inc., 2000, p. 32.
Arrangements Most Likely to be in Violation of Stark Law	(1) arrangements wherein physicians own shares of the practice under which they are employed; (2) arrangements wherein physicians are employed, hold directorships, or have other affiliations with hospitals and other organizations; (3) arrangements between physicians, medical practices, hospitals, or a combination of these wherein contractual services are negotiated, and (4) arrangements wherein space and rental agreements are made between designated health service entities	"The Legal Element," in "Physician Compensation Plans: State-of-the-Art Strategies," by Bruce A. Johnson, JD, MPA, and Deborah Walker Keegan, PhD, FACMPE, Medical Group Management Association, 2006, p. 147; "Stark Rule Proposals Finalized," by Cathy Dunlay and Kevin Hilvert, Schottenstein Zox & Dunn Resources, 8/13/08, www.szd.com/resources.php?NewsID=1184&method=unique (accessed August 14, 2008).
Common Mandate Enforced by all of the Safe Harbor Provisions	Physicians and practitioners must be compensated at fair market value and at rates considered commercially reasonable.	"The Legal Element," in "Physician Compensation Plans: State-of-the-Art Strategies," by Bruce A. Johnson, JD, MPA, and Deborah Walker Keegan, PhD, FACMPE, Medical Group Management Association, 2006, p. 147.

Key Concept	Definition	Citation
General Attributes of Commercially Reasonable Compensation Arrangements	(1) at fair market value, (2) contains a list of the duties actually performed by the physician, (3) listed services are reasonable necessary, and (4) services could not be adequately provided for less compensation	"Physician Compensation Arrangements," by Daniel K. Zismer, 1999, p. 204; "OIG Advisory Opinion No. 07-10," September 27, 2007, p. 10; "OIG Compliance Program For Individual and Small Group Physician Practices," Notice, 65 Fed. Reg. 59434 (Oct. 5, 2000); "Fair Market Value in Health Care Transactions," by Lewis Lefko, Haynes and Boone, LLP, July 20, 2007, www.worldservicesgroup.com/publications.asp?action=article&artid=2086 (accessed September 18, 2008).
Drivers of Revenue Accounted for Under a P4P System of Reimbursement:	(1) clinical productivity, (2) quality performance, and (3) efficiency	"The Broad Perspective—Physician Compensation Issues across Different Practice Settings," by Daniel K. Zismer, in "Physician Compensation Arrangements," by Daniel K. Zismer, An Aspen Publication, 1999, pp. 16–17.
Competitive Factors That Affect Compensation	(1) specialization and provider diversity, (2) consolidation, (3) practitioner experience, and (4) performance variation	"The Compensation Plan Development Process," p. 25; "Industry Trends In Physician Compensation," pp. 232–33; and "Special Issues in Physician Compensation" pp. 181–84 in "Physician Compensation Plans: State-of-the-Art Strategies," by Bruce A. Johnson, JD, MPA, and Deborah Walker Keegan, PhD, FACMPE, Medical Group Management Association, 2006.
Compensation Plan Life Cycle	Phase 1: The Current Plan; Phase 2: The Potential Plan; and Phase 3: The New Plan	"The Compensation Plan Development Process," in "Physician Compensation Plans: State-of-the-Art Strategies," by Bruce A. Johnson, JD, MPA, and Deborah Walker Keegan, PhD, FACMPE, Medical Group Management Association, 2006, pp. 19–20.
Duration of the development timeline	Depends on (1) the size of the practice; (2) how detrimental the redesign is to the organization's survival, legal compliance, or both; and (3) how difficult developing, transitioning, or both to a new plan will be.	"The Compensation Plan Development Process," in "Physician Compensation Plans: State-of-the-Art Strategies," by Bruce A. Johnson, JD, MPA, and Deborah Walker Keegan, PhD, FACMPE, Medical Group Management Association, 2006, p. 19.
Ten Steps to Developing a Compensation Plan	Step 1: Determining Governance, Goals, and Principles Step 2: Investigating the Available Options Step 3: Benchmarking Step 4: Establishing a Framework Step 5: Detailing the Plan Infrastructure Step 6: Generating a Financial Model Step 7: Defending Against Alternative Models Step 8: Outlining Transition and Implementation Steps Step 9: Proposing the New Plan Step 10: Arriving at a Consensus	"Physician Compensation: Models for Aligning Financial Goals and Incentives," by Kenneth M. Hekman, Medical Group Management Association, 2000; "The Compensation Plan Development Process," in "Physician Compensation Plans: State-of-the-Art Strategies," by Bruce A. Johnson, JD, MPA and Deborah Walker Keegan, PhD, FACMPE, Medical Group Management Association, 2006.
Governance of the Compensation Plan Development Process	Governance may be (1) top down (managerial) or (2) bottom up (physicians and practitioners elected to research alternative options). It can also follow (3) election of a compensation planning committee.	"The Compensation Plan Development Process," in "Physician Compensation Plans: State-of-the-Art Strategies," by Bruce A. Johnson, JD, MPA, and Deborah Walker Keegan, PhD, FACMPE, Medical Group Management Association, 2006, p. 18.

(continued)

(continued)

Key Concept	Definition	Citation
The Role of Consultants	(1) Aiding in the evaluation of the existing system—identifying strengths, as well as opportunities for improvement (2) Offering knowledge and experience related to the various arrangements and alternatives available (3) Helping to establish goals and principles (4) Investigating the various foundational and specific options the practice may wish to entertain (5) Assisting in financial modeling of the alternative plans (6) Creating the materials needed for communicating and presenting proposed plan(s) (7) Launching the decision making process	"Physician Compensation for Physicians in Hospital Employment," by M. Catherine Higgins and Theresa M. Raczak, in "Physician Compensation: Models for Aligning Financial Goals and Incentives," by Kenneth M. Hekman, Medical Group Management Association, 2000, pp. 118–19; "The Compensation Plan Development Process," in "Physician Compensation Plans: State-of-the-Art Strategies," by Bruce A. Johnson, JD, MPA, and Deborah Walker Keegan, PhD, FACMPE, Medical Group Management Association, 2006, p. 21.
General Goals Inherent to a Successful Compensation System	(1) Condoning productivity (2) Reinforcing involvement in professional services, ancillary practices, outreach, leadership, and other diverse and potentially nonclinical roles (3) Encouraging teamwork and group solidarity (4) Guaranteeing that the system is fiscally sound (5) Elucidating specific performance expectations and responsibilities (6) Easing the process of recruiting and retaining practitioners (7) Ensuring that compensation and reimbursement methodologies complement each other	"Physician's Compensation: Measurement, Benchmarking, and Implementation," by Lucy R. Carter, CPA, and Sara S. Lankford, CPA, John Wiley & Sons, Inc., 2000, pp. 57–61, 133–38, 176–78; "The Compensation Plan Development Process," in "Physician Compensation Plans: State-of-the-Art Strategies," by Bruce A. Johnson, JD, MPA, and Deborah Walker Keegan, PhD, FACMPE, Medical Group Management Association, 2006, p. 27–28.
Common Principles of Successful Compensation Plans	(1) Unbiased measurement systems (2) A concise number of performance metrics (3) Clearly defined and methodically enforced processes, expectations, repercussions, and objectives (4) Transparent documentation, communication, and enforcement (5) Clear and simple processes, expectations, repercussions, and objectives (6) Compensation stability (7) Appropriate weighting of individual and team accountability and responsibility (8) A feasible transition plan from current to future practices (9) Financial responsibility (10) Legal conformity	"Compensation Principles," in "Physician Compensation: Models for Aligning Financial Goals and Incentives," by Kenneth M. Hekman, Medical Group Management Association, 2000, pp. 20–21; "The Compensation Plan Development Process," in "Physician Compensation Plans: State-of-the-Art Strategies," by Bruce A. Johnson, JD, MPA, and Deborah Walker Keegan, PhD, FACMPE, Medical Group Management Association, 2006, p. 28.
Compensation Plan Alignment	Ensuring that a potential plan aligns with external and internal factors that must be taken into consideration	"Four Basic Principles of Compensation," in "Physician's Compensation: Measurement, Benchmarking, and Implementation," by Lucy R. Carter, CPA, and Sara S. Lankford, CPA, John Wiley & Sons, Inc., 2000, pp. 59–61; "Implementation of Physician Compensation Programs," in "Physician Compensation: Models for Aligning Financial Goals and Incentives," by Kenneth M. Hekman, Medical Group Management Association, 2000, p. 159–60.

Key Concept	Definition	Citation
External Factors	(1) Any changes to reimbursement, health plans, or other financial drivers of the market (2) The rates of practitioner compensation currently seen in the healthcare market (3) Any changes in population, demographics, or patient demand	Implementation," by Lucy R. Carter, CPA, and Sara S. Lankford, CPA, John Wiley & Sons, Inc., 2000, pp. 59–61; "Implementation of Physician Compensation Programs," in "Physician Compensation: Models for Aligning Financial Goals and Incentives," by Kenneth M. Hekman, Medical Group Management Association, 2000, pp. 159–60; "The Compensation Plan Development Process," in "Physician Compensation Plans: State-of-the-Art Strategies," by Bruce A. Johnson, JD, MPA and Deborah Walker Keegan, PhD, FACMPE, Medical Group Management Association, 2006, pp. 29–30.
Internal Factors	Essentially, the goals and principles that were set to guide the process	"Four Basic Principles of Compensation," in "Physician's Compensation: Measurement, Benchmarking, and Implementation," by Lucy R. Carter, CPA, and Sara S. Lankford, CPA, John Wiley & Sons, Inc., 2000, pp. 59–61; "The Compensation Plan Development Process," in "Physician Compensation Plans: State-of-the-Art Strategies," by Bruce A. Johnson, JD, MPA, and Deborah Walker Keegan, PhD, FACMPE, Medical Group Management Association, 2006, pp. 29–30.
Cultural Dimension of a Compensation Plan Matrix	The foundational structure and methodology of a practice's compensation plan is suggestive of the practice's culture, specifically, of whether the practice is just a collection of individual practitioners or does, in fact, promote a team-oriented group dynamic will manifest itself in the dynamic that the system of compensation fosters. Practices are placed in one of three categories depending on where they fall along the cultural axis of the compensation plan "plane," wherein the financial dimension is represented as one-dimensional.	"Cash Compensation in Medical Group Practices: Application of an RVU-Based Approach," in "Physician Compensation Arrangements," by Daniel K. Zismer, An Aspen Publication, 1999, pp. 37, 62; "Compensation Plan Options—The Compensation Plan Matrix," in "Physician Compensation Plans: State-of-the-Art Strategies," by Bruce A. Johnson, JD, MPA, and Deborah Walker Keegan, PhD, FACMPE, Medical Group Management Association, 2006, p. 63.
Categories in the Cultural Dimension	(1) team-oriented, (2) individualistic, and (3) middle ground	"Cash Compensation in Medical Group Practices: Application of an RVU-Based Approach," in "Physician Compensation Arrangements," by Daniel K. Zismer, An Aspen Publication, 1999, pp. 37, 62; "Compensation Plan Options—The Compensation Plan Matrix," in "Physician Compensation Plans: State-of-the-Art Strategies," by Bruce A. Johnson, JD, MPA, and Deborah Walker Keegan, PhD, FACMPE, Medical Group Management Association, 2006, p. 63.
Financial Dimensions of the Compensation Plan Matrix	The financial dimensions, or "plane," of the compensation plan matrix is juxtaposed against the cultural dimension of compensation planning on the basis of its two dimensions: (1) the means by which revenue is calculated and allocated, as it relates to the system of compensation, and (2) the means by which practice expense is calculated and allocated, as it relates to the system of compensation. These financial dimensions are collectively comprised of nine elements.	"Base Salary," in "Physician's Compensation: Measurement, Benchmarking, and Implementation," by Lucy R. Carter, CPA, and Sara S. Lankford, CPA, John Wiley & Sons, Inc., 2000, p. 86; "Compensation Plan Options—The Compensation Plan Matrix," in "Physician Compensation Plans: State-of-the-Art Strategies," by Bruce A. Johnson, JD, MPA, and Deborah Walker Keegan, PhD, FACMPE, Medical Group Management Association, 2006, p. 63.

(continued)

(continued)

Key Concept	Definition	Citation
Nine Financial Elements of the Compensation Plan Matrix	*Revenue Elements*	"Base Salary," in "Physician's Compensation: Measurement, Benchmarking, and Implementation," by Lucy R. Carter, CPA, and Sara S. Lankford, CPA, John Wiley & Sons, Inc., 2000, p. 86; "Compensation Plan Options—The Compensation Plan Matrix," in "Physician Compensation Plans: State-of-the-Art Strategies," by Bruce A. Johnson, JD, MPA, and Deborah Walker Keegan, PhD, FACMPE, Medical Group Management Association, 2006, p. 68.
	Element 1 allocates revenue or income using a unit-based method (that is, equal share, direct salary plans, or by utilizing a standardized value unit, like the work relative value unit, to which a dollar amount is assigned).	
	Element 2 assigns a baseline income or share of revenue which is guaranteed, while allowing for added compensation on the basis of incentive measures to account for performance based reward.	
	Element 3 is a combination of element 1 and element 4—a production-based compensation model (that is, a certain percentage of compensation will come from an equal allocation of revenue and the remaining compensation will come from a production-based allocation).	
	Element (4) utilizes strictly production-driven methods of allocating compensation—"you eat what you kill."	
	Element (5) uses a staggered or tiered method to allocate either revenue (and, thus, included in the previously discussed revenue elements) or expense (placing it in the following group of elements).	
	Expense Elements	
	Element (6) allocates expenses on an equal-share basis, and the calculation included in the compensation algorithm.	
	Element (7) allocates expenses in negotiation with a production-based leveraging component (that is, a certain percentage based on equal share and the remainder based on production levels as a means of expense allocation).	
	Element (8) is a means of modified cost accounting by which practice expenses are divided into physician-specific ("direct"), equal-share ("fixed"), and on the utilization-based ("variable") categories.	
	Element (9) allocates expenses strictly on the basis of utilization.	
General Compensation Plan Framework Categories	(1) team-oriented, (2) individualistic, and (3) middle ground.	"Compensation Plan Options—The Compensation Plan Matrix," p. 66; "Compensation Plan Architectures," p. 83 in "Physician Compensation Plans: State-of-the-Art Strategies," by Bruce A. Johnson, JD, MPA, and Deborah Walker Keegan, PhD, FACMPE, Medical Group Management Association, 2006; "Cash Compensation in Medical Group Practices: Application of an RVU-Based Approach," in "Physician Compensation Arrangements," by Daniel K. Zismer, An Aspen Publication, 1999, p. 62;
Team-Oriented Frameworks	Revenue − Expense = Funds Available for Compensation	"Cash Compensation in Medical Group Practices: Application of an RVU-Based Approach," in "Physician Compensation Arrangements," by Daniel K. Zismer, An Aspen Publication, 1999, p. 62; "Compensation Plan Architectures," in "Physician Compensation Plans: State-of-the-Art Strategies," by Bruce A. Johnson, JD, MPA, and Deborah Walker Keegan, PhD, FACMPE, Medical Group Management Association, 2006, p. 84.
Individualistic Frameworks	Allocated Revenue − Allocated Expense = Practitioner Compensation	"Compensation Plan Architectures," in "Physician Compensation Plans: State-of-the-Art Strategies," by Bruce A. Johnson, JD, MPA, and Deborah Walker Keegan, PhD, FACMPE, Medical Group Management Association, 2006, p. 92.

Key Concept	Definition	Citation
Purposes of Benchmarking	(1) Determine where a particular practice stands, in comparison to similar practices, in terms of overhead spending, staffing and staff distribution, supply expenditures, and so forth	"Measuring Physician Work and Effort," in "Physician Compensation Plans: State-of-the-Art Strategies," by Bruce A. Johnson, JD, MPA, and Deborah Walker Keegan, PhD, FACMPE, Medical Group Management Association, 2006, pp. 110–12.
	(2) Identify problematic areas of operation in which a practice may wish to improve efficiency	
	(3) Compare physician-specific rates of compensation for fairness	
	(4) Compare physician-specific rates of production	
	(5) Compare physician-specific rates of compensation to rates of production and determine if there is appropriate correlation	
	(6) Ensure that practices comply with Stark law and antikickback laws and rules, as well (when applicable) laws placed on tax-exempt organizations	
Two Levels on Which Benchmarking Is Performed	(1) organizational and (2) practitioner	"The Joint Commission's Perspective," by Paul M. Schyve, MD, in "Measuring Clinical Care: A Guide for Physician Executives," by Stephen C. Schoenbaum, MD, MPH, the American College of Physician Executives, 1995, pp. 51, 57; "The Shrinking Pie," in "Physician's Compensation: Measurement, Benchmarking, and Implementation," by Lucy R. Carter, CPA, and Sara S. Lankford, CPA, John Wiley & Sons, Inc., 2000, pp. 20–21; "The Compensation Plan Development Process," in "Physician Compensation Plans: State-of-the-Art Strategies," by Bruce A. Johnson, JD, MPA, and Deborah Walker Keegan, PhD, FACMPE, Medical Group Management Association, 2006, pp. 31–32.
Key Considerations When Detailing a Compensation Plan	Types of work performed by practitioners include: (1) clinical, (2) teaching, (3) research, and (4) service.	"The Physician Compensation in Academic Medical Practices," by Joseph H. Levitch and Daniel K. Zismer, in "Physician Compensation Arrangements," by Daniel K. Zismer, An Aspen Publication, 1999, p. 113. "The Compensation Plan Development Process," in "Physician Compensation Plans: State-of-the-Art Strategies," by Bruce A. Johnson, JD, MPA, and Deborah Walker Keegan, PhD, FACMPE, Medical Group Management Association, 2006, pp. 33–34.
	The basis for rewarding or providing incentives includes: (1) productivity, (2) quality outcomes, (3) managed care, (4) patient satisfaction, (5) clinical resource management, (6) teaching, (7) research, and (8) leadership.	
	The level at which incentives and evaluation of performance are set includes: (1) individual practitioner, (2) specialty groups, (3) entire practices, and (4) some combination of the previous.	
	Two incentives to factor into compensation include: (1) fixed or variable and (2) "at risk" portions.	
	The relationship between compensation and a practice's overall funding is determined by (1) degree of financial support for the various types of work activities and (2) the expenses associated with the various organizational levels.	
Stakeholders in Compensation Planning	Practitioners and the compensating enterprises	"The Joint Commission's Perspective," by Paul M. Schyve, MD, in "Measuring Clinical Care: A Guide for Physician Executives," by Stephen C. Schoenbaum, MD, MPH, the American College of Physician Executives, 1995, p. 51, 57; "Incentive Compensation," in "Physician's Compensation: Measurement, Benchmarking, and Implementation," by Lucy R. Carter, CPA, and Sara S. Lankford, CPA, John Wiley & Sons, Inc., 2000, p. 94; "Common Pitfalls," in "Physician's Compensation: Measurement, Benchmarking, and Implementation," by Lucy R. Carter, CPA, and Sara S. Lankford, CPA, John Wiley & Sons, Inc., 2000, pp. 176–77.

(continued)

(continued)

Key Concept	Definition	Citation
Factors for Which Compensation Plans Should Account	(1) The practitioner's clinical productivity (2) The practitioner's nonclinical productivity (3) The practice's characteristics, business structure, and legal considerations	"Physician Compensation Plans: State-of-the-Art Strategies," by Bruce A. Johnson, JD, MPA, and Deborah Walker Keegan, PhD, FACMPE, Medical Group Management Association, 2006, pp. 103–12, 179.
Benchmarking Clinical and Nonclinical Productivity of a Practitioner Addresses	(1) Where practitioner compensation falls with respect to the statistical distribution of other practitioners, either internally or externally (2) Where practitioner clinical production falls with respect to the statistical distribution of other practitioners, either internally or externally (3) Where practitioner performance in other areas (that is, nonclinical performance measures) falls with respect to the statistical distribution of other practitioners, either internally or externally	"The Compensation Plan Development Process," in "Physician Compensation Plans: State-of-the-Art Strategies," by Bruce A. Johnson, JD, MPA, and Deborah Walker Keegan, PhD, FACMPE, Medical Group Management Association, 2006, p. 31.
Factors Influencing Practitioner Performance	(1) clinical and (2) nonclinical productivity	"Measuring Physician Work and Effort," in "Physician Compensation Plans: State-of-the-Art Strategies," by Bruce A. Johnson, JD, MPA, and Deborah Walker Keegan, PhD, FACMPE, Medical Group Management Association, 2006, p. 104-5, 114–15.
Drivers of Clinical Productivity	(1) time, (2) efficiency, (3) volume, and (4) quality performance	"The Joint Commission's Perspective," by Paul M. Schyve, MD, in "Measuring Clinical Care: A Guide for Physician Executives," by Stephen C. Schoenbaum, MD, MPH, the American College of Physician Executives, 1995, p. 57; "Physician Compensation Arrangements," by Daniel K. Zismer, An Aspen Publication, 1999; "Pay for Performance: Quality- and Value- Based Reimbursement," by Norman (Chip) Harbaugh Jr., Pediatric Clinics of North America, Vol. 56, No. 4 (2009), pp. 997–98. "Physician Compensation: Models for Aligning Financial Goals and Incentives," by Kenneth M. Hekman, Medical Group Management Association, 2000; "Measuring Physician Work and Effort," in "Physician Compensation Plans: State-of-the-Art Strategies," by Bruce A. Johnson, JD, MPA, and Deborah Walker Keegan, PhD, FACMPE, Medical Group Management Association, 2006, pp. 114–15.
Drivers of Nonclinical Productivity	(1) service activities, (2) fiscal or financial variables, (3) quality of clinical and nonclinical work, (4) accessibility, (5) team-orientation, (6) teaching activities, and (7) research activities	"Special Issues in Physician Compensation," in "Physician Compensation Plans: State-of-the-Art Strategies," by Bruce A. Johnson, JD, MPA, and Deborah Walker Keegan, PhD, FACMPE, Medical Group Management Association, 2006, pp. 177–79.
Considerations When Conducting Benchmark Analyses on the Practice Level	(1) Whether or not the practice struggles with insurance collections and sponsor accounts (2) How the practice's payor mix bodes in comparison with other practices (3) Trends in reimbursement strategies observed within the practice's payor mix (4) The practice's aggregate and departmental operating expenditures as compared with other practices (5) How practice performance outcomes compare to those of other practices	"The Joint Commission's Perspective," by Paul M. Schyve, MD, in "Measuring Clinical Care: A Guide for Physician Executives," by Stephen C. Schoenbaum, MD, MPH, the American College of Physician Executives, 1995, p. 51, 57; "The Compensation Plan Development Process," in "Physician Compensation Plans: State-of-the-Art Strategies," by Bruce A. Johnson, JD, MPA, and Deborah Walker Keegan, PhD, FACMPE, Medical Group Management Association, 2006, p. 31.
Duration of Buy-In	For most physician-owned practices, one to three years; for larger groups, four or five years	"Buying In to Partnership: Make Arrangements Clear," in Partner Buy-ins, Physician's Advisory Vital Topic Series, 1999, p. 3.

Key Concept	Definition	Citation
Methods of Buy-In Payment	Before-tax funding, by which the buy-in amount is considered on a before-tax basis, and after-tax funding.	"Chapter 4—Group Partnerships, Clinics, and Corporations," in ""Selling or Buying a Medical Practice," by Gary R. Schaub, Medical Economics Books, 1988, pp. 67–74.
Determining the Fair Market Value of the Buy-In Payment and Process	The valuator must determine (1) the terms and amounts of payments made and (2) the conversion of all of these considerations to an economic basis, stated as a cash payment amount.	"Introduction," in "Section 2: Marketing valuation Services," in "Valuation of a Medical Practice," by Reed Tinsley, CPA, Rhonda Sides, CPA, Gregory D. Anderson, CPA, CVA, John Wiley and Sons, Inc., 1999, p. 8.
Methods Used for Compensating Nonclinical Services	(1) direct and (2) indirect	"Special Issues in Physician Compensation," in "Physician Compensation Plans: State-of-the-Art Strategies," by Bruce A. Johnson, JD, MPA, and Deborah Walker Keegan, PhD, FACMPE, Medical Group Management Association, 2006, pp. 177–79.
Common Objectives of Various Algorithms for Compensating Faculty Physicians Using Performance-Based Incentive Methods	(1) To design physician salaries such that a percentage is variable; (2) To motivate physicians and staff to participate in clinical, research-based, or academic activities that generate more revenue, either directly or indirectly; (3) To focus on certain performance indicators set by and specific to the organization; and (4) To compensate physicians based on their level of productivity.	"Adapting Industry-Style Business Model to Academia in a System of Performance-Based Incentive Compensation," E. Albert Reece, MD, PhD, MBA; Olan Nugent, MS; Richard P. Wheeler, MD; Charles W. Smith, MD; et al., Academic Medicine, Vol. 83, No. 1 (Jan 2008), p. 76.
XYZ model	Total Salary = X + X' + Y + Z	"Designing a Physician Compensation and Incentive Plan for an Academic Healthcare Center," by Donna Steinmetz, MSHA, FACMPE, the American College of Medical Practice Executives, Medical Group Management Association, September 2005; "Compensation and Incentive Plans for Physicians," by Charles Stiernberg, MD, MBA, November 2001, www.physicianspractice.com/ (accessed October 29, 2009).
Factors That Influence the Allocation of Time and Manpower to Nonclinical, Administrative, Managerial, and Executive Duties	(1) The number of practitioners (typically physicians) responsible for these duties (2) The amount of time each practitioner dedicates to his or her respective duties (3) The specific administrative duties performed	"Evaluation of Specialty Physician Workforce Methodologies," by the Council on Graduate Medical Education, U.S. Department of Health and Human Services, Health Resources and Services Administration, September 2000, p. 12.
Types of Shareholders or Partners	(1) senior and (2) junior. Senior shareholders have more responsibilities.	"Buying In to Partnership: The Stock Purchase," in Partner Buy-ins, Physician's Advisory Vital Topic Series, 1999, pp. 5–6.
Methods of Compensating Outreach Activities	(1) crediting travel time and (2) calculating efficiency of production	"Special Issues in Physician Compensation," in "Physician Compensation Plans: State-of-the-Art Strategies," by Bruce A. Johnson, JD, MPA, and Deborah Walker Keegan, PhD, FACMPE, Medical Group Management Association, 2006, p. 185.
Considerations When Assigning Credits to Travel Time	(1) estimate the approximate travel time from one practice site to another (2) establish an evaluation and management current procedural terminology (CPT) code that represents offsite work (3) estimate the standard number of CPT units per hour that a practitioner can be expected to perform	"Special Issues in Physician Compensation," in "Physician Compensation Plans: State-of-the-Art Strategies," by Bruce A. Johnson, JD, MPA, and Deborah Walker Keegan, PhD, FACMPE, Medical Group Management Association, 2006, pp. 185–86.

Overview

The first half of the twentieth century marked the emergence of consolidated business arrangements in healthcare professional practices. As a result, the means by which practitioners, namely physicians, were compensated evolved as well. Each emerging type of compensation plan became associated with certain benefits, as well as financial, legal, and clinical repercussions. In this chapter, compensation planning is dissected to identify the fundamental elements that are inherent to the development process, regardless of how future trends may influence healthcare professionals and their practices. These basic elements can be presented as they relate to Rudyard Kipling's *Six Honest Serving-Men*:[1]

> I KEEP six honest serving-men
>
> They taught me all I knew;
>
> Their names are *What* and *Why* and *When* and *How* and *Where* and *Who*

What?—The Definition of a Physician Compensation Plan

First and foremost, a **physician compensation plan** is a way of allocating an organization's revenues and expenses and determining appropriate methods of compensating professionals for the services they provide.[2] In an increasingly labyrinthine marketplace of misaligned priorities, physician compensation plans may (1) contribute to the incentive and performance feedback system, (2) assist in driving performance to achieve goals, and (3) facilitate more effective identification and communication of an organization's values, dynamic, productivity objectives, and performance expectations.[3]

Practitioner compensation is typically comprised of three components: (1) base salary, (2) incentive pay, and (3) benefits. The means by which compensation is allocated into these components may be driven by a number of factors, including (1) industry trends, (2) the four pillars (regulatory, reimbursement, competitive, and technological environments), (3) the practice dynamic and business structure, and (4) a practitioner's characteristic tendencies in both clinical and nonclinical professional areas.[4]

Why?—Is a New Compensation Plan Needed?

Internal Indicators

Several internal indicators, or practice characteristics, are suggestive of the success (or failure) of an existing compensation plan: (1) practitioner perceptions, (2) practice productivity, (3) financial standing, and (4) the existing level of compensation.[5] Practices can exhibit a spectrum of tendencies with regard to these characteristics; where a practice lies on this spectrum may indicate whether the practice's compensation plan is effective or inadequate.[6]

If the majority of practitioners in an organization are fairly content with the existing compensation structure, with only a few isolated qualms from individuals who feel they are subject to unfair circumstances, then, by in large, the compensation plan has served its purpose.[7] Alternately, if the practice–provider dynamic is extremely fragile and there exists a trend of constant threats, contract terminations, or unhealthy and vengeful competition, there may be cause to reassess the compensation plan that has been implemented.[8] Similarly, a consistent flow and pace of productivity is suggestive of a fairly uncontroversial compensation system, whereas, disparities in professional and personal productivity may be reason for concern.[9] Practices that have an appropriate operating margin are less likely than those in severe debt to reconsider their compensation plan.[10] Lastly, consistent rates of compensation may be a sign of a properly devised compensation plan, whereas a decreasing trend in compensation may suggest that it is time for a change.[11] Practices may exhibit characteristics that fall anywhere between these extremes. As a result, practices tend to fall into one of three categories: (1) practices that *must seek* an alternative compensation plan; (2) practices that *adopt* a dynamic compensation plan, which they actively refine to align with industry changes as well as internal changes in strategy, goals, or both; or (3) practices that fall somewhere in between, which could potentially benefit from a revamped compensation plan but will not fail otherwise.[12]

EXTERNAL INDICATORS (THE FOUR PILLARS)

In order to coexist symbiotically with an evolving healthcare industry, practices that wish to succeed will likely need evolve as well. As such, practices should assess the current (and projected) success or failure of a compensation plan in light of external indicators, that is, existing and impending industry trends, principally within the four pillars. Generally speaking, practices may want to review their existing compensation plan in light of economic and demographic changes in the workforce, as well as the patient population, in order to evolve according to changes in patient health outcomes and community needs.[13]

KEY REGULATORY CONSIDERATIONS

As discussed extensively in chapter 3 of *An Era of Reform*, the federal and state regulation of the corporate practice of medicine, fraud and abuse, licensure, insurance, and other aspects of healthcare professional practice typically has significant bearing on an organization's compensation arrangements.[14] Violations of these laws may result in civil or criminal penalties, that is, fines for impermissible remuneration.[15]

Fraud and Abuse

Fraud and abuse, namely as it relates to compensation, is regulated through a body of laws, among the most notable being the Stark law, the False Claims Act, and the antikickback statute.[16]

The Stark Law

The Stark law (detailed in chapter 3 of *An Era of Reform*) prohibits referral of designated health services (DHS) for Medicare and Medicaid patients to entities (that is, physicians, physician groups, independent contractors, and clinical laboratories) that have ownership interest in, or have affiliation with, a referring physician or billing hospital.[17] Permissible physician or practitioner compensation arrangements comply with the exceptions listed under Stark law (for more information related to Stark exceptions, see chapter 3 of *An Era of Reform*).[18] Enterprises or organizations engaging in the following arrangements are more likely to be implicated by Stark law:

1. Arrangements wherein physicians own shares of the practices by which they are employed (that is, any arrangement in which the referred physician or group has the right to receive financial benefits from the referring physician) (see chapter 3 of *An Era of Reform*).[19]

2. Arrangements wherein physicians are employed, hold directorships, or have other affiliations with hospitals and other organizations (see chapter 3 of *An Era of Reform*).[20]

3. Various contractual service arrangements (both direct and indirect) between physicians, medical practices, hospitals, or a combination of these.[21]

4. Space and equipment rental agreements between DHS entities (see chapter 3 of *An Era of Reform*).[22]

It is important that compensation plans and arrangements comply with one or more Stark exceptions (for a list of Stark exceptions, see chapter 3 of *An Era of Reform*).[23] In addition, many states have promulgated their own self-referral legislation.[24] For a list of states with self-referral legislation, see chapter 3 of *An Era of Reform*.

False Claims Act (FCA)

Another enforcement measure used to combat healthcare fraud and abuse is the federal False Claims Act (FCA). The FCA primarily targets fraudulent reimbursement claims (for example, upcoding or billing for unnecessary services).[25] Additionally, Stark law and antikickback statute violations may be prosecuted under the FCA (see chapter 3 of *An Era of Reform*).[26]

Antikickback Statute

The antikickback statute forbids offering, soliciting, or paying remuneration in exchange for the referral of patient services that are paid for by Medicare.[27] Enforcement agencies as well as the federal courts have found antikickback regulation and legislation to be broadly applicable. The Office of the Inspector General (OIG) adopted the "one purpose test," which states that only one motive (or purpose) of an arrangement need prescribe impermissible remuneration or referral to render the arrangement in violation of the antikickback statute.[28] Because many legitimate business arrangements may be affected, safe harbors and exceptions to the antikickback statute have been issued that describe compensation arrangements that may be permissible under antikickback laws (for a list of safe harbors and exceptions, see chapter 3 of *An Era of Reform*).[29] In addition to incorporating the one purpose test, the OIG routinely issues an advisory publication, "Special Fraud Alerts," that highlights questionable arrangements.[30] A common mandate enforced by all of the safe harbor provisions is that physicians or practitioners be compensated at fair market value and at rates considered commercially reasonable.[31] In general, compensation agreements are likely to be commercially reasonable as long as they

1. are at fair market value,

2. list the actual duties to be performed by the physician,

3. include services that are reasonably necessary to the provider based on provider circumstances, and

4. include services that could not be adequately provided for less compensation.[32]

Internal Revenue Service (IRS) Governance of Compensation

The Internal Revenue Service (IRS) requires that compensation arrangements be consistent with the fair market value of the associated service line and that the arrangement meets the threshold for commercial reasonableness.[33] For a list of several specific factors used to determine the commercial reasonableness of a physician compensation arrangement, see chapter 3 of *An Era of Reform*. Compensation rates that exceed fair market value and the thresholds for commercial reasonableness are implicated as payments for referrals.[34] These presumed violations of Stark law and the antikickback statute often result in civil or criminal penalties.[35]

Internal Revenue Code (IRC) Requirements

The **Internal Revenue Code (IRC)** provisions outline the tax-related implications of (1) compensation plan infrastructure, (2) compensation methodologies, and (3) how compensation methods may be treated by taxing authorities.[36] Healthcare professional practices are subject to different tax scenarios, depending on the type of business structure (as defined and discussed in chapter 1 of *Professional Practices*) they embody, which may include

1. sole proprietorships,

2. professional partnerships,

3. professional corporations (Subchapter S corporation or Subchapter C corporations),

4. limited liability partnerships, and

5. limited liability companies[37]

IRS Initiatives

Recently, tax exempt healthcare entities, namely nonprofit hospitals, have been subject to increased regulatory scrutiny. This heighted stringency may be largely attributable to what has been claimed to be the overcompensation of the executives employed by these organizations using government and community funds.[38] The rebuttable presumption is a safe harbor that allows tax-exempt organizations to avoid IRS penalties by assuming executive compensation is at fair market value if (1) compensation rates are approved by authorized bodies whose constituent members have no conflicts of interest, (2) compensation rates have been set based on a reliance of comparable data, and (3) authorizing bodies adequately, and concurrently, documented the basis for their decisions.[39]

> Recently, tax exempt healthcare entities, namely, nonprofit hospitals, have been subject to increased regulatory scrutiny.

"Enforcement Efforts Take Aim at Executive Compensation of Tax-Exempt Health Care Entities," by Candace L. Quinn and Jeffrey D. Mamorsky, 18 Health Law Reporter 1640, Dec. 17, 2009; "Employment Tax Audits of Exempt Hospitals Could Turn Up Other Issues, Attorneys Warn," 18 Health Law Reporter 1653, Dec. 24, 2009.

As an added measure of enforcement, the IRS developed a payroll audit, scheduled for February 2010, and it anticipated that 6,000 companies, including approximately 1,500 tax-exempt organizations (for example, nonprofit hospitals), would participate.[40] Among other things, one reason for auditing these and other types of healthcare organizations is to contain abuse of IRC safe harbors.[41] As a result of recently passed healthcare legislation, fraud and abuse regulation may be subject to more increased stringency on the federal and state level, namely with regard to nonprofit organizations.[42] In order to demonstrate continued compliance, entities should document their compliance programs and procedures and use current benchmarking data to routinely assess their compensation rates against fair market value thresholds.[43]

KEY REIMBURSEMENT CONSIDERATIONS

Changes in the reimbursement climate could negatively affect the adequacy of previously sufficient compensation plans.[44] Reimbursement methods and levels directly affect a practice's financial dynamic.[45] Because compensation may contribute considerably to the financial dynamic of healthcare professional practices and is a significant element of a practice's financial activity, changes to compensating methodologies and rates may be cause for practices to revisit their compensation plans.[46] Aligning compensation plans with reimbursement instruments not only reinforces fiscal solidarity, but it also allows practices to maximize the amount of revenue that they generate.[47]

> Aligning compensation plans with reimbursement instruments, not only to reinforce fiscal solidarity, but also to allow practices to maximize the amount of revenue that they generate.

"Factors Impacting Physician Compensation," in "Physician's Compensation: Measurement, Benchmarking, and Implementation," by Lucy R. Carter, CPA and Sara S. Lankford, CPA, John Wiley & Sons, Inc., 2000, p. 5; "Pay-for-Performance (P4P) and Physician Compensation," in "Physician Compensation Plans: State-of-the-Art Strategies," by Bruce A. Johnson, JD, MPA and Deborah Walker Keegan, PhD, FACMPE, Medical Group Management Association, 2006, p. 131.

Healthcare Professional Compensation and Pay-for-Performance (P4P)

The emergence of pay-for-performance (P4P) systems appears to have reinforced the importance of realigning compensation plans to complement reimbursement mechanisms.[48] As discussed extensively in chapter 2 of *An Era of Reform*, P4P is a reimbursement system wherein a fraction of the payment is derived from standardized performance measures.[49] Generally speaking, a P4P system will include (1) a set of performance objectives, (2) a metric system and performance standards from which criteria for evaluation can be derived, and (3) an incentive system, wherein the amount and method for allocating the payments among those who meet or exceed the reward threshold.[50] Typically, practices that are reimbursed on a P4P basis may attribute payment for services rendered (that is, generated revenue) to clinical productivity, as well as to quality and efficiency of performance. Practices under a P4P system that utilize compensation plans that almost entirely, if not solely, reward for clinical productivity may struggle to sufficiently synchronize their methodologies and revenue stream.[51] As such, a practice that reimburses based on a P4P system should also take into consideration quality, patient safety, and efficiency elements when compensating its practitioners.[52]

KEY COMPETITION CONSIDERATIONS

Compensation plans may affect and, in turn, be influenced by inter- and intra-practice competitive stressors that may take several forms. Practitioner recruitment and retention requires that practices compensate at rates that are competitive and consistent with the existing market.[53] Also, the competitive dynamic within a practice may be influenced by the existing system of practitioner compensation (for example, the level of transparency, fairness, and disparities and the incentive or reward for clinical and nonclinical performance), which may foster perceivably healthy or unhealthy practice relationships and may potentially have a positive effect, a negative effect, or both on practice performance.[54] Competitive drivers of compensation may include (1) the diversification and specialization of the workforce, (2) the increased complexity of healthcare organizational structures, (3) the way in which experience is accounted for in compensation, and (4) increased variability in practice tendencies.

Impact of Specialization and Provider Diversity on Compensation

Changes in the healthcare climate and workforce may influence inter- and intra-practice competition between and among primary care and specialty physicians, as well as between and among physician and nonphysician providers. For practices that wish to maintain pace with market competitors, it may be advantageous to implement compensation plans that cater to the demanded specialty mix and provider mix.[55]

Impact of Consolidation on Compensation

The proliferative array of existing business structures, arrangements and affiliations, and consolidated organization types may fuel the continued growth of a dynamic and increasingly diverse healthcare competitive market (see chapter 4 of *An Era of Reform and* chapters 1 and 2 of *Professional Practices*). Each of these various and emerging organizational structures may be distinguished, in part, on the basis of their unique compensation arrangements and methodologies. As a result, the competitive dynamic that exists between and among the diverse types of healthcare professional practices may be intrinsically tied to the methods of compensation and employment that best complement their organizational structure.[56]

Impact of Experience on Compensation

Experience and, to some effect, seniority may be strategically implemented into a compensation plan for several purposes. At one extreme, practices may wish to isolate new associates from the established system of compensating practitioners by insuring some form of set income for an established period of time.[57] This allows new practitioners to acclimate while protecting the interest of the remaining practitioners.[58] Alternately, some systems are designed to incentivize loyalty and heighten retention by compensating on the basis of experience and, to some effect, seniority.[59] Although, historically, seniority may have been a key factor in determining base salary, newer compensation plans do not necessarily account for senior ranking, even in academic practices, when establishing base salary.[60]

Practices may engage in buy or sell agreements, which may encourage the transition from associateship to partnership (known as buy-in arrangements,) the transition from partnership to retirement (referred to as buy-out arrangements), or both.[61] These agreements may incorporate experience-based compensation strategies in order to (1) enhance recruitment, (2) heighten retention, (3) fuel competitive drive, (4) ensure the satisfaction of existing partners and the quality of future ones, and (5) incentivize loyalty.[62]

Impact of Performance Variation on Compensation

For various reasons, including higher level of dedication to executive, administrative, academic, research, other nonclinical duties, or a combination of these, as well as variation in production levels, lifestyle expectations, and full- or part-time status, the diversity of provider practices and production levels has increased. These changes in workforce demographics and demands may continue to incite controversy over potentially biased performance measures.[63] Accordingly, this competitive element should be taken into consideration on a practice-specific basis.[64]

KEY TECHNOLOGY CONSIDERATIONS

The growth in both management and clinical technology has transformed the practitioner performance dynamic, and, as such, it should factor into the compensation methodology, especially if production is a key component of the plan.[65] New performance measures that reflect this added dimension to productivity should be derived as new technologies enter the healthcare market and become part of a particular practice.[66]

Alternately, as expenditures attributed to healthcare technological development, research, and implementation increase in quantity, complexity, and controversy, their affect on overall spending will depend on how the cost is allocated, how responsibility is allocated, how much and by whom the technology is utilized, and how its implementation affects productivity, quality, efficiency, or a combination of these.[67] Because these indicators may ultimately factor into the successes and failures of existing and future plans, they may be significant considerations for the strategic development of an effective compensation plan.

WHEN?—THE COMPENSATION PLAN LIFE CYCLE

PHASE 1: THE EXISTING PLAN

The existing compensation methods employed by many practices that seek to reevaluate their remunerative strategies are often rooted in the traditional infrastructures that these practices embrace.[68] As an organization grows in size and complexity, the original compensation plan may no longer suffice to meet the needs of the professionals employed by or affiliated with the practice.[69] Naturally, practices and their employees grow accustomed to the ingrained culture of the organization, and, despite the degree of unrest or dissatisfaction that may exist, they will, at least, struggle to identify the need for change—if not resist it entirely.[70] When a compensation plan has been recognized as inadequate on the basis of the criteria discussed in **Internal Indicators** and **External Indicators (The Four Pillars)**, the practice can move to pursue a more appropriate means of compensating its physicians and other healthcare professionals.[71]

PHASE 2: THE POTENTIAL PLAN: THE DEVELOPMENT TIMELINE

The duration of time necessary to develop, transition into, and fully implement a compensation plan is contingent upon the size of the practice; how detrimental the redesign may be to the organization's survival, legal compliance, or both; and how difficult the anticipated redesign and implementation processes are expected to be.[72] If the practice is unable to compensate its employees, or if it is out of legal compliance, the process may, in some cases, be expedited.[73] Alternately, larger or more complex practices typically may expect a longer timeline than the average practice.[74] However, for most practices, six to nine months may serve as subjective benchmark duration for the typical compensation plan development process.[75] Designing a compensation plan may taken between three to six months to complete (nine months for larger practices), and the remaining time typically is invested in transitioning out of the old plan and implementing the new one.[76] In general, timelines that are longer than these standard durations are indicative of a deeper problem that is being overlooked.[77] In these instances, and depending on the specific circumstances, it may be beneficial for practices to seek outside consulting advice.[78]

PHASE 3: THE NEW PLAN

Depending on the magnitude of change needed, and the way in which the proposed change is received by the practice employees and affiliates, transitioning into and implementing a new compensation plan in its entirety may take months—even years—longer than expected.[79] In some cases, organizational culture can be extremely difficult to change, especially if there is resistance to the proposed plan.[80] Also, perceptions and attitudes attributed to an old system might be difficult to relinquish, and they may persist long after the new plan is put in place.[81] Typically, it can take between three and five years for such issues to subside. Although some practices may endure even longer periods of unrest, very few are fortunate enough to see sufficient improvement in less than three years.[82]

HOW?—TEN STEPS TO DEVELOPING A COMPENSATION PLAN

Although the mechanical details of the development process may vary due to the diverse array of practice types and provider arrangements, the typical development process may include the ten steps discussed in the following sections.[83]

STEP 1: DETERMINING GOVERNANCE, GOALS, AND PRINCIPLES

Before a practice attempts to identify existing problems and potential solutions, certain foundational decisions should be made, specifically (1) who will be included in this decision making process and in what capacity, (2) what specific goals or objectives must be central to the process, and (3) what principles must shape the development process and drive all of the decisions that are made through to the implementation of an improved compensation plan.[84]

GOVERNANCE OPTIONS

Leadership in the development of compensation plans may take several forms, but results tend to be more favorable when physicians and other providers within the practice play a significant role in the decision making process.[85] Although practices may seek assistance from external resources (that is, attorneys, CPAs, and consultants), awareness, concern, support, and commitment from a strong group of practitioners is considered instrumental to the implementation and long-lived success of a new compensation plan.[86] Practices have several options when choosing ownership *and* oversight of the compensation development process; they may choose to adopt one method or choose a combination of several.[87] Some organizations may choose to take a *top down* approach to developing a new plan, wherein the decision lies in the hands of management or a governing board.[88] Other practices may wish to employ a *bottom up* approach, electing physicians to research alternatives to the existing compensation system.[89] The most common development strategy, however, appears to be the election of a compensation planning committee.[90] Both physician and nonphysician consultants may be recruited to facilitate the process. These consultants may function as part of a planning committee or independently throughout the process.[91]

The Compensation Planning Committee

A **compensation planning committee** is a collection of practice members that is representative of the practice population as a whole; physician executives and practitioners of all levels and specialty areas are appointed to mirror the practice distribution.[92] Compensation planning committees usually are responsible for executing the remaining steps in this process.[93]

The Consultant's Role

Consultants, in this context, provide any third-party assistance to the development process, addressing topics including, but not limited to, administration, healthcare consulting, accounting, and legal consulting.[94] In general, the role of a consultant may include such tasks as

1. aiding in the evaluation of the existing system, identifying strengths, as well as opportunities for improvement;

2. offering knowledge and experience related to the various arrangements and alternatives available;

3. helping to establish goals and principles;

4. investigating the various foundational and specific options the practice may wish to entertain;

5. assisting in financial modeling of the alternative plans;

6. creating the materials needed for communicating or presenting proposed plan(s); and

7. launching the decision making process.[95]

SETTING GOALS—TARGET OBJECTIVES

Establishing goals for the development process should be instrumental to the remaining steps and are intended to reflect the practice's culture, existing operation, and future aspirations.[96] Although the specific objectives of a practice's compensation plan will be unique, general goals that should be inherent to a successful system may include

1. encouraging productivity (in a fee-for-service environment);

2. reinforcing involvement in professional services, ancillary practices, outreach, leadership, and other diverse and potentially nonclinical roles;

3. encouraging teamwork and group solidarity;

4. guaranteeing that the system is fiscally sound;

5. elucidating specific performance expectations and responsibilities;

6. easing the process of recruiting and retaining practitioners; and

7. ensuring that compensation and reimbursement methodologies complement each other.[97]

DEVELOPING PRINCIPLES—IDEAL CHARACTERISTICS

Certain design principles should be chosen by the governing members of the development process, and the principles typically represent those characteristics that the members hope will resonate from their eventual design.[98] Again, although these principles are practice specific, successful compensation plans are typically characterized by certain mainstream qualities, such as

1. unbiased measurement systems;

2. a concise number of performance metrics;

3. clearly defined and methodically enforced processes, expectations, repercussions, and objectives;

4. transparent documentation, communication, and enforcement;

5. clear and simple processes, expectations, repercussions, and objectives;

6. compensation stability;

7. appropriate weighting of individual and team accountability and responsibility;

8. a feasible transition plan from current to future practices;

9. financial responsibility; and

10. legal conformity.[99]

STEP 2: INVESTIGATING THE AVAILABLE OPTIONS

The key to this step is ensuring that the plan committee, or other governing entity, is sufficiently educated on the matters of healthcare structures, dimensions, and trends as they relate to the practice in question. This involves aligning potential compensation plan(s) with existing external and internal conditions, as well as weighing financial and cultural variables to ensure that proposed plans best suit practice needs.[100]

COMPENSATION PLAN ALIGNMENT

External Factors: Aligning With the Environment
Understanding the external factors that could potentially affect the implementation of a new compensation plan is of similar significance as understanding the external indicators that suggest the need for a new plan in the first place. Without understanding how a practice-specific system will fare within the healthcare industry, the success of a compensation plan may be short-lived or nonexistent.[101] Important external factors include such considerations as

1. changes to reimbursement, health plans, or other financial drivers of the market;

2. the rates of practitioner compensation seen in the healthcare market; and

3. changes in population, demographics, or patient demand.[102]

Internal Factors: Aligning With the Established Goals and Principles
As previously discussed, in order to avoid settling on a plan that fails to meet the goals and principles set to guide the process, the available options should to be aligned to meet these internal factors.[103] See the suggested goals and principles in *Determining Governance, Goals, and Principles* for further guidance on areas in which alignment may be beneficial.

COMPENSATION PLAN MATRIX: CULTURAL VERSUS FINANCIAL DIMENSIONS

In addition to the external and internal variables that may be beneficial to consider when evaluating various available plan options, cultural and financial practice dimensions are often significant components of the basic infrastructures from which compensation plans can be derived.[104] These dimensions are interrelated and can be evaluated against each other to determine the general infrastructure that best suits any given practice, be it a team-oriented infrastructure, an individualistic infrastructure, or one that lies somewhere in between.[105]

Cultural Dimensions

Practice culture represents one dimension that can be used to classify the plethora of existing compensation plans. The foundational structure and methodology of a practice's compensation plan is suggestive of the practice's culture.[106] More specifically, whether the practice is just a collection of individual practitioners or if it promotes a team-oriented group approach will manifest itself in the dynamic that the system of compensation cultivates.[107] A well-developed plan can be instrumental to changing culture, as well, primarily by promoting practice goals and rewarding certain behaviors and activities.[108] As such, the practice culture should emulate the principles and goals defined in step 1 of this process.[109]

The large collection of existing compensation plans may be placed in three categories across the cultural dimension of the compensation plan plane: individualistic, team-oriented, and middle-ground.[110] Compensation within a team-oriented culture tends to be based on the practice's overall performance.[111] Alternately, those organizations that emphasize individual practitioner performance are more likely to adopt an individualistic culture.[112] Middle-ground encompasses a broad spectrum of practice types in which cultures differ significantly from each other.[113]

Financial Dimensions: The Nine Elements

The financial "plane" is juxtaposed against the cultural dimension of the compensation plan matrix, on the basis of its two dimensions: (1) the means by which *revenue* is calculated and allocated, as it relates to the system of compensation, and (2) the means by which practice *expense* is calculated and allocated, as it relates to the system of compensation.[114] A total of nine variables, or elements, drive these dimensions, four of which are attributed to revenue, four of which are attributed to expense, and one of which is attributed to both.[115] These nine elements represent the building blocks from which a plethora of general compensation plan frameworks (that is, architectures, blueprints, or foundations) can be devised.[116]

Revenue Elements

As previously mentioned, four revenue elements have been identified to address how income can be treated as a component of a compensation plan.[117] As included in the following list, the elements range from the most team-oriented with element 1 to the least team-oriented (or most individualistic) with element 4.[118]

1. Element 1 allocates revenue or income using a unit-based method (that is, equal share, direct salary plans, or by utilizing a standardized value unit, like the work relative value unit, to which a dollar amount is assigned);

2. Element 2 assigns a baseline income or share of revenue which is guaranteed and allows for added compensation on the basis of incentive measures to account for performance-based rewards;

3. Element 3 is a combination of element 1 and element 4, that is, it is a production-based compensation model (a certain percentage of compensation will come from an equal allocation of revenue and the remaining compensation will come from a production-based allocation); and

4. Element 4 utilizes strictly production-driven methods of allocating compensation, that is, a "you eat what you kill" approach.[119]

Element Five—Attributed to Both Revenue and Expense Dimensions

Element 5 uses a staggered, or tiered, method to allocate either *revenue* (and as a result included in the section *Revenue Elements*) or *expense* (placing it in the following group of elements).[120]

Expense Elements

Elements six through nine comprise the expense dimension and represent the different ways in which practice expense may be allocated and the effect of that allocation on compensation.[121] The highest level of team-orientation is accounted for in element 6, and the highest degree of individualistic culture is accounted for in element 9:[122]

6. Element 6 allocates expenses on an equal-share basis, and the calculation is included in the compensation algorithm;

7. Element 7 allocates expenses by negotiating with a production-based leveraging component (a certain percentage based on equal share and the remainder based on production levels as a means of expense allocation);

8. Element 8 is a means of modified cost accounting by which practice expenses are divided into physician-specific ("direct"), equal-share ("fixed"), and utilization-based ("variable") categories; and

9. Element 9 allocates expenses strictly on the basis of utilization.[123]

The Spectrum of Frameworks Derived From the Compensation Matrix

Figure 3-1 represents the matrix generated when these three dimensions interface. This matrix can be used to understand and align various major compensation plan infrastructures—on a very general level—implemented across the healthcare industry.[124] The revenue and expense dimensions, as they correlate with the three cultural classifications, result in eighteen basic frameworks that practices may choose to utilize once they have determined their target objectives, established an understanding of external and internal trends, and weighed their theoretical options.[125] As the description indicates, element 5 lies at the center of the matrix and aligns with both the revenue and expense dimensions.[126] The process by which a practice decides upon a general framework is discussed further in *Establishing the General Framework*, however, options may include the frameworks presented in the following sections.

Figure 3-1: Compensation Matrix

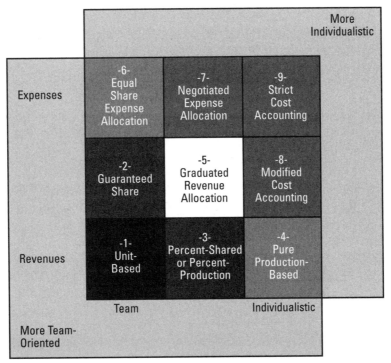

Table 3-1: Compensation Matrix—Team-Oriented Framework

Name	Element Equation	Description	Examples
Unit-Based Plans	Revenue Element 1	Compensation allocated on a basis of per-unit of service.	(1) Allocating revenue based on a straight salary (2) Allocating revenue based on 100 percent compensation (3) Allocating revenue based on compensation per unit of work (4) Allocating revenue based on a hourly wages
Guaranteed Share Plans	Revenue Element 2	Large portion of compensation allocated based on some form of fixed or market-driven salary.	(1) Allocating revenue based on a base salary plus incentives (2) Allocating revenue based on market determined salary plus incentive (3) Allocating revenue based on nonclinical production incentive based compensation measures
Percent-Shared or Percent-Production Plans	Revenue Element 3	Negotiated portion of compensation is distributed on a per-unit of service basis, with the rest allocated according to the amount of revenue generated.	Allocating revenue based on 70 percent equal share of net income, with a 30 percent incentive based on production (or other percentage combinations)
Purely Production-Based Plans	Revenue Element 4	Each practitioner is compensated individually based on their own level of production.	Allocating revenue based on total net income allocated at 100 percent (based on percent of total production)
Graduated Revenue Allocation Plans	Revenue Element 5	Practitioners are compensated using a tiered system of allocating revenue; not based on a graduated distribution of expense.	(1) Allocating revenue based on a graduated percentage of net revenues or collections (2) Allocating revenue based on a graduated dollars per work relative value unit of production (3) Allocating revenue based on a market determined overhead assessment with floor (4) Allocating revenue based on a graduated overhead assessment of production

Team-Oriented Frameworks

Team-oriented practices attempt to compensate using methodologies that are uniform and gain practice-wide acceptance. Essentially, the funds that remain from the practice revenue after all expenses (which are essentially shared under these frameworks) have been paid are distributed on the basis of an established methodology.[127] The following equation represents this framework:

$$\textit{Revenue} - \textit{Expense} = \textit{Funds Available for Compensation}^{128}$$

Rather than placing the emphasis on the strategized allocation of expense, team-oriented frameworks serve as various strategies by which revenue can be allocated within a practice.[129] As such, these frameworks rely solely on the revenue dimension, and the strategies by which compensation is allocated distinguish them from one another.[130] Several different frameworks may fall under this classification, such as unit-based plans, guaranteed share plans, percent-shared or percent-production plans, purely production-based plans, and graduated revenue allocation plans.[131] See figure 3-1. These infrastructures are described in subsequent sections, and the advantages and disadvantages to using such methodologies are outlined in table 3-1.

1. *Unit-based plans*, which align with revenue element 1, compensate on a per-unit of service basis, wherein the measure of service may vary (that is, a set salary, equal share, compensation per unit-measure of work, hourly rates, and so forth) but expense allocation is not factored into the methodology.[132]

Advantages	Disadvantages
(1) Easy plan administration. (2) Stable compensation for physicians. (3) Plan can include a production orientation for setting the level of unit-based compensation. (4) Because the individual's productivity and income are not emphasized, practices with straight salary arrangements may easily form a "care team" approach with multiple specialties caring for a single patient.	(1) Issues of fairness can arise between physicians who produce at varying levels in an equal share plan. (2) No direct incentives exist for performance outcomes. (3) Physicians who focus on individual issues may undermine group practice orientation. (4) Practice cost can be overlooked as physician compensation not tied to expenditures.
(1) The plan supports group practice orientation. (2) Stable compensation exists with prospect of addition income from incentives. (3) Incentives support diverse goals through performance measures.	(1) Nonguaranteed income may be too small to motivate behavioral change. (2) Incentives for clinical productivity easily addressed, but qualitative incentives are too subjective. (3) Multiple incentive measures require that medical administrative infrastructure and information systems are at levels consistent with data requirements.
(1) Compensation promotes both teamwork and group practice orientation. (2) No conflict exists regarding cost. (3) By combining various measures and approaches, plans can create different levels of sharing, revenue generation, and recognitions of physician work.	(1) No direct attention to practice operating costs exists. (2) The level of sharing between physicians must be negotiated to maintain fairness.
(1) Physicians perceive control over work levels and income. (2) Physicians are rewarded for productivity, so a practice is highly productive.	(1) Inequity may arise between revenue and physician effort due to payor mix variations. (2) Physicians too focused on production may lose sight of other important areas.
(1) The plan focuses on production with negotiated overhead assessment. (2) The plan allows for varying levels of compensation based on production or other measures to be consistent with financial realities. (3) Surrogate expense treatment may be used without expense micromanagement and disputes. (4) The plan links physicians desired defined income level with a minimum production level.	(1) Surrogate measures may be inconsistent with physician perceptions of fairness. (2) Reflected revenue variations may be inconsistent with payor mix. (3) Physicians too focused on production may lose sight of other important areas.

2. *Guaranteed share plans*, which align with revenue element 2, are not as team-oriented as unit-based plans, because they, in part, incorporate measures of production, quality, efficiency, other performance-based incentives, or a combination of these in their methodologies.[133] However, a significant fraction of compensation within this infrastructure is based on some form of fixed or market-driven salary, and expense is not taken into consideration, thereby keeping guaranteed share plans on the team-oriented end of the spectrum.[134]

3. *Percent-shared or percent-production plans*, which align with revenue element 3, are some hybrid of the unit-based and purely production-based plans in that a percent of compensation is distributed on a per-unit of service basis, while the remaining portion is allocated according to the amount of revenue generated.[135] As with the other team-oriented frameworks, expense allocation is not factored into the compensation methodologies these plans employ.[136]

4. *Purely production-based plans with no expense allocation*, which align entirely with revenue element 4, measure production on a practitioner-basis and compensate individual practitioners accordingly. However, practitioners do not control direct revenue shares, and, as such, practitioner-specific expenditures are not taken into consideration when calculating compensation.[137]

5. *Graduated revenue allocation plans*, which align with revenue element 5 as it lies within the revenue dimension, involve a tiered system of allocating revenue when compensating practitioners.[138] What distinguishes graduated revenue allocation plans from other plans that align solely with element 5 is that these plans do not compensate based on a graduated distribution of expense.[139]

Table 3-2: Compensation Matrix—Individualistic Framework

Name	Element Equation	Description	Examples
Purely Production-Based + Strict Cost Accounting Plans	Revenue Element 4 + Expense Element 9	Revenue is distributed according to individual practitioners' production and expense is determined using practitioner-specific direct expense allocation.	Allocating revenue based on personal production, paired with strict cost accounting of expenses based on utilization to maximum extent possible
Purely Production-Based + Modified Cost Accounting Plans	Revenue Element 4 + Expense Element 8	Revenue is directly based on production and expenditures allocated based on pre-set category [for example directly to practitioners, practitioner utilization, or fixed (equal-share) basis].	Allocating revenue based on percent of production, as well as with modified cost accounting of expenses (with combined shared and utilization-based expense allocation)
Purely Production-Based + Negotiated Expense Allocation Plans	Revenue Element 4 + Expense Element 7	A portion of cost is allocated on the basis of production and a negotiated methodology is used to allocate the rest.	Allocating revenue based on production, and allocating 50 percent of expense on the basis of equal share and the other 50 percent based on production
Purely Production-Based + Equal Share Expense Allocation Plans	Revenue Element 4 + Expense Element 6	Revenue completely tied to the amount generated, but expense is allocated on an equal share basis.	(1) Allocation of net income on the basis of personal production, and allocation of expense on a pure equal share basis
Purely Production-Based + Graduated Expense Allocation Plans	Revenue Element 4 + Element 5 as an Expense Element Only	Compensation is allocated on a tiered scale, applying staggering to expense rather than revenue.	(1) Allocating revenue based on pure production with market determined overhead assessment with floor (2) Allocating revenue based on a graduated overhead assessment determined established by production

Individualistic Frameworks

Plans characterized by an individualistic framework lie on the opposite end of the spectrum and account for both revenue and expense allocation in their methodologies.[140] The following equation represents this framework.

Allocated Revenue – Allocated Expense = Practitioner Compensation[141]

Taking into consideration both revenue and expense dimensions, individualistic frameworks compensate based on the each practitioner's generated revenue, as well as on some means of allocating practice expense.[142] The general infrastructures that fall under this classification include various combinations of revenue and expense elements.[143] Again, the various basic infrastructures are discussed in subsequent sections, and their respective advantages and disadvantages are addressed in table 3-2.

1. *Purely production-based plans + strict cost accounting plans*, as their name suggests, align with revenue element 4 and expense element 9.[144] These plans focus on allocating both financial elements, in the most direct way, to practitioners.[145] Under such plans, revenue is distributed according to practitioner-specific levels of production, and expense is accounted for using practitioner-specific direct expense allocation (a type of strict cost accounting, which typically includes professional liability insurance, continuing medical education, automobile expenses, cellular phones, and so forth).[146] Typically, this is limited to physician-specific direct expense allocation,

Advantages	Disadvantages
(1) Physicians are directly responsible for their own production and expenses. (2) Physicians are directly accountable for the cost of practice. (3) The framework is generally financially viable because costs are allocated before compensation is paid.	(1) Strict cost accounting systems require extensive administrative infrastructure. (2) Conflict may arise over specific expenditures requiring recurrent discussions or negotiations. (3) Strict cost accounting may lead to "illusion of precision" regarding practice costs.
(1) Physician compensation is directly linked to cost of practice. (2) Less complex administrative infrastructure is required. (3) The framework is generally financially viable because physicians are encouraged to be both productive and aware of costs.	(1) Cost allocation requires considerable discussion or negotiation. (2) Physicians may perceive they are being held accountable for expenditures over which they have little control.
(1) Physician compensation is linked to work effort and cost, but it does not require strict cost accounting. (2) In multispecialty practices, the plan allows primary care physicians to be supplemented by specialists with higher revenue potential. (3) Plans are simple and easy to understand. (4) Plans often are seen as fair under the theory that those who generate more should pay a larger share of operating costs.	(1) Cost allocation requires discussion or negotiation to determine percentages and methodologies. (2) Cost allocation based on production may not be consistent with actual resource use. (3) Specialists may resent subsidizing primary care physicians. (4) Physicians may perceive they are being held accountable for expenditures over which they have little control.
(1) The plan is simple to administer. (2) Most practice expenses are fixed. (3) Teamwork and production are promoted through expense allocation. (4) Less detail and micromanagement is required.	(1) The plan does not address variable expenses. (2) Physicians too focused on production may lose sight of other important areas. (3) Physicians may spend frivolously because expenses are divided equally.
(1) The plan rewards production. (2) The plan links compensation to cost without micromanagement. (3) Physicians, "pay their fair share," based on production, but also they reap the benefits of additional production. (4) The plan may incorporate market-based overhead. (5) The plan discourages excessive production.	(1) Possibility of frequent negotiations over perceived fairness exists. (2) The plan may require specific mix of specialties to succeed. (3) Utilization of market data may be both helpful (benchmarking) and problematic (not representative of specific practice). (4) Physicians may perceive they are only rewarded at the extremes.

with nonphysician practitioner expenses covered under the physician who benefits from the services provided by these nonphysician healthcare professionals.[147]

2. *Purely production-based plans + modified cost accounting plans* are derived from revenue element 4 and expense element 8. Just as with purely production-based plans + strict cost accounting plans, revenue is directly based on production, wherein physicians will earn, essentially, what revenue they generate. In contrast, however, purely production-based plans + modified cost accounting plans essentially place expenditures into broad categories, allocating certain types of expenditures directly to practitioners, other types of expenditures based on practitioner utilization, and the majority of expenditures on some form of fixed (equal-share) basis.[148]

3. *Purely production-based plans + negotiated expense allocation plans* are a combination of revenue element 4 and expense element 7.[149] Although direct allocation of revenue is characteristic of this system, a portion of expense is allocated on the basis of production and a negotiated methodology is used to allocate the rest.[150] An example of this infrastructure is a system wherein 50 percent of expense is allocated per equal share and the remaining 50 percent is allocated on a production basis.[151] An alternate system may allocate 50 percent of expense on a fixed basis, wherein practitioners are responsible for equal shares; 20 percent in equal shares to each division, at which time divisions would allocate their share of the expense among their practitioners; and 30 percent based on the ratio of practitioner production to total production.[152]

4. *Purely production-based plans + equal share expense allocation plans* are a hybrid of revenue element 4 and expense element 6, with revenue allocated entirely based on the amount generated but with expense allocated on an equal share basis [that is, 100 percent equal share allocation; allocation of practitioner-specific expenses to each practitioner, with the remaining expenses allocated equally; 100 percent equal share allocation per, adjusted based on clinical full-time equivalency (FTE)].[153]

5. *Purely production-based plans + graduated expense allocation plans* incorporate revenue element 4 and element 5 as an expense element only—as with many plans aligned to element 5, this plan lies very close to the center of the spectrum and plans that are considered middle ground.[154] While, like graduated revenue allocation plans, this system utilizes a tiered means of allocating compensation, the staggering is applied to *expense* rather than *revenue*.[155] Interestingly, by allocating revenue strictly based on production and graduating the allocation of expense, plans in this category are creating a direct relationship between practitioner production and expense allocation, wherein the distribution of expenditures is graduated based on production levels.[156]

Table 3-3: Compensation Matrix—Muddled Middle Ground

Element Equation	Examples
Revenue Element 2 + Expense Element 6	Allocating revenue based on a set salary plus incentives determined by allocated revenues minus expense, with expenses divided equally.
Revenue Element 3 + Expense Element 6	Allocating revenue based on a set salary plus incentive determined by allocated revenues minus expense, with expenses allocation either shared or based on percentage of production (negotiated beforehand).
Revenue Element 2 + Expense Element 7	Allocating revenue based on a market determined salary, coupled with an incentive based on graduated share of revenues over target.
Revenue Element 3 + Expense Element 7	Allocating revenue based on a defined equal share in revenue allocation with a graduated expense allocation.
Revenue Element 2 + Expense Element 8	Allocating revenue based on a set salary plus an incentive determined by allocated revenues minus expense, with expenses allocated based on modified cost accounting (some part based on utilization).
Revenue Element 3 + Expense Element 8	Allocating revenue based on 70 percent equal share and 30 percent determined by production, coupled with expenses allocated 60 percent equal share with 40 percent based on percentage of production (or other percentage combinations).
Revenue Element 2 + Expense Element 9	Allocating revenue based on a set specialty-specific salary, in addition to, a percentage of revenues based on production utilizing strict cost accounting of practice expenses.
Revenue Element 3 + Expense Element 9	Allocating revenue based on 70 percent equal share and 30 percent determined by production, coupled with explicit equal share expense allocation.

The Muddled Middle Ground

The distribution of infrastructures across the spectrum, as it is discussed previously with regard to the categorical extremities, is based on the tendencies associated with these types of team-oriented and individualistic plans.[157] However, as the previous descriptions and table 3-1 and table 3-2 suggest, this distribution is not concrete.[158] A particular plan may technically be classified as one of these two extremes, but the relationships a specific plan has with one or both dimensions and the actual methodology by which a particular practice implements a given plan may shift that application closer or further away from what is considered the middle ground.[159]

Plans classified as middle ground possess both team-oriented and individualistic attributes, and they incorporate elements from both revenue and expense dimensions.[160] Because a diverse array of middle ground infrastructures exist, some examples, their descriptions, and strengths and weaknesses may be found in table 3-3.[161]

STEP 3: BENCHMARKING

Benchmarking (discussed extensively in chapter 2, *Benchmarking*) is essential to the process of compensation planning; it involves the comparison of key performance indicators (for example, financial, productivity, and quality metrics) against a practice standard for organizations of similar or the same kind.[162] Benchmarking, as part of compensation plan development, serves such purposes as

1. determining where a particular practice stands, in comparison to similar practices, in terms of overhead spending, staffing and staff distribution, supply expenditures, and so forth;

2. identifying problematic areas of operation in which a practice may wish to improve efficiency;

3. comparing physician-specific rates of compensation for fairness;

4. comparing physician-specific rates of production;

5. comparing physician-specific rates of compensation to rates of production and determine if there is appropriate correlation; and

6. ensuring that practices comply with Stark law and antikickback laws and rules, as well (when applicable) laws placed on tax-exempt organizations.[163]

As it relates to compensation planning, benchmarking on the organizational and practitioner levels may be of significance, as discussed in *Practitioner Benchmarking* and *Practice Benchmarking*.[164]

STEP 4: ESTABLISHING THE GENERAL FRAMEWORK

As discussed in steps 2 and 3, the countless systems of compensation implemented in the healthcare industry can be identified through extensive research, evaluated alongside external and internal environments and benchmarking metrics, and categorized within the cultural domain and financial range of the three-dimensional compensation matrix.[165] Based on this research and evaluation, the plans best suited for a given practice can be identified and the foundation, or general framework, for a compensation plan can be developed.[166] The various combinations across the cultural, revenue-based, and expense-based dimensions (see *The Spectrum of Frameworks Derived From the Compensation Matrix*) serve to represent a significant number of foundational options from which a practice may choose as its general framework.[167] An overarching system definition should be consistent with the goals and principles established in step 1.[168] This framework serves as a high-level blueprint of the proposed compensation plan, ensuring that all the appropriate variables and alignment factors are taken into account before delineating the plan details.[169]

STEP 5: DETAILING THE PLAN INFRASTRUCTURE

With an infrastructure established, the details of the plan can be determined by keeping the following overarching questions and their subordinate considerations in mind:[170]

1. How will practitioners be compensated for the work that they do? When addressing this question, the following activities must be taken into consideration:

   a. Clinical

   b. Teaching

   c. Research

   d. Service

2. What should rewards and incentives be based on? Key considerations include:

   a. Productivity

   b. Outcomes and quality

   c. Managed care

   d. Patient satisfaction

   e. Clinical resource management

   f. Teaching

   g. Research

   h. Leadership

3. What should be the standard level of incentive and evaluation? Key levels to consider include:

   a. Individual practitioner

   b. Specialty groups

   c. Entire practice

   d. A combination of these various levels

4. How should incentives factor into compensation? Key considerations include:

   a. Fixed or variable

   b. A certain amount "at risk"

5. What is the correlation between compensation and the practice's overall funds? Key considerations include:

   a. The degree of financial support for the various activities listed in question 1

   b. Expenses for the various levels listed in question 3[171]

By addressing such key questions and considerations within the context of the practice setting, the details of a plan customized to the needs of that practice can be outlined.[172]

STEP 6: GENERATING A FINANCIAL MODEL

The financial model typically is generated by the accounting and finance staff upon request of the committee or other governing entities.[173] A financial model is necessary to ensure that the plan would be fiscally dependable from the practice and practitioner perspectives.[174] In order to generate a financial model of a potential compensation plan, the staff should account for various components taken into consideration up until this point in the process.[175] Historical practice data and industry benchmarks should be used to make projections about the practice's compensation rates within the context of market-based compensation plan levels, measures of productivity, and other performance indicators.[176] A model can effectively demonstrate practitioner shifts in compensation and allow for justification through comparison with market benchmarking data.[177] Though regulatory doubt has been raised with regard to the use of benchmark data in determining the fair market value and commercial reasonableness of a given compensation arrangement, these financial measures have played a significant role in ensuring compliance with legal expectations.[178]

> A financial model is necessary to ensure that the plan would be fiscally dependable from practice and practitioner perspectives.

"Administering the Compensation Plan," p. 137; "Common Pitfalls," pp. 176–77, in "Physician's Compensation: Measurement, Benchmarking, and Implementation," by Lucy R. Carter, CPA, and Sara S. Lankford, CPA, John Wiley & Sons, Inc., 2000; The Compensation Plan Development Process," in "Physician Compensation Plans: State-of-the-Art Strategies," by Bruce A. Johnson, JD, MPA, and Deborah Walker Keegan, PhD, FACMPE, Medical Group Management Association, 2006, p. 34.

The general frameworks of proposed plans typically are evaluated prior to assessing financial models, because the committees and governing entities may wish to assess their plans as they align with predetermined goals and principles in conjunction with the financial consequences of applying the proposed plans in practice.[179]

STEP 7: DEFENDING AGAINST ALTERNATIVE MODELS

Not only is it important to model the changes that a proposed plan, or multiple proposed plans, will encounter, but it is also necessary to compare these changes to the effect that alternative models may have on the practice compensation plan, as well.[180] By comparing various models to each other and removing any cause for bias by approaching the financial data in a "blinded" manner, the committee will not be moved by any personal or misaligned motivations (that is, removing individual physician names to ensure that compensation is not biased unfairly).[181]

STEP 8: OUTLINING TRANSITION AND IMPLEMENTATION STEPS

Once the committee decides on a plan to propose to the practice as best suited to meet the group's needs, a reasonable and thorough plan for transitioning into this new plan must be developed.[182] As previously mentioned, this process may be very gradual, depending on the amount of change that the practice and its members are undertaking.[183] Such means of transitioning may include incrementally planned changes to the plan infrastructure and mechanics over the course of several months or years or the provision of data to practitioners a certain amount of time prior to the actual implementation of the new plan.[184] In doing so, the practice and its members are given what has been determined as ample time to acclimate to the proposed change.[185]

STEP 9: PROPOSING THE NEW PLAN

With the foundational goals, principles, and leadership; supporting rationale and research; and the span of options and the elimination criteria by which the most appropriate plans were identified, benchmarking data and financial models, unbiased evaluations, and reliable action plan, the committee or governing entities of the compensation plan development process are ready to present their proposed plan to the practice as a whole.[186] There must be a means by which practice members can voice their questions, comments, or concerns, be it by way of further meetings with administrative authorities, via e-mail correspondence, through practitioner forums, or by some other means of communication.[187] Before presenting a proposed plan, the development committee or governing entities can reasonably ensure that they have accounted for the primary facets of the development process by utilizing the checklist found in the appendix.[188]

Step 10: Arriving at a Consensus

Arriving at some form of a consensus is the final—and key—step to developing a new compensation plan.[189] The term "consensus" is used lightly in this context, because these plans often are faced with skepticism by practice members. A proposal is considered successful if it is met with mild approval and regarded as tolerable by the majority of practitioners.[190] Assuming the plan was established in a methodical, transparent, and unbiased manner, it should likely be received in this manner.[191]

> The term consensus is used lightly in reference to compensation planning, because these plans are often faced with skepticism to say the least. A proposal is considered successful if it is met with mild approval—regarded as tolerable by the majority of practitioners.

"Four Basic Principles of Compensation," in "Physician's Compensation: Measurement, Benchmarking, and Implementation," by Lucy R. Carter, CPA, and Sara S. Lankford, CPA, John Wiley & Sons, Inc., 2000, p. 56; "The Compensation Plan Development Process," in "Physician Compensation Plans: State-of-the-Art Strategies," by Bruce A. Johnson, JD, MPA, and Deborah Walker Keegan, PhD, FACMPE, Medical Group Management Association, 2006, p. 37.

Where?—The Compensating Enterprise

The various stakeholders concerned with a practice's means of compensation continue to become increasingly interrelated, especially as the level of organizational consolidation and affiliation within the healthcare industry continues to increase and diversify. This section and the one following, discuss practice and practitioner entities separately and as they relate to each other, in order to establish an understanding of the performance, productivity, and practice drivers of compensation planning.

In addition to the factors that influence practitioner performance, the elements that characterize various practice types may be investigated when determining whether a more suitable means of compensation is needed, and they may be taken into consideration when choosing an appropriate compensation plan. Practitioner performance and productivity are largely dependent on a practice's characteristics. Accordingly, a practice should be evaluated as a unit in order to (1) understand the practice infrastructure and environment, (2) assess the staff dynamic and practitioner interactions within the existing organization, and (3) apply this frame of reference to establish standards on the practice level and apply them at the practitioner level.[192]

Practice Benchmarking

On the organizational level, benchmarking is a tool for measuring financial and productivity performance, among other variables, against similar organizations.[193] There are several key considerations that should drive practice-level benchmarking analyses and, therefore, compensation planning, including:

1. whether the practice struggles with insurance collections and sponsor accounts,
2. how the practice's payor mix compares with other practices,
3. what trends in reimbursement strategies are observed within the practice's payor mix,

4. how the practice's aggregate and departmental operating expenditures compare with other practices, and

5. how the practice's performance outcomes compare to those of other practices.[194]

FACTORS INFLUENCING PRACTICE PERFORMANCE

The key benchmarking considerations listed in the prior section are influenced by several characteristics specific to a practice's culture, objectives, and dynamic, namely, the practice's organizational structure (that is, site of service, business structure, and form of governance), community orientation (various aspects of the practice culture), facility metrics (that is, staffing distribution and dynamics), and facilities and services (see chapter 1 of *Professional Practices* for a detailed discussion of these various characteristics of a healthcare organization). Also, factors discussed as the four pillar drivers of productivity and compensation may influence the practice culture and dynamic [for example, the competitive climate among the various practitioners, see *External Indicators (The Four Pillars)*].

ORGANIZATIONAL STRUCTURE

Hospital-Based Versus Office-Based Practices

As discussed in *External Indicators (The Four Pillars)*, the increasingly complex affiliation, consolidation, and ownership arrangement options afforded to healthcare professional practices have significant implications for compensation planning. A practice's level of affiliation and consolidation may be, largely, a result of its organizational structure, because the site of service, business structure, and ownership and governance dynamic will drive (and be driven by) the relationships that the enterprise has with its practitioners.

An organization's characteristic site of service, that is, office- or hospital-based, drives its fundamental affiliations, arrangements, and productivity dynamic and, therefore, its methods of compensation. More important, the distinction between these sites of service has certain legal implications, for example, Stark law restricts the applicability of certain compensation arrangements to specific practice types. Practice business structure and governance (specifically, where ownership lies, employment status, revenue streams, and whether a practice is for-profit or nonprofit) are suggestive of the specific physician and physician-executive compensation and ownership arrangements characteristic of each organization. The legal implications are specified further as they relate to these particular affiliation and ownership dynamics. The legal considerations regarding compensation plans related to certain key organizational structures are discussed in the subsequent section. For more detail related to these regulatory standards, please see *Key Regulatory Considerations*.

Hospital-Based Compensation Arrangements

All hospital-based compensating enterprises must comply with antikickback regulations as well as with state laws and rules governing fraud and abuse. Hospital regulation of this nature will focus (not exclusively) on alignment with thresholds for fair market value and commercial reasonableness (see *Key Regulatory Considerations*).[195]

Hospital-Executive Compensation Arrangements

Given the trend in excess hospital executive compensation, as well as the public outcry against abuse of hospital funds in the nonprofit sector, alleged violators are subject to particularly severe scrutiny.[196] For more information on current IRS initiatives against excessive executive compensation, see *IRS Initiatives.*

Hospital-Employed Physician Compensation Arrangements

Hospital-employed physician compensation arrangements are held to the same stringent expectations, that is, they must be at fair market value and commercially reasonable.[197] Stark law may not be as detrimental under these circumstances, because it does not apply to practitioners employed by only one hospital.[198] These issues are discussed in further detail in *Key Regulatory Considerations.*

Hospital-Outside Provider Compensation Arrangements: Independent Contractors Versus Group Practice Physicians

When hospitals form contractual relationships with outside practitioners (namely physicians), both entities must be weary of potential fraud and abuse violations, as well as noncompliance with corporate practice of medicine guidelines.[199]

Under Stark IV, any hospital that bills for services provided by an outside source (physician practice, contractor, clinical laboratory, and so forth) is considered a DHS entity; as a result, interactions between billing hospitals and physicians providing health services are classified as "under arrangements" and must comply with one or more Stark exceptions or safe harbor laws.[200] Most frequently, contractual arrangements align with the ownership exception to the Stark law (for more information on Stark law and its exceptions, see *The Stark Law* or chapter 3 of *An Era of Reform*).[201]

Per-Click Arrangements

Additionally, the exceptions for space and equipment leases, fair market value compensation, and indirect compensation arrangements were altered under Stark IV to prohibit charging for rented space and equipment on a "per-click," or per-unit basis.[202] This amendment, enacted in October 2009, forbids the billing of lessees for services provided by proxy of referrals from the DHS entity lessors (for more information on per-click arrangements, see chapter 3 of *An Era of Reform*).[203]

Gainsharing

Gainsharing, though formally undefined, refers to arrangements whereby hospital cost savings for patient care are allocated by some negotiated means to the appropriate physician(s).[204] Although the OIG has issued advisory reports that suggest its approval of gainsharing arrangements, the Centers for Medicare and Medicaid (CMS) has released guidance that may suggests otherwise, cautioning against gainsharing arrangements under which the Stark law may be implicated.[205] Organizations may fall out of compliance as a result of impermissible incentive payment, shared savings programs (for more information of gainsharing and its regulations see chapter 3 of *An Era of Reform*), or both.[206]

Office-Based Compensation Arrangements

Office-based compensation arrangements are subject to the same regulations as are hospitals.[207] Multi-specialty practices and referrals between physicians with ownership interest are arrangements subject to heightened scrutiny and enforcement of regulations and laws related to fraudulent Medicare and Medicaid reimbursement claims.[208] The following section regarding business structure as a determinant in compensation planning, while applicable to both hospital- and office-based practices, is of most significance to the latter.

Business Structure: Balancing Long- Versus Short-Term Partnership Goals[209]

As mentioned in *Impact of Experience on Compensation*, methods of compensation may differ for new associates (as well as for celebrated and long-term practitioners). The entry of new associates into a practice setting, namely a physician-owned practice setting, is often met by the skepticism of veteran practitioners, because the transition may be at the expense of their compensation and shareholdings. Weighting the long-term investment of incentivizing established practitioners against the short-term compromise of introducing new physicians into the practice may be a necessary consideration in determining how such transitions will factor into practitioner compensation.

This is of particular significance with respect to associates transitioning into ownership. Over the years, established group practices have often presented **buy-in** offers to new associates as one of the understood terms of their employment. As a measure of precaution laced with incentive, physician-owned group practices may incorporate buy-in conditions into the understood terms of an their associate employment agreements.[210] Most often, this is contingent upon the satisfactory completion of one to three years of employment as an employed associate physician within the practice.[211] Physicians contemplating entry into an associateship or employment arrangement with a group practice may place a significant amount of weight on the terms and contingencies of transitioning from associateship to ownership.[212] See figure 3-2 for a medical practice buy-in flow chart.

Practice Buy-In Process: Considerations

Employment agreements for associate physicians tend to include only vague and conditional provisions regarding the potential for buy-in to ownership interest in the practice.[213] The interim nature of this loosely termed "agreement" theoretically allows the practice more flexibility should the operational, financial, or market circumstances of the practice change or should the associate physician fail to meet the expectations of the practice, partners, or both.[214] The contingency of a tentative buy-in may protect healthcare professional practices from violating certain tax regulations.[215] Despite legitimate reasons for not specifying the details of the transactions, both owners and aspiring or current associates should, from the onset of buy-in discussions with potential associates, exhibit a cursory understanding of the potential buy-in calculation methods that may be utilized in the circumstances under which an associate transitions into ownership, as well as how such buy-in amounts will be paid.[216] The subsequent employment relationship will be much improved if the practice can preempt potential problems when the matter is ultimately negotiated.[217]

Period of Buy-In

The period of buy-in is variable and circumstantial. For most physician-owned practices, the buy-in period should last between one to three years, however, larger groups are encouraged to consider extending the duration to four or five years.[218] Additionally, it is not uncommon for enterprises in some markets, namely office-based, physician-owned practices, to defer the decision to offer a buy-in until *after* the first two years of employment, up to three years.[219] Primary care practices typically require shorter first employment periods than do specialty and surgical practices primary care practices (for example, after one to two years of employment), due to high demand for superior quality manpower.[220] Alternately, prolonged transitions into partnership characteristic of less pressed specialties and larger group practices, may be due in part to the challenge of determining whether a new physician is a suitable candidate for long-term ownership after only one year of employment and in part to the required length of time to allow the associate physician to achieve the required buy-in amount through a **foregone compensation**

Figure 3-2: Medical Practice Buy-In Flow Chart

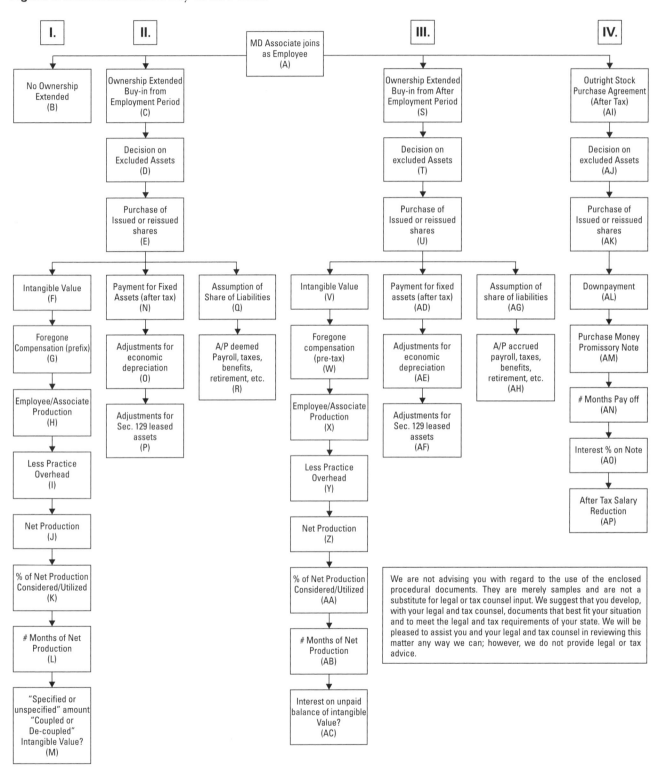

formula.[221] However, in many situations, a new physician may clearly demonstrate all of the characteristics and the commitment necessary to become an owner after, for example, one year.[222] Should the employment contract include a clause permitting the owner or owners to assess the situation at year end, a buy-in offer may be extended (or withheld) at this time. This type of clause provides flexibility to the practice and incentivizes to the associate to demonstrate his or her desire for ownership.

> Primary care practices typically require shorter first employment periods than specialty and surgical practices (for example, after one to two years of employment), due to high demand for high-quality manpower.

"Buying In to Partnership: Make Arrangements Clear," in Partner Buy-ins, Physician's Advisory Vital Topic Series, 1999, pp. 3–4.

Ownership Percentage of the Practice

Most often physicians ultimately own equal shares in the practice; however, it is not unusual to encounter group practices with ownership or equity allocated between "senior" and "junior" shareholders or partners.[223] The "one-doc-one shareholder" approach ordinarily is simpler to administer and maintain and is, therefore, more realistic for small groups.

Methods of Buy-In Payment

The decision regarding how the new physician will pay the buy-in amount is often considered in the context of two general categories, that is, "before-tax funding" and "after-tax funding."[224] The practice should consider payment for the new physician's share of the practice's fixed assets (and perhaps, specified other balance sheet assets) on an after-tax basis, which action will create an appropriate tax basis for the new physician's ownership.[225] The buy-in amount that relates to the practice's intangible value (often misguidedly called "goodwill") is often paid for on a before-tax basis, accomplished though the implementation of income differentials between the new physician and the existing owners of the practice for a specified period of time.[226] Because the buy-in transaction may have to be reported to the IRS, appropriate tax research and documentation are required to support the structure of the buy-in.[227]

> The buy-in amount that relates to the practice's intangible value (often misguidedly called "goodwill") is often paid on a before-tax basis, accomplished though the implementation of income differentials between the new physician and the existing owners of the practice for a specified period of time.

"Chapter 4—Group Partnerships, Clinics, and Corporations," in ""Selling or Buying a Medical Practice," by Gary R. Schaub, Medical Economics Books, 1988, pp. 67–74; "How to Structure a New Partner's 'Buy-In'," and "What Does Growing Uncertainty Over Goodwill Value Mean to New Partner Buy-Ins," in Partner Buy-Ins, Physician's Advisory Vital Topic Series, 1999, pp. 7–8, 11–12.

Instead of including accounts receivable in the buy-in, often parties have found that a more efficient way to handle the practice's current accounts receivable (at the time of the buy-in) may be to declare a bonus of the net realizable receivable to inure to the sole benefit of the current owners. This amount can be paid out over a period of years and becomes a regular overhead item of the practice, effectively reducing the cost of the buy-in to the new physician-owner. If accounts receivable are not included in the buy-in formula, the existing owners are compensated for their share of the practice's intangibles, separate and aside from the accounts receivable, which inure to the benefit of the current owners.[228]

Regardless of whether a specific buy-in amount is negotiated and the nature of the buy-in payment(s) and process, the valuation consultant must analyze the transaction in terms of fair market value.[229] This requires determining the terms and amounts of payments made and the conversion of all of these considerations (if possible) to an economic basis, stated as a cash payment amount.[230]

Each and every detail of the subject practice's transactions or offers should be investigated and analyzed to determine whether they are relevant, valid, and unskewed indications of value. Be aware of the economic realities of transactional related consulting agreements that do not require the seller to perform actual services and may actually represent part of the sale proceeds. Further adjustments may be required for changes since the date of the sale or offer within the practice, the healthcare industry, the specialty, the managed care environment, or other factors, including differences in the size of the respective interests involved in the transactions. Prior transactions also may include acquisitions by the practice as a useful guideline in the valuation process.

Consolidation and Integration

Fee-For-Service Versus Capitation

As discussed in *Key Reimbursement Considerations* and *Impact of Consolidation on Compensation*, compensation is influenced by the payment systems under which practices are reimbursed, which are becoming increasingly diverse with increased consolidation and integration, resulting in MCOs, emerging practice models, and reform initiatives. Fee-for-service systems of reimbursement typically foster practices that incentivize productivity inasmuch as services are reimbursed on the basis of a predetermined fee schedule. Alternately, capitation is based on beneficiary enrollment, and, as such, the fixed amount a practice is reimbursed for a given time is meant to contain costs and control utilization by mandating how much the practice can be expected to perform under the existing fee schedule. Such systems do not intrinsically encourage practitioners to increase productivity, and unless other efforts are made to channel practice focus, may lead practitioners to treat administration of care as secondary to maximizing patient enrollment and minimizing utilization to heighten revenue. Reimbursement reform efforts intended to contain costs (for example, bundled payments and P4P) also may have an effect on practice compensation methodologies, due to the performance objectives they emphasize and the incentives with which practitioners are provided.

Community Orientation

Compensating Nonclinical Services

Two general kinds of methods for compensating nonclinical services may be implemented: (1) a direct method and (2) an indirect method.[231] Direct methods involve compensating based on performance of specific and defined tasks. Indirect methods are methods that are inherent to the infrastructure of a compensation plan, that is, agreed upon nonclinical performance expectations and incentives are built into the compensation plan in and of itself.[232] For example, compensation plans that exhibit indirect methods of nonclinical compensation may detail contingent performance requirements of base salary compensation or eligibility for incentives.

Some of the most common types non-clinical activities taken into consideration when developing compensation plans are listed in **Nonclinical Productivity**, and the performance measures used to quantify nonclinical productivity for each type of activity are outlined in table 3-4.[233]

Compensating Academic Activities and Clinical Research

As of 2010, economic trends in healthcare have led department administrators to revisit the means by which physicians are compensated for academic and research-based services.[234] Reduced reimbursement and heightened regulatory stringency have led to diminutive increases in cost-of-living salaries. As such, physicians seeking pay raises have focused on activities that generate revenue, letting research fall by the wayside. As a result, many administrators are abandoning the "cost of doing business" approach to compensation and are instead implementing performance-based incentive methodologies.[235] Several successful algorithms have been cited in the literature. However, these strategies all derive from the same objectives: (1) to design physician salaries such that a percentage is variable; (2) to motivate physicians and staff to either directly or indirectly participate in clinical, research-based, or academic activities that generate more revenue; (3) to focus on certain performance indicators set by and specific to the organization; and (4) to compensate physicians based on their level of productivity.[236] The model an organization chooses to implement depends on the organization's specific priorities and objectives.

The XYZ model[237] is considered among the oldest and most commonly used compensation and incentive plan:

$$Total\ Salary = X + X' + Y + Z$$

Table 3-4: Performance Expectations for Measuring Productivity and Determining Compensation

Performance Expectation Categories	Measures
Service Activities	Administrative responsibilities, leadership roles, committee involvement, professional activities, community outreach
Fiscal or Financial Variables	Cost of practice, cost per work relative value unit, cost as a percent of total medical revenue, billing and coding compliance
Quality of Clinical and Nonclinical Work	Healthcare Effectiveness Data and Information Set measures, emergency department utilization, laboratory utilization, pharmacy utilization, referrals, medical record documentation, patient satisfaction
Accessibility	Next third available appointment, physician availability, wait times
Team Orientation	Interpersonal effectiveness, teamwork, levels of engagement, esprit de corps
Teaching Activities	Hours of teaching, assigned service as a preceptor, resident supervision, medical student lectures
Research Activities	Extramural funding, percent grants submitted versus rewarded

> The XYZ model is considered among the oldest and most commonly used compensation and incentive plan.

"Designing a Physician Compensation and Incentive Plan for an Academic Healthcare Center," by Donna Steinmetz, MSHA, FACMPE, the American College of Medical Practice Executives, Medical Group Management Association, September 2005; "Compensation and Incentive Plans for Physicians," by Charles Stiernberg, MD, MBA, November 2001, www.physicianspractice.com/ (accessed October 29, 2009).

In this formula, X is the fixed and guaranteed base-salary (based upon the amount of time worked), X' is specific to academic medical institutions and represents an expanded base-salary (based on physician's academic rank, step, and academic programmatic unit, which is quantified on a 0–9 scale and multiplied by a health sciences differential), Y represents a negotiable salary (may be variable or fixed), and Z represents a variable, incentive-based salary component (based on productivity) that usually accounts for 5 to 20 percent of total compensation.[238]

Productivity can be quantified collectively for all activities or separately for each type of activity. Activities may be categorized in several ways, typically accounting for clinical practice, research, and academic performance and leadership. Productivity can be quantified relative to the organization's prioritized performance indicators and, therefore, can be based on work relative value units (wRVUs), gross charges, net charges, or collections, or a weighted combination of these variables.[239] The purest of these metrics is the wRVU and perhaps the least pure is collections, because it is sensitive to nonphysician staff performance and collections as well as payor mix, and, as a result, it is subject to the most statistical variability.

A point system may be implemented to allow for the combinatorial quantification of productivity. The X' and Y components are set each year and derive from (1) nonnegotiable practice requirements (that is, patient care and, for academic medical centers, teaching) and (2) supplementary activities. Should employees fail to fulfill the nonnegotiable requirements, they may be penalized with negative points in the X' category, Y category, or both. Alternately, employees that exceed baseline expectations for one or more practice activities will be awarded points in the appropriate classification(s).[240] Administrators establish point values based on the availability of funds. Unlike X, X', and Y components, which are negotiated annually, the Z component is negotiated quarterly, based upon professional fee balances.[241]

A relative value unit (RVU) methodology also may be used to quantify clinical and research productivity, whereby RVUs are assigned to, for example, the salary support generated through grants and contracts and are weighted according to the amount of support received. Compensation for a particular research venture is then calculated based on the established RVU and each employee's role or level of involvement.[242] The implementation of an RVU system that quantifies productivity independently for each activity category reportedly increased the reserve balance 244 percent, increased total compensation 20 percent for all employees, and increased grant funding from the National Institutes of Health by a factor of 1.7.[243]

Compensating Leadership and Administrative Tasks

The appropriate allocation of time and manpower to nonclinical, administrative, managerial, and executive duties is often dependent upon

1. the number of practitioners (typically physicians) responsible for these duties,
2. the amount of time each practitioners dedicates to their respective duties, and
3. the specific administrative duties performed.[244]

The first step in the general methodology used to determine compensation for leadership and administrative tasks is to identify the practitioners partaking in these activities and to list and describe their related tasks, duties, responsibilities, and accountabilities.

Next, existing benchmark data can be used to conduct an analysis of existing market conditions and determine the amount of time and compensation needed to perform nonclinical, administrative, and executive tasks in the designated type of medical practice. Data is available in several forms, and, as such, several algorithms may be considered in determining the most appropriate means by which to conduct this analysis.

Depending on the data and algorithm used, as well as the amount of data available, the estimates generated can be general or customized to reflect department characteristics, the number of physicians, and the distribution of tasks among the involved physicians. Next, suggested compensation plans can be evaluated based on the distribution of tasks.

Due to increasingly stringent regulation of executive compensation (see *Hospital-Executive Compensation Arrangements*), it is important that hospitals allocating payment for administrative, directorship, and executive duties are extremely methodical and thorough in their benchmarking, financial analysis, and continued assessment of their compensation plans and that their compensation practices are transparent and well documented.

Compensating Outreach

To an even greater degree than other nonclinical activities, a negative connotation is often linked to outreach activities, because some physicians believe that the productivity and quality of their work–life balance will be subpar at their service site, especially in comparison to their home base practice site.[245] As such, practitioners may "cherry pick" locations based on their perceived comparability to other locations. In order to minimize the bias associated with the provision of outreach services, the following compensation methodologies intended to incentivize this form of nonclinical activities have been developed: (1) crediting travel time and (2) calculating efficiency of production.[246]

By negotiating a system of travel time crediting, practitioners who engage in outreach activities may be compensated for what many consider to be a "lost opportunity for clinical practice production."[247] When assigning credit to travel time,

1. estimate the approximate travel time from one practice site to another;

2. establish an evaluation and management Current Procedural Terminology (CPT) code that represents offsite work; and

3. estimate the standard number of CPT units per hour that a practitioner can be expected to perform.[248]

To calculate efficiency of production,

1. designate a defined fraction of the total compensation pool to be allocated using an efficiency component;

2. determine the amount of time each practitioner dedicates to activities in traditional clinical *and* outreach locations;

3. define and list each practitioner's primary locations, that is, all locations that are *not* outreach locations;

4. measure each practitioner's clinical production at primary location(s) using measures specific to those location(s);

5. establish a standardized measure of clinical production at primary locations representative of all practitioners;

6. determine each practitioner's clinical production at primary location(s) using the standardized measure established in the previous step and calculate rate of production (for example, WRVU per hour); and

7. allocate efficiency component according to (a) WRVUs per hour of scheduled time at the primary practice location and (b) time assigned to outreach sites—in doing so, practitioners not only get rewarded for their outreach involvement but also for their ability to contribute to nonclinical production without forfeiting clinical productivity.[249]

Facility Metrics: Physician Staffing Versus Nonphysician Staffing

The distribution of physician-to-nonphysician employees and contractors, as outlined in the practice's facility metrics, will likely influence the practice's compensation dynamic, because each provider type is compensated differently.[250] As first described in the *Introduction* and reinforced over the course of *volume 1*, **nonphysician providers (NPPs)** play a diverse role in the provision of healthcare services. They may work synergistically with physicians, as a physician supplement for the provision of select services, or in parallel to physicians for the provision of services that, though comparable to physician services, are entirely outside the scope of physician practices. As such, NPPs may be further divided into three categories based on the types of services they provide:

1. *Allied health professionals* (also known as *parallel providers*) have a scope of professional practice that is separate, distinct, and, essentially, parallel to the scope of physician practice.

2. *Mid-level providers* (also known as *triage providers*) are trained to provide a specific subset of physician services, with the *original* objective of providing "triage" relief for physicians by enhancing patient throughput.[251] Mid-level providers are afforded a significant level of autonomy within their scope of practice, and, as such, they may act alongside—or independent of—physicians under certain conditions for the provision of previously determined services.

3. *Technicians and paraprofessionals* (also known as *physician extenders*) that either provide manpower support or highly technical services both necessary for and contingent upon the provision of certain specialized physician services.

A practitioner that is placed in one of these categories is not always providing the services that distinguish them from practitioners in the other categories. For example, mid-level providers are relied upon for the provision of specialized services that are incident to physician services, but they also exercise a certain measure of independence because they can autonomously provide a specific scope of services *in lieu* of physicians.[252]

An appropriate measure of NPP productivity should reflect the type of services *performed*, not the type of services *permitted* under law. Accordingly, several methods are used to compensate nonphysician professionals:

1. *Unit-based compensation infrastructures*: wherein nonphysician providers receive a straight salary, contingent upon certain performance expectations and based on their schedule, patient intake, and generated revenue. Under this methodology, nonphysician providers would be informed of the expectations they are required to meet. Reciprocally, the practice will honor the negotiated budget for NPP compensation, benefits, and expenses;

2. *Guaranteed share compensation infrastructures*: wherein nonphysician provider compensation is derived according to market rates and contingent with certain baseline performance expectations;

3. *Pure production compensation infrastructures*: wherein nonphysician provider compensation is derived from a separate pool of revenue generated entirely by the characteristic nonphysician providers, who are also expected to cover their own expenditures; or

4. *Purely production-based plans + modified cost accounting compensation infrastructures* essentially place expenses into several broad categories, allocating certain types of expenditures directly to practitioners and allocating other types of expenditures on the basis of practitioner utilization, with the majority of expenditures on a fixed or equal-share basis.[253]

The plan utilized is contingent upon the role played by the employed or contracted NPPs. For example, despite the expansion of mid-level provider autonomy, the supportive role of NPPs, as part of specialized medical or surgical teams, remains particularly significant.[254] In such settings, NPPs provide specialized manpower support to aid in the provision of physician services rather than independently providing billable services that generate revenue. As a result, NPPs employed as, for example, surgical assistants may be considered a direct expense to the physician(s) that are benefiting from their services and may be accounted for using purely production-based + modified cost accounting compensation infrastructures.[255]

In addition to accounting for the services that are delegated to healthcare professionals within a practice setting, market indicators and benchmark data should be consulted to ensure that compensation methods align with the market norm.

The process of compensating mid-level providers as well as technicians and paraprofessionals differs from physician compensation because mid-level providers are not a DHS entity under Stark law.[256] Because paraprofessionals are still provided with a Medicare provider number, they are subject to the antikickback statute, as well as to federal and state fraud and abuse laws.[257] In addition, reimbursement for mid-level providers and paraprofessionals is subject to specific CMS percentages based on circumstance and service.

FACILITIES AND SERVICES: SINGLE SPECIALTY VERSUS MULTISPECIALTY PRACTICE

Lastly, the specialty dynamic and mix will affect the means by which each type of physician or nonphysician practitioner is compensated. Additionally, the continuum of care afforded across single specialty *and* multispecialty practices will likely influence market control and, therefore, practice incentives and compensation.

WHO?—THE PRACTITIONER

Traditional methods of practitioner compensation are structured as though clinical productivity is the sole indicator of performance. As a result of various external drivers (see *External Indicators (The Four Pillars)*), the increasingly complex and diverse practice dynamics (discussed in *Where?—The Compensating Enterprise*), and the evolution, diversification, and expansion of practitioner tasks, duties, responsibilities, and accountabilities, productivity-based benchmarks are no longer a sufficient means of measuring practitioner performance, and, therefore, compensation methodologies derived on the basis of such assumptions may be inadequate.[258] Instead, the method a practice uses to compensate a practitioner should account for

1. the practitioner's clinical productivity,

2. the practitioner's nonclinical productivity, and

3. the practice's characteristics, business structure, and legal considerations (see *Where?—The Compensating Enterprise*).[259]

> Traditional methods of practitioner compensation are structured as though clinical productivity is the sole indicator of performance.

"The Effects of Consolidation on Physician Compensation: Expectations and Future Challenges," by Daniel K. Zismer and David A. Kaplan, in "Physician Compensation Arrangements," by Daniel K. Zismer, An Aspen Publication, 1999, pp. 6–8.

PRACTITIONER BENCHMARKING

The roles and responsibilities of practitioners have diversified to complement an array of healthcare organization types. In other words, an individual's practice performance is, in part, a result of the practice environment.[260] Practitioners that emulate a practice's clinical or nonclinical objectives are contributing to the success of the organization.[261] The elements that should be factored into measuring practitioner performance are substrata of clinical and nonclinical productivity.[262]

Benchmarking clinical and nonclinical productivity on the practitioner level can help address several key considerations when developing a compensation plan, namely

1. where practitioner compensation falls with respect to the statistical distribution of other practitioners, either internally or externally;

2. where practitioner clinical production falls with respect to the statistical distribution of other practitioners, either internally or externally; and

3. where practitioner performance in other areas (that is, nonclinical performance measures) falls with respect to the statistical distribution of other practitioners, either internally or externally.[263]

PRACTITIONER PROFILING

By assessing practitioner data, the proper balance of quality, efficiency, and clinical or nonclinical productivity can be established, and a compensation plan can be constructed accordingly.[264] However, it is also essential to keep the process of data communication transparent. **Practice profiling** is the reporting of raw, unbiased practice data to practitioners.[265]

Specifically, practitioners receive periodic report cards that enable them to assess their performance relative to their peers, by comparing utilization data, quality indicators, satisfaction measures, and office review data.[266] Keeping practitioners engaged in initial and continued benchmarking and performance assessments will not only reduce tension and controversy but also will motivate practitioners to improve their performance.[267]

FACTORS INFLUENCING PRACTITIONER PERFORMANCE

CLINICAL PRODUCTIVITY

Clinical productivity is one of the primary benchmarking considerations that should navigate the development of a compensation plan. There are four practitioner-specific drivers of clinical productivity: time, efficiency, volume, and quality performance.[268] These factors should comprise a significant portion of the benchmark analysis conducted during the compensation plan development process. Plotting productivity against each of these factors will allow the practice to assess the practitioner's performance in each area and will determine the standard distribution of each variable across the staff in order to establish methods of weighting the areas against each other, by which productivity can be quantified across the practice.[269]

Time

The amount of time a practitioner dedicates to clinical activity will, naturally, influence the practitioner's level of clinical productivity. Because much benchmarking is done on the basis of a full-time equivalent norm, regardless of what other measures of work and effort are taken into consideration when establishing a system of compensation, the amount of time worked will, inevitably, affect how a practitioner is compensated.[270] However, a growing emphasis is being placed on academic, administrative, executive, volunteer and other nonclinical activities in measuring practitioners' performance and compensating practitioners for their work.[271] The time dedicated to such tasks inevitably affects the amount of time spent on clinical activities. Nonclinical activities as a growing portion of practitioner responsibilities will be discussed further in *Nonclinical Productivity* and *Community Orientation*.

Efficiency

A practitioner's level of efficiency will also, invariably, contribute to his or her level of productivity and, therefore, his or her level of compensation,[272] that is, the amount of time dedicated to clinical tasks and the amount produced will likely reflect a practitioner's contribution to the practice's clinical throughput.[273] Taking efficiency into consideration will, in part, account for the discrepancy introduced by nonclinical time worked, as well as the variability introduced by fewer hours worked or part-time practitioners. However, a variable that may contribute to efficiency and should, therefore, be taken into consideration is the degree or type of practitioner specialization and what implications that may have on the degree of difficulty of work, type of work, or both that a practitioner performs.[274] When determining how to compensate practitioners for their services, efficiency may need to be measured using graduated performance expectations that take into consideration higher levels of specialization.[275] This element of competition is discussed in *Key Competition Considerations*.

Volume

The volume of clinical production is a third variable contributing to the measure of practitioner productivity, though similar considerations, such as time and efficiency, should be taken into consideration.[276] As with time considerations, nonclinical "production" may deter from clinical production, and it should be taken into consideration when calculating productivity from any measure of volume.[277] Also, the area and degree of specialization will likely contribute to the amount of patient throughput, because more complex areas of practice will require more time and, therefore, appear less "efficient."[278] The practitioner's level of experience also will have a positive or negative effect on the amount of work produced, as well as on time and efficiency measures.[279] As previously indicated, these practitioner characteristics are discussed further in *Key Competition Considerations*.

Quality

The quality of care administered to a patient is the fourth—and final—personal driver of productivity. Quality benchmarking has taken and increasingly predominant place in measuring practitioner performance and compensating accordingly.[280] As discussed in *Key Reimbursement Considerations*, P4P methods of reimbursement have emerged in recent years. Because compensation plans are largely aligned to reimbursement trends, quality of care measures have become increasingly important to quantifying productivity.[281]

NONCLINICAL PRODUCTIVITY

Drivers of nonclinical productivity, or rather, nonclinical activities that may factor into practitioner performance may include

1. service activities,

2. fiscal or financial variables,

3. quality of clinical and nonclinical work,

4. accessibility,

5. team-orientation,

6. teaching activities, and

7. research activities.[282]

A practitioner's performance in any of these areas is driven by personal motivators as well as the by various practice attributes, as discussed in *Where?—The Compensating Enterprise*. Measures used when determining compensation for these activities are listed in table 3-4.[283] The methods, considerations, and concerns related to compensating nonclinical performance are discussed in *Community Orientation*.

CONCLUSION

With the diversification of healthcare professional practice enterprises and workforce practitioners, compensation for services rendered went from being fairly simple to invariably complex and delicate. An array of compensation options, as demonstrated in the previous sections, became available to meet the emerging challenges associated with the demand for shorter hours and increased leave times; reduced demand for productivity; increased emphasis on noncash benefits; increased opportunity for, and emphasis on, professional development in nonclinical areas (that is, research, teaching, and management); and emphasis on professional training and development. With those countless options emerged countless legal violations, business faux pas, competitive strains, and financial variables that factored into the development of practice-tailored compensation plans. With movements in healthcare reform, increased enforcement of fraud and abuse compliance and emphasis on a more fluid and effective continuum of care will likely add to the weight attributed to these drivers of compensation planning.

🔑 Key Sources

Key Source	Description	Citation	Hyperlink
"Special Fraud Alerts"	Advisory publications issued by the Office of the Inspector General. As pertinent to this chapter, some editions of this publication address arrangements that may violate laws and regulations governing fraud and abuse.	"Fraud Alerts," by the U.S. Department of Health and Human Services, Office of the Inspector General, January 13, 2010, http://oig.hhs.gov/fraud/fraudalerts.asp (accessed February 2, 2010).	http://oig.hhs.gov/fraud/fraudalerts.asp
Internal Revenue Service (IRS)	The IRS is organized to carry out the responsibilities of the secretary of the Treasury under section 7801 of the Internal Revenue Code.		www.irs.gov/
Council on Graduate Medical Education	Authorized by Congress in 1986 to provide ongoing assessment of physician workforce trends	"Physician Compensation Plans: State-of-the-Art Strategies," by Bruce A. Johnson, JD, MPA and Deborah Walker Keegan, PhD, FACMPE, Medical Group Management Association, 2006, p. v.	www.cogme.gov/
Cost Survey	Surveys performed and published by the Medical Group Management Association		www.mgma.com
Cost Survey for Single-Specialty Practices			www.mgma.com
Cost Survey for Multi-Specialty Practices			www.mgma.com
Cost Survey for Cardiovascular/Thoracic Surgery and Cardiology			www.mgma.com
Cost Survey for Orthopedic Practices			www.mgma.com
Cost Survey for Integrated Delivery System Practices			www.mgma.com
Medical Group Compensation and Financial Survey			www.mgma.com
Ambulatory Surgery Center Performance Survey			www.mgma.com
Physician Compensation and Production Survey			www.mgma.com
Management Compensation Survey			www.mgma.com
Physician Placement Starting Salary Survey			www.mgma.com
Academic Practice Compensation and Production Survey for Faculty and Management			www.mgma.com
Financial Ratios	Ratios calculated and published by Schonfeld & Associates, Inc., based on public reports published by the IRS	"IRS Corporate Financial Ratios" Twenty-Fourth Edition, Schonfeld & Associates, Inc., April 15, 2009.	www.saibooks.com/
ASC Financial Benchmarking Survey	Survey performed and published by the Foundation for Ambulatory Surgery in America, Advantage Consulting, Inc.		https://members.ascassociation.org/eweb/DynamicPage.aspx?Site=ASC&WebKey=e1b0a66d-f0d3-4894-a342-77d419ae716b

(continued)

Key Source	Description	Citation	Hyperlink
Hospital Salary & Benefits Report	Surveys performed and published by the Hospital & Healthcare Compensation Service; John R. Zabka Associates, Inc.		www.hhcsinc.com/hcsreports.htm
Physician Salary Survey Report			www.hhcsinc.com/hcsreports.htm
Physician Compensation Survey Results	Surveys performed and published by Sullivan Cotter and Associates, Inc.		www.sullivancotter.com/surveys/purchase.php
Physician On-Call Pay Survey Report			www.sullivancotter.com/surveys/purchase.php
Physician Compensation and Productivity Survey Report			www.sullivancotter.com/surveys/purchase.php
Survey of Manager and Executive Compensation in Hospital and Health Systems			www.sullivancotter.com/surveys/purchase.php
Medical Group Executive Compensation Survey			www.sullivancotter.com/surveys/purchase.php
Physician Executive Compensation Survey	Survey performed and published by The American College of Physician Executives		www.acpe.org/membersonly/compensationsurvey/index.aspx?theme=c
Report on Medical School Faculty Salaries	Survey performed and published by the American Academy of Medical Colleges		https://services.aamc.org/publications/index.cfm?fuseaction= Product.displayForm&prd_id=252
Intellimarker ASC Benchmarking Study	Survey performed and published by the VMG		www.vmghealth.com/

⚑ Associations

Type of Association	Professional Association	Description	Citation	Hyperlink
National	Medical Group Management Association (MGMA)	"Since 1926, MGMA has delivered networking, professional education and resources and political advocacy for medical practice management." MGMA's mission is to constantly "improve the performance of medical group professionals."	"About the Medical Group Management Association," Medical Management Group Association, www.mgma.com/about/ (accessed February 19, 2010).	www.mgma.com
National	American Academy of Medical Colleges (AAMC)	"The AAMC represents all 131 accredited U.S. and 17 accredited Canadian medical schools; approximately 400 major teaching hospitals and health systems, including 68 Department of Veterans Affairs medical centers; and nearly 90 academic and scientific societies. Through these institutions and organizations, the AAMC represents 125,000 faculty members, 75,000 medical students, and 106,000 resident physicians."	"About the AAMC," by the American Academy of Medical Colleges, www.aamc.org/about/start.htm (accessed February 19, 2010)	www.mgma.com
National	American Medical Group Association (AMGA)	"AMGA represents medical groups and organized systems of care, including some of the nation's largest, most prestigious integrated healthcare delivery systems." AMGA's mission is to improve "health care for patients by supporting multispecialty medical groups and other organized systems of care."	"About AMGA," American Medical Group Association, www.amga.org/AboutAMGA/index_aboutAMGA.asp (accessed February 19, 2010).	www.amga.org

APPENDIX:

WAIT! The Compensation Plan Checklist

☐ Alignment with Internal Environment

    ☐ Have the goals of the proposed plan been outlined?

    ☐ Does the proposed plan emulate the practice mission, vision, principles, and goals?

    ☐ Does it strive for a balanced system of compensation?

☐ Clear Performance Expectations

    ☐ Have minimum performance expectations been established?

    ☐ Do these performance expectations take administrative, teaching, research-related, and/or other non-clinical activities into consideration?

☐ Fiscally Reliable

    ☐ Is the practice afforded certain safeguards and securities in case the plan is unsuccessful?

    ☐ Does the plan take into consideration the flow of money through the practice, across both clinical and non-clinical activities?

    ☐ Have future practice development, cash flow, reserves, and/or other needs been accounted for?

    ☐ In the circumstance of a shortage, how will the compensation plan change? (Reduced base salaries? Supplement? Equivalent percentage or dollar? An algorithmic means?)

☐ Legally Permissible

    ☐ Is the plan in compliance with Stark Law and Anti-Kickback Statute?

    ☐ Is the plan in line with *fair market value* and *commercial reasonableness*?

    ☐ Has up-to-date documentation been generated?

☐ Clear and Consistent, With No Room for Convolution

    ☐ Is there a written plan?

☐ Have specific rules and parameters been outlined?

☐ For any potential areas of ambiguity that may arise, has some form of structure or ownership been delineated?

☐ **Simple: Easily Understood and Conveyed**

☐ Will this plan easily be disseminated between and among practitioners and practice administrators?

☐ **Practice-Wide Transparency and Consistency**

☐ Have a set of rules been established within the plan for practice-wide application?

☐ Are quantifiable and replicable examples been included in the plan?

☐ Does the plan call for perpetual reporting on the basis of management, productivity, efficiency, etc.?

☐ **Well-Weighted Individual and Group Accountability**

☐ In what way does the plan allocate responsibility? On the basis of a team oriented culture? Weighted entirely on the individual? Both?*

---

* "Compensation Plan Decision and Implementation," in "Physician Compensation Plans: State-of-the-Art Strategies," by Bruce A. Johnson, JD, MPA and Deborah Walker Keegan, PhD, FACMPE, Medical Group Management Association, 2006, p. 46.

Endnotes

1 "Just so Stories" By Rudyard Kipling and J.M. Gleeson, Garden City, NY: Doubleday and Company, Inc., 1902, p. 65.

2 "Physician Compensation Plans: State-of-the-Art Strategies," By Bruce A. Johnson and Deborah Walker Keegan, Englewood, CO: Medical Group Management Association, 2006, p. 9.

3 "Physician Compensation Plans: State-of-the-Art Strategies," By Bruce A. Johnson and Deborah Walker Keegan, Englewood, CO: Medical Group Management Association, 2006, p. 9; "Physician Compensation: Models for Aligning Financial Goals and Incentives" By Kenneth M. Hekman, New York, NY: McGraw-Hill, 2000, p. 153-157.

4 "Physician's Compensation: Measurement, Benchmarking, and Implementation," by Lucy R. Carter and Sara S. Lankford, New York, NY: John Wiley & Sons, Inc., 2000, p. 62.

5 "Physician Compensation Plans: State-of-the-Art Strategies," By Bruce A. Johnson and Deborah Walker Keegan, Englewood, CO: Medical Group Management Association, 2006, p. 10.

6 "Physician Compensation Plans: State-of-the-Art Strategies," By Bruce A. Johnson and Deborah Walker Keegan, Englewood, CO: Medical Group Management Association, 2006, p. 10; "Physician Compensation: Models for Aligning Financial Goals and Incentives" By Kenneth M. Hekman, New York, NY: McGraw-Hill, 2000, p. 153-154.

7 "Physician Compensation Plans: State-of-the-Art Strategies," By Bruce A. Johnson and Deborah Walker Keegan, Englewood, CO: Medical Group Management Association, 2006, p. 10.

8 "Physician Compensation Plans: State-of-the-Art Strategies," By Bruce A. Johnson and Deborah Walker Keegan, Englewood, CO: Medical Group Management Association, 2006, p. 10; "Physician Compensation: Models for Aligning Financial Goals and Incentives" By Kenneth M. Hekman, New York, NY: McGraw-Hill, 2000, p. 156-157; "Physician's Compensation: Measurement, Benchmarking, and Implementation," by Lucy R. Carter and Sara S. Lankford, New York, NY: John Wiley & Sons, Inc., 2000, p. 26-27.

9 "Physician Compensation Plans: State-of-the-Art Strategies," By Bruce A. Johnson and Deborah Walker Keegan, Englewood, CO: Medical Group Management Association, 2006, p. 10.

10 *Ibid.*

11 *Ibid.*

12 "Physician Compensation Plans: State-of-the-Art Strategies," By Bruce A. Johnson and Deborah Walker Keegan, Englewood, CO: Medical Group Management Association, 2006, p. 9-10.

13 "Physician Compensation Plans: State-of-the-Art Strategies," By Bruce A. Johnson and Deborah Walker Keegan, Englewood, CO: Medical Group Management Association, 2006, p. 25.

14 "Medicare and State Health Care Programs: Fraud and Abuse" 42 CFR Part 1001 (July 29, 1991); "Physician's Compensation: Measurement, Benchmarking, and Implementation," By Lucy R. Carter and Sara S. Lankford, New York, NY: John Wiley & Sons, Inc., 2000, p. 32; "Advisory Opinion 07-10A", Office of Inspector General, Advisory Opinion (September 27, 2007), Accessed at http://oig.hhs.gov/fraud/docs/advisoryopinions/2007/AdvOpn07-10A.pdf (Accessed 5/7/10) p. 8.

15 "Medicare and Medicaid Patient & Program Protection Act of 1987" Pub. L. 100-93 (August 18, 1987).

16 "Physician's Compensation: Measurement, Benchmarking, and Implementation," By Lucy R. Carter and Sara S. Lankford, New York, NY: John Wiley & Sons, Inc., 2000, p. 32.

17 "Physician's Compensation: Measurement, Benchmarking, and Implementation," By Lucy R. Carter and Sara S. Lankford, New York, NY: John Wiley & Sons, Inc., 2000, p. 45.

18 "Physician Compensation Plans: State-of-the-Art Strategies," By Bruce A. Johnson and Deborah Walker Keegan, Englewood, CO: Medical Group Management Association, 2006, p. 146.

19 "Physician Compensation Plans: State-of-the-Art Strategies," By Bruce A. Johnson and Deborah Walker Keegan, Englewood, CO: Medical Group Management Association, 2006, p. 147.

20 *Ibid.*

21 "Partner Buy-Ins" The Physician's Advisory: Vital Topic Series, Advisory Publications, Conshohocken, PA: Leif C. Beck, LL.B, C.P.B.C, 1999, p. 3-4; "Physician Compensation Plans: State-of-the-Art Strategies," By Bruce A. Johnson and Deborah Walker Keegan, Englewood, CO: Medical Group Management Association, 2006, p. 147.

22 "Stark Rule Proposals Finalized" By Cathy Dunlay and Kevin Hilvert, Schottenstein Zox & Dunn Resources, August 13, 2008, http://www.szd.com/resources.php?NewsID=1184&method=unique (Accessed 8/14/08).

23 "Physician Compensation Plans: State-of-the-Art Strategies," By Bruce A. Johnson and Deborah Walker Keegan, Englewood, CO: Medical Group Management Association, 2006, p. 147.

24 "Health Care Fraud: Enforcement and Compliance" By Robert Fabrikant, et al., New York, NY: Law Journal Press, 2007, p. 2-62, 2-64.

25 "Fraud Enforcement and Recovery Act of 2009: Sec. 4 Clarifications to the False Claims Act to Reflect the Original Intent of the Law" S.386, Congress, February 5, 2009, Accessed at http://thomas.loc.gov/cgi-bin/query/D?c111:1./temp/~c111Xp38c3:: (Accessed 5/1/09); "What is the False Claims Act and Why is it Important?" The False Claims Act Legal Center, 2009, http://www.taf.org/whyfca.htm (Accessed 09/8/09).

26 "Health Care Fraud and Abuse: Practical Perspectives" By Linda A. Baumann, Washington, DC: The American Bar Association, 2002, p. 112-113.

27 "Physician Compensation Plans: State-of-the-Art Strategies," By Bruce A. Johnson and Deborah Walker Keegan, Englewood, CO: Medical Group Management Association, 2006, p. 147; "Physician's Compensation: Measurement, Benchmarking, and Implementation," By Lucy R. Carter and Sara S. Lankford, New York, NY: John Wiley & Sons, Inc., 2000, p. 37.

28 United States of America v. A. Alvin Greber, 760 F.2d 68 (April 30, 1985).

29 "Physician Compensation Plans: State-of-the-Art Strategies," By Bruce A. Johnson and Deborah Walker Keegan, Englewood, CO: Medical Group Management Association, 2006, p. 147; "Physician's Compensation: Measurement, Benchmarking, and Implementation," By Lucy R. Carter and Sara S. Lankford, New York, NY: John Wiley & Sons, Inc., 2000, p. 38; "The Hypocrisy of the One Purpose Test in Anti-Kickback Enforcement Law" By Eugene E. Elder, BNA Health Care Fraud Report, Vol. 4, No. 15 (July 26, 2000), http://www.akingump.com/files/Publication/ef37d179-30e2-4266-b4f8-a8481641073c/Presentation/PublicationAttachment/eada4c55-dae7-498d-befa-adefb6d82b9d/445.html (Accessed 10/06/09), p. 546.

30 "Special Fraud Alerts" Office of Inspector General, Department of Health and Human Services, Fed. Reg. Vol. 65, (December 19, 1994).

31 "Physician Compensation Plans: State-of-the-Art Strategies," By Bruce A. Johnson and Deborah Walker Keegan, Englewood, CO: Medical Group Management Association, 2006, p. 147.

32 "Advisory Opinion 07-10A" Office of Inspector General, Advisory Opinion (September 27, 2007), Accessed at http://oig.hhs.gov/fraud/docs/advisoryopinions/2007/AdvOpn07-10A.pdf (Accessed 5/7/10) p. 10; "OIG Compliance Program For Individual and Small Group Physician Practices" 65 Fed. Reg. 59434 (October 5, 2000).

33 "Medicare and Medicaid Programs; Physicians' Referrals to Health Care Entities With Which They Have Financial Relationships" 63 Fed. Reg. 1700-1703 (January 9, 1998).

34 American Lithotripsy Society v. Thompson, 215 F.Supp.2d 23, 27 (D.D.C. July 12, 2002).

35 *Ibid.*

36 "Physician Compensation Plans: State-of-the-Art Strategies," By Bruce A. Johnson and Deborah Walker Keegan, Englewood, CO: Medical Group Management Association, 2006, p. 148; "Physician's Compensation: Measurement, Benchmarking, and Implementation," by Lucy R. Carter and Sara S. Lankford, New York, NY: John Wiley & Sons, Inc., 2000, p. 62.

37 "Physician's Compensation: Measurement, Benchmarking, and Implementation," by Lucy R. Carter and Sara S. Lankford, New York, NY: John Wiley & Sons, Inc., 2000, p. 62; "S Corp, C Corp, LLC, LLP which is best?" By Dennis Murray, Medical Economics, March 5, 2004, http://license.icopyright.net/user/viewFreeUse.act?fuid=NDIxMzI4MA%3D%3D (Accessed 7/30/09).

38 "Employment Tax Audits of Exempt Hospitals Could Turn Up Other Issues, Attorneys Warn" 18 Health Law Reporter 1653, (December 24, 2009), Accessed at http://news.bna.com/hlln/display/batch_print_display.adp (Accessed 12/28/09) p. 1-4; "Enforcement Efforts Take Aim at Executive Compensation of Tax-Exempt Health Care Entities" by Candace L. Quinn and Jeffrey D. Mamorsky, 18 Health Law Reporter 1640, (December 17, 2009) Accessed at http://news.bna.com/hlln/display/batch_print_display.adp (Accessed 12/28/09), p.1, 7.

39 "An Introduction to I.R.C. 4958 (Intermediate Sanctions)" By Lawrence M. Brauer et al., Internal Revenue Service (2002), http://apps.irs.gov/pub/irs-tege/eotopich02.pdf (Accessed 12/28/09), p. 270-273.

40 "Employment Tax Audits of Exempt Hospitals Could Turn Up Other Issues, Attorneys Warn" 18 Health Law Reporter 1653, (December 24, 2009), Accessed at http://news.bna.com/hlln/display/batch_print_display.adp (Accessed 12/28/09) p. 1-4; "Enforcement Efforts Take Aim at Executive Compensation of Tax-Exempt Health Care Entities" by Candace L. Quinn and Jeffrey D. Mamorsky, 18 Health Law Reporter 1640, (December 17, 2009) Accessed at http://news.bna.com/hlln/display/batch_print_display.adp (Accessed 12/28/09).

41 Ibid.

42 "Sec. 4959—Taxes on Failures by Hospital Organization" Pub. L. 111-148 (March 23, 2010) Accessed at http://frwebgate.access.gpo.gov/cgi-bin/getdoc.cgi?dbname=111_cong_bills&docid=f:h3590enr.txt.pdf (Accessed 5/13/10).

43 "Enforcement Efforts Take Aim at Executive Compensation of Tax-Exempt Health Care Entities" by Candace L. Quinn and Jeffrey D. Mamorsky, 18 Health Law Reporter 1640, (December 17, 2009) Accessed at http://news.bna.com/hlln/display/batch_print_display.adp (Accessed 12/28/09).

44 "Physician Compensation Plans: State-of-the-Art Strategies," By Bruce A. Johnson and Deborah Walker Keegan, Englewood, CO: Medical Group Management Association, 2006, p. 25; "Physician Compensation: Models for Aligning Financial Goals and Incentives" By Kenneth M. Hekman, New York, NY: McGraw-Hill, 2000, p. 156-157; "Physician's Compensation: Measurement, Benchmarking, and Implementation" By Lucy R. Carter and Sara S. Lankford, New York, NY: John Wiley & Sons, Inc., 2000, p. 5.

45 "Physician Compensation Plans: State-of-the-Art Strategies," By Bruce A. Johnson and Deborah Walker Keegan, Englewood, CO: Medical Group Management Association, 2006, p. 25.

46 "Physician Compensation Plans: State-of-the-Art Strategies," By Bruce A. Johnson and Deborah Walker Keegan, Englewood, CO: Medical Group Management Association, 2006, p. 131; "Physician Compensation: Models for Aligning Financial Goals and Incentives" By Kenneth M. Hekman, New York, NY: McGraw-Hill, 2000, p. 156-157.

47 "Physician Compensation Plans: State-of-the-Art Strategies," By Bruce A. Johnson and Deborah Walker Keegan, Englewood, CO: Medical Group Management Association, 2006, p. 131; "Physician's Compensation: Measurement, Benchmarking, and Implementation" By Lucy R. Carter and Sara S. Lankford, New York, NY: John Wiley & Sons, Inc., 2000, p. 5.

48 "Physician Compensation Plans: State-of-the-Art Strategies," By Bruce A. Johnson and Deborah Walker Keegan, Englewood, CO: Medical Group Management Association, 2006, p. 131.

49 "Pay-for-Performance in Health Care" By Jim Hahn, CRS Report for Congress, Washington D.C.: Congressional Research Service, November 2, 2006, p. CRS-2.

50 Ibid.

51 "Pay for Performance: Quality- and Value- Based Reimbursement," By Norman (Chip) Harbaugh Jr., Pediatric Clinics of North America, Volume 56, Number 4, (2009),Accessed at http://www.pediatric.theclinics.com/article/S0031-3955(09)00057-1/pdf Accessed 5/7/10), p. 997-998; "Physician Compensation Arrangements: Management & Legal Trends" By Daniel K. Zismer, Gaithersburg, MD: Aspen Publishers, Inc., 1999, p. 16-17; "Physician Compensation Plans: State-of-the-Art Strategies," By Bruce A. Johnson and Deborah Walker Keegan, Englewood, CO: Medical Group Management Association, 2006, p. 131.

52 Ibid.

53 "Physician Compensation Plans: State-of-the-Art Strategies," By Bruce A. Johnson and Deborah Walker Keegan, Englewood, CO: Medical Group Management Association, 2006, p. 25; "Physician's Compensation: Measurement, Benchmarking, and Implementation" By Lucy R. Carter and Sara S. Lankford, New York, NY: John Wiley & Sons, Inc., 2000, p. 83.

54 "Physician Compensation Arrangements: Management & Legal Trends," By Daniel K. Zismer, Gaithesburg, MD: Aspen Publishers, Inc., 1999, p. 113.

55 "Physician Compensation Arrangements: Management & Legal Trends" By Daniel K. Zismer, Gaithersburg, MD: Aspen Publishers, Inc., 1999, p. 14-15; "Physician Compensation Plans: State-of-the-Art Strategies," By Bruce A. Johnson and Deborah Walker Keegan, Englewood, CO: Medical Group Management Association, 2006, p. 25; "Physician's Compensation: Measurement, Benchmarking, and Implementation," By Lucy R. Carter and Sara S. Lankford, New York, NY: John Wiley & Sons, Inc., 2000, p. 16, 26-27.

56 "Physician Compensation: Models for Aligning Financial Goals and Incentives" By Kenneth M. Hekman, New York, NY: McGraw-Hill, 2000, p. 19; "Physician Compensation Plans: State-of-the-Art Strategies" By Bruce A. Johnson and Deborah Walker Keegan, Englewood, CO: Medical Group Management Association, 2006, p. 232-233.

57 "Physician Compensation Plans: State-of-the-Art Strategies," By Bruce A. Johnson and Deborah Walker Keegan, Englewood, CO: Medical Group Management Association, 2006, p. 181-184; "Physician Compensation: Models for Aligning Financial Goals and Incentives" By Kenneth M. Hekman, New York, NY: McGraw-Hill, 2000, p. 156-157; "Physician's Compensation: Measurement, Benchmarking, and Implementation," By Lucy R. Carter and Sara S. Lankford, New York, NY: John Wiley & Sons, Inc., 2000, p. 55, 83-84.

58 "Physician Compensation Plans: State-of-the-Art Strategies," By Bruce A. Johnson and Deborah Walker Keegan, Englewood, CO: Medical Group Management Association, 2006, p. 181; "Physician Compensation: Models for Aligning Financial Goals and Incentives" By Kenneth M. Hekman, New York, NY: McGraw-Hill, 2000, p. 156-157; "Physician's Compensation: Measurement, Benchmarking, and Implementation," By Lucy R. Carter and Sara S. Lankford, New York, NY: John Wiley & Sons, Inc., 2000, p. 55, 83-84.

59 "Physician Compensation Arrangements: Management & Legal Trends," By Daniel K. Zismer, Gaithesburg, MD: Aspen Publishers, Inc., 1999, p. 7; "Physician Compensation Plans: State-of-the-Art Strategies," By Bruce A. Johnson and Deborah Walker Keegan, Englewood, CO: Medical Group Management Association, 2006, p. 181-184; "Physician Compensation: Models for Aligning Financial Goals and Incentives," By Kenneth M. Hekman, New York, NY: McGraw-Hill, 2000, p. 55, 58-59, 77, 159-160; "Physician's Compensation: Measurement, Benchmarking, and Implementation" By Lucy R. Carter and Sara S. Lankford, New York, NY: John Wiley & Sons, Inc., 2000, p. 59-61.

60 "Physician Compensation Plans: State-of-the-Art Strategies," By Bruce A. Johnson and Deborah Walker Keegan, Englewood, CO: Medical Group Management Association, 2006, p. 181-184.

61 "Partner Buy-Ins" The Physician's Advisory: Vital Topic Series, Advisory Publications, Conshohocken, PA: Leif C. Beck, LL.B, C.P.B.C, 1999, p. 2, 3-4, 7-8, 11-12; "Physician Compensation Plans: State-of-the-Art Strategies," By Bruce A. Johnson and Deborah Walker Keegan, Englewood, CO: Medical Group Management Association, 2006, p. 181; "Physician Compensation: Models for Aligning Financial Goals and Incentives" By Kenneth M. Hekman, New York, NY: McGraw-Hill, 2000, p. 156-157; "Physician's Compensation: Measurement, Benchmarking, and Implementation," By Lucy R. Carter and Sara S. Lankford, New York, NY: John Wiley & Sons, Inc., 2000, p. 55, 83-84.

62 Ibid.

63 "Physician Compensation Plans: State-of-the-Art Strategies" By Bruce A. Johnson and Deborah Walker Keegan, Englewood, CO: Medical Group Management Association, 2006, p. 232-233.

64 Ibid.

65 "Paying Physicians: Options for Controlling Cost, Volume, and Intensity of Services," by Mark V. Pauly, et al., Ann Arbor, MI: Health Administration Press, 1992, p. 31; "Physician Compensation Plans: State-of-the-Art Strategies" By Bruce A. Johnson and Deborah Walker Keegan, Englewood, CO: Medical Group Management Association, 2006, p. 232-233.

66 "Physician Compensation Plans: State-of-the-Art Strategies" By Bruce A. Johnson and Deborah Walker Keegan, Englewood, CO: Medical Group Management Association, 2006, p. 232-233.

67 "Paying Physicians: Options for Controlling Cost, Volume, and Intensity of Services," by Mark V. Pauly, et al., Ann Arbor, MI: Health Administration Press, 1992, p. 31.

68 "Physician Compensation Plans: State-of-the-Art Strategies," By Bruce A. Johnson and Deborah Walker Keegan, Englewood, CO: Medical Group Management Association, 2006, p. 40-41.

69 "Physician Compensation: Models for Aligning Financial Goals and Incentives" By Kenneth M. Hekman, New York, NY: McGraw-Hill, 2000, p. 23; "Physician Compensation Plans: State-of-the-Art Strategies," By Bruce A. Johnson and Deborah Walker Keegan, Englewood, CO: Medical Group Management Association, 2006, p. 40-41.

70 "Physician Compensation Plans: State-of-the-Art Strategies," By Bruce A. Johnson and Deborah Walker Keegan, Englewood, CO: Medical Group Management Association, 2006, p. 40-41; "Physician's Compensation: Measurement, Benchmarking, and Implementation" By Lucy R. Carter and Sara S. Lankford, New York, NY: John Wiley & Sons, Inc., 2000, p. 56.

71 "Physician Compensation Plans: State-of-the-Art Strategies," By Bruce A. Johnson and Deborah Walker Keegan, Englewood, CO: Medical Group Management Association, 2006, p. 40-41.

72 "Physician Compensation Plans: State-of-the-Art Strategies," By Bruce A. Johnson and Deborah Walker Keegan, Englewood, CO: Medical Group Management Association, 2006, p. 19.

73 *Ibid.*

74 *Ibid.*

75 *Ibid.*

76 *Ibid.*

77 "Physician Compensation Plans: State-of-the-Art Strategies," By Bruce A. Johnson and Deborah Walker Keegan, Englewood, CO: Medical Group Management Association, 2006, p. 19-20.

78 *Ibid.*

79 "Physician Compensation Plans: State-of-the-Art Strategies," By Bruce A. Johnson and Deborah Walker Keegan, Englewood, CO: Medical Group Management Association, 2006, p. 19.

80 "Physician Compensation Plans: State-of-the-Art Strategies," By Bruce A. Johnson and Deborah Walker Keegan, Englewood, CO: Medical Group Management Association, 2006, p. 41; "Physician's Compensation: Measurement, Benchmarking, and Implementation" By Lucy R. Carter and Sara S. Lankford, New York, NY: John Wiley & Sons, Inc., 2000, p. 56.

81 "Physician Compensation: Models for Aligning Financial Goals and Incentives" By Kenneth M. Hekman, New York, NY: McGraw-Hill, 2000, p. 26; "Physician Compensation Plans: State-of-the-Art Strategies," By Bruce A. Johnson and Deborah Walker Keegan, Englewood, CO: Medical Group Management Association, 2006, p. 41.

82 "Physician Compensation Plans: State-of-the-Art Strategies," By Bruce A. Johnson and Deborah Walker Keegan, Englewood, CO: Medical Group Management Association, 2006, p. 41; "Physician's Compensation: Measurement, Benchmarking, and Implementation" By Lucy R. Carter and Sara S. Lankford, New York, NY: John Wiley & Sons, Inc., 2000, p. 56.

83 "Physician Compensation Plans: State-of-the-Art Strategies," By Bruce A. Johnson and Deborah Walker Keegan, Englewood, CO: Medical Group Management Association, 2006, p. 24.

84 "Physician Compensation Plans: State-of-the-Art Strategies," By Bruce A. Johnson and Deborah Walker Keegan, Englewood, CO: Medical Group Management Association, 2006, p. 17-19, 21, 27, 28; "Physician Compensation: Models for Aligning Financial Goals and Incentives," By Kenneth M. Hekman, New York, NY: McGraw-Hill, 2000, p. 65-67; "Physician's Compensation: Measurement, Benchmarking, and Implementation," By Lucy R. Carter and Sara S. Lankford, New York, NY: John Wiley & Sons, Inc., 2000, p. 59-61, 133-138.

85 "Physician Compensation Plans: State-of-the-Art Strategies," By Bruce A. Johnson and Deborah Walker Keegan, Englewood, CO: Medical Group Management Association, 2006, p. 17; "Physician's Compensation: Measurement, Benchmarking, and Implementation," By Lucy R. Carter and Sara S. Lankford, New York, NY: John Wiley & Sons, Inc., 2000, p. 133.

86 "Physician Compensation Plans: State-of-the-Art Strategies," By Bruce A. Johnson and Deborah Walker Keegan, Englewood, CO: Medical Group Management Association, 2006, p. 17-18; "Physician Compensation: Models for Aligning Financial Goals and Incentives" By Kenneth M. Hekman, New York, NY: McGraw-Hill, 2000, p. 158; "Physician's Compensation: Measurement, Benchmarking, and Implementation" By Lucy R. Carter and Sara S. Lankford, New York, NY: John Wiley & Sons, Inc., 2000, p. 133-138.

87 "Physician Compensation Plans: State-of-the-Art Strategies," By Bruce A. Johnson and Deborah Walker Keegan, Englewood, CO: Medical Group Management Association, 2006, p. 18.

88 *Ibid.*

89 *Ibid.*

90 "Physician Compensation Plans: State-of-the-Art Strategies," By Bruce A. Johnson and Deborah Walker Keegan, Englewood, CO: Medical Group Management Association, 2006, p. 18; "Physician Compensation: Models for Aligning Financial Goals and Incentives," By Kenneth M. Hekman, New York, NY: McGraw-Hill, 2000, p. 118-119.

91 *Ibid.*

92 *Ibid.*

93 "Physician Compensation Plans: State-of-the-Art Strategies," By Bruce A. Johnson and Deborah Walker Keegan, Englewood, CO: Medical Group Management Association, 2006, p. 18-19.

94 "Physician Compensation Plans: State-of-the-Art Strategies," By Bruce A. Johnson and Deborah Walker Keegan, Englewood, CO: Medical Group Management Association, 2006, p. 21; "Physician Compensation: Models for Aligning Financial Goals and Incentives," By Kenneth M. Hekman, New York, NY: McGraw-Hill, 2000, p. 118-119.

95 "Physician Compensation Plans: State-of-the-Art Strategies," By Bruce A. Johnson and Deborah Walker Keegan, Englewood, CO: Medical Group Management Association, 2006, p. 29-30.

96 "Physician Compensation Plans: State-of-the-Art Strategies," By Bruce A. Johnson and Deborah Walker Keegan, Englewood, CO: Medical Group Management Association, 2006, p. 27; "Physician Compensation: Models for Aligning Financial Goals and Incentives," By Kenneth M. Hekman, New York, NY: McGraw-Hill, 2000, p. 66-67; "Physician's Compensation: Measurement, Benchmarking, and Implementation" By Lucy R. Carter and Sara S. Lankford, New York, NY: John Wiley & Sons, Inc., 2000, p. 133-135.

97 "Physician Compensation Plans: State-of-the-Art Strategies," By Bruce A. Johnson and Deborah Walker Keegan, Englewood, CO: Medical Group Management Association, 2006, p. 27-28; "Physician's Compensation: Measurement, Benchmarking, and Implementation," By Lucy R. Carter and Sara S. Lankford, New York, NY: John Wiley & Sons, Inc., 2000, p. 57-61, 133-138, 176-178.

98 "Physician Compensation Plans: State-of-the-Art Strategies," By Bruce A. Johnson and Deborah Walker Keegan, Englewood, CO: Medical Group Management Association, 2006, p. 28.

99 "Physician Compensation: Models for Aligning Financial Goals and Incentives" By Kenneth M. Hekman, New York, NY: McGraw-Hill, 2000, p. 20-21; "Physician Compensation Plans: State-of-the-Art Strategies," By Bruce A. Johnson and Deborah Walker Keegan, Englewood, CO: Medical Group Management Association, 2006, p. 28.

100 "Physician Compensation Arrangements: Management & Legal Trends" By Daniel K. Zismer, Gaithersburg, MD: Aspen Publishers, Inc., 1999, p. 25-27; "Physician Compensation Plans: State-of-the-Art Strategies," By Bruce A. Johnson and Deborah Walker Keegan, Englewood, CO: Medical Group Management Association, 2006, p. 29-30, 59-69; "Physician Compensation Strategies" By Craig W. Hunter and Max Reiboldt, Second Edition, American Medical Association, 2004, p. 52; "Physician Compensation: Models for Aligning Financial Goals and Incentives" By Kenneth M. Hekman, New York, NY: McGraw-Hill, 2000, p. 83-85.

101 "Physician Compensation: Models for Aligning Financial Goals and Incentives" By Kenneth M. Hekman, New York, NY: McGraw-Hill, 2000, p. 159-160.

102 "Physician Compensation Plans: State-of-the-Art Strategies," By Bruce A. Johnson and Deborah Walker Keegan, Englewood, CO: Medical Group Management Association, 2006, p. 29-30; "Physician Compensation: Models for Aligning Financial Goals and Incentives" By Kenneth M. Hekman, New York, NY: McGraw-Hill, 2000, p. 159-160.

103 "Physician Compensation Plans: State-of-the-Art Strategies," By Bruce A. Johnson and Deborah Walker Keegan, Englewood, CO: Medical Group Management Association, 2006, p. 29-30; "Physician's Compensation: Measurement, Benchmarking, and Implementation" By Lucy R. Carter and Sara S. Lankford, New York, NY: John Wiley & Sons, Inc., 2000, p. 59-61.

104 "Physician Compensation Plans: State-of-the-Art Strategies," By Bruce A. Johnson and Deborah Walker Keegan, Englewood, CO: Medical Group Management Association, 2006, p. 62.

105 *Ibid.*

106 "Physician Compensation Plans: State-of-the-Art Strategies," By Bruce A. Johnson and Deborah Walker Keegan, Englewood, CO: Medical Group Management Association, 2006, p. 61.

107 "Physician Compensation Arrangements: Management & Legal Trends," By Daniel K. Zismer, Gaithersburg, MD: Aspen Publishers, Inc., 1999, p. 160; "Physician Compensation Plans: State-of-the-Art Strategies," By Bruce A. Johnson and Deborah Walker Keegan, Englewood, CO: Medical Group Management Association, 2006, p. 61; "Physician Compensation: Models for Aligning Financial Goals and Incentives" By Kenneth M. Hekman, New York, NY: McGraw-Hill, 2000, p. 36-40.

108 "Physician Compensation Plans: State-of-the-Art Strategies," By Bruce A. Johnson and Deborah Walker Keegan, Englewood, CO: Medical Group Management Association, 2006, p. 61; "Physician Compensation: Models for Aligning Financial Goals and Incentives" By Kenneth M. Hekman, New York, NY: McGraw-Hill, 2000, p. 38-40.

109 "Physician Compensation Plans: State-of-the-Art Strategies," By Bruce A. Johnson and Deborah Walker Keegan, Englewood, CO: Medical Group Management Association, 2006, p. 61; "Physician's Compensation: Measurement, Benchmarking, and Implementation" By Lucy R. Carter and Sara S. Lankford, New York, NY: John Wiley & Sons, Inc., 2000, p. 59-61.

110 "Physician Compensation Arrangements: Management & Legal Trends" By Daniel K. Zismer, Gaithersburg, MD: Aspen Publishers, Inc., 1999, p. 62; "Physician Compensation Plans: State-of-the-Art Strategies," By Bruce A. Johnson and Deborah Walker Keegan, Englewood, CO: Medical Group Management Association, 2006, p. 63.

111 "Physician Compensation Arrangements: Management & Legal Trends," By Daniel K. Zismer, Gaithersburg, MD: Aspen Publishers, Inc., 1999, p. 27-28, 37-40, 62; "Physician Compensation Plans: State-of-the-Art Strategies," By Bruce A. Johnson and Deborah Walker Keegan, Englewood, CO: Medical Group Management Association, 2006, p. 63.

112 "Physician Compensation Arrangements: Management & Legal Trends," By Daniel K. Zismer, Gaithersburg, MD: Aspen Publishers, Inc., 1999, p. 37, 62; "Physician Compensation Plans: State-of-the-Art Strategies," By Bruce A. Johnson and Deborah Walker Keegan, Englewood, CO: Medical Group Management Association, 2006, p. 63.

113 "Physician Compensation Arrangements: Management & Legal Trends" By Daniel K. Zismer, Gaithersburg, MD: Aspen Publishers, Inc., 1999, p. 62; "Physician Compensation Plans: State-of-the-Art Strategies," By Bruce A. Johnson and Deborah Walker Keegan, Englewood, CO: Medical Group Management Association, 2006, p. 63.

114 "Physician Compensation Plans: State-of-the-Art Strategies," By Bruce A. Johnson and Deborah Walker Keegan, Englewood, CO: Medical Group Management Association, 2006, p. 64; "Physician's Compensation: Measurement, Benchmarking, and Implementation" By Lucy R. Carter and Sara S. Lankford, New York, NY: John Wiley & Sons, Inc., 2000, p. 86-88.

115 "Physician Compensation Plans: State-of-the-Art Strategies," By Bruce A. Johnson and Deborah Walker Keegan, Englewood, CO: Medical Group Management Association, 2006, p. 64.

116 "Physician Compensation Arrangements: Management & Legal Trends" By Daniel K. Zismer, Gaithersburg, MD: Aspen Publishers, Inc., 1999, p. 69; "Physician Compensation Plans: State-of-the-Art Strategies," By Bruce A. Johnson and Deborah Walker Keegan, Englewood, CO: Medical Group Management Association, 2006, p. 69.

117 "Physician Compensation Plans: State-of-the-Art Strategies," By Bruce A. Johnson and Deborah Walker Keegan, Englewood, CO: Medical Group Management Association, 2006, p. 68; "Physician's Compensation: Measurement, Benchmarking, and Implementation" By Lucy R. Carter and Sara S. Lankford, New York, NY: John Wiley & Sons, Inc., 2000, p. 86.

118 "Physician Compensation Plans: State-of-the-Art Strategies," By Bruce A. Johnson and Deborah Walker Keegan, Englewood, CO: Medical Group Management Association, 2006, p. 68.

119 *Ibid.*

120 "Physician Compensation Plans: State-of-the-Art Strategies," By Bruce A. Johnson and Deborah Walker Keegan, Englewood, CO: Medical Group Management Association, 2006, p. 70.

121 "Physician Compensation Plans: State-of-the-Art Strategies," By Bruce A. Johnson and Deborah Walker Keegan, Englewood, CO: Medical Group Management Association, 2006, p. 68; "Physician's Compensation: Measurement, Benchmarking, and Implementation" By Lucy R. Carter and Sara S. Lankford, New York, NY: John Wiley & Sons, Inc., 2000, p. 88.

122 "Physician Compensation Plans: State-of-the-Art Strategies," By Bruce A. Johnson and Deborah Walker Keegan, Englewood, CO: Medical Group Management Association, 2006, p. 68.

123 "Physician Compensation Plans: State-of-the-Art Strategies," By Bruce A. Johnson and Deborah Walker Keegan, Englewood, CO: Medical Group Management Association, 2006, p. 68-69.

124 "Physician Compensation Plans: State-of-the-Art Strategies," By Bruce A. Johnson and Deborah Walker Keegan, Englewood, CO: Medical Group Management Association, 2006, p. 66.

125 "Physician Compensation Plans: State-of-the-Art Strategies," By Bruce A. Johnson and Deborah Walker Keegan, Englewood, CO: Medical Group Management Association, 2006, p. 83.

126 "Physician Compensation Plans: State-of-the-Art Strategies," By Bruce A. Johnson and Deborah Walker Keegan, Englewood, CO: Medical Group Management Association, 2006, p. 70.

127 "Physician Compensation Plans: State-of-the-Art Strategies," By Bruce A. Johnson and Deborah Walker Keegan, Englewood, CO: Medical Group Management Association, 2006, p. 84.

128 "Physician Compensation Arrangements: Management & Legal Trends" By Daniel K. Zismer, Gaithersburg, MD: Aspen Publishers, Inc., 1999, p. 62; "Physician Compensation Plans: State-of-the-Art Strategies," By Bruce A. Johnson and Deborah Walker Keegan, Englewood, CO: Medical Group Management Association, 2006, p. 84.

129 "Physician Compensation Plans: State-of-the-Art Strategies," By Bruce A. Johnson and Deborah Walker Keegan, Englewood, CO: Medical Group Management Association, 2006, p. 84.

130 "Physician Compensation Plans: State-of-the-Art Strategies," By Bruce A. Johnson and Deborah Walker Keegan, Englewood, CO: Medical Group Management Association, 2006, p. 84-85.

131 "Physician Compensation Plans: State-of-the-Art Strategies," By Bruce A. Johnson and Deborah Walker Keegan, Englewood, CO: Medical Group Management Association, 2006, p. 84-91.

132 "Physician Compensation Plans: State-of-the-Art Strategies," By Bruce A. Johnson and Deborah Walker Keegan, Englewood, CO: Medical Group Management Association, 2006, p. 84-86

133 *Ibid.*

134 *Ibid.*

135 "Physician Compensation Plans: State-of-the-Art Strategies," By Bruce A. Johnson and Deborah Walker Keegan, Englewood, CO: Medical Group Management Association, 2006, p. 88.

136 *Ibid.*

137 "Physician Compensation Plans: State-of-the-Art Strategies," By Bruce A. Johnson and Deborah Walker Keegan, Englewood, CO: Medical Group Management Association, 2006, p. 89.

138 "Physician Compensation Plans: State-of-the-Art Strategies," By Bruce A. Johnson and Deborah Walker Keegan, Englewood, CO: Medical Group Management Association, 2006, p. 90.

139 *Ibid.*

140 "Physician Compensation Plans: State-of-the-Art Strategies," By Bruce A. Johnson and Deborah Walker Keegan, Englewood, CO: Medical Group Management Association, 2006, p. 92.

141 *Ibid.*

142 *Ibid.*

143 *Ibid.*

144 "Physician Compensation Plans: State-of-the-Art Strategies," By Bruce A. Johnson and Deborah Walker Keegan, Englewood, CO: Medical Group Management Association, 2006, p. 92-93.

145 *Ibid.*

146 *Ibid.*

147 *Ibid.*

148 "Physician Compensation Plans: State-of-the-Art Strategies," By Bruce A. Johnson and Deborah Walker Keegan, Englewood, CO: Medical Group Management Association, 2006, p. 93-94.

149 "Physician Compensation Plans: State-of-the-Art Strategies," By Bruce A. Johnson and Deborah Walker Keegan, Englewood, CO: Medical Group Management Association, 2006, p. 95.

150 *Ibid.*

151 *Ibid.*

152 *Ibid.*

153 "Physician Compensation Plans: State-of-the-Art Strategies," By Bruce A. Johnson and Deborah Walker Keegan, Englewood, CO: Medical Group Management Association, 2006, p. 96-97.

154 "Physician Compensation Plans: State-of-the-Art Strategies," By Bruce A. Johnson and Deborah Walker Keegan, Englewood, CO: Medical Group Management Association, 2006, p. 97-98.

155 *Ibid.*

156 *Ibid.*

157 "Physician Compensation Plans: State-of-the-Art Strategies," By Bruce A. Johnson and Deborah Walker Keegan, Englewood, CO: Medical Group Management Association, 2006, p. 98-99.

158 *Ibid.*

159 *Ibid.*

160 *Ibid.*

161 *Ibid.*

162 "Physician Compensation Arrangements: Management & Legal Trends," By Daniel K. Zismer, Gaithesburg, MD: Aspen Publishers, Inc., 1999, p. 113-115; "Physician Compensation Plans: State-of-the-Art Strategies," By Bruce A. Johnson and Deborah Walker Keegan, Englewood, CO: Medical Group Management Association, 2006, p. 31-32; "Physician Compensation Strategies" By Craig W. Hunter and Max Reiboldt, Second Edition, American Medical Association, 2004, p. 52-54.

163 "Physician Compensation Plans: State-of-the-Art Strategies," By Bruce A. Johnson and Deborah Walker Keegan, Englewood, CO: Medical Group Management Association, 2006, p. 110-112.

164 "Measuring Clinical Care: A Guide for Physician Executives" By Stephen C. Schoenbaum, Tampa, FL: American College of Physician Executives, 1995, p. 51, 57; "Physician Compensation Plans: State-of-the-Art Strategies," By Bruce A. Johnson and Deborah Walker Keegan, Englewood, CO: Medical Group Management Association, 2006, p. 31-32; "Physician's Compensation: Measurement, Benchmarking, and Implementation," by Lucy R. Carter and Sara S. Lankford, New York, NY: John Wiley & Sons, Inc., 2000, p. 20-21.

165 "Physician Compensation Plans: State-of-the-Art Strategies," By Bruce A. Johnson and Deborah Walker Keegan, Englewood, CO: Medical Group Management Association, 2006, p. 32.

166 *Ibid.*

167 *Ibid.*

168 "Physician Compensation Plans: State-of-the-Art Strategies," By Bruce A. Johnson and Deborah Walker Keegan, Englewood, CO: Medical Group Management Association, 2006, p. 32; "Physician's Compensation: Measurement, Benchmarking, and Implementation" By Lucy R. Carter and Sara S. Lankford, New York, NY: John Wiley & Sons, Inc., 2000, p. 61.

169 "Physician Compensation Plans: State-of-the-Art Strategies," By Bruce A. Johnson and Deborah Walker Keegan, Englewood, CO: Medical Group Management Association, 2006, p. 32-33; "Physician's Compensation: Measurement, Benchmarking, and Implementation" By Lucy R. Carter and Sara S. Lankford, New York, NY: John Wiley & Sons, Inc., 2000, p. 60-61.

170 "Physician Compensation Plans: State-of-the-Art Strategies," By Bruce A. Johnson and Deborah Walker Keegan, Englewood, CO: Medical Group Management Association, 2006, p. 33-34.

171 "Physician Compensation Arrangements: Management & Legal Trends," By Daniel K. Zismer, Gaithesburg, MD: Aspen Publishers, Inc., 1999, p. 113; "Physician Compensation Plans: State-of-the-Art Strategies," By Bruce A. Johnson and Deborah Walker Keegan, Englewood, CO: Medical Group Management Association, 2006, p. 33-34.

172 "Physician Compensation Plans: State-of-the-Art Strategies," By Bruce A. Johnson and Deborah Walker Keegan, Englewood, CO: Medical Group Management Association, 2006, p. 33-34.

173 "Physician Compensation Plans: State-of-the-Art Strategies," By Bruce A. Johnson and Deborah Walker Keegan, Englewood, CO: Medical Group Management Association, 2006, p. 33.

174 "Physician Compensation Plans: State-of-the-Art Strategies," By Bruce A. Johnson and Deborah Walker Keegan, Englewood, CO: Medical Group Management Association, 2006, p. 34; "Physician's Compensation: Measurement, Benchmarking, and Implementation" By Lucy R. Carter and Sara S. Lankford, New York, NY: John Wiley & Sons, Inc., 2000, p. 137, 176-177.

175 "Physician Compensation Plans: State-of-the-Art Strategies," By Bruce A. Johnson and Deborah Walker Keegan, Englewood, CO: Medical Group Management Association, 2006, p. 33.

176 "Physician Compensation Plans: State-of-the-Art Strategies," By Bruce A. Johnson and Deborah Walker Keegan, Englewood, CO: Medical Group Management Association, 2006, p. 33; "Physician Compensation: Models for Aligning Financial Goals and Incentives" By Kenneth M. Hekman, New York, NY: McGraw-Hill, 2000, p. 83-89; "Physician's Compensation: Measurement, Benchmarking, and Implementation" By Lucy R. Carter and Sara S. Lankford, New York, NY: John Wiley & Sons, Inc., 2000, p. 56-61.

177 "Physician Compensation Plans: State-of-the-Art Strategies," By Bruce A. Johnson and Deborah Walker Keegan, Englewood, CO: Medical Group Management Association, 2006, p. 34-35.

178 "Physician Compensation Plans: State-of-the-Art Strategies," By Bruce A. Johnson and Deborah Walker Keegan, Englewood, CO: Medical Group Management Association, 2006, p. 33; "Physician Compensation: Models for Aligning Financial Goals and Incentives," By Kenneth M. Hekman, New York, NY: McGraw-Hill, 2000, p. 37.

179 "Physician Compensation Plans: State-of-the-Art Strategies," By Bruce A. Johnson and Deborah Walker Keegan, Englewood, CO: Medical Group Management Association, 2006, p. 35; "Physician Compensation: Models for Aligning Financial Goals and Incentives" By Kenneth M. Hekman, New York, NY: McGraw-Hill, 2000, p. 84-92.

180 "Physician Compensation Plans: State-of-the-Art Strategies," By Bruce A. Johnson and Deborah Walker Keegan, Englewood, CO: Medical Group Management Association, 2006, p. 36; "Physician Compensation: Models for Aligning Financial Goals and Incentives," By Kenneth M. Hekman, New York, NY: McGraw-Hill, 2000, p. 119.

181 "Physician Compensation Plans: State-of-the-Art Strategies," By Bruce A. Johnson and Deborah Walker Keegan, Englewood, CO: Medical Group Management Association, 2006, p. 36.

182 "Physician Compensation Plans: State-of-the-Art Strategies," By Bruce A. Johnson and Deborah Walker Keegan, Englewood, CO: Medical Group Management Association, 2006, p. 36; "Physician Compensation: Models for Aligning Financial Goals and Incentives," By Kenneth M. Hekman, New York, NY: McGraw-Hill, 2000, p. 119.

183 "Physician Compensation Plans: State-of-the-Art Strategies," By Bruce A. Johnson and Deborah Walker Keegan, Englewood, CO: Medical Group Management Association, 2006, p. 36; "Physician Compensation: Models for Aligning Financial Goals and Incentives," By Kenneth M. Hekman, New York, NY: McGraw-Hill, 2000, p. 119-120.

184 "Physician Compensation Plans: State-of-the-Art Strategies," By Bruce A. Johnson and Deborah Walker Keegan, Englewood, CO: Medical Group Management Association, 2006, p. 36; "Physician Compensation: Models for Aligning Financial Goals and Incentives" By Kenneth M. Hekman, New York, NY: McGraw-Hill, 2000, p. 153.

185 "Physician Compensation Plans: State-of-the-Art Strategies," By Bruce A. Johnson and Deborah Walker Keegan, Englewood, CO: Medical Group Management Association, 2006, p. 36.

186 "Physician Compensation Plans: State-of-the-Art Strategies," By Bruce A. Johnson and Deborah Walker Keegan, Englewood, CO: Medical Group Management Association, 2006, p. 37.

187 "Physician Compensation Plans: State-of-the-Art Strategies," By Bruce A. Johnson and Deborah Walker Keegan, Englewood, CO: Medical Group Management Association, 2006, p. 37; "Physician Compensation: Models for Aligning Financial Goals and Incentives" By Kenneth M. Hekman, New York, NY: McGraw-Hill, 2000, p. 163; "Physician's Compensation: Measurement, Benchmarking, and Implementation" By Lucy R. Carter and Sara S. Lankford, New York, NY: John Wiley & Sons, Inc., 2000, p. 61.

188 "Physician Compensation Plans: State-of-the-Art Strategies," By Bruce A. Johnson and Deborah Walker Keegan, Englewood, CO: Medical Group Management Association, 2006, p. 46.

189 "Physician Compensation Plans: State-of-the-Art Strategies," By Bruce A. Johnson and Deborah Walker Keegan, Englewood, CO: Medical Group Management Association, 2006, p. 37; "Physician's Compensation: Measurement, Benchmarking, and Implementation" By Lucy R. Carter and Sara S. Lankford, New York, NY: John Wiley & Sons, Inc., 2000, p. 60-61.

190 "Physician Compensation Plans: State-of-the-Art Strategies," By Bruce A. Johnson and Deborah Walker Keegan, Englewood, CO: Medical Group Management Association, 2006, p. 37; "Physician's Compensation: Measurement, Benchmarking, and Implementation" By Lucy R. Carter and Sara S. Lankford, New York, NY: John Wiley & Sons, Inc., 2000, p. 56.

191 "Physician Compensation Plans: State-of-the-Art Strategies," By Bruce A. Johnson and Deborah Walker Keegan, Englewood, CO: Medical Group Management Association, 2006, p. 37; "Physician's Compensation: Measurement, Benchmarking, and Implementation" By Lucy R. Carter and Sara S. Lankford, New York, NY: John Wiley & Sons, Inc., 2000, p. 59-61.

192 "Physician Compensation Plans: State-of-the-Art Strategies," By Bruce A. Johnson and Deborah Walker Keegan, Englewood, CO: Medical Group Management Association, 2006, p. 110-112.

193 "Physician Compensation Plans: State-of-the-Art Strategies," By Bruce A. Johnson and Deborah Walker Keegan, Englewood, CO: Medical Group Management Association, 2006, p. 31.

194 "Measuring Clinical Care: A Guide for Physician Executives" By Stephen C. Schoenbaum, Tampa, FL: American College of Physician Executives, 1995, p. 51, 57; "Physician Compensation Plans: State-of-the-Art Strategies," By Bruce A. Johnson and Deborah Walker Keegan, Englewood, CO: Medical Group Management Association, 2006, p. 31.

195 "Valuing Physician and Executive Compensation Arrangements: Fair Market Value & Commercial Reasonableness Thresholds" By Robert James Cimasi and David Grauer, National Association of Certified Valuation Analysts, June 26, 2009, p. 4.

196 "Employment Tax Audits of Exempt Hospitals Could Turn Up Other Issues, Attorneys Warn" 18 Health Law Reporter 1653, (December 24, 2009), Accessed at http://news.bna.com/hlln/display/batch_print_display.adp (Accessed 12/28/09) p. 1-4; "Enforcement Efforts Take Aim at Executive Compensation of Tax-Exempt Health Care Entities" by Candace L. Quinn and Jeffrey D. Mamorsky, 18 Health Law Reporter 1640, (December 17, 2009) Acessed at http://news.bna.com/hlln/display/batch_print_display.adp (Accessed 12/28/09), p. 1, 7.

197 "Valuing Physician and Executive Compensation Arrangements: Fair Market Value & Commercial Reasonableness Thresholds" By Robert James Cimasi and David Grauer, National Association of Certified Valuation Analysts, June 26, 2009, p. 4.

198 "Exceptions to the Referral Prohibition Related to Ownership or Investment Interests" 42 C.F.R. 411.357 (October 1, 2008).

199 "Medicare Program; Changes to the Hospital Inpatient Prospective Payment Systems and Fiscal Year 2009 Rates; Final Rule" 73 Fed. Reg. 48723-48724, 48730 (August 19, 2008).

200 Ibid.

201 Ibid.

202 "Stark Rule Proposals Finalized" By Cathy Dunlay and Kevin Hilvert, Schottenstein Zox & Dunn Resources, August 13, 2008, http://www.szd.com/resources.php?NewsID=1184&method=unique (Accessed 8/14/08).

203 Ibid.

204 "An Analysis of Gainsharing Arrangements Under Stark Law" By Albert W. Shay, Health Lawyers News, Vol. 9, No. 7 (July 2005), http://www.sonnenschein.com/docs/docs_healthcare/Shay_et_al_--_HLN_Ju.pdf (Accessed 02/19/10), p. 5-13.

205 Ibid.

206 "Stark Rule Proposals Finalized" By Cathy Dunlay and Kevin Hilvert, Schottenstein Zox & Dunn Resources, August 13, 2008, http://www.szd.com/resources.php?NewsID=1184&method=unique (Accessed 8/14/08).

207 Ibid.

208 "False Claims" 31 U.S.C.A. § 3729(a) (July 5, 1994).

209 "Healthcare Transactions: A Description of the Process and Considerations Involve," By Robert J. Cimasi, Health Capital Consultants, p. 3-5.

210 "Partner Buy-Ins" The Physician's Advisory: Vital Topic Series, Advisory Publications, Conshohocken, PA: Leif C. Beck, LL.B, C.P.B.C, 1999, p. 3.

211 "Partner Buy-Ins" The Physician's Advisory: Vital Topic Series, Advisory Publications, Conshohocken, PA: Leif C. Beck, LL.B, C.P.B.C, 1999, p. 4.

212 "Partner Buy-Ins" The Physician's Advisory: Vital Topic Series, Advisory Publications, Conshohocken, PA: Leif C. Beck, LL.B, C.P.B.C, 1999, p. 3.

213 Ibid.

214 "Partner Buy-Ins" The Physician's Advisory: Vital Topic Series, Advisory Publications, Conshohocken, PA: Leif C. Beck, LL.B, C.P.B.C, 1999, p. 2, 3-4.

215 "Partner Buy-Ins" The Physician's Advisory: Vital Topic Series, Advisory Publications, Conshohocken, PA: Leif C. Beck, LL.B, C.P.B.C, 1999, p. 7, 8 , 11, 12; "Partner Buy-Ins" The Physician's Advisory: Vital Topic Series, Advisory Publications, Conshohocken, PA: Leif C. Beck, LL.B, C.P.B.C, 1999, p. 7, 11, 12.

216 "Partner Buy-Ins" The Physician's Advisory: Vital Topic Series, Advisory Publications, Conshohocken, PA: Leif C. Beck, LL.B, C.P.B.C, 1999, p. 7, 11-12; "Partner Buy-Ins" The Physician's Advisory: Vital Topic Series, Advisory Publications, Conshohocken, PA: Leif C. Beck, LL.B, C.P.B.C, 1999, p. 3.

217 "Partner Buy-Ins" The Physician's Advisory: Vital Topic Series, Advisory Publications, Conshohocken, PA: Leif C. Beck, LL.B, C.P.B.C, 1999, p. 2-4, 7-8, 11-12; "Partner Buy-Ins" The Physician's Advisory: Vital Topic Series, Advisory Publications, Conshohocken, PA: Leif C. Beck, LL.B, C.P.B.C, 1999, p. 3-4; "Physician Compensation Plans: State-of-the-Art Strategies," By Bruce A. Johnson and Deborah Walker Keegan, Englewood, CO: Medical Group Management Association, 2006, p. 191-192.

218 "Partner Buy-Ins" The Physician's Advisory: Vital Topic Series, Advisory Publications, Conshohocken, PA: Leif C. Beck, LL.B, C.P.B.C, 1999, p. 3.

219 Ibid.

220 "Partner Buy-Ins" The Physician's Advisory: Vital Topic Series, Advisory Publications, Conshohocken, PA: Leif C. Beck, LL.B, C.P.B.C, 1999, p. 3-4.

221 "Partner Buy-Ins" The Physician's Advisory: Vital Topic Series, Advisory Publications, Conshohocken, PA: Leif C. Beck, LL.B, C.P.B.C, 1999, p. 3, 4; "Selling or Buying a Medical Practice," By Gary R. Schaub, Oradell, NJ: Medical Economics Books, 1988, p. 191-192.

222 "Selling or Buying a Medical Practice," By Gary R. Schaub, Oradell, NJ: Medical Economics Books, 1988, p. 3-4.

223 "Partner Buy-Ins" The Physician's Advisory: Vital Topic Series, Advisory Publications, Conshohocken, PA: Leif C. Beck, LL.B, C.P.B.C, 1999, p. 5, 6.

224 "Partner Buy-Ins" The Physician's Advisory: Vital Topic Series, Advisory Publications, Conshohocken, PA: Leif C. Beck, LL.B, C.P.B.C, 1999, p. 7, 8 , 11, 12; "Partner Buy-Ins" The Physician's Advisory: Vital Topic Series, Advisory Publications, Conshohocken, PA: Leif C. Beck, LL.B, C.P.B.C, 1999, p. 7, 8 , 11, 12; "Selling or Buying a Medical Practice," By Gary R. Schaub, Oradell, NJ: Medical Economics Books, 1988, p. 67-74.

225 "Partner Buy-Ins" The Physician's Advisory: Vital Topic Series, Advisory Publications, Conshohocken, PA: Leif C. Beck, LL.B, C.P.B.C, 1999, p. 7,8 , 11,12; "Valuation of a Medical Practice" By Reed Tinsley, Rhonda Sides, Gregory D. Anderson, New York: John Wiley and Sons, Inc., 1999, p. 8; "Selling or Buying a Medical Practice," By Gary R. Schaub, Oradell, NJ: Medical Economics Books, 1988, p. 67-74.

226 "Physician Compensation Plans: State-of-the-Art Strategies," By Bruce A. Johnson and Deborah Walker Keegan, Englewood, CO: Medical Group Management Association, 2006, p. 177-179; "Physician Compensation Plans: State-of-the-Art Strategies," By Bruce A. Johnson and Deborah Walker Keegan, Englewood, CO: Medical Group Management Association, 2006, p. 177-179; "Valuation of a Medical Practice" By Reed Tinsley, Rhonda Sides, Gregory D. Anderson, New York: John Wiley and Sons, Inc., 1999, p. 8.

227 "Designing a Physician Compensation and Incentive Plan for an Academic Health-care Center" By Donna Steinmetz, Medical Group Management Association, 2006; "Physician Compensation Plans: State-of-the-Art Strategies," By Bruce A. Johnson and Deborah Walker Keegan, Englewood, CO: Medical Group Management Association, 2006, p. 177-179.

228 "Adapting Industry-Style Business Model to Academia in a System of Performance-Based Incentive Compensation" By E. Albert Reece et al., Academic Medicine, Vol. 83, No. 1 (January 2008), p. 76; "Adapting Industry-Style Business Model to Academia in a System of Performance-Based Incentive Compensation" By E. Albert Reece et al., Academic Medicine, Vol. 83, No. 1 (January 2008), p. 77; "Adapting Industry-Style Business Model to Academia in a System of Performance-Based Incentive Compensation" By E. Albert Reece et al., Academic Medicine, Vol. 83, No. 1 (January 2008), p. 76.

229 "Designing a Physician Compensation and Incentive Plan for an Academic Health-care Center," By Donna Steinmetz, Medical Group Management Association, 2006.

230 "Compensation and Incentive Plans for Physicians" By Charles Stiernberg, November 2001, http://www2.utmb.edu/otoref/Grnds/Compensation_11-2001/Compensation_11-2001.pdf (Accessed 04/30/10), p. 1, 4.

231 "Physician Compensation Plans: State-of-the-Art Strategies," By Bruce A. Johnson and Deborah Walker Keegan, Englewood, CO: Medical Group Management Association, 2006, p. 177-179.

232 Ibid.

233 Ibid.

234 "Designing a Physician Compensation and Incentive Plan for an Academic Health-care Center," By Donna Steinmetz, Medical Group Management Association, 2006.

235 "Adapting Industry-Style Business Model to Academia in a System of Performance-Based Incentive Compensation" By E. Albert Reece et al., Academic Medicine, Vol. 83, No. 1 (January 2008), p. 78.

236 "Adapting Industry-Style Business Model to Academia in a System of Performance-Based Incentive Compensation" By E. Albert Reece et al., Academic Medicine, Vol. 83, No. 1 (January 2008), p. 78; "Designing a Physician Compensation and Incentive Plan for an Academic Healthcare Center," By Donna Steinmetz, Medical Group Management Association, 2006.

237 "Designing a Physician Compensation and Incentive Plan for an Academic Health-care Center," By Donna Steinmetz, Medical Group Management Association, 2006.

238 "Compensation and Incentive Plans for Physicians" By Charles Stiernberg, November 2001, http://www2.utmb.edu/otoref/Grnds/Compensation_11-2001/Compensation_11-2001.pdf (Accessed 04/30/10), p. 1-4.

239 "Adapting Industry-Style Business Model to Academia in a System of Performance-Based Incentive Compensation" By E. Albert Reece et al., Academic Medicine, Vol. 83, No. 1 (January 2008), p. 78; "An Incentive Compensation System That Rewards Individual and Corporate Productivity" By Deanna R. Willis et al., Family Medicine, Vol. 36, No. 4 (April 2004), p. 272.

240 "Adapting Industry-Style Business Model to Academia in a System of Performance-Based Incentive Compensation" By E. Albert Reece et al., Academic Medicine, Vol. 83, No. 1 (January 2008), p. 78.

241 "Evaluation of Specialty Physician Workforce Methodologies," By the Council on Graduate Medical Education, U.S. Department of Health and Human Services, Health Resources and Services Administration, September 2000, p. 12; "Physician Compensation Plans: State-of-the-Art Strategies," By Bruce A. Johnson and Deborah Walker Keegan, Englewood, CO: Medical Group Management Association, 2006, p. 185-186.

242 "Physician Compensation Plans: State-of-the-Art Strategies," By Bruce A. Johnson and Deborah Walker Keegan, Englewood, CO: Medical Group Management Association, 2006, p. 185-186; "Physician Compensation Plans: State-of-the-Art Strategies," By Bruce A. Johnson and Deborah Walker Keegan, Englewood, CO: Medical Group Management Association, 2006, p. 185-186.

243 "Physician Compensation Plans: State-of-the-Art Strategies," By Bruce A. Johnson and Deborah Walker Keegan, Englewood, CO: Medical Group Management Association, 2006, p. 185-186; "Physician Compensation Plans: State-of-the-Art Strategies," By Bruce A. Johnson and Deborah Walker Keegan, Englewood, CO: Medical Group Management Association, 2006, p. 187-188.

244 "An Incentive Compensation System That Rewards Individual and Corporate Productivity" By Deanna R. Willis et al., Family Medicine, Vol. 36, No. 4 (April 2004), p. 272; "Physician Compensation Plans: State-of-the-Art Strategies," By Bruce A. Johnson and Deborah Walker Keegan, Englewood, CO: Medical Group Management Association, 2006, p. 193-194.

245 "Physician Compensation Plans: State-of-the-Art Strategies," By Bruce A. Johnson and Deborah Walker Keegan, Englewood, CO: Medical Group Management Association, 2006, p. 185.

246 Ibid.

247 "Physician Compensation Plans: State-of-the-Art Strategies," By Bruce A. Johnson and Deborah Walker Keegan, Englewood, CO: Medical Group Management Association, 2006, p. 185-186.

248 Ibid.

249 Ibid.

250 "Physician Compensation Plans: State-of-the-Art Strategies" By Bruce A. Johnson and Deborah Walker Keegan, New York, NY: Medical Group Management Association, 2006, p. 193-194.

251 "Physician Compensation Plans: State-of-the-Art Strategies," By Bruce A. Johnson and Deborah Walker Keegan, Englewood, CO: Medical Group Management Association, 2006, p. 103-112, 179.

252 "Physician Compensation Plans: State-of-the-Art Strategies," By Bruce A. Johnson and Deborah Walker Keegan, Englewood, CO: Medical Group Management Association, 2006, p. 104-105.

253 "Physician's Compensation: Measurement, Benchmarking, and Implementation" By Lucy R. Carter and Sara S. Lankford, New York, NY: John Wiley & Sons, Inc., 2000, p. 176-177.

254 "Physician Compensation Plans: State-of-the-Art Strategies," By Bruce A. Johnson and Deborah Walker Keegan, Englewood, CO: Medical Group Management Association, 2006, p. 31; "Physician's Compensation: Measurement, Benchmarking, and Implementation," By Lucy R. Carter and Sara S. Lankford, New York, NY: John Wiley & Sons, Inc., 2000, p. 94.

255 "Physician Compensation Arrangements: Management & Legal Trends," By Daniel K. Zismer, Gaithesburg, MD: Aspen Publishers, Inc., 1999, p. 111-113.

256 "Physician Compensation Plans: State-of-the-Art Strategies," By Bruce A. Johnson and Deborah Walker Keegan, Englewood, CO: Medical Group Management Association, 2006, p. 137.

257 Ibid.

258 "Physician Compensation Arrangements: Management & Legal Trends," By Daniel K. Zismer, Gaithesburg, MD: Aspen Publishers, Inc., 1999, p. 111-113.

259 Ibid.

260 "Physician Compensation Plans: State-of-the-Art Strategies," By Bruce A. Johnson and Deborah Walker Keegan, Englewood, CO: Medical Group Management Association, 2006, p. 114-115.

261 "Physician Compensation Plans: State-of-the-Art Strategies," By Bruce A. Johnson and Deborah Walker Keegan, Englewood, CO: Medical Group Management Association, 2006, p. 104-105; 114-115.

262 "Physician Compensation: Models for Aligning Financial Goals and Incentives" By Kenneth M. Hekman, New York, NY: McGraw-Hill, 2000, p. 86.

263 "Physician Compensation Arrangements: Management & Legal Trends," By Daniel K. Zismer, Gaithesburg, MD: Aspen Publishers, Inc., 1999, p. 6, 8.

264 "Physician Compensation Plans: State-of-the-Art Strategies," By Bruce A. Johnson and Deborah Walker Keegan, Englewood, CO: Medical Group Management Association, 2006, p. 114-115.

265 "Measuring Clinical Care: A Guide for Physician Executives" By Stephen C. Schoenbaum, Tampa, FL: American College of Physician Executives, 1995, p. 51, 57.

266 "Physician Compensation Plans: State-of-the-Art Strategies," By Bruce A. Johnson and Deborah Walker Keegan, Englewood, CO: Medical Group Management Association, 2006, p. 114-115; "Physician Compensation Plans: State-of-the-Art Strategies," By Bruce A. Johnson and Deborah Walker Keegan, Englewood, CO: Medical Group Management Association, 2006, p. 114-115.

267 "Physician Compensation: Models for Aligning Financial Goals and Incentives" By Kenneth M. Hekman, New York, NY: McGraw-Hill, 2000, p. 49-50.

268 "Physician Compensation Plans: State-of-the-Art Strategies," By Bruce A. Johnson and Deborah Walker Keegan, Englewood, CO: Medical Group Management Association, 2006, p. 114-115.

269 *Ibid.*

270 "Measuring Clinical Care: A Guide for Physician Executives" By Stephen C. Schoenbaum, Tampa, FL: American College of Physician Executives, 1995, p. 51, 57.

271 "Physician Compensation Plans: State-of-the-Art Strategies," By Bruce A. Johnson and Deborah Walker Keegan, Englewood, CO: Medical Group Management Association, 2006, p. 114-115; "Physician Compensation Plans: State-of-the-Art Strategies," By Bruce A. Johnson and Deborah Walker Keegan, Englewood, CO: Medical Group Management Association, 2006, p. 114-115.

272 "Physician Compensation Arrangements: Management & Legal Trends" By Daniel K. Zismer, Gaithersburg, MD: Aspen Publishers, Inc., 1999, p. 20-21; "Physician Compensation Plans: State-of-the-Art Strategies," By Bruce A. Johnson and Deborah Walker Keegan, Englewood, CO: Medical Group Management Association, 2006, p. 114-115.

273 "Pay for Performance: Quality- and Value- Based Reimbursement," By Norman (Chip) Harbaugh Jr., Pediatric Clinics of North America, Volume 56, Number 4, (2009), Accessed at http://www.pediatric.theclinics.com/article/S0031-3955(09)00057-1/pdf (Accessed 5/7/10), p. 997-998.

274 "Pay for Performance: Quality- and Value- Based Reimbursement," By Norman (Chip) Harbaugh Jr., Pediatric Clinics of North America, Volume 56, Number 4, (2009),Accessed at http://www.pediatric.theclinics.com/article/S0031-3955(09)00057-1/pdf (Accessed 5/7/10), p.997-998; "Physician Compensation Plans: State-of-the-Art Strategies," By Bruce A. Johnson and Deborah Walker Keegan, Englewood, CO: Medical Group Management Association, 2006, p. 114-115.

275 "Physician Compensation Plans: State-of-the-Art Strategies," By Bruce A. Johnson and Deborah Walker Keegan, Englewood, CO: Medical Group Management Association, 2006, p. 114-115.

276 "The Broad Perspective—Physician Compensation Issues across Different Practice Settings," by Daniel K. Zismer, in "Physician Compensation Arrangements," By Daniel K. Zismer, An Aspen Publication, 1999, p. 20-21; "Measuring Physician Work and Effort," in "Physician Compensation Plans: State-of-the-Art Strategies," by Bruce A. Johnson, JD, MPA and Deborah Walker Keegan, PhD, FACMPE, Medical Group Management Association, 2006, p. 114-115.

277 "Physician Compensation Plans: State-of-the-Art Strategies," By Bruce A. Johnson and Deborah Walker Keegan, Englewood, CO: Medical Group Management Association, 2006, p. 114-115; "Physician Compensation Plans: State-of-the-Art Strategies," By Bruce A. Johnson and Deborah Walker Keegan, Englewood, CO: Medical Group Management Association, 2006, p. 177-179; "Physician Compensation: Models for Aligning Financial Goals and Incentives" By Kenneth M. Hekman, New York, NY: McGraw-Hill, 2000, p. 52.

278 "Physician Compensation Plans: State-of-the-Art Strategies," By Bruce A. Johnson and Deborah Walker Keegan, Englewood, CO: Medical Group Management Association, 2006, p. 177-179; "Physician Compensation Plans: State-of-the-Art Strategies," By Bruce A. Johnson and Deborah Walker Keegan, Englewood, CO: Medical Group Management Association, 2006, p. 9.

279 "Physician Compensation Plans: State-of-the-Art Strategies," By Bruce A. Johnson and Deborah Walker Keegan, Englewood, CO: Medical Group Management Association, 2006, p. 148; "Physician Compensation: Models for Aligning Financial Goals and Incentives," By Kenneth M. Hekman, New York, NY: McGraw-Hill, 2000, p. 118-119.

280 "Physician Compensation Plans: State-of-the-Art Strategies," By Bruce A. Johnson and Deborah Walker Keegan, Englewood, CO: Medical Group Management Association, 2006, p. 137; "Physician Compensation: Models for Aligning Financial Goals and Incentives," By Kenneth M. Hekman, New York, NY: McGraw-Hill, 2000, p. 118-119.

281 "Physician Compensation: Models for Aligning Financial Goals and Incentives" By Kenneth M. Hekman, New York, NY: Medical Group Management Association, 2000, p. 52; "Physician Compensation Plans: State-of-the-Art Strategies," By Bruce A. Johnson and Deborah Walker Keegan, Englewood, CO: Medical Group Management Association, 2006, p. 191-192.

282 "Physician Compensation Plans: State-of-the-Art Strategies" By Bruce A. Johnson and Deborah Walker Keegan, New York, NY: Medical Group Management Association, 2006, p. 177-179.

283 *Ibid.*

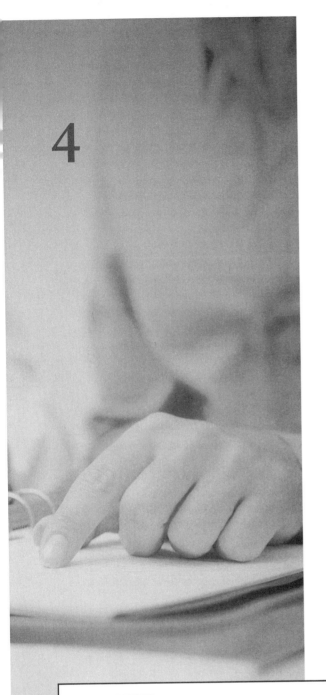

4

Financial Valuation of Enterprises, Assets, and Services

It is impossible to estimate the value of the services given by the medical profession to the people of the United States during the past century. It would be easy to compute the service given by the charity hospitals. But who can compute the value of the services given in improving national and domestic sanitation and hygiene; in doubling the span of life; in destroying the sources of many of the worst epidemics; in warring against personal actions liable to induce common diseases, and in making plain to everyone the importance of strengthening the body and preserving the health? These important services have been given as free gifts to the American people.

Theodore Wiprud, 1937

KEY TERMS

- Capitalization Rate
- Cash Flow
- Control Premium
- Cost of Capital
- Discount for Lack of Control
- Discount for Lack of Marketability
- Discount Rate
- Equity Risk Premium
- Excess Earnings
- Forced Liquidation Value
- Going Concern Value
- Goodwill
- Intangible Assets
- Invested Capital
- Investment Value
- Liquidation Value
- Liquidity
- Market Multiple
- Net Book Value
- Orderly Liquidation Value
- Premise of Value
- Standard of Value
- Tangible Assets
- Valuation Date
- Value in Exchange
- Value in Use
- Weighted Average Cost of Capital

Key Concept	Definition	Citation
Asset (Asset-Based) Approach	A general way of determining a value indication of a business, business ownership interest, or security using one or more methods based on the value of the assets net of liabilities.	"ASA Business Valuation Standards," American Society of Appraisers, 2008, p. 25.
Capitalization of Earnings Method	A method within the income approach whereby economic benefits for a representative single period are converted to value through division by a capitalization rate.	"ASA Business Valuation Standards," American Society of Appraisers, 2008, p. 26.
Cost Approach	A general way of determining a value indication of an individual asset by quantifying the amount of money required to replace the future service capability of that asset.	"ASA Business Valuation Standards," American Society of Appraisers, 2008, p. 26.
Discounted Cash Flow Method	A method within the income approach whereby the present value of expected net cash flows is calculated using a discount rate.	"ASA Business Valuation Standards," American Society of Appraisers, 2008, p. 27.
Excess Earnings Method	A specific way of determining a value indication of a business, business ownership interest, or security determined as the sum of (1) the value of the assets derived by capitalizing excess earnings and (2) the value of the selected asset base; also frequently used to value intangible assets.	"ASA Business Valuation Standards," American Society of Appraisers, 2008, p. 27.
Guideline Public Company Method	A method within the market approach whereby market multiples are derived from market prices of stocks of companies that are engaged in the same or similar lines of business and that are actively traded on a free and open market.	"ASA Business Valuation Standards," American Society of Appraisers, 2008, p. 28.
Income (Income-Based) Approach	A general way of determining a value indication of a business, business ownership interest, security, or intangible asset using one or more methods that convert anticipated economic benefits into a present single amount.	"ASA Business Valuation Standards," American Society of Appraisers, 2008, p. 28.
Market (Market-Based) Approach	A general way of determining a value indication of a business, business ownership interest, security, or intangible asset by using one or more methods that compare the subject to similar businesses, business ownership interests, securities, or intangible assets that have been sold.	"ASA Business Valuation Standards," American Society of Appraisers, 2008, p. 29.
Merger and Acquisition Method	A method within the market approach whereby pricing multiples is derived from transactions of significant interests in companies engaged in the same or similar lines of business.	"ASA Business Valuation Standards," American Society of Appraisers, 2008, p. 30.

OVERVIEW

Many events may set the stage for the valuation (appraisal) of healthcare enterprises, assets, or services, with the scope of valuation services ranging from comprehensive, formal written reports with certified opinions to limited, restricted use analyses and valuation consultations, as well as valuation review.

Opinions of value related to healthcare enterprises may be provided in both the for-profit and tax-exempt arenas for the purposes of sale or transfer, merger and acquisition, lending and capital formation, or liquidation and dissolution. These services also may be provided for management planning, insurance claims, gift and estate tax planning, and for other related purposes.

In addition to healthcare enterprise valuations, opinions of value may be provided related to the valuation of two types of assets:

1. Tangible assets, which include accounts receivable; cash and real property; supplies and inventory; tangible personal property, including furniture, fixtures, and equipment; and leasehold improvements

2. Intangible assets, which include marketing property; intellectual property; human capital; regulatory, financial, and technological intangible assets; and goodwill

See *Classification and Valuation of Assets* for further discussion of tangible and intangible assets.

Also, within the heightened scrutiny of the ever-changing regulatory environment in which healthcare enterprises and providers operate, transactions involving the employment of physicians are of increasing importance. A certified opinion regarding fair market value and commercial reasonableness is required to support the compensation arrangements between physician providers and enterprises that employ these providers (often tax-exempt hospital organizations) in order to withstand scrutiny from state and federal agencies regarding the stringent statutory requirements under antikickback, fraud and abuse, and related laws.

Although the valuation of healthcare enterprises, assets, and services is a complex, evolving topic in professional practice methodology, standards, and sources, it is a rapidly growing area of consultancy in the healthcare field that is expected to continue to expand. In light of this, significant valuation concepts, methods, and processes will be discussed in subsequent sections.

BASIC ECONOMIC VALUATION TENETS: VALUATION OF HEALTHCARE ENTERPRISES

The valuation of healthcare enterprises, for example, professional practices, hospitals, and ambulatory outpatient centers, requires an understanding of the economic and market forces, that is, the reimbursement, regulatory, competition, and technology environments in which these provider entities operate (see chapters 2, 3, 4, and 5 of *An Era of Reform*, respectively). Specifically, this chapter will discuss the selection and application of the approaches and methodologies typically utilized in the valuation of professional practice enterprises.

Market perceptions of value of an enterprise are based on investors' knowledge of the historical and existing environment, but more important, the anticipated trends of the industry sector and transactional or capital marketplace within which the subject professional practice enterprise operates. An understanding of the importance of trends as related to the valuation process is illustrated by the following basic valuation tenets:

- All value is the expectation of future benefit; therefore, value is forward looking.
- The best indicator of future performance is usually the performance of the immediate past.
- Historical accounting and other data are useful primarily as a road map to the future.

In the past, professional practice valuation methodologies relied heavily upon the analysis of historical accounting and other data as predictive of performance and value. Increasingly, however, circumstances surrounding the professional practice's specific specialty and the market within which it operates may have the potential to make the "historical" past a less reliable indicator of the practice's future financial performance. The turbulent status of the healthcare industry during the past three decades has introduced intervening events and circumstances that may have a dramatic effect on the revenue, benefit stream, or operating expense and margin outlook for the subject professional practice. In that event, the "road map of historical performance" becomes less predictive of future performance. An illustration of how events may change a valuator's prediction of a subject professional practice's performance is set forth in the following figure 4-1.

Figure 4-1: Reliance on Historical Data for Valuations

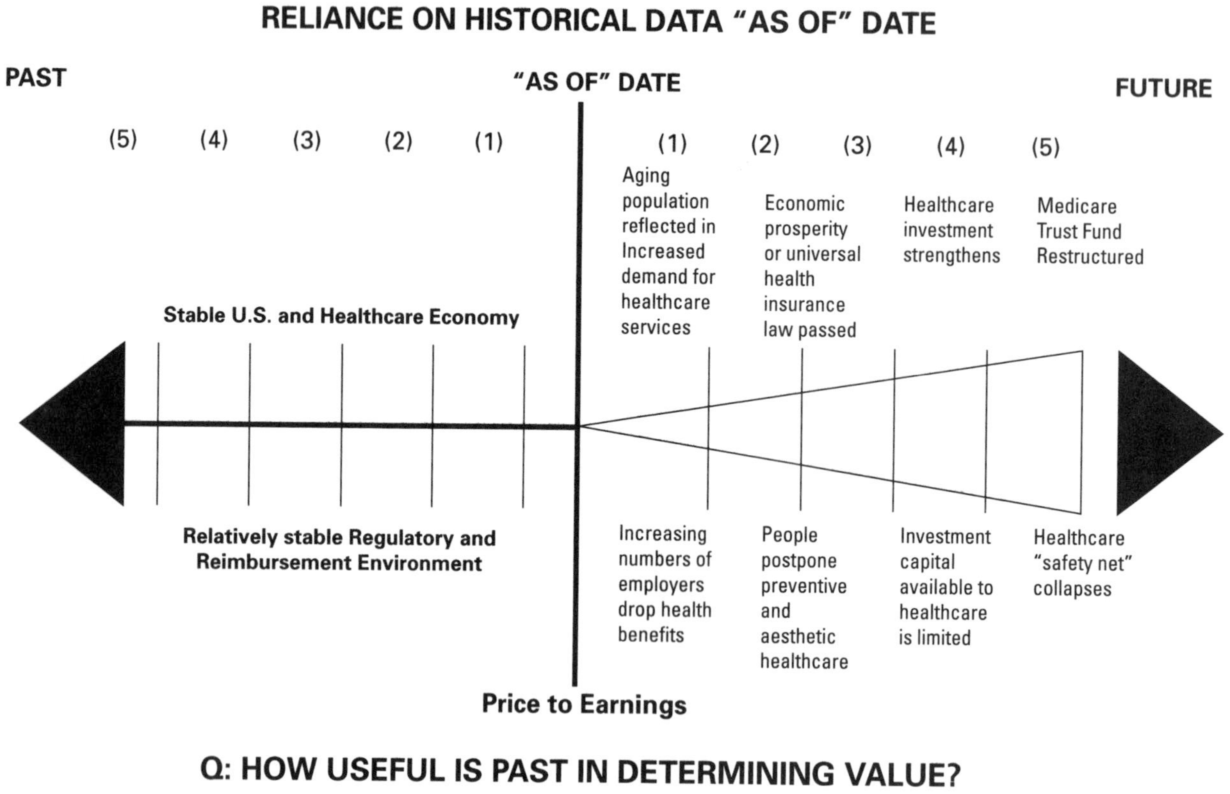

RELIANCE ON HISTORICAL DATA "AS OF" DATE

| PAST | "AS OF" DATE | FUTURE |

(5) (4) (3) (2) (1) | (1) (2) (3) (4) (5)

(1) Aging population reflected in Increased demand for healthcare services

(2) Economic prosperity or universal health insurance law passed

(4) Healthcare investment strengthens

(5) Medicare Trust Fund Restructured

Stable U.S. and Healthcare Economy

Relatively stable Regulatory and Reimbursement Environment

(1) Increasing numbers of employers drop health benefits

(2) People postpone preventive and aesthetic healthcare

(4) Investment capital available to healthcare is limited

(5) Healthcare "safety net" collapses

Price to Earnings

Q: HOW USEFUL IS PAST IN DETERMINING VALUE?

THE VALUE PYRAMID

Key "value drivers" of professional practice enterprises may be viewed within the context of the following "Value Pyramid" (figure 4-2), that is, the process related to the financial valuation of these enterprises generally can be discussed within the context of two distinct determinants: I, the determination of the appropriate economic income, earnings, or net benefit stream for the subject enterprise, and R, the development and selection of the appropriate risk-adjusted required rate of return (typically expressed as a discount rate, capitalization rate, or valuation multiple), to apply to the net benefit stream selected. For further discussion of calculations related to I and R, see *Developing a Forecast and Net Economic Benefit: Projection of Net Cash Flow* and *Cost Capital: Developing the Risk-Adjusted Required Rate of Return,* respectively.

Figure 4-2: The Value Pyramid

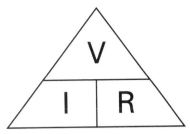

I → Income/Earnings/Benefit Stream as defined by appraiser & appropriate to assignment

R → Risk Adjusted Discount Rate/Cap Rate/Multiple risk adjusted and applicable to selected income stream

V → VALUE

BUY OR BUILD?—VALUE AS AN INCREMENTAL BENEFIT

Another important value concept is driven by the economic principle of substitution, which states that the cost of an equally desirable substitute (or one of equivalent utility) tends to set the ceiling of value; that is, it is the maximum price that a knowledgeable buyer would be willing to pay for a given asset or property. As applied to the professional practice valuation process, this concept is embodied in selecting and applying valuation methods in a manner that recognizes that the fair market value of a professional practice (for example, a healthcare professional practice) is the aggregate present value of the total of all future benefits of ownership to be derived, in excess of (and incremental to) the level of net economic benefits that may be projected to accrue from an alternative, hypothetical, start-up enterprise of the same type, setting, format, and location. This benefit of "buying" rather than "building" is referred to as the "incremental benefit." Figure 4-3 illustrates the concept of total incremental benefit.

Figure 4-3: Total Incremental Benefit

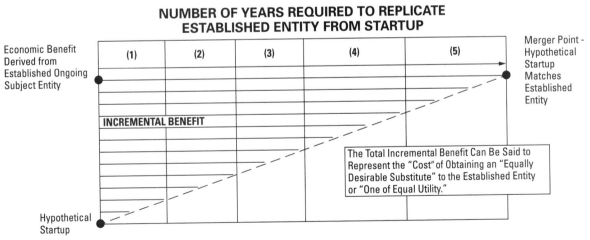

The "equally desirable substitute" that is required by the principle of substitution may be more difficult to hypothesize or project at a time when historical trends and assumptions may no longer be deemed valid by prospective purchasers or investors. Measuring the depth of the marketplace's perception regarding the probability of success for start-ups being diminished by reimbursement and regulatory pressures is subject to similar uncertainties.

THE STANDARD OF VALUE AND PREMISE OF VALUE

At the outset of each valuation engagement, it may be important to appropriately define and have all parties agree to the **standard of value** that outlines the type of value to be determined (for example, fair market value, fair value, market value, investment value, book value, and so forth) and is often described as answering the question, "value to whom?" It is also imperative that the **premise of value**, an assumption further defining the standard of value to be used and under which a valuation is conducted, be determined at the outset of the valuation engagement. The premise of value defines the hypothetical terms of the sale and answers the question, "value under what further defining circumstances?" (for example, value-in-use as a going concern or value-in-exchange, ranging from orderly disposition of an assemblage of the assets to forced liquidation, and so forth, as discussed in *Value in Use* and *Value in Exchange*, respectively).

THE STANDARD OF VALUE AND THE UNIVERSE OF TYPICAL BUYERS

The standard of fair market value is defined as the most probable price that the subject interest should bring if exposed for sale on the open market, as of the valuation date, but exclusive of any element of value arising from the accomplishment or expectation of the sale. This standard of value assumes an anticipated hypothetical transaction, in which the buyer and seller are each acting prudently with a reasonable equivalence of knowledge, and that the price is not affected by any undue stimulus or coercion. Implicit in this definition are the following additional assumptions:

(1) The hypothetical transaction considered contemplates a *universe* of typical potential purchasers for the subject property and not a *specific* purchaser or specific class of purchaser.

(2) Buyer and seller are typically motivated.

(3) Both parties are well informed and acting in their respective rational economic self-interests.

(4) Both parties are professionally advised, and the hypothetical transaction is assumed to be closed with the typical legal protections in place to safeguard the transfer of ownership of the legal bundle of rights that define and encompass the transacted property or interest.

(5) A sufficiently reasonable amount of time is allowed for exposure in the open market.

(6) A reasonable availability of transactional capital in the marketplace.

(7) Payment is made in cash or its equivalent.

In the case of a professional practice, which operates in an industry that is subject to more regulatory restraints, the following additional assumptions are implicit in the definition of fair market value:

(1) The anticipated hypothetical transaction would be conducted in compliance with Stark I and Stark II legislation, prohibiting physicians from making referrals for designated health services reimbursable under Medicare to an enterprise with which the referring physician has a financial relationship.[1] Stark II defines fair market value as "the value in arms length transactions, consistent with the general market value . . ."[2] It is further assumed that the transaction falls within Stark II's specific exception for "isolated financial transaction[s]" when "the amount of the remuneration under the employment . . . [(1)] is consistent with . . . fair market value of the services, . . . [(2)] is not determined in a manner that takes into account (directly or indirectly) the volume or value of any referrals by the referring physician, [(3)] . . . is provided pursuant to an agreement which would be commercially reasonable even if no referrals were made to the

employer, . . . and [(4)] the transaction meets such other requirements as the Secretary [of HHS] may impose by regulation as needed to protect against program or patient abuse[.]"[3]

(2) The anticipated hypothetical transaction would be conducted in compliance with the federal antikickback statute, making it illegal to knowingly pay or receive any remuneration in return for referrals.[4] The federal antikickback statute requires the payment of "fair market value in arm's-length transactions and . . . [that any compensation] is not determined in a manner that takes into account the volume or value of any referrals or business otherwise generated between the parties for which payment may be made in whole or in part under Medicare, Medicaid or other Federal health care programs[.]"[5]

(3) Related to the second point, the following definitions of terms apply: "In an excess benefit transaction, the general rule for the valuation of property, including the right to use property, is fair market value."[6] "A disqualified person [regarding any transaction,] is any person who was in a position to exercise substantial influence over the affairs of the applicable tax-exempt organization at any time during [a five-year period ending on the date of the transaction]."[7] "An excess benefit transaction is a transaction in which an economic benefit is provided by an applicable tax-exempt organization, directly or indirectly, to or for the use of a disqualified person, and the value of the economic benefit provided by the organization exceeds the value of the consideration received by the organization."[8]

For additional discussion of fair market value relevant to the valuation of healthcare services, specifically, see *Fair Market Value: The Principle of Substitution and Principle of Utility*. Additionally, see *Definition of Fair Market Value (IRS, Anti-Kickback, Stark)* for additional information related to how fair market value is generally defined by certain regulatory edicts.

THE PREMISE OF VALUE AND THE INVESTMENT TIME HORIZON

The premise of value, under which a valuation is conducted, is an assumption further defining the standard of value to be used. The premise of value defines the hypothetical terms of the sale and answers the question, "value under what further defining circumstances?" Two general concepts relate to the consideration and selection of the premise of value: (1) value in use and (2) value in exchange.

Value in Use

Value in use is the premise of value that assumes that the assets will continue to be used as part of an ongoing business enterprise, producing profits as a benefit of ownership of a going concern. It should be noted that, to support a valuation premise of **going concern value**, that premise would require a reasonable likelihood that the subject enterprise would generate, in the reasonably foreseeable future, sufficient net margin to generate a sufficient economic cash flow to support the value of the investment represented by the tangible assets utilized to generate the revenue stream of the provider enterprise.

Accordingly, in the absence of a reasonable expectation of such sufficient economic cash flow to support the value of the investment represented by the tangible assets utilized to generate the revenue stream of the provider enterprise, the valuator may select a premise of value of [v]alue-in-exchange as an orderly disposition of a mass assemblage of assets, in place. This premise of value does not include existing use in the production of net economic cash flow, and it will not include consideration of the assets as a going concern business enterprise.

It should be noted that the decision to utilize the value in exchange premise of value instead of the value in use premise of value does not preclude the existence of a requisite valuation of the value of intangible assets. Intangible assets may well exist and hold significant economic value in exchange. See *Classification and Valuation of Assets* for discussion of the classification and valuation of tangible and intangible assets.

Value in Exchange

The first type of **value in exchange** appraises a business as part of a mass assemblage of the assets in place, not as a going concern enterprise. This is in contrast to value in exchange, often referred to as "liquidation value," for which liquidation can be on the basis of an orderly disposition of the assets, which considers each asset on an individual basis, or on the basis of **forced liquidation**. Costs of liquidation should be considered in the value estimate when using this premise of value. Shortening the investment time horizon may have a deleterious effect on the valuation of the subject enterprise because it presents a restriction on the available pool of buyers and investors and the level of physician ownership, as required under the standard of fair market value. As stated by James Zukin

> The underlying asset approach can be done on either a net liquidation basis or by using *the value of the underlying assets in continued use*. The former basis is normally applicable when there is a distinct possibility that the business is worth more 'dead' than 'alive.' . . . value in use is the appropriate starting point for an analysis of a going business enterprise's fixed assets. However, the values reported on this basis must be tested to show that the income stream justifies the values reported. When that situation exists, value in use on an unadjusted basis is appropriate. When the net profits are not sufficient to justify the values reported, a downward adjustment to these values in use must be made. Ultimately, the underlying asset approach must consider the net profits or cash flow of a business when expressing an opinion of value other than liquidation value. *It is important that the income or benefit stream justify the values of the fixed assets in order to properly employ this approach.*[9] (emphasis added)

VALUATION ADJUSTMENTS FOR RISK

The selection of the appropriate risk adjustment to market derived required rates of return utilized in the development of selected discount rates, capitalization rates, market multiples in healthcare valuation, or a combination of these requires a thorough understanding of several underlying investment concepts. When developing a discount or **capitalization rate** to be applied in income approach methods, the following should be considered:

(1) Investors in professional practices have alternative investments available to them. Therefore, the investment justification for a given professional practice should be considered in comparison to rates of return available from a broad array of other types of investments.

(2) High risk factors are considered to have a greater than average chance of negatively affecting the enterprise's earning power, while low risk factors are considered less likely to reduce the enterprise's ability to generate profits and cash flow as a future benefit of ownership, and, accordingly, elements that increase risk decrease the value of the enterprise. Conversely, elements that decrease risk increase the value of the enterprise.

(3) Knowledgeable investors in a professional practice with an accompanying high degree of risk should require a greater return on investment to compensate for the greater risk.

(4)   There will be differences of opinion regarding how much risk is represented by any single characteristic of the professional practice, and the risk tolerance of each individual investor is, to a large extent, dependent upon the return on investment required to compensate for his or her perceived level of risk.

> Elements that increase risk decrease the value of the enterprise, and, conversely, elements that decrease risk increase the value of the enterprise.

"Options Pricing," The Options Industry Council, www.optionseducation.org/basics/options_pricing.jsp (accessed January 15, 2010).

In addition to the informed consideration (that is, consideration of the four pillars) of the effect of what may be volatile market changes on the perception of risk and resulting adjustment to the required rate of return for investment, the most probable income, earnings, or benefit stream that is forecasted to be available for a return to the subject enterprise's investors also should be analyzed carefully. This analysis helps to determine appropriate adjustments to reported results derived from historical performance, such that they reflect the most accurate and appropriate information available on the valuation date of the most probable performance, often referred to as normalized earnings. To arrive at an estimate of the normalized earnings for the subject enterprise, the adjustments considered should include but should not necessarily be limited to

(1)   actual or expected increase(s) or decrease(s) in fees and reimbursement for services by regulatory edict or competitive market pressures;

(2)   projected increase(s) or decrease(s) in operating expenses based on new operating parameters and market realities, for example, provider taxes and disclosure requirements; and

(3)   expectations of the future stability and growth of the revenue streams and the sustainability of the subject enterprise's earnings within the context of an ever-changing industry and marketplace.

In the final analysis, the valuator should make an assessment of a universe of typical buyers' existing "perceptions of the market" regarding the future performance of the subject enterprise, as well the market's assessment of risk related to an investment in such an enterprise. The valuator can then, based on an informed, realistic, and unsparing consideration of these conditions, make an assessment of an appropriate risk-adjusted required rate of return on investment and the forecast of the most probable income, earnings, or benefit stream.

VALUATION STEPS TO COMPLETE A TYPICAL CASE[10]

Prior to beginning a valuation, the valuator should consider the following several broad concepts at the outset of every engagement:

(1)   No single approach or method, or combination thereof, is universally applicable to every valuation engagement. Each case must be considered as a unique exercise of informed judgment, based upon careful analysis and supported by documented evidence and reasoned argument.

(2)   Each valuation endeavor should be considered within the context of the idea that "our process is our product." The valuation process does not lend itself to *ad hoc* decision making. A valuator

does well to remember the concept of "form before function," as well as the admonition of "the six Ps," that is "Proper Prior Planning Prevents Poor Performance."

(3)   The appraiser must "know the business," that is, he or she must have a thorough understanding of the healthcare industry and market sector within which the subject enterprise exists and operates.

In consideration of these concepts as all-encompassing tenets of the valuation engagement, the following sections discuss the steps of a valuation project. Note that a more formal description of the valuation engagement process is discussed in chapter 1, *Business Development for Consulting Services.*

DEFINING THE VALUATION ENGAGEMENT: RANGE OF VALUATION ASSIGNMENTS AND REPORT CONTENTS

At the outset of a valuation assignment, the valuator should match the deliverables of the valuation assignment to the specific purpose, objective, use, and any other special requirements of the project.

Two basic, yet distinct elements in defining the valuation engagement also should be considered:

(1)   the range of valuation assignments, which may include a written or oral appraisal report, appraisal consulting, or appraisal review; and

(2)   the scope of valuation reports, which under the 2008-2009 *Uniform Standards of Professional Appraisal Practice and Advisory Opinions* (USPAP), Scope of Work Rule,[11] it is noted that for each appraisal, appraisal review, and appraisal consulting assignment, an appraiser must:

1.   identify the problem to be solved;

2.   determine and perform the scope of work necessary to develop credible assignment results; and

3.   disclose the scope of work in the report.

An appraiser must properly identify the problem to be solved in order to determine the appropriate scope of work. The appraiser must be prepared to demonstrate that the scope of work is sufficient to produce credible assignment results.

Comment: Scope of work includes, but is not limited to:

1.   the extent to which the property is identified;

2.   the extent to which tangible property is inspected;

3.   the type and extent of data researched; and

4.   the type and extent of analyses applied to arrive at opinions or conclusions.

PRE-ENGAGEMENT

Pre-engagement steps for a valuation assignment require consideration of several definitions and project parameters required to fully denote the scope and purpose of the engagement, prior to beginning work related to the project. For example, it is necessary to

(1)   identify all parties involved in the engagement and whether there exist any conflicts of interest for the appraiser;

(2)   determine a definition and detailed description of the enterprise and interest being appraised;

(3)   determine the nature, objective, and use of appraisal and the standard of value and premise of value to be used in the course of the engagement; and

(4)   determine the effective date, or "as of" date for which the value is being determined.

Typical examples of project parameters that should be established at the outset of the engagement include the scope of assignment, timetable for appraisal, type of report to be issued, schedule of fees, any hypothetical conditions (that is, assumptions contrary to that which exist but, for the purposes of the report, have been, at the direction of the client, assumed to be that which would typically be expected by the universe of typical acquirers in a transfer of the enterprise interest), and the assumptions and limiting conditions relevant to the project and valuation.

DURING THE ENGAGEMENT

GATHERING NECESSARY DATA

An appraiser may collect two types of data for a valuation project:

(1)   *General data*, which consists of general industry research and information relative to the economic, demographic, industry, competition, healthcare industry, and medical specialty trends and managed care environments surrounding the subject entities, as well as transactional data, investment risk or return information, and market environment reports.

(2)   *Specific data*, which consists of data specific to, and obtained from, the subject entities, including, but not limited to financial statements, tax returns, productivity reports, supply inventories, accounts receivable schedules, payor mix, fixed asset schedules, service agreements, prior valuation or consulting reports, budgets and projections, and documentation on transactions involving the subject enterprise.

Data regarding the subject enterprise appropriate for the engagement may be obtained via submission of written documents and materials requests prior to site visits, phone interviews, or questionnaires. The opinion of value determined in the engagement will depend on the availability, completeness, accuracy, and reliability of this information.

PREPARING AND SUBMITTING THE VALUATION REPORT

The next steps of the valuation engagement will typically include selection of an appropriate valuation method and analysis of the gathered data, methods for which are discussed further in *Valuation Approaches, Methods, and Techniques*. After a preliminary draft report is reviewed by the client for any factual errors of omission or commission, the report is quality checked via internal review, and a signed and sealed certification report may then be submitted to the client.

POST-ENGAGEMENT

After submitting the final valuation report in full to the client, the appraiser should conduct a post-engagement review of the project with the client for the purposes of evaluating the quality of work for future engagements and for the purpose of obtaining reference permission from the client. Additionally, it is essential that all workpapers, data sources, and other engagement-related documents be retained " . . . for a period of at least five (5) years after preparation or at least two (2) years after final disposition of any judicial proceeding in which the appraiser provided testimony related to the assignment, whichever period expires last."[12] This is done for safekeeping and potential use or in the event of a dispute.

VALUATION APPROACHES, METHODS, AND TECHNIQUES

REVENUE RULING 59-60

Among the wide array of sources of guidance with which business valuation consultants should be familiar to conduct an accurate business valuation, the pronouncements of the Internal Revenue Service (IRS) may be the most widely cited. The IRS provides insights regarding its positions on business valuation issues through various mediums: Internal Revenue Code, the Treasury Regulations to the Code, Technical Advice Memorandums, Private Letter Rulings, and various Revenue Rulings. Revenue Ruling 59-60 (RR 59-60) has been a significant topic of discussion in the valuation community, because it provides basic guidance for the valuation of closely held common stocks. RR 59-60 provides a general outline and review to "the approach, methods and factors to be considered in valuing shares of the capital stock of closely held corporations for estate tax and gift tax purposes."[13]

In the valuation of the stock of closely held corporations or corporate stock that lacks market quotations, all available financial data along with significant factors affecting the fair market value should be considered. The following are fundamental factors that should be analyzed in each business valuation:

(1) "The nature of the business and the history of the enterprise from its inception;

(2) The economic outlook in general and the condition and outlook of the specific industry in particular;

(3) The book value of the stock and the financial condition of the business;

(4) The earnings capacity of the company;

(5) The dividend-paying capacity;

(6) Whether or not the enterprise has goodwill or other intangible value;

(7) Sales of stock and the size of the block of stock to be valued; and

(8) The market price of stocks of corporations engaged in the same or a similar line of business having their stocks actively traded in a free and open market, either on an exchange or over-the-counter."[14]

The choice of methodology depends primarily on the purpose of the valuation report and the specific characteristics of the professional practice. For example, the standard of value to be estimated in a divorce case is often fair market value; however, the standard may be different from state to state, because some states set a standard of fair value that is either judicially or legislatively defined. This idea is demonstrated by the state of Michigan, which has developed a concept known as the "holder's interest theory of value." The value to the holder concept is most often associated, although not frequently articulated, with investment or intrinsic value. Application of this standard of value contemplates value to the holder (or particular buyer) rather than value to a potential hypothetical buyer, that is "**investment value** [is distinguished] from fair market value in that it . . . provide[s] a going concern value to the current owner . . . [and thereby] identifies assets that have an . . . intrinsic worth to the owner, which may not be transferable to another [person]."[15]

Once the valuation consultant clearly understands the purpose of the appraisal assignment, has determined the standard of value and the premise of value, and has determined the availability and reliability of data, he or she must select one or more applicable methods. These methods can be classified by three major valuation approaches: (1) income, (2) cost, and (3) market.

> The three categories of major valuation approaches for the purpose of appraisal: income, cost, and market.
>
> *"Valuation Discounts for Lack of Marketability," by Robert James Cimasi, Physician's News Digest, Aug. 2007, www.physiciansnews.com/business/807cimasi.html (accessed December 11, 2010).*

INCOME APPROACHES

Two income approach methods are discussed in the following sections: (1) the discounted cash flow method and (2) the single period capitalization method.

DISCOUNTED CASH FLOW METHOD

The *discounted cash flow method* is a multiperiod discounting income approach based method, which estimates the present value of expected cash flows distributable to the owners of the enterprise being appraised, with a residual or "terminal" value ascribed to all periods beyond the estimated projection.

The value of an investment in an operating company is often considered to be equal to the present value of all its pro rata share of expected future cash flows. Therefore, when selecting the discounted cash flow method, the valuation consultant recognizes that the fair market value of a medical practice is the aggregate present value of the total of all cash flows likely to be achieved from the practice.

The net present value is calculated by applying a weighted average cost of capital or a risk-adjusted built-up discount rate to the total debt-free net cash flow generated by the practice. This total debt-free net cash flow is the gross collected revenues of the practice less all cash and nonowner or nonofficer compensation-related expenses adjusted for depreciation, capital expenditures, and working capital. This represents the real cash flow of the practice.

These cash flows are then discounted over the selected years of the projection at the risk-adjusted discount rate. All cash flows after the final year of the projection are accounted for in the terminal period and are calculated by utilizing the adjusted debt-free cash flow of the final projected year capitalized at the selected capitalization rate (discount rate less the long term growth rate) and then discounted at the selected risk-adjusted discount rate to arrive at the present value of all of the terminal-period cash flows. The total present value of all the cash flows will be equal to the estimated fair market value of the practice under this method.

Because the discounted net cash flow method typically results in a Subchapter C corporation equivalent level of value due to both the tax structure typically used in projections, as well as the use of a build-up method to develop a discount rate derived from empirical market transactional data shares of publicly traded C corporations, an adjustment to reflect a pass-through entity minority equity interest level of value may be appropriate. An adjustment to reflect the additional incremental net economic benefits derived from an entity's pass-through status also may be applicable to the indicated results derived from other methods, including the guideline public company method and the direct market comparable transactions method, which are discussed further in subsequent sections.

SINGLE PERIOD CAPITALIZATION METHOD

This method, also known as the "capitalization of earnings method," estimates the present value of the enterprise being appraised by capitalizing a single representative (normalized) year of economic benefits to the owner, in contrast to the multiple period discounting method.[16] The three variables on which a capitalization method depends are: (1) projected base level economic income flow, (2) **cost of capital**, and (3) expected long-term growth rate.[17] As such, it should be noted that inherent in the single period capitalization method is the expectation of stable, constant growth, and it is sensitive to unpredictable volatility or otherwise erratic changes in economic income. In cases in which the anticipated economic benefits are expected to be unstable, the valuator will most likely utilize the discounted multiple period discounted cash flow method rather than the single period capitalization method. In contrast, the single period capitalization method is often useful for entities expecting a stable or relatively even growth in economic benefits.[18]

Market Approaches

Several market approach based methods exist, including (1) the merger and acquisition method, (2) the guideline public company method, and (3) the prior subject entity transactions method. The first two of these market approach based methods are premised on the concept that actual transactions provide guidance to value rooted in the principle of substitution, which states that the value of a subject property is the cost of an equally desirable substitute or one of equal utility. Healthcare professional practice owners are perhaps more comfortable with the market approach based methods in concept, because they may be more readily comprehended, being based on observable evidence of prior transactions of comparable entities in a manner somewhat similar to how homes are appraised. Although practice owners often prefer a simplistic and easily comprehended market approach based method for appraising a healthcare professional practice, this desire for valuation convenience, in light of the paucity of reliable transactional data of homogenous, comparable enterprises, it is still often the case that (to use the old adage), "if wishes were horses, then beggars would ride!"

Although market approach based methods are conceptually desirable, there may be significant impediments to their use in valuing closely-held enterprises. As stated by Dr. Shannon Pratt:

> The opportunities to go awry in the implementation of the market approach are legion. Sometimes the toughest ones to spot are the errors of omission, such as failure to consider the full population of potentially useful guideline companies, failure to make certain adjustments, or failure to use all of the best data available to support certain adjustments, such as reasonable compensation, or a discount for lack of marketability. Some of the most common errors are: . . . failure to analyze and adjust guideline company data; . . . applying multiples to inconsistently defined data; . . . failure to account for excess or deficient cash; . . . using an "asset plus" rule when a company's returns are not adequate to support the assets employed; . . . not applying proper discounts and premiums or not adequately supporting the amounts of the discounts or premiums applied.[19]

In other words, the market-based approaches of valuation are contingent upon the homogeneity of comparable enterprises. The increasing degree of market diversity and complexity, paired with the lack of comparable and reliable data that may be attributed to potentially challenging methods of transaction price allocation may make it difficult to achieve the ideal level of homogeneity. As an example of this challenge, the Goodwill Registry, a widely known database published annually by the Health Care Group, Inc., is advertised as a source for transactional benchmarking data. It lists what it terms "goodwill percent," which is designed to serve as an indicator of value for healthcare professional practices and is reported as "the sum total of practice intangibles under *a term of convenience, 'goodwill'*" (emphasis added). More specifically, goodwill percent is based on *goodwill value*, defined as "the portion of the total value/sales price, including patient charts, leasehold interests, use of seller's name, going concern value, patient lists, credit records, restrictive covenants, consulting payments to seller, patient care contracts, etc."

The following criticisms are encountered when using data from the Goodwill Registry for market-based valuation methods:

(1) When maintaining the Goodwill Registry's definition of "goodwill value," all intangible assets of a practice are defined as goodwill (See *Goodwill and Patient-Related Intangible Assets* for further discussion of generally accepted definitions of goodwill for valuation purposes).

(2) By asserting that all practice intangible assets should be considered goodwill, as well as in its derivation of goodwill, the Goodwill Registry does not address the very nature of how tangible and intangible assets coexist and relate to each other in the value of professional practices.[20]

(3) It does not offer an explanation regarding the source of the method of allocation of the reported practice transaction price between the subject enterprise's tangible and intangible assets and the subsequent reported amount of goodwill value.

(4) It does not reveal or address whether the allocation of intangible asset value was based on the separate, discreet valuation of those respective asset classes, or whether it was calculated by the practice advisor or survey respondent merely by subtracting the tax basis depreciated book value of tangible assets that happen to appear on the practice's balance sheet (in contrast to their economic fair market value) from the reported sale price and then simply assuming that the residual amount of the sale price after that subtraction equals the value of intangible assets.

Similar challenges in interpretation of data are inherent in other widely used transaction databases.

Further discussion of differing definitions of goodwill may be found in *Conflicting Definitions of Intangible Assets Versus Goodwill*, and a discussion regarding the classification of tangible and intangible assets may be found in *Classification and Valuation of Assets*. The following sections discuss several of the market-based methods utilized in valuation engagements and further illustrate the challenges associated with this genre of approaches.

MERGER AND ACQUISITION METHOD

The merger and acquisition method, also known as the "market data comparable method," the "analysis of transactional data method," and the "direct market comparable transactions method," analyzes the terms (price, terms, interest, assets included, and so forth) of specific transactions involving the acquisition of substantial, control positions (most often the entirety) of similar assets. This method is founded on the conceptual basis of the economic principles of efficient markets and substitution. The merger and acquisition method may be applied when a relatively efficient and unrestricted secondary market for comparable properties exists and when that market accurately represents the activities of a representative number of willing buyers and willing sellers.

The principle of substitution holds that the cost of an equally desirable substitute, or one of equal utility, tends to set the ceiling of value, that is, it is the maximum that a knowledgeable buyer would be willing to pay for a property or business. However, the concept is burdened by the circumstance that, because no two companies are exactly the same, a valuator must look for transactions of homogeneous companies, similar to the subject enterprise, to use as substitutes or "guidelines" to lead to an indication of value for the subject practice.[21]

An application of the merger and acquisition method is outlined in box 4-1.

Box 4-1: The Merger and Acquisition Valuation Method

The following steps should be considered when using the merger and acquisition valuation method.

1. Select the appropriate look-back period prior to the valuation date from which to select transactions (that is, select a look-back period during which economic and industry conditions are similar to those at the valuation date).

2. Identify transactions in which the target company is similar to the subject enterprise (for example, same specialty, services, and so forth).

3. Obtain data regarding the transactions (for example, transaction consideration or price, transaction terms, target practice's financial information, number of physicians, services provided, geographic location, interest in the target company acquired, and so forth).

4. Select appropriate transactions to utilize in the methodology based upon similarity to subject practice and sufficiency of data and information related to the transaction.

5. Adjust transaction price for noncash terms of the deal. As mentioned previously in *The Standard of Value and the Universe of Typical Buyers*, implicit in the definition of fair market value is "payment is made in cash or its equivalent." Therefore, if any of the transaction consideration in the guideline transactions was paid in company stock, management or consulting agreements, earnouts, notes, or a combination of these, the transaction price may require an adjustment to reflect cash value.

6. Calculate appropriate valuation ratios. The valuator must determine whether the ratios derive an equity level of value (for example, price/EBT Earnings Before Tax or price/earnings) or an invested capital or asset level of value (for example, market value of invested capital (MVIC)/revenue or MVIC/EBITDA).

7. Analyze the data for several statistical measures of central tendency, for example, mean, median, high, low, upper quartile, and lower quartile. The valuator also may consider the relationship of the ratios to other characteristics of the target companies (for example, perform a regression analysis between the MVIC/revenue ratio and the target companies' profitability).

8. Choose the appropriate ratio to apply to the subject enterprise's proper benefit stream (for example, multiply the subject practice's net revenue to the chosen MVIC/revenue ratio).

9. Decide the appropriate weight of consideration to be given to each valuation technique, if multiple techniques are utilized (for example, MVIC/revenue and MVIC/EBITDA). The valuator should consider the nature of the universe of typical purchasers of enterprises similar to the subject enterprise, that is, are potential investors or hypothetical acquirers of the subject practice most likely be "horizontal consolidators" (that is, companies whose motivations are to increase revenue within product lines offered at the time of comparison and would affect their own expense structure to the acquired revenue stream) or "vertical integrators" (that is, companies whose motivations are to add new product lines that are not offered at the time of comparison).

10. Adjust for any assets or liabilities included or excluded in the subject practice valuation but included or excluded in the guideline transactions.

11. Apply any premiums, discounts, or both, if appropriate, to reach the level of value as set forth in the valuation engagement.

The merger and acquisition method may be selected because, conceptually, an analysis of actual transactions of comparable healthcare practices and a comparison in the aggregate to the practice "make good sense." However, the method may have drawbacks. Because no two companies are exactly the same, the transactions of homogeneous companies, similar to any given subject enterprise, typically are used as substitutes or "guidelines" to lead to an indication of value for that subject enterprise. Also, due to the developing and perceivably unreliable nature of reported comparable transactional data for healthcare practices, as well as the significant and substantive dissimilarity and individual uniqueness of healthcare practices (which tend to be unique enterprises lacking easily divisible, homogenous units for comparison), the abstraction of useful and valid data may be problematic.

GUIDELINE PUBLICLY TRADED COMPANY APPROACH

The guideline publicly traded company approach is based upon the theory that an indication of value of the subject enterprise can be derived by analyzing historical transactional data to develop several transactional ratios of shares of common stock in publicly traded companies that provide services comparable to those provided by the subject enterprise. As a result, the utility of this approach may be contingent upon the availability of a sufficient number of comparable publicly traded companies. This method assumes that pricing relationships, based on measurements of these selected transactional ratios of comparable publicly traded companies, can provide useful and relevant indications of investor expectations and, accordingly, useful indications of value for the services provided by the subject enterprise. In the circumstance that subject entities and comparable publicly traded companies exhibit largely dissimilar revenues and asset sizes, this method may not be ideal.

After a sufficient number of comparable guideline companies are identified, the market value of invested capital (MVIC) is calculated for each of the guideline publicly traded companies. MVIC is the value of equity capital (that is, market value of common stock and preferred stock outstanding) and interest-bearing debt capital (that is, market value of both long-term and short-term interest-bearing debt and capital leases). Then, the MVIC/revenue and MVIC/EBITDA **market multiples** may be calculated for each of the publicly traded comparable entities.

Smaller companies often have more business and financial risk than larger companies and tend to have lower pricing multiples than larger companies.[22] Therefore, using the previously stated equations (that is, MVIC/revenue and MVIC/EBITDA), as well as data from larger publicly traded companies to derive pricing multiples, can distort the indications of value of smaller companies (if not appropriately adjusted) when these multiples are utilized (multiplied by the subject enterprise's appropriate economic benefit stream) to develop indications of value of the subject practice. When necessary, the valuation multiples may be adjusted to reflect size disparities that may exist between the subject enterprise and the comparable publicly traded companies.

One of the size adjustment techniques which may be utilized involves the measurement of differences in the historical equity returns of smaller companies as compared to larger companies (measured by market value of equity) from data compiled and reported by credible sources [for example, the *Stocks, Bonds, Bills and Inflation Yearbook, Valuation Edition* (SBBI)]. The following equations may be utilized to adjust both the MVIC/revenue and MVIC/EBITDA multiples to reflect size disparities previously discussed:[23]

$$\textit{Adjusted MVIC/Revenue Multiple} = \cfrac{1}{\cfrac{(1)}{\textit{Unadj. Multiple}} + \left(\textit{Variant Factor (\%Equity / MVIC) x Size Premium}\right)}$$

$$\textit{Adjusted MVIC/EBITDA Multiple} = \cfrac{1}{\cfrac{(1)}{\textit{Unadj. Multiple}} + \left((\%Equity / MVIC) \text{ x Size Premium}\right)}$$

where:

Unadjusted Multiple =	*Multiple derived from guideline public company data*
% Equity/MVIC =	*Market value of equity of the guideline public company divided by market value of total invested capital of the guideline public company*
Size Premium =	*Difference between the arithmetic mean return of the guideline public company size decile compared to the subject enterprise size decile as reported by "Morningstar"*
Variant Factor =	*Net revenue of the guideline public company divided by EBITDA of the guideline public company*

Several measures of central tendency, that is, mean, median, high, low, and the upper and lower quartiles, may be calculated and used to analyze the generated adjusted multiples in order to determine the optimal means of comparing the publicly traded market transactions of the guideline companies' shares to a hypothetical transaction involving the subject enterprise. Several other considerations may factor into this analysis, such as (1) comparison of the subject enterprise's operations to those of the guideline public companies, (2) stability of the physicians and providers of the subject enterprise, (3) the practice infrastructure and dynamic (for example, as a department within a larger practice or a stand-alone entity, as well as any other arrangements, affiliations, or contracts), and (4) risk related to the probability of achieving management's projections utilized by this valuation.

Prior Subject Entity (Practice) Transactions

Prior sales of the subject enterprise, whether in its entirety or partial, can provide a good estimate of value. As one of eight factors to be considered in appraising closely held businesses, RR 59-60[24] states:

> Sales of stock of a closely held corporation should be carefully investigated to determine whether they represent transactions at arm's length. Forced or distress sales do not ordinarily reflect fair market value nor do isolated sales in small amounts necessarily control as the measure of value. This is especially true in the valuation of a controlling interest in a corporation. Since, in the case of closely held stocks, no prevailing market prices are available, there is no basis for making an adjustment for blockage. It follows, therefore, that such stocks should be valued upon a consideration of all the evidence affecting the fair market value. The size of the block of stock itself is a relevant factor to be considered. Although it is true that a minority interest in an unlisted corporation's stock is more difficult to sell than a similar block of listed stock, it is equally true that control of a corporation, either actual or in effect, representing as it does an added element of value, may justify a higher value for a specific block of stock.

Purchase and sale agreement offers related to prior transactions, or bona-fide offers or letters of intent to sell or purchase an interest in the enterprise to be appraised, may provide indications of the enterprise's fair market value and should be carefully reviewed to determine if the data is relevant as an indicator of value.

However, for several reasons, including the following, this is not always the case:

1. The size of the interest in the prior transaction may be substantially and significantly different from that of the interest being valued.

2. Transactions and offers may be few (if any) and the most recent transaction or offer may be dated years before the valuation date.

3. Significant differences can occur in the operations of the enterprise being appraised subsequent to the prior transactions.

4. It cannot be established that the selling price was negotiated in an arm's-length manner.

5. Prior transactions, including those within the company, are sometimes motivated by a desire to either reward performance and retain talent on the part of the seller or to ensure job security, on the part of the buyer, by offering an interest at a discount or premium unrelated to the fair market value of the subject enterprise. This is "undue motivation," which is proscribed in the definition of fair market value.

ASSET AND COST APPROACHES

Asset and cost approaches seek an indication of value by determining the cost of reproducing or replacing an asset. These methods are commonly utilized when there is no significant income stream to capitalize, that is, the enterprise has little value beyond the tangible assets or in the event that the enterprise is not a going concern enterprise. Several methods may be utilized under the asset approach, including (1) the asset accumulation method, (2) the liquidation value method, and (3) the excess earnings method.

ASSET ACCUMULATION METHOD

The asset accumulation method, also known as the adjusted net asset value method, estimates the value of the total **invested capital** of an enterprise by identifying, distinguishing, disaggregating, and summing the fair market value of both *tangible* and *intangible* component assets. Also refer to *Value in Exchange*, which discusses the valuation tenet of value in exchange as an orderly disposition of the assets.

Challenges with this method include determining which assets can legally be sold and to whom. Further, determining the fair market value of goodwill and intangible assets and residual goodwill requires the use of some type of capitalization of earnings method, with the same difficulties noted previously. See *Goodwill and Patient-Related Intangible Assets* for further discussion of the definition(s) and classification of intangible assets versus goodwill.

LIQUIDATION VALUE METHODS

Liquidation value methods, either by orderly or forced disposition, estimate the value of an enterprise by determining the present value of the net proceeds from liquidating the company's assets and paying off liabilities. The "orderly" method is used to describe a situation in which the sell-off process is conducted in an organized and systematic fashion under a reasonable timeline constructed by the seller. In this scenario a lesser degree of urgency exists. Under the "forced" method, the seller no longer is in a situation to proceed at its own discretion, with all, or the majority of, the assets being sold at approximately the same time in a relatively quick fashion. Generally, the *orderly liquidation value* method will yield a value greater than the value which may be determined under the forced liquidation value method.

EXCESS EARNINGS METHOD

The *excess earnings method*, also called the "treasury method" or the "IRS formula method," is based on RR 68-609 and is considered by many in the valuation community to be a hybrid method, combining elements of the asset- and cost-based approach methods with elements of income approach methods.

The excess earnings method values the intangible assets of the enterprise being appraised utilizing a residual technique. First, a portion of the benefit stream (for example, net free cash flow or net income) is attributed to a return on net tangible assets utilizing a market derived cost of capital for similar tangible assets. Then, an appropriate portion of the benefit stream is attributed to the fair market value of the replacement cost of services provided by the owner as "owner compensation." Finally, the dollar amount of the benefit that remains after the deduction of these two amounts (the "residual") is then presumed to be attributable to the intangible assets. This amount of the benefit stream, which has been determined to be attributable to the intangible assets of the subject enterprise, is then capitalized using a risk-adjusted equity rate of return, and the resulting indicated value of the intangible assets is combined with (added to) the value of the tangible assets of the enterprise being appraised to arrive at an estimate of overall asset value for the subject enterprise as a going concern.

Challenges in using the excess earnings method include (1) determining the net tangible asset value, (2) determining the earnings base to be capitalized, (3) determining a reasonable rate of return on tangible assets, and (4) determining the capitalization rate to be applied to the "excess earnings." Additionally, common errors in utilizing the excess earnings method include (1) failing to allow for owner's salary, (2) failing to use realistic normalized earnings, (3) utilizing unadjusted book values of assets, and (4) selecting the inappropriate capitalization rate.[25]

APPLICATION OF THE VALUE PYRAMID TO THE VALUATION OF A PROFESSIONAL PRACTICE ENTERPRISE

As referenced in figure 4-2, several steps must be taken in order to determine the value of the various components of the value pyramid (that is, *I, R,* and *V*), described in *The Value Pyramid*. The value represented by *I* is defined as the net economic benefit stream available to the investors in the subject practice (for example, pre-tax net income, after-tax net income, net cash flow, and so forth). A description for the determination of the net cash flow to be utilized as the *I* in the application of the value pyramid to the valuation of a professional practice enterprise is discussed in the following sections.

DEVELOPING A FORECAST AND NET ECONOMIC BENEFIT: PROJECTION OF NET REVENUE

The projection of net revenue typically is based upon two significant variables: (1) changes in reimbursement yield, which reflect the expected change in revenue per unit of procedure volume (discussed further in *Fluctuation in Reimbursement Yield: Sustainable Growth Rate: (SGR)*), and (2) changes in utilization demand and market share, which reflect the expected change in procedure volume.

When considering the former, the projection of revenue per unit of procedure volume (that is, reimbursement) should include, but should not be limited to, consideration of such aspects as the practice's payor mix and the practice management's change in commercial reimbursement, potential Congressional action regarding Medicare and Medicaid reimbursement, and changes to the types of procedures eligible for payment as designated by Current Procedural Terminology (CPT) codes (for example, the addition of new codes or the subtraction or bundling of existing codes).

Projected changes in utilization demand and market share should include, but should not be limited to, consideration of such aspects as the expected change in the service area's population, the expected change in the age demographics and social economic characteristics of the service area's population, the introduction and acceptance of new technologies, the entrance or exit of competitors, changes to the types of procedures eligible for payment as they are defined by CPT codes, the practice management's expectation of change in volume, and the capacity of the practice's facilities.

Fluctuation in Reimbursement Yield: Sustainable Growth Rate (SGR)

As a factor with a direct effect on the projection of a practice's net revenue, it is important for a valuation consultant to consider the variables that determine annual reimbursement yield. Since 1998, Medicare annual fee schedules have been determined by a methodology known as the sustainable growth rate (SGR). This method, based on a forecast of inflation, Medicare enrollment, growth of the gross domestic product (GDP), and specified regulatory developments, sets a target level for healthcare expenditures under Medicare Part B. Payment schedules for the subsequent year are adjusted either up or down depending on what actual healthcare expenditures are, as compared to the target. As discussed further in chapter 2 of *An Era of Reform*, since 2002, healthcare expenditures have consistently exceeded SGR target levels, resulting in increasingly larger cuts to the physician payment schedules in subsequent years. However, due to Congressional action, the proposed cuts to reimbursement have been overridden each year (see table 4-1 for annual changes to the conversion factor from 2004–9), and often increased by approximately 1 percent. However, should Congress fail to act in accordance with its historical precedents, a significant negative change in reimbursement yield could have a significant impact on projections for the enterprise's net revenue.

DEVELOPING A FORECAST AND NET ECONOMIC BENEFIT: PROJECTION OF EXPENSES

Once the revenue has been projected, the economic expense burden utilized to generate that revenue must be projected. The first step for projecting expenses is to determine whether the expense is a *fixed expense* or a *variable expense*. A fixed expense is one that does not change from period to period, or changes very little (for example, rent). In contrast, a variable expense changes with the consumption of the good or service of interest (for example, utilities). When projecting expenses, a valuator also may consider a mix of both fixed and variable expenses.

Once expenses are determined to be fixed or variable, the valuator may then determine which growth index to utilize. A fixed expense can be grown at an indexed rate (for example, a medical care inflation rate), although a variable expense can be grown based on several methods of allocation, for example, at the rate of growth of net revenue, at the rate of growth of procedure volume, or at an increase in square footage, and so forth. In addition, in those circumstances in which an expense may be considered a mix of both fixed and variable expenses, it can be grown at a hybrid rate of growth, including the fixed indexed rate and the variable rate, or an expense can be projected based on management's expectation.

DEVELOPING A FORECAST AND NET ECONOMIC BENEFIT: PROJECTION OF NET CASH FLOW

The statement of net **cash flow** reports an enterprise's sources and uses of cash for a specific period of time. A projected economic statement of net cash flows (represented by I in the value pyramid) for the professional practice may be derived from the practice's forecasted income statements.

First, the practice's net income after taxes typically is converted to a debt-free level of cash flow by the following method:

(1) Adding noncash expenses, such as depreciation and amortization expense;

(2) Subtracting increases in working capital; and

(3) Subtracting projected capital expenditures during each respective projected period.

The resulting net cash flow on a debt-free (asset) basis reflects the measure of economic benefit to the owner of assets in the professional practice, which is utilized in the discounted net cash flow method. However, note that if the valuator is not proceeding with the analysis on a debt-free basis and is instead utilizing a "net of debt" technique in a subsequent step, debt must be considered as an addition to cash flow.

Table 4-1: Medicare Updates: Changes in Conversion Factors[*]

Year	Update
2004	1.5%
2005	1.5%
2006	0.2%
2007	0.0%
2008	0.5%
2009	1.1%
Average change:	
2004–2009	0.8%

[*] "Estimated Sustainable Growth Rate and Conversion Factor, for Medicare Payments to Physicians in 2010," Centers for Medicare and Medicaid Services, November 2009, p. 7.

It should be noted that, to support a valuation premise of value-in-use as a going concern would require a reasonable likelihood that the subject enterprise would generate, in the reasonably foreseeable future, sufficient net margin distributable first to those physician producers of the practice revenue stream, second to support the nonphysician compensation related overhead, and third to provide a sufficient economic cash flow that supports the value of the investment represented by the tangible assets utilized to generate the revenue stream of the practice enterprise.

In some circumstances, analysis of the past and existing performance of the subject enterprise, in consideration of the most probable revenue forecast and expense structure for the practice (and within the context of prevailing market conditions related to physician and staff compensation and other practice expenses), fails to indicate a reasonable likelihood that the subject enterprise, as a going concern enterprise, would generate sufficient net economic cash flow to support the value of the investment represented by the tangible assets utilized to generate the revenue stream of the practice. Such circumstances present a significant boundary for the consideration of the premise of value.

Maintaining with the value of the underlying assets in continued use, as stated by Zukin (see *Value in Exchange*), in the absence of a reasonable expectancy of such net economic cash flow to support the value of the investment represented by the tangible assets utilized to generate the revenue stream of the subject enterprise, the premise of value of "value in exchange as an orderly disposition of a mass assemblage of assets, in place" may be selected, wherein premise of value typically excludes existing use in the production of net economic cash flow, as well as consideration of the assets as a going concern business enterprise.

Utilizing valuation approaches and methods consistent with an underlying asset approach to value may account for the component parts of a business enterprise, but it remains contingent upon the definition of the premise of value of "value in exchange as an orderly disposition of a mass assemblage of assets, in place." Pratt stated:[26]

> The selection of the appropriate premise of value is an important step in defining the appraisal assignment. Typically, in a controlling interest valuation, the selection of the appropriate premise of value is a function of the highest and best use of the collective assets of the subject business enterprise. Each of these alternative premises of value may apply under the same standard, or definition, of value. For example, the fair market value standard calls for a 'willing buyer' and a 'willing seller.' Yet, these willing buyers and sellers have to make an informed economic decision as to how they will transact with each other with regard to the subject business. In other words, is the subject business worth more to the buyer and the seller as a going concern that will continue to operate as such, or as a collection of individual assets. . . . In either case, the buyer and seller are still 'willing.' And, in both cases, they have concluded a set of transactional circumstances that will maximize the value of the collective assets of the subject business enterprise.

Further support for the selected premise of value of "value in exchange as an orderly disposition of a mass assemblage of assets, in place" may, for some practices, stem from the possibility that, in lacking the immediate ability to obtain fair market compensation, a significant number of physicians would depart from the practice, thereby making it unlikely to be sustained as a going concern enterprise.

COST CAPITAL: DEVELOPING THE RISK-ADJUSTED REQUIRED RATE OF RETURN

In the discussion of the value pyramid (see *The Value Pyramid* and *Application of the Value Pyramid to the Valuation of a Professional Practice Enterprise*), having forecasted future net economic benefit to the owner, the next step in the valuation process is to apply a risk-adjusted required rate of return (that is, the *R* of the value pyramid), by which to the net benefit stream is capitalized to economic value at a date certain, also known as the **valuation date**. Risk is discussed further in *Assessing Risk*.

COMPARATIVE FINANCIAL DATA AND BENCHMARKING

Information used to compare the subject enterprise's financial statements with industry averages is available through a variety of industry sources. Some of the standard sources which cover all industry categories include: *RMA Annual Statement Studies*, published by the Risk Management Association; *Financial Studies of the Small Business*, published by Financial Research Associates; and *Statistics of Income: Partnership Source Book* and *Statistics of Income: Sole Proprietor Source Book*, both of which are available from the National Archives of the IRS. Other sources of this data include trade associations and various industry studies.

Benchmarking techniques often are used to compare financial data and determine the degree to which the enterprise of interest (for example, professional practice) varies from comparable healthcare industry (market) norms, providing an indication of the subject enterprise's internal performance and financial status, among other metrics for the purpose of assessing risk related to the investment in the subject enterprise. See chapter 2, *Purpose of Benchmarking* for further discussion of benchmarking techniques utilized in valuation and their purpose. Additionally, see chapter 2, *Financial Benchmarking*, for more discussion regarding the process and metrics utilized for financial benchmarking techniques. Note that benchmarking also is used when comparing compensation data; see chapter 2, *Compensation Benchmarking* for further discussion of this benchmarking type. Sources for financial and compensation benchmarking data are described further in chapter 2, *Sources of Benchmarking Data*.

RETURN ON INVESTMENT—DISCOUNT RATE OR COST OF EQUITY

The **discount rate**, at which the measured expected stream of economic benefit of ownership is discounted to present value, is selected by the valuation consultant to represent the rate of return a typical investor in the professional practice would require in discounting the expected stream of the economic benefits of equity ownership of the subject professional practice, given the systematic risk of the market, as well as the unsystematic risk of investment in the subject professional practice. In contrast, the capitalization rate is the rate by which a single estimate of benefit is divided to determine value. Inherent in the single period capitalization formula is the assumption of continuity of the benefit stream in perpetuity. Typically, the capitalization rate is calculated by deducting the projected annual long-term growth rate of the subject healthcare practice from the selected discount rate.

Discount Rate

<less growth>

= Capitalization (CAP) Rate

As mentioned previously, the discount rate is a measure of return required of an equity investor, therefore, in effect, it is the cost of equity of a specific business enterprise. The cost of equity combined with the cost of debt comprise the weighted average cost of capital (WACC) of a specific business enterprise (discussed further in *Weighted Average Cost of Capital*), which is utilized when estimating the return on investment of total invested capital (both equity and debt).

WEIGHTED AVERAGE COST OF CAPITAL

The discount rate or cost of equity typically is applied when determining the present value of future economic benefits in deriving the equity value (that is, the **net book value**) of the enterprise being appraised, or, a "net-of-debt" basis:

equity = assets − liabilities

When applying an income approach method to value the assets of the enterprise, that is, on a "debt-free" basis, the valuator would typically use a WACC as the expected rate of return on the investment:

assets = equity + liabilities

The WACC is a blend of the cost of an enterprise's various capital components, including the cost of debt capital and the cost of equity capital of the enterprise.

The WACC is calculated by the formula:

$$WACC = (k_e * W_e) + (k_d [1-t] * W_d)$$

where:

k_e = *Cost of Equity*

W_e = *Weight of Equity*

k_d = *Cost of Debt*

t = *Effective Tax Rate*

W_d = *Weight of Debt*

RISK-FREE RATE

The starting point for developing an appropriate discount rate is the alternative investment opportunities in risk-free or relatively risk-free investments. The interest paid by U.S. government securities is often considered to be a close substitute or proxy for a risk-free rate (for example, a twenty-20-year treasury bond).

INVESTMENT ALTERNATIVE (EQUITY RISK PREMIUM)

This adjustment reflects the extra return, or premium, that is expected by the typical equity investor in large company stocks in excess of the return on a riskless asset. Morningstar has studied and estimated the historical (since 1926) realized **equity risk premium (ERP)** associated with the risk of investment in common stock in SBBI.

Various valuation publications have compared the expected growth in GDP, earnings, or dividends with realized returns reported by sources such as Morningstar, noting that "investors could not have expected as large an ERP as the equity premiums actually realized."[27] These studies suggest that investors reasonably would not have expected as large an ERP as that which was actually realized, and it may be appropriate to adjust downward a historical realized ERP to estimate an expected ERP, based on the aforementioned studies and recent research.[28]

INDUSTRY RISK PREMIUM

This adjustment measures the risk of the healthcare industry (Standard Industrial Classification (SIC) code 80) against the market index as a whole by applying an industry risk premium to the "build-up" method. Morningstar has developed an industry premium methodology from tracking the returns and related betas, which are measurements of relative volatility, of companies in a number of industries in SBBI, and it estimated the industry risk premium for SIC 801 "Offices and Clinics of Doctors of Medicine" to be -0.79 percent.[29]

SIZE RISK PREMIUM

The combination of the risk-free rate and the equity risk premium estimates the return required by the investor in large company stocks. Morningstar measures the additional return of small company stocks over the market as a whole.[30]

COMPANY-SPECIFIC RISK (CSR) PREMIUM

The combination of the risk-free rate and the equity risk premium estimates the return required by the investor in large company stocks. Ibbotson measures the additional return of small company stocks over the market as a whole.

This adjustment is somewhat more subjective in that it reflects the valuation consultant's informed assessment of the various risk factors that are inherent and specific to the subject professional practice. Additional risk factors, specific to a subject healthcare practice include, but are not limited to, operational performance (as evidenced by benchmarking), market or competition, technological obsolescence, uncertainty related to reimbursement from government and managed care providers, provider and staff stability, access to capital, risk related to key persons or key suppliers, depth of management, and geographic distribution.

Research challenges related to determining the appropriate discount rate or cost of equity include (1) finding research to support the quantification of subject healthcare practice specific risk premiums, (2) obtaining size premium data for small companies, and (3) determining industry risk adjustments for certain professional practice industry subsectors.

A calculator has been released using the Butler-Pinkerton method to measure total cost of equity and public company specific risk.[31] It provides empirical benchmarks for selecting the correct company-specific risk (CSR) premium for the subject enterprise, mixing subjective and objective techniques. This process begins by reviewing the public company's form 10-K to understand the disclosures related to company-specific factors. The valuator can then place the private company within, above, or below the calculated benchmarks based on the degree to that the private company faces the same risks as the public company. Also, although Pinkerton and Butler do not recommend using the NASDAQ index as a proxy, it is available in their calculator. The calculator can only be used to calculate implicit volatilities exactly matching the private company's total cost of equities. Canadian public companies also can be used in the calculator. If the companies are publicly traded in the United States, pricing data will be available. Otherwise, historical data must be utilized. The calculator pulls closing prices of indices and can handle pricing adjusted for dividends. Data is available for the previous five years (or 261 weeks), and the creators recommend using at least the past three years when calculating beta. Also, selecting public company comparables in the model using the calculator does not differ from selecting them for the market approach.

One of the most innovative abilities of the calculator is the way it pulls the prior 261 weeks of closing prices for a particular company. For example, if the effective date is Monday, the calculator will return 261 Mondays of closing prices. The technique has not been reviewed by the Security Exchange Commission or the IRS.[32]

Pinkerton and Butler were questioned about the necessity of having good public company comparables when using the calculator for a $40 million enterprise when the opposing party valued it at $90 million. They responded by explaining that the calculator has empirical data, although alternatives to calculating CSR lack this type of data. Although the calculator may have "'not-so great' guidelines," the component observation method offers no empirical data. Because the calculator computes the CSR from the same publicly traded companies included in the income approach, it should not be discounted when there are no good guideline companies to use, because the income approach is not abandoned when this occurs.[33]

ASSESSING RISK

When assessing the amount of risk associated with the given professional practice enterprise being valued (component R of the value pyramid), it is important for the valuator to keep the following items in mind:

(1) Because uncertainty breeds the perception of risk, under which circumstances a higher rate of return is demanded by potential purchasers, even high quality, risk averse, stable growth, highly profitable, and eminently transferable professional practices may have the potential to be "tar-brushed" by the perception of overall market uncertainty, as well as risk related to the particular subject enterprise's industry sector.

(2) Other market motivating factors often drive transactional pricing multiples, for example, investors' fear of being shut out of their ability to legally maintain or sell their investment, represents an undue stimulus or special motivation and synergy that may drive the deal resulting in prices below or above value.

(3) The selection of risk-adjusted rates to capitalize an earnings or benefit stream into value requires more than just a cursory analysis of underlying data related to market systematic risk, as a nonsystematic, subject enterprise risk adjustment also may be appropriate.

The valuator should aware that the assessment of risk by investors is related to both the actualities and (perhaps more substantially) the perceptions of the market, related to external economic, demographic, and industry conditions, as well as to aspects of the specific subject professional practice and the prospective transaction.

ANALYSIS OF RISK

As discussed previously, it is important to first analyze and reach a supportable conclusion regarding the relationship between risk and return for a specific type of practice investment which is characteristic of the specific dynamics of the market in which it operates at any point in time before selecting a discount or capitalization rate.

It should be kept in mind that although this estimate of investor perceived risk is necessarily based, to a great degree, on the subjective judgment of the valuation consultant, objective methods and teachings are available and should be employed to the extent possible to arrive at a valid and supportable discount or capitalization rate. The assessment of risk is inexorably related to and should be based upon an informed consideration of the most probable expectations and perceptions of a universe of typical buyers regarding the future performance of the subject enterprise, as well as material changes in substantive value drivers.

In the final analysis, the assessment of risk must be correlated carefully to an informed, realistic, and unsparing assessment of existing "buyer perceptions in the market."

LEVEL OF VALUE—DISCOUNTS AND PREMIUMS

With each method utilized, certain adjustments should be considered based upon the specific requirements of each engagement and the inherent indication of value, that is, the "level of value" that results from each method.

When a "closely held" level of value (in contrast to "freely traded," "marketable," or "publicly traded" level) is sought, the valuation consultant may need to make adjustments to the indicated valuation results. Inherent risks exist and are relative to the **liquidity** of investments in closely held, nonpublic companies that are not relevant to the investment in companies whose shares are publicly traded (freely traded). Investors in closely held companies do not have the ability to dispose of an invested interest quickly if the situation is called for, for example, forecasted unfavorable industry conditions or the investor's personal immediate need for cash. This relative lack of liquidity of ownership in a closely held company is accompanied by risks and costs associated with the selling of an interest in said company (that is, locating a buyer, negotiation of terms, advisor or broker fees, risk of exposure to the market, and so forth). Conversely, investors in the stock market most often are able to sell their interest in a publicly traded company within hours and receive cash proceeds in a few days. Accordingly, a discount may be applicable to the value of a closely held company due to the inherent illiquidity of the investment. Such a discount is commonly referred to as a **discount for lack of marketability**.

> Inherent risks exist and are relative to the liquidity of investments in closely held, nonpublic companies that are not relevant to the investment in companies whose shares are publicly traded.

"Valuation Discounts for Lack of Marketability," by Robert James Cimasi, Physician's News Digest, Aug. 2007, www.physiciansnews.com/business/807cimasi.html (accessed December 11, 2010).

Over the years, several empirical studies have been performed that attempt to quantify a discount for lack of marketability, typically in three categories: (1) transactions involving restricted stock of publicly traded companies, (2) private transactions of companies prior to their initial public offering, and (3) an analysis and comparison of the price to earnings ratios of acquisitions of public and private companies.

With a noncontrolling interest, in which the holder cannot solely authorize and cannot solely prevent corporate actions (in contrast to a controlling interest), a **discount for lack of control**, (DLOC), may be appropriate. In contrast, a **control premium** may be applicable to a controlling interest. A control premium is an increase to the pro rata share of the value of the business that reflects the impact on value inherent in the management and financial power that can be exercised by the holders of a control interest of the business (usually the majority holders). Conversely, a DLOC or minority discount is the reduction from the pro rata share of the value of the business as a whole that reflects the impact on value of the absence or diminution of control that can be exercised by the holders of a subject interest.

Several empirical studies have been done to attempt to quantify DLOC from its antithesis, control premiums. The studies include the *Mergerstat Review*, an annual series study of the premium paid by investors for controlling interest in publicly traded stock, and the *Control Premium Study*, a quarterly series study that compiles control premiums of publicly traded stocks by attempting to eliminate the possible distortion caused by speculation of a deal.[34]

CLASSIFICATION AND VALUATION OF ASSETS

As related to the valuation of assets, once the subject enterprise and interest have been defined, the appropriate classification of assets and the goodwill related to the professional practice is critical to the valuation process. The classification of assets may be initiated by condensing the existing assets within the context of two categories: tangible and intangible. See a general definition of both terms in *Overview*. Figure 4-4 depicts a representative classification of tangible and intangible assets in the context of a professional practice.

Figure 4-4: Classification of Intangible and Tangible Assets

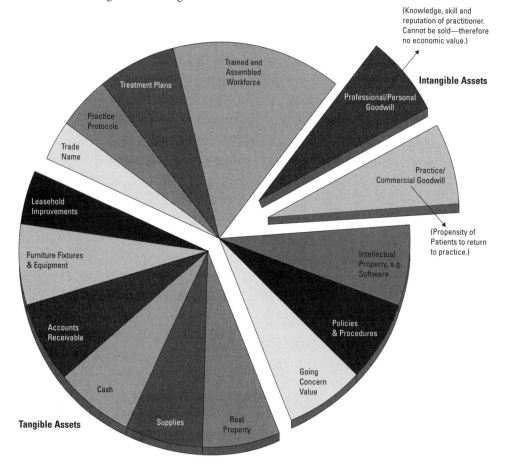

Professional healthcare practices are only one of a wide range of many different and unique healthcare service sector enterprises, and each will have a unique and distinct profile regarding the likelihood of existence of the various specific assets. Although the existence or nonexistence of any of these distinct assets in the various types of healthcare service sector enterprises is specific to the subject enterprise being valued, it may be useful to review some general observations that may be made regarding that likelihood, based on the historical development, changes in the industry, and subsequent changes in organizational structure and operation of the various types.

Figure 4-5 provides an illustrative analysis of the likelihood of the existence of specific assets of professional practice or physician-related organizations. Following a listing of the types of tangible assets is a listing of the types of intangible assets often considered, as classified into ten main categories. It should be noted that this representative listing is for illustrative purposes only.

Figure 4-5: Likelihood of Existence of Specific Assets of Physician Organizations

LIKELIHOOD OF EXISTENCE OF SPECIFIC ASSETS OF PHYSICIAN ORGANIZATIONS 1. Almost always 2. Often 3. Sometimes 4. Almost never, minimal	Solo	Office Based Group	Academic	Hospital Based Group	IPA	GPWW	MSO	PPMC	Hospitalist
Tangible									
1) Accounts Receivable	1	1	3	1	4	4	4	2	2
2) Cash, Investments	3	2	4	2	4	4	3	2	2
3) Furniture, Fixtures, and Equipment	1	1	4	4	4	4	1	2	4
4) Leasehold Improvements	3	1	4	4	4	4	3	2	4
5) Real Property	3	3	4	4	4	4	3	3	4
6) Supplies	1	1	3	4	4	4	3	2	4
7) Medical Library	4	2	2	3	4	4	4	4	4
Intangible									
1) Payor/Customer-Related									
a) Managed-Care Agreements	1	1	1	1	1	3	4	2	1
b) Provider Service Agreements/Medical Directorships	3	2	1	1	4	3	4	3	1
c) Direct Contracting Customer Lists	3	2	3	4	2	4	4	3	3
d) HMO Enrollment Lists	4	3	3	4	2	4	4	2	4
2) Goodwill and Patient-Related									
a) Custody of Medical Charts and Records	1	1	3	4	4	4	4	3	4
b) Personal/Professional Goodwill	1	1	1	2	4	4	4	3	2
c) Practice/Commercial Goodwill	3	2	3	3	3	3	3	3	3
d) Patient Lists/Recall Lists	2	2	3	4	4	4	4	3	4
3) Human Capital-Related									
a) Employment/Provider Contracts	4	1	1	1	3	4	3	2	1
b) Trained and Assembled Workforce	2	1	4	3	3	4	2	2	4
c) Policies and Procedures	3	2	3	2	2	3	2	2	3
d) Depth of Management	4	2	3	4	3	3	2	2	4
4) Intellectual Property-Related									
a) Practice Protocols	4	2	2	2	3	3	4	3	2
b) Treatment Plans/Care Mapping	3	2	2	2	3	3	4	3	2
c) Procedural Manuals/Laboratory Notebooks	4	2	2	3	4	4	3	2	3

(continued)

(continued)

LIKELIHOOD OF EXISTENCE OF SPECIFIC ASSETS OF PHYSICIAN ORGANIZATIONS 1. Almost always 2. Often 3. Sometimes 4. Almost never, minimal	Solo	Office Based Group	Academic	Hospital Based Group	IPA	GPWW	MSO	PPMC	Hospitalist
d) Technical and Specialty Research	4	3	2	4	4	4	3	3	3
e) Patents and Patent Applications	4	3	2	3	4	4	4	4	4
f) Copyrights	4	3	3	4	4	4	4	4	4
g) Trade Names	3	2	4	4	3	3	3	1	4
h) Trade Secrets	4	3	3	4	3	3	4	3	4
i) Royalty Agreements	4	4	3	4	3	3	3	3	4
5) Locations and Operations-Related									
a) Management Information/Executive Decision	4	2	3	3	2	3	2	1	4
b) Favorable Leases-Leasehold interests	2	3	3	4	4	4	3	3	4
c) Going Concern Value	3	2	3	4	3	4	2	2	4
d) Asset Assemblage Factors	3	2	4	4	4	4	2	2	4
e) Historial Documents/Charts/RVU Studies	2	2	2	3	3	4	3	3	4
f) Supplier Contracts, e.g. Group Purchasing Orgs.	3	2	2	4	4	3	2	2	4
6) Governance/Legal Structure-Related									
a) Organizational Documents	4	1	2	1	3	2	1	1	4
b) Non-Compete Covenants	4	1	2	1	4	3	1	1	3
c) Income Distribution Plans	4	1	1	1	4	1	1	1	4
7) Marketing and Business Development-Related									
a) Print Ads, Telephone #s, Billboards, etc.	2	2	3	4	4	3	2	3	4
b) Franchise/License Agreements	3	3	4	4	4	4	3	3	4
c) Joint Ventures/Alliances, e.g. "Call-a-nurse"	3	2	2	4	4	3	3	2	4
d) Market Entrance Barriers/Factors	3	2	2	2	3	3	3	3	3
8) Regulatory/Legal-Related									
a) Facility Licenses	4	3	4	4	4	3	3	3	4
b) Medical Licenses	1	1	1	1	4	4	4	4	1
c) Permits—Real Estate Special Use	3	3	4	4	4	3	3	3	4
d) Litigation Awards and Liquidated Damages	4	3	4	3	3	3	3	3	4
e) Certificates of Need	4	3	4	4	4	3	3	3	4
f) Medicare Certification/UPIN	1	1	1	1	4	4	4	3	1
g) Certifications—e.g. NCQA, AAAHC, JCAHO	3	3	3	3	3	4	4	3	1
9) Financial/Revenue Stream-Related									
a) Office Share	3	3	4	4	4	2	2	3	4
b) Management Services Contracts	4	3	4	4	4	2	1	1	1
c) Financing Agreements	4	3	4	4	4	3	3	3	4
d) Underwriting/Private Placement Memoranda	4	3	4	4	4	3	2	1	4
e) Budgets/Forecasts/Projections	4	2	3	3	2	3	2	1	4
10) Technology-Related									
a) Computer Software/Network Integration	4	2	4	4	2	3	2	1	4
b) Technical/Software Documentation	4	3	4	4	2	3	2	1	4
c) Maintenance/Support Relationships	2	1	4	4	1	2	1	1	4

Additional discussion and definitions regarding a representative list of intangible assets of a professional practice (referenced in figure 4-5) may be found in *Classification and Valuation of Intangible Assets*.

This relationship of the respective values of tangible and intangible assets relative to the value of the entire practice enterprise was illustrated in the classic 1937 text by James C. Bonbright, *The Valuation of Property: A Treatise on the Appraisal of Property for Different Legal Purposes*:[35]

> What is the value of the left-hand member of a pair of $4 gloves? Practically nothing if the part is valued separately from the whole; approximately $4 if the part is valued as a part of the larger whole. Obviously, neither of these figures—zero of $4 per glove—can be multiplied by two as an expression of the value of a pair of gloves. On the other hand, if we start with the $4 value of the entire pair and prorate that figure between the two gloves by dividing by two, we get a value per glove that is utterly meaningless.
>
> The example of the gloves presents an almost perfect illustration of a case where each part of an organic whole must be valued either at zero or else at the full value of the whole, depending on whether the part is valued as a separate commodity or as a part of the larger unit. This situation prevails whenever each of three conditions is met: (a) when each part is utterly worthless except as a part of the whole, (b) when no one part can be replaced except at a cost at least equal to the value of the whole, or except after a fatal delay, and, (c) when each part is indispensable to the functioning of the whole. Seldom, however, are all these conditions met with in the valuation of property. Many of the assets of a business enterprise, for example, can be disposed of, separately from the business, at a substantial price; most of them can be replaced in time to save the business and at a cost much less than the value of the whole business; many of them are not indispensable to the business—the enterprise could get along without them, though with a loss of earning power. Each asset, therefore, is worth neither zero on the one basis of valuation, nor the full value of the entire enterprise on the other basis.
>
> It is nevertheless true that, with rare exceptions, there is a wide disparity between the value of an entire business enterprise and the sum of the values of its various assets or parts. This truth is well recognized when the comparison is between the value of the whole business and the separate liquidation values of the assets.[36] But it has been frequently overlooked, or even expressly denied, when the comparison is between the value of the business and the sum of the values of the assets, valued as parts of the whole. Misled by the mathematical postulate, applied to spatial relationships, that 'the whole is equal to the sum of its parts,' many courts, and even some expert appraisers, have falsely inferred that the value of an economic whole is equal to the sum of the values of the parts. They have therefore often assumed that the value of the intangible assets of a business is equal to the value of the business itself minus the value of the tangibles . . .

Tangible assets of a subject enterprise often are defined as those items owned by the subject enterprise that possess a physicality, that is, they can be seen or touched. The intangible assets of the subject enterprise often are defined as those nonphysical items that grant certain specified property rights and privileges of ownership and that have or promise economic benefits to the owner(s) of the subject enterprise.

Although the major distinction between these definitions of tangible and intangible assets is the aspect of their "physicality," this is not an exclusive definitional barrier. In fact, "physical" tangible assets also possess an "intangible" aspect with respect to the legal rights of property ownership attached to them. Further, some physical evidence or element of an intangible asset often exists that reassures its economic existence. For example, relationships between an employer and its employees that form the basis of "trained-and-assembled-workforce-in-place" are intangible, however, they may be evidenced by employment agreements. Intellectual property rights, such as trade names, trademarks, service marks, patents, and copyrights, are intangible assets, however, they may be evidenced by certificates, licenses, and other related documents.

When determining whether some aspect of a business enterprise, or some factor of the operation and performance of that enterprise in the market, qualifies as an intangible asset, the aspect or factor should be endowed with several attributes characteristic of "property" that may be ascribed to it and that allow it to rise to the definition of "intangible asset."

These traits, qualities, attributes, and characteristics include:

(1) The item should exist and be identified in a manner that allows it to be recognized as a legal property right that can be defended in court as private property and the ownership of which can be sold or transferred.

(2) The item should have some element of evidentiary support and documentation for its existence, including both the inception and the termination of its existence in relation to an action, circumstance, or event that can be legally described and identified.

(3) The item should, despite its lack of physical substance, generate a measure of economic benefit to its owner.

With regard to the concept of property as an economic physicality, James C. Bonbright states:

> These perplexing questions as to the nature of the thing to be valued might seem to be of no concern to the student of valuation, however . . . [h]ow one shall define property in a given case is bound up with the question how one shall find value in that same case. The two problems must be treated together by persons who understand their interrelationship.[37]

From a valuation and economic perspective it may be useful to consider property within the context of four principal categories:

(1) Personal property that is tangible

(2) Personal property that is intangible

(3) Real estate property that is tangible

(4) Real estate property that is intangible

In recognition that real property has been defined as, " . . . the bundle of legal rights which people have in . . . the very objects, particularly the tangible objects to which these rights attach," and with the given that any given legal right is "intangible," it is a logical deduction that "real property" is intangible.[38] However, the real estate appraisal industry has distinguished "real property" ("the intangible bundle of rights, interests, and benefits inherent in the ownership of real estate") from "real estate" ("the tangible, physical entity").

In addition to the complexity of distinguishing between "intangible real property" and "intangible personal property," the issue of "property as an economic physicality" involves other aspects of the definition of intangible assets. These include such attributes as whether the item is able to be touched and felt (tangible) and seen or observed (visible) and whether it has a physical, material body (corporeal).

Having determined how to adequately classify tangible versus intangible assets, the following sections further discuss the classification and valuation of types of tangible and intangible assets.

VALUATION OF TANGIBLE PERSONAL PROPERTY

When performing a valuation analysis, the purpose of the recast analysis and restatement of the balance sheet of the enterprise being valued is to determine the economic assets and liabilities of the subject enterprise, including tangible personal property, or **tangible assets**. The standard of value often utilized for valuation of tangible personal property (for example, furniture, fixtures, and equipment, or FF&E) is fair market value and assumes a debt-free cash sale on an as is, where is basis. This concept or standard of value presupposes the continued utilization of each of the items in conjunction with all other installed items of FF&E that are included within the scope of the analysis and that a revenue stream exists sufficient to justify their utilization. The highest and best use for FF&E can be defined as "the most probable and legal use of a property, which is physically possible, appropriately supported, financially feasible, and that results in the highest value."[39] An illustrative example of a typical FF&E analysis is described in following paragraphs and depicted in table 4-2.

The subject enterprise assets can be depicted through a depreciation expense report, which may include asset descriptions, dates of acquisition, acquisition costs, accumulated depreciation, deprecation methods, and taxable lives for the FF&E of the practice. In addition, the valuation consultant typically performs a physical inventory and inspection of the practice's assets.

When utilizing the asset or cost approach to valuing assets, the replacement cost new (index price) is determined by multiplying appropriate asset inflation factors to historical cost. Following the determination of the index price for the practice assets, the economic value of the assets is calculated by applying a devalue percentage, based on the economic useful life and age of the asset, to the index price. The devalue percentage is calculated as the age of the asset (in years) divided by the economic useful life of the asset.

Functional and economic obsolescence also may be considered in the analysis of the practice assets. Functional obsolescence occurs when the replacement assets would have greater utility, that is, improved production processes or lower operating costs, than the original or existing equipment. Economic obsolescence occurs when some event or circumstance, "external" to the equipment itself, is responsible for a decreased ability of the equipment to properly perform its intended task. Examples of economic factors contributing to an impairment of an asset include decreased demand for a product, limited production life, and environmental or governmental regulations imposed on a type of asset that might limit or impede its operation.

VALUATION OF ACCOUNTS RECEIVABLE

Similar to the restatement of tangible personal property, the accounts receivable for a subject enterprise are restated to reflect an actual expected collections rather than the book value. An adjustment for net accounts receivable to reflect the fair market value typically include some adjustment(s) to the historical collection rate, the cost of collection, and a present value adjustment to the book value of gross charges allocated to the enterprise.

Table 4-2: Example of Cost Approach to Furniture, Fixtures, and Equipment (FF&E)

A Type	B Description	C Number of Items	D Economic Life	E Asset Condition	F Year Acquired
M	Deluxe Ultrasound Table	1	15	5	1990
M	Philips Ie33 Echo System	1	5	3	2007
M	Midmark TEE Procedure Treatment Cart	1	10	4	1991
M	Tilt Table	1	15	2	—
M	Patient Step Stools	3	15	3	2001
M	Exam Chairs	3	15	3	2000
Historical Price					
Restated Value					
Fair Market Value of FF&E per Cost Approach					

When:

A: Classified as medical (M) or office (O) equipment
B or C: Description of equipment and quantity
D: Economic useful life (3, 4, 5, 7, 10, 15, 20, 25, 30, or 40 years)
E: Condition factor weight
F: Acquisition date, per review of data
G: Acquisition price, per review of data
H: [Current index for type (M) or (O)]/(index at acquisition * acquisition price)
I: Replacement cost new estimate, if applicable
J: Devaluage percentage based on economic life
K: Condition factor
L: Restated value, indexed price * (1 − devaluation percentage) * condition factor = valuation

Source: "Valuation Quarterly," Marshall & Swift

CLASSIFICATION AND VALUATION OF INTANGIBLE ASSETS

In the context of the valuation of healthcare professional practices, the typical focus of the classification of assets begins with quantifying and determining the existence of **intangible assets**. In addition to tangible assets, there are several types of intangible assets, which are described in more detail in the following sections, may be considered in the valuation of a professional practice.

PAYOR OR CLIENT-RELATED INTANGIBLE ASSETS

Intangible assets that may be classified as relating to payors or clients include contracts, such as managed care agreements, provider service agreements, direct contracting customer lists, and HMO enrollment lists. Managed care agreements provide the subject enterprise with the probability of a continued revenue stream that will provide economic benefit to the owner(s) in the future and thereby hold value.

In the same manner, provider service agreements, as well as medical directorships, can provide the subject enterprise and its providers with a competitive advantage through, for example, preferred block scheduling times in hospital operating rooms or diagnostic clinics. By contracting services directly to businesses and other groups, the subject enterprise can shield itself from continuing discounts and other cost containment pressures as well as rising administrative costs applied by third-party managed care contracts. Participation on HMO enrollment lists provides healthcare professional practices and other providers access to a predefined patient base, that is, a block of HMO enrollees, that they otherwise would have access to at a higher cost per enrollee (through out-of-network co-pays and premiums).

G	H	I	J	K	L
Acquisition Price	Indexed Price	Replacement Cost New	Devaluage Percentage	Condition Factor	Restated Value
$3,629.73	$ 5,915.70	—	85.00%	80.00%	$ 709.88
—	—	$65,000.00	48.83%	100.00%	$33,258.33
$2,354.00	$ 3,731.31	—	85.00%	90.00%	$ 503.73
—	—	$ 3,500.00	18.11%	110.00%	$ 3,152.72
$ 255.00	$ 339.67	—	54.28%	100.00%	$ 155.30
$ 900.00	$ 1,221.56	—	58.94%	100.00%	$ 501.52
$7,138.73	—	—	—	—	—
	$11,208.24	—	—	—	—
					$38,281.48

GOODWILL AND PATIENT-RELATED INTANGIBLE ASSETS

Once the identifiable and separately quantifiable intangible assets are valued, the residual amount of intangible asset value that remains is often referred to as **goodwill**. This term may appropriately be considered as the propensity of patients (and the revenue stream thereof) to return to the practice incremental to that which is quantified as the contribution of the other tangible and intangible assets in the assemblage of assets which comprises the enterprise. Keep in mind that goodwill is only one of the several intangible assets that may be found to exist in a professional practice; it is not a "catch-all-moniker" for all intangible assets in the aggregate.

Intangible assets that are sometimes considered as part of goodwill and relating to patients include custodial rights to medical charts and records, electronic medical records, patient recall lists, and both personal or professional goodwill, practice or commercial goodwill, or both. The custody of medical charts, electronic medical records, and patient recall lists may be identified separately and quantified as a distinct intangible asset aside from goodwill, however, they often are considered together with goodwill because they create the background that supports the propensity for the continued patient–provider relationship.

Sources for guidance on the definition of goodwill can be found in IRS RR 59-60 and established judicial opinions from valuation related case law. In the event that the valuator first determines the existence of intangible asset value in the subject enterprise and then determines the existence of goodwill as one of the intangible assets, the next step is to identify, distinguish, disaggregate, and allocate the relevant potion of the existing goodwill to either professional or personal goodwill or practice or commercial goodwill. Note that further discussion of goodwill and the conflicting definitions used to define it, as it relates to valuation, is found in *Conflicting Definitions of Intangible Assets Versus Goodwill.*

Professional or Personal Goodwill

Professional or personal goodwill results from the charisma, education, knowledge, skill, board certification, and reputation of a specific physician practitioner. Professional or personal goodwill is generated by the physician's reputation and personal attributes that accrue to that individual physician. Because these attributes "go to the grave" with that specific individual physician and, therefore, cannot be sold, they have no economic value.

Professional or personal goodwill is not transferable. Even with long transition periods of introduction for a new acquiring physician owner, the charisma, skills, reputation, and personal attributes of the seller cannot, by definition, be transferred.

It is often stated that with assisted transfer (that is, extended transition period) a large portion of professional goodwill may be transferred. The transferability violates the definition of professional or personal goodwill. That portion of goodwill that may be transferred is defined as practice (or commercial) goodwill and is described in the following section.

Practice or Commercial Goodwill

Practice or commercial goodwill, as distinguished from professional or personal goodwill, is transferred frequently. Practice or commercial goodwill may be described as the unidentified, unspecified, residual attributes of the practice as an operating enterprise that contribute to the propensity of patients (and the revenue stream thereof) to return to the practice. Several significant factors should be considered when determining the existence and quantity of practice or commercial goodwill related value.

It must be determined whether patients return to the practice because of attributes of the practice or because they are mandated to do so by their managed care insurance coverage. The practice's participation on a given managed care panel of providers may be subject to rapid and unexpected change. In that circumstance, the valuator needs to decide whether the value of the practice that may be attributable to managed care organization relationships should perhaps be considered as an identifiable, specific contract related asset, and separately valued, as opposed to being treated as practice or commercial goodwill.

HUMAN CAPITAL-RELATED INTANGIBLE ASSETS

Intangible assets that may be classified as relating to human capital include staff or employee and provider employment agreements, trained and assembled workforce in place, policies and procedures, and depth of management. Staff or employee and provider employment agreements provide the subject enterprise with certain assurances under which the employee or provider fulfills his or her role as a representative of the subject enterprise. The value of recruiting, hiring, and assembling employees and their training, as well as their practice experience, is encompassed in the intangible asset referred to as "trained and assembled workforce in place." This is a growing type of investment due to the high-tech nature of managing and operating practices and the complexity involved in the coding, billing, or claims resolution process and other related tasks. The policies and procedures of a subject enterprise are usually developed and refined over an extended period of time and at a cost to the owner(s) of the subject enterprise. These policies and procedures lend to the efficiencies and productivity of the subject enterprise. Typically, the success of any organization is significantly reliant upon the leadership of the organization. Accordingly, the qualifications and experience brought to the subject enterprise by management personnel may provide depth-of-management value to the subject enterprise.

INTELLECTUAL PROPERTY-RELATED INTANGIBLE ASSETS

Intangible assets that may be classified as intellectual property related may include practice protocols, treatment plans or care mapping, procedure manuals and laboratory notebooks, technical and specialty research, patents and patent applications, copyrights, trade names, trade secrets, and royalty agreements. Practice protocols and treatment plans, or care mapping, are standardized steps and an agreed upon process to diagnose and manage a patient's care through the term of the medical need. These assets are usually developed over time based upon tested and researched patient outcome data, which may require significant investment. They may bring value to the subject enterprise, if continuously followed, recorded, and reported, in as much as they provide evidence of a higher quality or more cost-effective delivery of services, which gains competitive advantage in the market. Procedure manuals outline the steps necessary to perform the various tasks required for the operation of the subject enterprise. When followed, procedure manuals can assure the continuous productivity and consistency of performance of the staff even when there is turnover or cross-training of staff.

Technical and specialty research are considered the "work-in-progress" of patents, copyrights, or other intangible assets. Patents acquired by healthcare professional practices may include specialized equipment and instruments that may lend to the increased care and beneficial quality outcomes of the practice's patients. Copyrights acquired by healthcare practices include proprietary software that can generate schedules and track patient care across multiples providers and disciplines, producing utilization and outcome reports based upon the treatment provided for use in negotiating reimbursement from managed care companies. Copyrights also may include books, patient information brochures, websites, and similar communication-related assets. Such software may increase productivity, patient care outcomes, and reimbursement at the practice. Trade names, such as the name of the subject enterprise, can bring recognition and brand loyalty to the subject enterprise. Royalty agreements, usually related to copyrights or patents owned, can provide a continuing revenue stream not subject to healthcare reimbursement risks.

LOCATIONS AND OPERATIONS-RELATED INTANGIBLE ASSETS

Intangible assets that may be classified as relating to locations and operations may include computerized management information systems that produce customized reports on the financial, operating, and patient outcome performance of the subject enterprise to aid in management decision-making and strategic planning. Favorable leases, and the leasehold interests they generate, can contribute to the value of a subject enterprise, depending upon the ability of the subject enterprise to sublease its leased space at a rate higher than it is paying. The subject enterprise, as a going concern, is a revenue-generating business enterprise and has the immediate ability to create economic benefit for the owner(s). The assemblage of assets may refer to the value of all of the practice's assets in place and working together to generate revenue. Historical documents, such as financial statements, patient charts, and productivity reports create a historical record for which future records can be compared for the purpose of management decision-making and strategic planning. Supplier contracts, typically those obtained through group purchasing organizations, can provide the subject enterprise with pricing and service assurances that can provide increased accuracy and reliability for budgeting of the practice's operations and with a competitive cost advantage for producing and providing its services.

GOVERNANCE OR LEGAL STRUCTURE RELATED INTANGIBLE ASSETS

Intangible assets that may be classified as relating to governance or legal structure may include organizational documents, income distribution plans, and noncompete covenants. Organizational documents, such as corporate by-laws, operating agreements, and shareholders agreements, are a written record of the "rules" by which the organization operates and provides certain privileges and protections to the owner(s) or shareholder(s) on an individual, as well as a collective, basis. Income distribution plans are the agreed upon formula(s) by which the owner(s) or shareholder(s), as well as other providers, are compensated. Noncompete covenants may provide some competitive protection to the subject enterprise from employees or colleagues who may, at their departure to a competitor, put the practice at risk of losing patients, referrals, or both.

Marketing and Business Development-Related Intangible Assets

Intangible assets that may be classified as marketing and business development may include advertising, franchise or licensing agreements, joint ventures or alliances, and market entrance barriers. Advertising (e.g., websites, Yellow Pages and print media ads, telephone numbers, and billboards) serves, much like trade names do, to create a desired image of the organization in an effort to create brand loyalty. Franchise or license agreements can enable an organization to access markets (either geographical or service) that may not have been feasible previously, for example, licensing the rights to operate a nationally developed cancer treatment center. In much the same way, joint ventures and alliances with other organizations may enable an organization to gain access to additional revenue streams. For example, a healthcare professional practice may partner with a local hospital to develop an ambulatory surgery center. The healthcare practice gains access to the facility fees that, in the past, have been flowing solely to hospital, while it shares the capital responsibility for the development with the hospital.

The stringent requirements for licensing act to restrict the number of practicing professionals, which in turn acts as a limit to competition and sets barriers to participation in the profession. Credentialing restrictions and medical staff requirements of certain hospitals, ambulatory surgery centers, diagnostic imaging centers, and other outpatient facilities also may present a "barrier to entry" for providers in a given location or setting, which provides an element of value for the practice that is the "gatekeeper" for access to the credentialing. Established referral patterns and closed panel managed care contracts also can act as an entry barrier to practices within certain markets.[40] Depending on the specific circumstances, this can either add or detract from practice value. Additionally, allied health professionals and alternative medicine practitioners increasingly are being accepted and recognized by payors and patients as a legitimate alternative to traditional providers and services. A healthcare practice that has already overcome these potential barriers can provide added value to the subject enterprise.

Regulatory or Legal-Related Intangible Assets

Intangible assets that may be classified as relating to regulatory or legal matters may include facility licenses, medical licenses, permits, litigation awards and liquidated damages, certificates of need (CONs), Medicare certification, and other certifications and accreditations. Facility and medical licenses, as well as permits, are consistently under the review of regulatory and legal authorities. Just as they may be a barrier to entry, continued possession can be a competitive advantage. Litigation awards can be in the form of a tangible benefit (for example, cash) or an intangible benefit (for example, upholding a noncompete dispute). A CON, or similar program, is one in which government determines where, when, and how capital expenditures will be made for healthcare facilities and major equipment. A CON acts in a manner similar to a license or permit to allow a provider to offer certain services. Medicare certification of a facility or provider allows reimbursement by the government for patients subscribed to Medicare. The revenue stream of some healthcare organizations (that is, nursing homes, cardiology practices, and hospitals) are heavily dependent upon the revenue stream of Medicare patients, as a result, the ability to bill and receive reimbursement for services provided to these patients is of great value to these organizations. Attainment of other certifications and accreditations, such as the National Committee for Quality Assurance (NCQA), the Accreditation Association for Ambulatory Health Care (AAAHC), and the Joint Commission on Accreditation of Healthcare Organizations (The Joint Commission), can create an added image of quality or superior service for an organization. In addition some third-party payors may require certain accreditations for participation on their panels.

FINANCIAL OR REVENUE STREAM-RELATED INTANGIBLE ASSETS

Intangible assets that may be classified as relating to financial or revenue streams may include office share arrangements, management services agreements, financing agreements, underwriting or private placement memoranda, and budgets, forecasts, or projections. Office share arrangements, whereby a healthcare practice may share office space and staff with another healthcare practice, can enable a practice to see patients in different geographical areas on a periodic basis without bearing the entire overhead costs related to the "satellite" office. Management services agreements (MSAs) define the terms (for example, timeliness and cost) under which an outside organization provides certain management services (for example, accounting, billing, and managed care contracting) to a healthcare practice. In the event that the specific MSA provides a competitive financial advantage to the practice, it may hold economic value to the owner(s). Financing agreements may prove to have value if the favorable terms (for example, amount of credit, interest rate, and amortization of loan) by which an organization may obtain additional capital to grow the organization, through additional working capital, capital purchases, acquisitions, and so forth. Budgets, forecasts, and projections often serve as a road map for the financial performance of an organization. These budgets can assist management in making strategic decisions, such as equipment purchases and provider recruiting, which enhances the probability of future net economic benefit to the owner(s).

TECHNOLOGY-RELATED INTANGIBLE ASSETS

Intangible assets that may be classified as relating to technology may include computer software or network integration, technical or software documentation, and maintenance or support agreements. With the increase in productivity provided by office automation, computer software and network integration contribute to the efficient operations of an organization. The documentation of the computer software or network integration of an organization is a written record of these assets in use. The technology in an organization can create economic benefit and value to the organization only if it is working effectively to increase productivity, thereby decreasing costs and enhancing the net economic benefit of ownership. Maintenance and support relationships, typically through written agreements, provide an organization with assurances that the technology will consistently perform as expected and required during the term of the relationship or agreement. The existence and implementation of these agreements may prevent "downtime" with the resulting loss of productivity and related revenue opportunity costs.

CONFLICTING DEFINITIONS OF INTANGIBLE ASSETS VERSUS GOODWILL

As discussed in *Goodwill and Patient-Related Intangible Assets*, goodwill is one type of intangible asset that may be considered in the valuation of professional practices. Goodwill is considered by some valuation professionals to be the residual amount of intangible asset value that may exist after the separately identified, separately distinguishable, and separately appraised elements of intangible value have been determined.

In June 2001, the Financial Standards Accounting Board (FASB) instituted Statement of Financial Accounting Standard (SFAS) Nos. 141 and 142. Prior to these standards, companies generally reported as goodwill the entire difference between the purchase price and the book value of identified tangible assets. Intangible assets typically were capitalized as part of overall acquire goodwill and amortized over a finite period; they were *not* required to be separately identified. SFAS Nos. 141 and 142 now require that goodwill be calculated as the overall purchase price minus the value of both tangible and identifiable intangible assets that have a finite useful life.[41] Additionally, traditional accounting allocation for valuing intangible assets, such as replacement costs or book values that fail to consider the market negotiation framework, may lead to indefensible measures of value.[42]

Accounting Versus Appraisal Definition

In the accounting world intangible asset values most often are viewed and characterized in a different manner than the valuation profession. For example, goodwill often is still referred to accountants as "the difference between the book value of assets on the healthcare entity's balance sheet and what the entity would sell for" or as "the going concern value which results from an organized assemblage of revenue-producing assets."

It should be noted that, in economic fact, goodwill is only one of many identifiable and quantifiable intangible assets related to healthcare service sector entities. In healthcare service sector entities, for example, professional practices, goodwill should be more appropriately defined as the propensity of patients and customers (and the revenue stream thereof) to return to the entity.

Valuation of Healthcare Services

During the 1990s, hospitals began employing primary care physicians and acquiring private practices in response to the emergence and perceived threat of managed care and the gatekeeping function. Recently, the growth of hospital employment of physicians has been accelerating. However, the focus is now on employing physician specialists as a key business strategy, in order for hospitals to coordinate care, as well as for physician practices to alleviate the significant financial pressures they are encountering due to rising costs, reimbursement pressures, and the changing lifestyle choices of a newer generation of physicians who have different work–life priorities.[43]

Concurrently, there has been parallel growth in the number of hospitals compensating physicians for their performance of hospital administrative functions (for example, medical directorships and administrative or executive management positions), as well as a growing trend toward compensating physicians for coverage and call agreements.[44]

Corresponding with the growing trend toward hospital employment of physicians, there has been an increase in regulatory scrutiny related to the legal permissibility of these arrangements under the federal fraud and abuse laws as they relate to transactions between healthcare providers. Similar to transactions involving, for example, the sale of a healthcare practice, physician compensation arrangements are scrutinized under both the valuation standard of fair market value, as well as the related threshold of "commercial reasonableness," which are described in more detail in *Definition of Fair Market Value (IRS, Antikickback, Stark)* and *Definition of Commercial Reasonableness (IRS, Antikickback, Stark)*, respectively.[45] Fair market value and commercial reasonableness, as they relate specifically to the valuation process, are detailed further in the following sections.

Fair Market Value: The Principle of Substitution and Principle of Utility

Although in the past, compensation for physician executive, management, and administrative services may have been based on the physician's historical clinical practice earnings, there appears to be increasing concern that compensating medical directors based on lost opportunity cost may not meet regulatory scrutiny under Stark and, rather, should be based on the actual services performed.[46] Although in most circumstances the opportunity cost of a physician provider of clinical services should not serve as the sole basis for determining physician executive compensation for performance of administrative services, it is nevertheless important for the consultant providing an opinion regarding the fair market value and commercial reasonableness of a physician executive or medical director compensation arrangement to keep the "willing buyer-willing seller" requirement of the fair market value standard in mind. Also, the valuator should appropriately apply the economic concepts found in the principle of substitution and the principle of utility when performing the analysis.

The fundamental economic facts or economic behavior that will occur under certain conditions form the basis of the economic laws of what will happen objectively in certain economic situations. Within this concept, it can be said that the basis of all economic value derives from some form of economic usefulness, also termed utility, for example, the benefits, satisfaction, or both derived from the use of properties and services, the use of money, the use and consumption of goods, and the use of intangibles for investment purposes.[47] As a result, it has been said that the principle of utility may be stated as "[a]n object can have no value unless it has utility."[48] This concept, described previously in *Value in Use*, is often referred to as "value-in-use."

The dynamics concerning how economic value is created in this use and exchange continuum may be understood within the context of three additional basic principles related to the economic benefits to be derived from the right to control the subject services to be performed under the contractual arrangement. First, the principle of substitution posits that what normally sets the limit of what would be paid for property is the cost of an equally desirable substitute or one of equal utility. This principle is the basis for the decision regarding whether to "buy or build" a product or service. Second, the principle of investment limits posits that resources are not normally spent in pursuit of diminishing returns from property.[49] Third, and perhaps, most important, the principle of anticipation posits that the economic benefits of ownership of, or the contractual rights to control, the subject services to be performed under the contractual agreement are created from the expectation of those benefits or rights to be derived in the future; therefore, all economic value is forward looking.[50]

Specifically, the economic value analysis for determining fair market value should be focused on the economic benefits reasonably expected to be derived from the use or utility of the physician executive services, bounded by the cost of an equally desirable substitute, or one of equal utility, for each of the elements of economic benefit (or utility) to be derived from the right to control the physician executive services to be performed on behalf of the enterprise. It follows that a detailed examination of the attributes of the subject physician executive performing the administrative services must be undertaken, with each element of the attributes of the subject physician executive first identified regarding their existence, and then classified regarding the specific factors and traits (that is, the tasks, duties, responsibilities, and accountabilities) related to each attribute. This classification would exhibit the means by which they would reasonably be expected to provide utility to the hospital contracting for the physician executive services to be performed going forward.

Intrinsic to the discussion of identifying and appropriately classifying each attribute by which the physician executive will provide utility to the subject healthcare enterprise, is selecting the appropriate metric to be utilized in measuring the utility provided. Although such attributes as tasks and duties have discretely identifiable metrics that are more amenable to being quantified and measured (for example physician hour requirements and work relative value unit (wRVU) production), those attributes related to a physician executive's responsibility and accountability for ensuring his or her performance

Box 4-2: Documents Required to Perform Valuation Service by Sector

Physician Clinical Services

(1) The proposed agreement(s) for clinical professional services (including a detailed description of all tasks, duties, responsibilities, and accountabilities related to the services to be performed)

(2) The number of shifts per week and hour requirements per week anticipated under the proposed agreement

(3) All agreements for other similar positions at the employer entity, including the scope of services to be performed under each of those agreements

(4) The curriculum vitae for the physician performing the clinical services

(5) Documentation regarding the board certification, qualifications, and tenure of those physicians performing the services under all similar agreements

(6) Medical staff bylaws and roster

(7) Documentation of historical clinical productivity, measured in work relative value units (wRVUs), gross charges, net revenue, or count by Current Procedural Terminology (CPT) code for the past two years

Physician On-Call Services

(1) The proposed agreement(s) for on-call services (stating whether call is restricted or unrestricted and including a detailed description of all tasks, duties, responsibilities, and accountabilities related to the services to be performed)

(2) The number of shifts per week and on-call hour requirements per week anticipated under the proposed agreement

(3) The number of times the existing (specialty specific) on-call physician was (a) paged and (b) required to be present at the employer for the past two years

(4) All agreements for other similar positions at the employer entity, including the scope of services to be performed under each of those agreements

(5) The curriculum vitae for the physician performing the on-call

(6) Documentation regarding the board certification, qualifications, and tenure of those physicians performing on-call services under all similar agreements

(7) Medical staff bylaws and roster

(8) Documentation of historical clinical productivity, measured in wRVUs, gross charges, net revenue, or count by CPT code for the past two years

Physician Administrative, Management, and Executive Services

(1) The proposed agreement(s) for administrative, executive, and management services (including a detailed description of all tasks, duties, responsibilities, and accountabilities related to the services to be performed)

(2) All agreements for other similar positions at the employer entity, including the scope of services to be performed under each of those agreements

(3) Documentation regarding the board certification, qualifications, and tenure or those physicians performing the services under all similar medical directorship agreements

(4) Documentation of offers made to previous (or other existing) physician executives

(5) Documentation regarding the medical staff's need for administrative direction (based on activities, hospital research efforts, community outreach programs, and so forth)

(6) The employer's medical staff bylaws and roster

(7) The employer's medical directorship agreement(s), listing the annual hour requirements and annual compensation paid to each medical director

(8) Time sheet records and the time spent and work performed by the physician on each administrative function and service, subject to the position

(9) The size of employer, number of patients, acuity levels of patients, and the specific needs related to the particular service line

(10) The number of committees and meetings that require the physician executive's involvement, attendance, or both and the average frequency and duration of each committee and meeting

(11) Documentation that the employer (at least) annually assesses the effectiveness of the physician executive in performing his or her tasks, duties, and responsibilities, as well as commercial reasonableness of the contract

(12) Description of quality programs, including centers of excellence and "never event"* committees

---

* "Fair Market Value: Analysis and Tools to Comply with Stark and Anti-kickback Rules" By Robert A. Wade and Marcie Rose Levine, Audioconference: HC Pro, Inc., Mar. 19, 2008, p. 59.

under the given contract are more complex and varied in their scope, thereby resulting in these attributes not being easily quantified, despite often being the attribute of utility that produces an equal or greater economic benefit for the organization. Accordingly, the value related to the utility attached to the physician executive's responsibilities and accountabilities will often provide greater economic benefit to the contracting organization vis-à-vis the risk and reward continuum and the physician executive's relative risk in undertaking the given responsibility and accountability attached to the terms of the given contract.

ROLE FOR THE VALUATION CONSULTANT

Typically, legal counsel does not provide a legal opinion regarding the fair market value or commercial reasonableness of a compensation arrangement and will most often retain an independent valuation consultant to provide a certified valuation opinion regarding fair market value, commercial reasonableness, or both of a compensation arrangement for a given employment or services agreement, including agreements for clinical professional services, medical directorships, and on-call coverage, as well as other administrative, management, and executive management services.[51]

When developing the valuation analysis, the valuation consultant will need to obtain the requisite documents related to the proposed compensation arrangement(s), which typically include the items found in box 4-2.

The valuation professional's review of these documents, as well as results from interviews with employer management and physicians, will serve as the basis for supporting the development of the valuation analysis related to the scope of services to be performed, that is, whether the physician will be providing administrative services in addition to clinical services.

VALUATION METHODOLOGY FOR SUPPORTING OPINIONS OF FAIR MARKET VALUE AND COMMERCIAL REASONABLENESS

Compensation arrangements may include combinations of the following elements:

(1) Base salary, that is, equal compensation paid to each physician

(2) Productivity-based compensation (for example, cap compensation and a given productivity percentile by specialty)

(3) Compensation based on a per RVU method

(4) Incentive bonus based on productivity

(5) An annual stipend for performance of administrative services, for example, medical directorships, departmental management, and oversight

(6) Incentive payments based on achieving quality of patient and beneficial outcomes based on agreed upon measures

(7) Incentive payments based on specified permissible gainsharing arrangements, for example, achieving certain cost savings and efficiencies

(8) Incentive payments paid based on the contributions and economic inputs of the employed physician(s) to achieve specified enhancement of the performance of the enterprise, for example, development of a "Center of Excellence"[52]

A selected listing of representative compensation surveys utilized for benchmarking physician clinical, executive, and on-call compensation are outlined in table 4-3. A more comprehensive listing of physician and executive compensation surveys may be found in *Sources of Physician Compensation Data* and *Sources of Healthcare Executive Compensation Data*. A critical step in utilizing these compensation surveys to benchmark the given compensation arrangement is to accurately establish the homogenous units of economic contribution to be used in the metrics of comparability. Additionally, the valuation professional must be careful to determine whether the particular compensation survey utilized includes data for ancillary services and technical component revenue, in addition to professional fee revenue, in its indication of "salary."

Table 4-3: List of Selected Generally Accepted Surveys Utilized for Benchmarking Physician and Executive Compensation

Survey Type	Title	Source Title	Most Recent Publication Date
Clinical Compensation & Benefits	Medical Group Compensation and Financial Survey	American Medical Group Association (AMGA)	2009
	Physician Compensation Report	Hay Group	Sep–08
	Hospital Salary & Benefits Report	Hospital & Healthcare Compensation Service; John R. Zabka Associates, Inc.	2009-2010
	Physician Salary Survey Report	Hospital & Healthcare Compensation Service; John R. Zabka Associates, Inc.	Apr–09
	Physician Compensation and Production Survey	Medical Group Management Association (MGMA)	2009
	Staff Salary Survey	The Health Care Group, Inc.	2009
	Physician Compensation and Productivity Survey Report	Sullivan Cotter and Associates, Inc.	2009
Management Services	Physician Executive Compensation Survey	The American College of Physician Executives; Cejka Search	2007
	Health Care Executive Compensation Survey	Clark Consulting (Healthcare Group)	2007
	Management Compensation Survey	Medical Group Management Association (MGMA)	2009
	Medical Directorship and On-Call Compensation Survey Report	Medical Group Management Association (MGMA)	2009
	Survey Report on Hospital & Health Care Management Compensation	Watson Wyatt Data Services	2007/2008
	Survey of Manager and Executive Compensation in Hospitals and Health Systems	Sullivan Cotter and Associates, Inc.	2009
	Top Management and Executive	Abbott, Langer Association Surveys	2009
	Integrated Health Networks Compensation Survey	William M. Mercer, Inc.	2009
Coverage & Call	Physician On-Call Pay Survey Report	Sullivan Cotter and Associates, Inc.	2009
	Medical Directorship and On-Call Compensation Survey Report	Medical Group Management Association (MGMA)	2009

PHYSICIAN CLINICAL SERVICES

In benchmarking compensation for physician professional clinical services, the range (percentile) of the compensation to be measured must be researched and established, the specialty or subspecialty needs to be matched, and the metric of comparability must be selected (for example, charges, collections, relative value units (RVUs), and so forth). At that point, it is necessary to determine how the hourly rate (if applicable) and full-time equivalency are calculated.[53] Additionally, when considering productivity-based elements of the compensation arrangement, careful attention should be paid to whether the compensation is based on a (1) percentage of collections, (2) percentage of gross charges, or (3) per RVU basis. Although compensation based on gross charges has the benefit of not being based on the patient–payor mix, the employer's gross charges may not necessarily be aligned with collections, and the physician's compensation may fluctuate significantly depending on the employer's increase or decrease in gross charges.[54] However, if compensation is based on an employer's collections, there may be a high incentive for physicians to treat patients with higher paying payors as opposed to treating Medicaid or indigent patients.[55] In those compensation arrangements in which compensation is based on a per RVU basis, there is the benefit of compensation being based upon the physician's productivity, that is, work effort, regardless of the employer's payor mix or collection rate. However, careful consideration should be paid to account for whether the compensation is based on a total RVU basis (work, practice, and medical-malpractice components comprising total RVU per CPT code) or whether it is based solely on a wRVU basis.[56] See *Clinical Benchmarking* for further discussion of some available clinical metrics and indicators for use in benchmarking analyses.

PHYSICIAN ON-CALL SERVICES

Hospitals typically utilize several time periods, including (1) hourly, (2) daily, (3) weekly, and (4) annually, as a metric in developing the basis of compensation for physicians for on-call services.

Additionally, consideration must be given to whether the on-call services are restricted (that is, the physician is required to stay on hospital premises during call) or unrestricted (that is, the physician is not required to stay on hospital premises during call). It should be noted that most facilities that employ physicians for unrestricted on-call services require physicians to remain within fifteen to thirty minutes of hospital premises during call.

PHYSICIAN EXECUTIVE, MANAGEMENT, AND ADMINISTRATIVE SERVICES

The process of determining the fair market value of physician executive, management, and administrative services compensation lends itself to the need for the documentation of the specific tasks, duties, responsibilities, and accountabilities required for those services. The principle of substitution and principle of utility, which were discussed previously in this chapter, should be integral in the consideration of the physical and cognitive skill level input required in performing these services. For example, each task required by the executive, management, and administrative services may involve one or both of the following elements: (1) medical knowledge and experience and (2) business and management acumen. Therefore, it is imperative that each task, duty, responsibility, and accountability of the subject services be compared to the industry compensation level(s) requisite of the skill and knowledge input to perform the specific task, duty, responsibility, and accountability of the subject services.

CONCLUSION

In financial valuation, no single approach or method, or combination thereof, is universally correct or that applies to every engagement. Each case must be considered as a unique exercise of informed judgment, based upon careful analysis and supported by documented evidence and reasoned argument.

However, all the sophisticated arithmetic and brilliant theoretical constructs in the valuation world will not support a credible valuation if the appraiser does not have a thorough understanding of the market sector within which the subject enterprise exists and operates, that is, the four pillars. In particular, it is critical to obtain and maintain appropriate documentation that the given compensation arrangement (whether it be for clinical services, administrative services, on-call services, or a combination of services) meets both the thresholds of being at fair market value and commercially reasonable in order to withstand increased scrutiny from the U.S. Office of Inspector General, Department of Justice, and the IRS. This is particularly important in the heightened and ever-changing regulatory environment in which healthcare enterprises and providers operate, with the potential severity of penalties, as well as related business consequences for entering into transactions and arrangements which may subsequently be found to be legally impermissible.

> A valuation is only credible if developed with a thorough understanding of the four pillars within the market sector of interest for that valuation.

HCC Terminology

Healthcare entities and providers should work closely and in a timely manner with competent healthcare legal counsel and certified valuation professionals to ensure that the proposed transaction, whether related to an enterprise, assets, or services, meets regulatory thresholds. A certified opinion regarding whether the proposed transaction is both at fair market value and commercially reasonable, prepared by an independent certified valuation professional, reviewed by legal counsel, and supported by adequate documentation, will significantly enhance the efforts of healthcare providers to establish a defensible position that their proposed transactional arrangement is in compliance.

Finally, a valuator should remember to question everything and everyone, but he or she should be prepared to utilize reasoned and informed professional judgment to review the valuation report. In the end, when arriving at the opinion of value, remember to [l]ove everyone, trust no one, and paddle your own canoe!

Key Sources

Key Source	Description	Citation	Hyperlink
"Valuing a Business: The Analysis and Appraisal of Closely Held Companies," 4th ed., by Shannon P. Pratt, Robert F. Reilly, & Robert P. Schweihs, McGraw-Hill, 2000	Resource for business valuation and appraisal theory and application.	"Valuations for Estate and Gift Tax Purposes," *in* "Valuing a Business: The Analysis and Appraisal of Closely Held Companies," 4th ed., by Shannon P. Pratt, Robert F. Reilly, & Robert P. Schweihs, McGraw-Hill, 2000, p. 585.	n/a
"Standards of Value: Theory and Applications," by Jay E. Fishman, Shannon P. Pratt, & William J. Morrison, John Wiley & Sons, Inc., 2007	Resource for business valuation and appraisal theory and application.	"Standards of Value: Theory and Applications," by Jay E. Fishman, Shannon P. Pratt, & William J. Morrison, John Wiley & Sons, Inc., 2007, pp. 167, 181.	n/a
"RMA Annual Statement Studies," published by the Risk Management Association	Standard source covering practice financial statements with industry averages for a variety of industry categories.	"About RMA," Risk Management Association, rmahq.org, 2009, www.rmahq.org/RMA/AboutRMA/ (accessed December 1, 2009).	www.rmahq.org/RMA/AboutRMA
"Financial Studies of the Small Business," published by Financial Research Associates	Standard source covering practice financial statements with industry averages for a variety of industry categories.	"About FRA," Financial Research Associates, LLC, frallc.com, 2009, www.frallc.com/about.aspx (accessed December 1, 2009).	www.frallc.com/about.aspx
"Statistics of Income: Partnership Source Book" and "Statistics of Income: Sole Proprietor Source Book" available through the Internal Revenue Service	Standard source covering practice financial statements with industry averages for a variety of industry categories.	"About Statistics of Income Sourcebooks," Internal Revenue Service, irs.gov, 2009, www.archives.gov/research/irs-data.html#psb (accessed December 1, 2009).	www.archives.gov/research/irs-data.html#psb

Key Source	Description	Citation	Hyperlink
Mergerstat Review	Annual series study of the premium paid by investors for controlling interest in publicly traded stock.	Published by FactSet Mergerstat, LLC. "FactSet Mergerstat Publications," FactSet Mergerstat, www.mergerstat.com/newsite/bookStore.asp (accessed November 4, 2009).	www.mergerstat.com/newsite bookStore.asp
Control Premium Study	Quarterly series study that compiles control premiums of publicly traded stocks by attempting to eliminate the possible distortion caused by speculation of a deal.	Compiled by Mergerstat/Shannon Pratt's BV Resources. "Mergerstat/BVR Control Premium Study - Quantify Minority Discounts and Control Premiums," Business Valuation Market Data, www.bvmarketdata.com/defaulttextonly.asp?f=CPS%20Intro (accessed November 4, 2009).	www.bvmarketdata.com/defaulttextonly. asp?f=CPS%20 Intro
Business Valuation Resources (BVR)	"Every top business valuation firm depends on BVR for authoritative market data, continuing professional education, and expert opinion. Rely on BVR when your career depends on an unimpeachable business valuation. Our customers include business appraisers, certified public accountants, merger and acquisition professionals, business brokers, lawyers and judges, private equity and venture capitalists, owners, CFOs, and many others. Founded by Dr. Shannon Pratt, BVR's market databases and analysis have won in the courtroom—and the boardroom—for over a decade."	"About Business Valuation Resources," www.bvresources.com/ (accessed October 12, 2009).	www.bvresources.com
American Institute of Certified Public Accountants (AICPA)	"The American Institute of Certified Public Accountants is the national, professional organization for all Certified Public Accountants. Its mission is to provide members with the resources, information, and leadership that enable them to provide valuable services in the highest professional manner to benefit the public as well as employers and clients. In fulfilling its mission, the AICPA works with state CPA organizations and gives priority to those areas where public reliance on CPA skills is most significant."	"AICPA Mission," www.aicpa.org/About+the+AICPA/AICPA+Mission/ (accessed October 12, 2009).	www.aicpa.org
Institute of Business Appraisers (IBA)	"The Institute of Business Appraisers is the oldest professional society devoted solely to the appraisal of closely-held businesses. Established in 1978, the Institute is a pioneer in business appraisal education and professional accreditation."	"The Institute of Business Appraisers," www.go-iba.org/ (accessed October 12, 2009).	www.go-iba.org

(continued)

(continued)

Key Source	Description	Citation	Hyperlink
The Canadian Institute of Chartered Business Valuators (CICBV)	"Established in 1971, The Canadian Institute of Chartered Business Valuators is nationally and internationally recognized as the pre-eminent business valuation organization in Canada. The Institute develops and promotes high professional standards governing a membership of more than 1,200 professionals who provide expertise in the areas of securities valuation, compliance, disputes and corporate finance."	"Welcome to the CICBV," https://www.cicbv.ca/ (accessed October 12, 2009).	https://www.cicbv.ca/

Associations

Type of Association	Professional Association	Description	Citation	Hyperlink	Contact Information
National	National Association of Certified Valuation Analysts (NACVA)	"NACVA's Mission is to provide resources to members and to enhance their status, credentials, and esteem in the field of performing valuations, financial forensics, and other related advisory services. To further this purpose, NACVA will advance these services as an art and science, establish standards for membership in the Association, provide professional education and research, foster practice development, advance ethical and professional practices, enhance public awareness of the Association and its members, and promote working relationships with other professional organizations."	"The Association," National Association of Certified Valuation Analysts, 2008, p. 4, www.nacva.com/PDF/association_brochure.pdf (accessed October 12, 2009).	www.nacva.com	**National Association of Certified Valuation Analysts** 1111 Brickyard Road, Suite 200 Salt Lake City, UT 84106 Phone: 801-486-0600 Fax: 801-486-7500 E-mail: nacva1@nacva.com
National	American Society of Appraisers (ASA)	"The American Society of Appraisers is an international organization of appraisal professionals and others interested in the appraisal profession. ASA is the oldest and only major appraisal organization representing all of the disciplines of appraisal specialists. The society originated in 1936 and incorporated in 1952. ASA is headquartered in the metropolitan Washington, D.C., area."	"American Society of Appraisers," www.appraisers.org/ASAHome.aspx (accessed October 12, 2009)	www.appraisers.org	**American Society of Appraisers** 555 Herndon Parkway, Suite 125 Herndon, VA 20170 Phone: 800- ASA-VALU (800-272-8258) or 703-478-2228 Fax: 703-742-8471

Endnotes

1   "Limitation on Certain Physician Referrals" 42 U.S.C.A. § 1395nn(a) (2006).

2   "Limitation on Certain Physician Referrals" 42 U.S.C.A. § 1395nn(h)(3) (2006).

3   "Limitation on Certain Physician Referrals" 42 U.S.C.A. § 1395nn(e)(2)(B), (C), (6) (2006).

4   "Criminal Penalties for Acts Involving Federal Health Care Programs" 42 U.S.C.A. § 1320a-7b(b) (2004).

5   "Program Integrity: Medicare and State Health Care Programs" 42 C.F.R. §1001.952(d)(5) (2004).

6   "Intermediate Sanctions—Excess Benefit Transactions" Internal Revenue Service, August 13, 2009, http://www.irs.gov/charities/charitable/article/0,,id=123303,00. html (Accessed 02/09/10).

7   "Disqualified Person" Internal Revenue Service, http://www.irs.gov/charities/ charitable/article/0,,id=154667,00.html (Accessed 09/02/08). ; "Lookback Period" Internal Revenue Service, 2008, http://www.irs.gov/charities/charitable/ article/0,,id=154670,00.html (Accessed 09/02/08).

8   "Intermediate Sanctions - Excess Benefit Transactions" Internal Revenue Service, August 13, 2009, http://www.irs.gov/charities/charitable/article/0,,id=123303,00. html (Accessed 02/09/10).

9   "Financial Valuation: Businesses and Business Interests" By James H. Zukin, New York, NY: Maxwell MacMillan, 1990, p. 42-44.

10 The material for this section is adapted from "Valuation of Healthcare Ancillary Services Providers" By Robert James Cimasi, Health Capital Consultants, National Association of Certified Valuation Analysts Consultants' Training Institute: San Diego, CA, December 12, 2008.

11 "Uniform Standards of Professional Appraisal Practice," Appraisal Standards Board, January 1, 2008, p. U-12.

12 "Uniform Standards of Professional Appraisal Practice," Appraisal Standards Board, January 1, 2008, p. U-9.

13 "Valuing a Business: The Analysis and Appraisal of Closely Held Companies" By Shannon P. Pratt, Robert F. Reilly, and Robert P. Schweihs, Fourth Edition, New York, NY: McGraw-Hill, 2000, p. 585.

14 *Ibid.*

15 "Standards of Value: Theory and Applications" By Jay E. Fishman, Shannon P. Pratt, and William J. Morrison, Hoboken, NJ: John Wiley & Sons, Inc., 2007, p. 167, 181.

16 "ASA Business Valuation Standards" American Society of Appraisers, 2008, p. 26.

17 "Valuing a Business: The Analysis and Appraisal of Closely Held Companies" By Shannon P. Pratt, and Alina V. Niculita, Fifth Edition, New York, NY: McGraw-Hill, 2008, p. 256.

18 "Valuing a Business: The Analysis and Appraisal of Closely Held Companies" By Shannon P. Pratt, and Alina V. Niculita, Fifth Edition, New York, NY: McGraw-Hill, 2008, p. 244-245.

19 "The Market Approach to Valuing Businesses" By Shannon Pratt, Second Edition, Hoboken, NJ: John Wiley & Sons, Inc., p. 273.

20 As mentioned previously, this method apparently relies on subtracting the tax basis depreciated book value of tangible assets which happen to appear on the practice's balance sheet (in contrast to their economic fair market value) from the reported sale price, and then assuming that the residual amount of the sale price after that subtraction equals the value of intangible assets (which, as a term of convenience, it defines as "goodwill").

21 Homogeneous: the same in structure, quality, etc; similar; uniform.

22 "Financial Valuation, Applications and Models," James R. Hitchner, 2nd ed., John Wiley & Sons, Inc., 2006, p. 311, Exhibit 8.

23 "Adjusting Multiples from Guideline Public Companies, Teleconference Presentation, August 31, 2006, Business Valuation Resources, LLC, 2006, Exhibit 8; "Financial Valuation: Applications and Models" By James R. Hitchner, Second Edition, Hoboken, NJ: John Wiley & Sons, Inc., 2006, p. 310-315.

24 Revenue Ruling 59-60, 1959-1, Internal Revenue Service, Cumulative Bulletin p. 237.

25 "Valuing Small Businesses and Professional Practices" By Shannon P. Pratt, Robert F. Reilly, and Robert P. Schweihs, Second Edition, Homewood, IL: Business One Irwin, 1998, p. 223-227.

26 "Valuing a Business: The Analysis and Appraisal of Closely Held Companies" By Shannon P. Pratt, and Alina V. Niculita, Fifth Edition, New York, NY: McGraw-Hill, 2008, p. 47-48.

27 "Equity Risk Premium: What Valuation Consultants Need to Know About Recent Research: 2005 Update" By Roger J. Grabowski and David W. King, Valuation Strategies, Sep/Oct 2005, p. 14, 16, 18-20, 48.

28 *Ibid.*

29 "2008 Ibbotson Stocks Bonds, Bills, and Inflation Valuation Yearbook" Morningstar: Chicago, IL, 2008, p. 39, 54.

30 "2008 Valuation Yearbook: Market Results for Stock, Bonds, Bills, and Inflations 1926-2007" Morningstar: Chicago, IL, 2008, p. 42, 268.

31 The calculator was created by Keith Pinkerton and Peter Butler based on the Butler-Pinkerton model, and is available on the Business Valuation Resource website (http://www.bvmarketdata.com/defaulttextonly.asp?f=bpmintro).

32 "Using the Butler Pinkerton Model - Total Cost of Equity and Public Company Specific Risk Calculator" By Keith Pinkerton and Peter Butler, Business Valuation Resources Webinar, March 6, 2008.

33 "Butler/Pinkerton Update Questions on Comparables" Business Valuation Library, March 5, 2008, http://bvlibrary.com/BVWire/BVWireArticlesPrint.aspx?docRef=575 (Accessed 05/27/10).

34 "FactSet Mergerstat Publications" FactSet Mergerstat, https://www.mergerstat. com/newsite/bookStore.asp (accessed 11/4/2009); "Mergerstat/BVR Control Premium Study - Quantify Minority Discounts and Control Premiums" Business Valuation Resources, http://www.bvmarketdata.com/defaulttextonly.asp?f= CPS%20Intro (Accessed 11/04/09).

35 [Internal note in Bonbright]—"Hence, in enterprise valuations, the fixed assets are seldom appraised at the liquidation values."

36 "The Valuation of Property: A Treatise on the Appraisal of Property for Different Legal Purposes, Volume I" By James C. Bonbright, New York, NY: McGraw-Hill, 1937, p. 76-77.

37 "The Valuation of Property: A Treatise on the Appraisal of Property for Different Legal Purposes, Volume I" By James C. Bonbright, New York, NY: McGraw-Hill, 1937, p. 99.

38 "The Valuation of Property: A Treatise on the Appraisal of Property for Different Legal Purposes, Volume I" By James C. Bonbright, New York, NY: McGraw-Hill, 1937, p. 100-101.

39 "Valuing Machinery and Equipment: The Fundamentals of Appraising Machinery & Technical Assets" Machinery and Technical Specialties Committee of the American Society of Appraisers, Second Edition, Washington, D.C., 2005, p. 570.

40 A closed panel is a managed care plan that contracts with only selected physicians on an exclusive basis for services, not allowing members to see physicians outside of the limited exclusive panel of providers for routine care. Examples include staff and group model Health Maintenance Organizations, but also apply to private medical groups that contract with an HMO.

41 "Financial Valuation: Applications and Models" By James R. Hitchner, Second Edition, Hoboken, NJ: John Wiley & Sons, Inc., 2006, p. 311.

42 "Grasping the Value of Intangible Assets" By Phillip A. Beutel and Bryan Ray, International Tax Journal, Vol. 30, No. 1, (Winter 2004), p. 35-36.

43 "Facilities are Learning from Past Physician Management and Compensation Mistakes: Hospital Employment Makes a Comeback" By Brad Rauh and Travis Singleton, Healthleaders Media, http://www.healthleadersmedia.com/content. cfm?topic=HOM&content_id=76934&item_id=3285&CFID=26220567&CFTO

KEN=48092385 (Accessed 5/28/10); "Grasping the Value of Intangible Assets" By Phillip A. Beutel and Bryan Ray, International Tax Journal, Vol. 30, No. 1, (Winter 2004), p. 37; "Managing Physician Compensation in Integrated Health Systems: A Focus on the Clinical Specialties" By Daniel K. Zismer, Essentia Health Consulting Perspective Newsletter (September 2007), http://www.sph.umn.edu/programs/mhaexec/execresources/articles/ESSE7_Perspective.pdf (Accessed 05/27/10), p. 1; As reported in an October 2008 Heath Affairs article, the findings from the Center for Studying Health System Change's most recent Community Tracking Study states that interviews in 12 nationally representative metropolitan areas indicate that hospitals are increasingly employing physicians, particularly specialists. "Hospital-Physician Relations: Two Tracks And The Decline of The Voluntary Medical Staff Model" By Lawrence P. Casalino et al., Health Affairs, Vol. 27, No. 5, (September/October 2008), p. 1305.

44 "The Managed Health Care Handbook" By Peter R. Kongstvedt, Third Edition, Gaithersburg, MD: Aspens Publishers, Inc., 1996, p. 147-48, 158.

45 In those business transactions or arrangements where either threshold is not met, there is also the possibility for a finding of legal impermissibility under the Federal False Claims Act (FCA) if a healthcare provider knowingly submits a claim for reimbursement to a government entity for services under compensation arrangements which are deemed to be Stark and Anti-Kickback violations. (See Exhibit A: Chronology of Significant Legal and Regulatory Events Related to Fair Market Value and Commercial Reasonableness, and Exhibit B: Summary of Regulatory Definitions Related to Fair Market Value and Commercial Reasonableness.)

46 "Beyond Anti-Markup: 'Stand in the Shoes' and Other Practical Implications" By Michael W. Paddock, The American Bar Association Health Law Section and the ABA Center for Continuing Legal Education, February 6, 2008, http://www.crowell.com/documents/Stark-Phase-III_Anti-Markup-Rules_Mike-Paddock.pdf (Accessed 10/14/08), p. 22; "Health Care Fraud and Abuse: Practical Perspectives" By Linda A. Baumann, Washington, D.C.: The American Bar Association Health Law Section and The Bureau of National Affairs, Inc., 2002, p. 255-57; "The Managed Health Care Handbook" By Peter R. Kongstvedt, Third Edition, Gaithersburg, MD: Aspens Publishers, Inc., 1996, p. 159.

47 "Appraisal and Valuation: An Interdisciplinary Approach" By Richard Rickert, Washington, D.C.: American Society of Appraisers, 1987, p. 24.

48 "Principles of Economics, Volume I" By F. W. Taussig, Second Edition, New York, NY: The MacMillan Company, 1917, pg. 120.

49 "Appraisal and Valuation: An Interdisciplinary Approach" By Richard Rickert, Washington, D.C.: American Society of Appraisers, 1987, p. 24.

50 Ibid.

51 "Fair Market Value: Analysis and Tools to Comply with Stark and Anti-kickback Rules" By Robert A. Wade and Marcie Rose Levine, Audioconference: HC Pro, Inc., Mar. 19, 2008, p. 49.

52 As reported by a May 18, 2006 CMS Media Release entitled Eliminating Serious, Preventable, and Costly Medical Errors—Never Events, 'never events' are errors in medical care that are clearly identifiable, preventable, and serious in their consequences for patients," thereby indicating a serious problem in the safety and credibility of the health care provider. Additionally, CMS indicated that such 'never events,' like surgery on the wrong body part or mismatched blood transfusion, cause serious injury or death to beneficiaries, and result in increased costs to the Medicare program to treat the consequences of the error."

53 "Valuing Physician and Executive Compensation Arrangements: Fair Market Value & Commercial Reasonableness Thresholds" By Robert James Cimasi and David Grauer, National Association of Certified Valuation Analysts, June 26, 2009, p. 50; See also "Fair Market Value: Analysis and Tools to Comply with Stark and Anti-kickback Rules" By Robert A. Wade and Marcie Rose Levine, Audioconference: HC Pro, Inc., Mar. 19, 2008, p. 51, 56-61.

54 "Fair Market Value: Analysis and Tools to Comply with Stark and Anti-kickback Rules" By Robert A. Wade and Marcie Rose Levine, Audioconference: HC Pro, Inc., Mar. 19, 2008, p. 55.

55 "Fair Market Value: Analysis and Tools to Comply with Stark and Anti-kickback Rules" By Robert A. Wade and Marcie Rose Levine, Audioconference: HC Pro, Inc., Mar. 19, 2008, p. 56-57.

56 "Fair Market Value: Analysis and Tools to Comply with Stark and Anti-kickback Rules" By Robert A. Wade and Marcie Rose Levine, Audioconference: HC Pro, Inc., Mar. 19, 2008, p. 58.

Glossary

Activity Ratio: A measure that indicates how efficiently the organization utilizes its resources or assets, including cash, accounts receivable, salaries, inventories, properties, plants, and equipment.

Audit: A formal examination and verification of financial accounts.

Benchmarking to Industry Norms: A subset of financial benchmarking used to compare internal company-specific data to survey data from other organizations within the same industry.

Benchmarking: A method of finding and implementing best practices by comparing a business or healthcare entity against the best in order to reach new goals and pursue continuous improvement.

Buy-in: A process by which established group practices allow associates to transition into ownership.

Capitalization Rate: Any divisor (usually expressed as a percentage) used to convert anticipated economic benefits of a single period into value.

Cash Flow: Cash that is generated over a period of time by an asset, group of assets, or business enterprise. It may be used in a general sense to encompass various levels of specifically defined cash flows. When the term is used, it should be supplemented by a qualifier (for example, "discretionary" or "operating") and a specific definition in the given valuation context.

Charge Description Master: The list of codes that reflect the various services offered by a particular healthcare professional practice which is used for billing these services to payers.

Charting: The process of putting medical treatments and diagnosis into the medical record (physical or electronic).

Clients: Targets whose preliminary proposal is negotiated to an engagement agreement (contract) are considered clients.

Clinical Benchmarking: A type of benchmarking, often dependent upon the level of investment and multidisciplinary efforts across several levels of care, is utilized for continuous development and maintenance of quality healthcare, attaining targeted patient-focused outcomes, and identifying evidence-based benchmarks for best practices, among other clinical outcomes.

Clinical Quality Indicators: Benchmarking metrics used to measure any clinical outcome or patient treatment. Three types of indicators fall under the umbrella of clinical quality indicators: (1) generic indicators, (2) disease-specific indicators, and (3) functional indicators.

Coding: The process of using the *International Classification of Diseases, Ninth Revision, Clinical Modification* and the Healthcare Common Procedure Coding System to assign a numeric value to medical diagnoses, procedures and surgery, signs and symptoms of disease and ill-defined conditions, poisoning and adverse effects of drugs, and complications of surgery and medical care.

Collaborative Benchmarking: A rapidly growing form of benchmarking distinguished by its development of an atmosphere that facilitates learning and sharing of knowledge.

Compensation Planning Committee: A collection of practice members that is representative of the practice population as a whole; physician executives and practitioners of all levels and specialty areas are appointed to mirror the practice distribution.

Competitive Benchmarking: A type of benchmarking used for the purpose of gaining superiority over competitors.

Competitor Benchmarking: A type of external benchmarking used for comparing work processes with those of that industry's best competitor to determine new target performance levels and develop a clear understanding of its direct competition.

Complex or Compound: A multifaceted analysis that incorporates different types of tools to synthesize an overall conclusion.

Consultants: Any third-party assistance to the development process.

Control Premium: An amount or a percentage by which the pro rata value of a controlling interest exceeds the pro rata value of a noncontrolling interest in a business enterprise, in a reflection of the power of control.

Corporate Compliance Services: Services that analyze a corporation's activities and reports whether they are in compliance with federal and state regulations; if not, present suggestions on how to become compliant through the implementation of compliance programs.

Cost of Capital: The expected rate of return that the market requires in order to attract funds to a particular investment.

Discount for Lack of Control: An amount or percentage deducted from the pro rata share of value of 100 percent of an equity interest in a business to reflect the absence of some or all of the powers of control.

Discount for Lack of Marketability: An amount or percentage deducted from the value of an ownership interest to reflect the relative absence of marketability.

Discount Rate: A rate of return used to convert a future monetary sum into present value.

Disease-Specific Indicators: A subset of clinical quality indicators used to classify patients with regard to either a specific diagnosis or procedure,

for example, the number of patients undergoing an elective surgery.

Economic Benchmarking: A type of benchmarking that concerns itself with research in market forces or comparison of business operation efficiency based on economic principles in a particular market.

Employee Retirement and Income Security Act: "A federal law that sets minimum standards for most voluntarily established pension and health plans in private industry to provide protection for individuals in these plans."

Equity Risk Premium: A rate of return added to a risk-free rate to reflect the additional risk of equity instruments over risk-free instruments (a component of the cost of equity capital or equity discount rate).

Excess Earnings: That amount of anticipated economic benefits that exceeds an appropriate rate of return on the value of a selected asset base (often net tangible assets) used to generate those anticipated economic benefits.

External Benchmarking: Consists of several different subcategories of benchmarking and includes any inter-entity comparison.

Fee Arrangements: The payment system agreed upon between consultant and client based on the amount of time and resources an engagement requires and its profitability for the consultant. Generally flat fees and hourly rates are used for consulting.

Financial Benchmarking: A method of financial analysis that may be used to understand the operational and financial status of a healthcare organization. Financial benchmarking consists of three steps: (1) historical subject benchmarking, (2) benchmarking to industry norms, and, (3) financial ratio analysis.

Financial Ratio Analysis: A subset of financial benchmarking that uses ratios, calculated as measurements of various financial and operational characteristics that represent the financial status of an enterprise, which are then evaluated in terms of their relative comparison to generally established industry norms.

Forced Liquidation Value: Liquidation value at which all, or the majority, of the assets will be sold at approximately the same time in a relatively quick fashion.

Forecasting: Using trend analysis to produce a prediction of future values or performance.

Foregone Compensation Formula: Allows associate physicians to achieve the minimum required buy-in amount for partnerships.

Functional Benchmarking: A derivative form of process benchmarking used to compare two or more organizations (that are not necessarily direct competitors) via comparison of specific business functions.

Functional Indicators: A subset of clinical quality indicators that utilize outcomes as a proxy for patient quality of life or overall population health, for example, patient functional performance following a procedure.

General Research: Comprised of the industry conditions, demographics, compensation trends, transactions, guideline publicly traded companies, industry specific trends, and other research not specifically related to the organization, practice, business, or enterprise of interest.

Generic Benchmarking: A type of benchmarking applicable to a variety of industries, that focuses on the identification, classification, and comparison of key business processes to those of the leading competitor(s).

Generic Indicators: A subset of clinical quality indicators based on a rate of occurrence within the patient population and includes measures of morbidity, mortality, and readmission.

Global Benchmarking: A type of external benchmarking that determines a comparison organization(s) based on geographic boundaries and location.

Going Concern Value: The value of a business enterprise that is expected to continue to operate. The intangible elements of going concern value result from factors such as having a trained work force, an operational plant, and the necessary licenses, systems, and procedures in place.

Goodwill: That intangible asset arising as a result of name, reputation, customer loyalty, location, products, and similar factors not separately identified.

Historical Subject Benchmarking: A subset of financial benchmarking that compares an organization's current or most recently reported performance with its past performance. This is used to identify changes of performance within the organization and to predict future performance.

Industry Benchmarking: A type of external benchmarking process used to compare an organization with its direct competitors and industry noncompetitors.

Institutional Quality Indicators: Benchmarking metrics used to determine the degree to which a provider adheres to regulatory standards set by accreditation agencies, associations, and other regulatory bodies.

Intangible Assets: Nonphysical assets, such as franchises, trademarks, patents, copyrights, goodwill, equities, mineral rights, and securities and contracts (as distinguished from physical assets), that grant rights and privileges and have value for the owner.

Internal Benchmarking: The comparison of different subdivisions or analogous products within one organization, by which comparison is limited to within-company projects and processes in order to identify best practices.

Internal Revenue Code: Outline tax-related implications of (1) how compensation plans are set up, (2) how compensation is paid, (3) how compensation is characterized, and (4) how compensation is treated by taxing authorities.

Invested Capital: The sum of equity and debt in a business enterprise. Debt is typically (1) all interest bearing debt or (2) long-term interest-bearing debt. When the term is used, it should be supplemented by a specific definition in the given valuation context.

Investment Value: The value to a particular investor based on individual investment requirements and expectations. (In Canada, the term used is "value to the owner.")

Leverage Ratio: A ratio of long-term debt to net fixed assets, which is used to illustrate the proportion of funds, or capital, provided by shareholders (owners) and creditors to aid analysts in assessing the appropriateness of an organization's current level of debt.

Liquidation Value: The present value of the net proceeds from liquidating the company's assets and paying off liabilities.

Liquidity Ratio: A metric that measures the ability of an organization to meet cash obligations as they become due, that is, to support operational goals.

Liquidity: The ability to quickly convert property to cash or pay a liability.

Management Advisory Services: Consulting services in the improvement of practice efficiency and efficacy.

Market Multiple: The market value of a company's stock or invested capital divided by a company measure (such as economic benefits or number of customers).

Net Book Value: With respect to a business enterprise, the difference between total assets (net of accumulated depreciation, depletion, and amortization) and total liabilities as they appear on the balance sheet (synonymous with "shareholder's equity"). With respect to a specific asset, the capitalized cost less accumulated amortization or depreciation as it appears on the books of account of the business enterprise.

Operational Benchmarking: A form of benchmarking similar to both process and performance benchmarking that targets noncentral work or business processes for improvement based on the application of the results.

Orderly Liquidation Value: Liquidation value at which the asset or assets are sold over a reasonable period of time to maximize proceeds received.

Organizational Development: The development of the internal systems and culture of an organization.

Performance Benchmarking: A more common form of benchmarking that utilizes outcome characteristics as benchmarking metrics (for example, price, speed, and reliability).

Physician Compensation Plan: A way of allocating an organization's revenues and expenses while determining appropriate methods of compensating professionals for the services they provide.

Practice Management: Consulting that involves a breakdown of the day-to-day management of the healthcare professional practice and analysis of the processes in place in order to identify areas of improvement.

Practice Profiling: Reporting of raw, unbiased practice data to practitioners.

Premise of Value: An assumption regarding the most likely set of transactional circumstances that may be applicable to the subject valuation (for example going concern or liquidation).

Presentation: The final phase of a consulting project during which the consultant reports results to clients or other parties.

Process Benchmarking: A type of benchmarking that focuses on the identification of particular key business processes or operational characteristics that require improvement.

Profitability: A measure of the overall net effect of managerial efficiency of the enterprise.

Prospects: Those suspects whose information leads the consultant to believe they could be potential clients.

Qualified Domestic Relations Orders (QDRO): "A judgment, decree, or order that is made pursuant to state domestic relations law," that creates, recognizes, or assigns an alternate payee's right to receive, a percentage of benefits payable to a participant under a retirement plan."

Risk Management: Adjusting exposures to stabilize variability while trimming dominant exposure to spread out and minimize risk.

Service Quality Indicators: Benchmarking metrics used to measure customer satisfaction regarding provided healthcare services.

Specific Research: Data pertaining specifically to the entity of interest that must usually be obtained from that entity.

Standard of Value: The identification of the type of value being used in a specific engagement (for example, fair market value, fair value, or investment value).

Strategic Benchmarking: A form of external benchmarking, similar to process benchmarking, that has the potential to fundamentally change business process by focusing upon identification and comparison of decision-making operations that affect the observed business outcomes.

Strategic Initiatives: A company's set objectives that, if met, would satisfy the vision of the organization.

Summarization: Using tables, matrices, abstracts, and so forth to distill a body of information into one or more of its essential characteristics in order to gain a general overview or compare information.

Suspects: Suspects are potential clients that have been identified by the consultant. Once indentified information is gathered on them, including: size of practice, location, site, specialty(s), services, ownership, financial status, and so forth This information is often stored in the consultant's contacts database.

Tactical Plans: A company's formal description of how, when, and where the strategic initiatives will be met.

Tangible Assets: Physical assets (such as cash, accounts receivable, inventory, property, plant and equipment, and so forth).

Targets: Prospects are surveyed on a case-by-case basis and those whose information meets the limiting qualifications set by the consultant have preliminary proposals prepared and can be considered targets.

The Joint Commission: An independent, non-profit organization responsible for the certification and accreditation of healthcare organizations across the United States.

"Tick and Tie": The mechanical process of checking every figure and process for errors, a term often used in accountancy.

Valuation Date: The specific point in time as of which a valuator's opinion of value applies (also referred to as the "effective date" or "appraisal date").

Valuation: "The act or process of determining the value of a business, business ownership interest, security, or tangible asset."

Value in Exchange: An orderly disposition of a mass assemblage of the assets in place but not as a going concern enterprise; also known as "liquidation value."

Value in Use: Premise of value that assumes that the assets will continue to be used as part of an ongoing business enterprise, producing profits as a benefit of ownership.

Vision: A company's vision should answer the long-term question: "why are we in business?"

Weighted Average Cost of Capital: The cost of capital (discount rate) determined by the weighted average, at market value, of the cost of all financing sources in the business enterprise's capital structure.